To entrepreneur
is to celebrate the
possible.

bulldog

bulldog

SPIRIT OF THE NEW ENTREPRENEUR

Ellie Rubin

HarperBusiness
HarperCollins*Publishers*Ltd

http://www.harpercanada.com

HarperCollins books may be purchased for educational, business,
or sales promotional use. For information please write:
Special Markets Department, HarperCollins Canada,
55 Avenue Road, Suite 2900, Toronto, Ontario, Canada M5R 3L2.

Lyrics by Rachel Kane (Gift of the Magi, from the album *Groundwire*,
produced by Adam's Rib Productions) are used by permission of the artist

Book design by Shauna Rae / Stingrae Design
Author photo by Sam Barnes

First edition

Canadian Cataloguing in Publication Data

Rubin, Ellie
Bulldog, spirit of the new entrepreneur

Includes index.

ISBN 0-00-638553-2

1. Entrepreneurship. 2. Success in business. 3. Rubin, Ellie
1. Title

HB615.R82999   658.4'21   C98-932584-9

99 00 01 02 03 04 WEB 8 7 6 5 4 3 2 1

Printed and bound in Canada

to Alex Rubin

WHO GAVE ME THE WHEREWITHAL TO
CONSTANTLY TEST MY ENTREPRENEURIAL SPIRIT WITH HIS LOVE,
HIS DREAMS, AND HIS CHAMPIONSHIP.

contents

The Bulldog

the lightness of entrepreneuring 3

relentless convergence 23

my trip to mecca 42

The Professional Eclectic

profile of the sensitive extrovert 63

the developing entrepreneur 81

the f(email) factor 107

The Chaos Pilot

secret recipes for a disordered world 129

exceptional emblems 143

the to-do list of architects and heroes 169

the advantageous burden of money 201

Storytelling

the beauty of imbalance 247

a never-ending act of doing 275

endnotes 293

thank you's 306

index 310

Whatever you can do,
or dream you can, begin it.
Boldness has genius, power
and magic in it.

GOETHE

bulldog

the bull-
dog

the bulldog the bull
the bulldog the bulldog the bull
bulldog the bulldog the bull
the bulldog the bulldog the bull
e bulldog the bulldog the bull bulldog the bulldog the bulldog
bulldog the bulldog the bulldog the bulldog the bulldog the bull
the bulldog the bulldog the bulldog the bulldog the bulldog the bulldog
g the bulldog the bulldog the bulldog the bulldog the bulldog the bulldog
the bulldog the bulld dog the bulldog the bulldog the bulldog the
lldog the bulldog the bulldog the bulldog the bulldog the bulldog the bulldog
the bulldog the bulldog the bulld bulldog the bulldog the bulldog the
lldog the bulldog the bulldog the bulldog the bull

the
bulldog

dog the bulld the bulldog the bulldog the bulldog the bull
ldog the bul he bulldog the bulldog the bulldog the bull
g the bull lldog the bulldog the bulldog the bulldog the bulld
oulldog th the bulldog the bulldog the bulldog the bulldog
lldog the bulldog the bulldog the bulldog the bulldog the
bulldog the bulldog the bulldog the bulldog the bulldog
dog the bulldog the bulldog the bull dog the bulldog the
he bull the bulldog the bu g the bulld
lldog t lldog the bulldog ullldog th
the bull e bulldog the b g the bull
ulldog t lldog the bulld bulldog t
the bull e bulldog the bulld he bulldo
ulldog th lldog the bull lldog the
g the bull ulldog the bull he bulldog
e bulldog bg the bul g the bulld
e bulldog lldog the l
the b

chapter 1 The Lightness of Entrepreneuring

I'd never seen so many lawyers and accountants sharing the same space. Our windowless boardroom held barely enough air. But I knew that wasn't why I was starting to feel queasy. I was suddenly and miserably struck by a painful truth: We couldn't do this deal. We had to say no to money, and without it, we could not survive.

I convinced the group at large that we needed to take a half-hour break in a separate room. The Bulldog team adjourned to the next room: me, my partners Chris Strachan (chief executive officer) and Tom Howlett (chief operating officer), our lawyer, and our key advisor and board member, my father.

Meanwhile, I was trying to decide how to break it to everyone that the deal I'd brought to the table was not going to work. Worse, how were we going to get the money we needed before running out of what was left—with only 10 days to spare?

Beginning in 1991, we had steadily built a company called the Bulldog Group that had evolved from a traditional design firm into one of the top multimedia production houses in Canada. Although we had grown dramatically (from a staff of 2 to 30 and from $0 to approximately $4 million in sales), we had visions of creating new products. More specifically, we dreamed of translating the knowledge we had accumulated as a service business—in the creation of CD-ROMs, Web sites for banks, and multimedia marketing programs for retailers—into tangible software. For the first few months of 1993, we had been wandering in circles trying to figure out how a multimedia design group could possibly get into the software business.

Then, after months of networking with various telco organizations, we got a call from Northern Telecom and New Brunswick Telecom (NB Tel). One of their customers—a company named MEDITrust—had been trying to find someone to build a prototype for a kiosk that would enable the company to sell its pharmacy services remotely over ISDN lines to its call center in Fredericton, New Brunswick. MEDITrust could not find anyone who could build it, and they needed the prototype immediately. So we signed a contract to build the world's first video-conferencing kiosk using ISDN. Naïve as we were, we agreed to create it from scratch in three months, even though we had never even met the customer or the Nortel engineers who were based in Minnetonka, Minnesota. And anyone who has ever created a software product knows how crazy it is to attempt to build an application without first communicating with the customer. But we did have three video-conferencing systems installed in our offices to keep the flow of information coming. It would have to do.

Three months later, at midnight on what seemed a long Tuesday, we were all sweating profusely as our designer tried to work out why he couldn't get the prototype to reboot. With wires pulled out of the back of our hand-made kiosk and the chairs set up for the big demo the next morning, we had no idea if we were going to lose every iota of credibility that we had painstakingly managed to create.

The next morning, with 30 pairs of eyes watching, Chris Strachan walked the executives from Nortel, NB Tel, MEDITrust, and Bell Canada through the demo, while our designer sat behind the kiosk and prayed. The demonstration went off without a hitch. In fact, the president of MEDITrust stood up and said, "I would like to have worldwide rights to this." Nortel executives nodded their heads, NB Tel executives applauded, and our designer hoped against all odds that they wouldn't ask for a rerun of the demo—it had just crashed, and he had no way of quickly reviving it.

That afternoon, the executives from NB Tel took Chris and me out for lunch. The most senior executive at the table, John MacDonald, congratulated us on our ability to make technology work within a business context. I remember that lunch to this day, because it was the first time we were acknowledged for Bulldog's particular skill—the ability to create a marketing model that would allow technology to shine. The next time we saw the NB Tel gang was at the press conference in Paquetville, New Brunswick, six months later. Frank McKenna (the premier at the time) opened the press conference, cameras clicked, and with the proper amount of development time, our application was very stable. We were heroes. John MacDonald was there, and we were delighted with his interest in us as people and as a company. Little did we know how important he would be to our future.

fast forward

Two years later, by late 1995, Bulldog had gone $600,000 in debt in an attempt to build a new software product. This time, our project had nothing to do with video conferencing or kiosks. Instead, our new product was to focus on the management, cataloging, and distribution of digital media files (video, audio, hypertext mark-up language, etc.) for the entertainment and broadcast industries. To bring the product to market, however, we were desperately in need of more money. Our existing service business could not keep up with our cash-flow requirements, and we had about five months before the company was going to sink. My job? Find funding—and fast.

Invention happens at the interface between the world and the creative mind.

GEOFFREY MOORE, CHAIRMAN AND FOUNDER, THE CHASM GROUP

In September 1995, I began discussions with a company that had read about Bulldog and was interested in investing in a firm that showed leadership in the multimedia design and production business. We seemed to be the perfect match. The only problem was that this company wanted to invest in and manage a multimedia design company, namely Bulldog, and we wanted a noncontrolling investor who was interested in a software company. This wasn't a sound basis for an investment strategy, but, as novices, we figured this out only after two months of negotiations. That's how I came to be sitting in an overheated boardroom, wondering how we were going to save our company and get out of the mess we were in.

We had asked for a half-hour recess. As soon as we closed the door of the adjoining boardroom, Chris and I looked at each other, and I knew I was not alone in my thinking. We both took a deep breath and said, "We can't do the deal."

"What do you mean? You have to do the deal! You have no other takers, and you are going to go under within about 10 days," pleaded our level-headed legal counsel.

"Ditto," said our levelheaded COO.

We knew that the deal on the table had us in a standstill agreement that expired on that very day. The other company was pressuring us to sign a standstill agreement for another 10 days, allowing them to complete their due diligence and finalize the paperwork. If we could delay the signing of the second standstill, we would legally be free to look for other investors. It had taken us two months to nurse this deal along, Christmas was looming, and there were no other prospects on the table. Who did we know? Where could we go to find the money that was going to save our company? We had to find someone who knew us, believed in us, and had the power to make something happen within this tight time frame.

Then it dawned on us. We had maintained our relationship with John MacDonald from NB Tel over the years. In fact, Chris and I had traveled to Ottawa a month earlier to have lunch with him and talk about how we'd need an infusion of capital. By now, he was the chief technology officer of Bell. It was worth a call.

The lawyers were getting restless in the boardroom. We asked for 10 more minutes. We held our breaths while I called John's number. Miraculously, we got him.

"John, we're in a real bind. We have a product that is revolutionary. It's in product development and coming along. We have put in $600,000 of our own money and are about 10 days away from going under. We're going to have to sign up the wrong investor, who is waiting in the next room, and give away our company to cover the additional funds it is going to take to complete the beta version of this product—unless we can come up with an alternative."

John already knew about our product from our last meeting. He didn't ask a lot of questions about who the investor was, or how we had gotten ourselves into this situation. Instead, he said, "I know that if you are that close to finalizing a product and have put that much of your own money and livelihood on the line, then it has got to be something worthwhile. I got a sense of the work you are doing from our lunch in Ottawa last month, and I believe in you as people. I think I can get you air time with the president and chief executive officer of BCE Capital Inc., who might be interested in the product. I can't guarantee anything. All I can do is make the connection. If need be, I will find a way to help you until BCE or some other investor can determine if you are a worthy investment."

Putting the phone on mute, we all looked at each other and gasped.

We returned to the boardroom and (with nerves of steel) told the group that we could not sign the deal and needed to revisit it once more before signing the standstill extension. They gave us 48 hours. We took it, based on a verbal commitment from John MacDonald and nothing more. No papers, no nondisclosure agreement, no signatures, no guarantees.

Twenty-four hours later, Peter Crombie, the president of BCE Capital, walked into our offices to look over our prototype. After conducting the appropriate due diligence, he verbally committed to providing us with seed money to cover the initial development period. Six weeks later, on January 15, 1996, we signed our deal with BCE Capital and were on our way to becoming a software company. Today, Bulldog software is sold internationally. We have over $17 million invested in our company; Sony Pictures Entertainment is a minority investor and our biggest customer. We are poised for leadership in our niche software category—media asset management.

Why did I tell you these stories? To impress you with all the companies we were able to get face time with? To tell you about our good fortune in finding financing? To support the myth that entrepreneurs are able to take advantage of fluke situations?

The answer to all of these questions is no. There was nothing fluky about how we got John MacDonald's support. Nor was there anything random about how I let my company get into the dire situation we found ourselves in that day. I told you these stories to show where my journey as an entrepreneur began. The story of saving my company exemplifies many of the key characteristics required of an entrepreneur in this day and age, characteristics that reflect the spirit and the tactics of the "new" entrepreneur in action.

These experiences and others like them have helped me to develop, hone, and confirm many of my most profound revelations about what it means to be an entrepreneur. I have reevaluated these lessons again and again in my attempt to define *entrepreneuring* as a relevant concept for anyone who wants to create their own "story"—whether that means starting one's own company, managing someone else's, or simply trying to incorporate a spirit of entrepreneurship into the work one does.

definitions are only temporary; self-destiny is not

Today, when technological advances have upped the ante on our "hurry-up-and-wait" sense of time, when downsizing and mega-mergers are unpredictable and dramatic, there is a heightened need for self-reliance. The one thing that is certain and constant is that each of us will accumulate experiences and has the opportunity to gain perspective and insight by actively pursuing knowledge. In the end, this knowledge is the one thing that is wholly our own. Some recent facts and figures reflect this. In the U.S., the temporary staffing industry represents a $50 billion a year business, and more than 2.5 million people report to work each day as a sole contractor. This rise in the number of "free agents" only reinforces my sense that in tumultuous times (which *are* constant) we must take the onus to create our destiny. Enter the need for active entrepreneuring.

I began this book by trying to figure out how to define the term *entrepreneur;* how to put words and concepts around it in a way that would make sense to people and motivate them to want to be one. Then I realized how off-track this approach was. One cannot take a linear approach to something that is essentially a nonlinear concept. Rather than ask, "How can I become an entrepreneur?" ask yourself, "What have I learned? What am I determined to learn? And how can I apply this knowledge to a new situation?"

Active entrepreneuring starts by letting go of our culture's overglamorized version of entrepreneurship, taking it off the shelf as a category that you either fall into or out of and recognizing that everyone has within them the ability to "entrepreneur" on some level.

In today's world of free agents, in a sense all of us are in the IPO game. In this case IPO does not refer to "initial public offering" but "independent professional offering," whereby each of us views our accumulated knowledge and talent like a stock—and not a commodity—and we are looking for ways to increase our own personal equity as we move forward. If this is the case, then those who learn how to leverage their talent and accumulated knowledge will be poised for greater success. For the ambitious among us, those who actively entrepreneur as a verb will reap the rewards in this personal equity game. And for good reason. The statistics on entrepreneurship are staggering.

An entrepreneur is "one who creates a product on his own account." The word has its roots in the French verb *entreprendre,* which means "to enterprise, to undertake, to begin and attempt to perform, and to venture upon" and dates back to 1430. The German word for enterprising individuals is *unternehmer,* and the Afrikaans translation is *ondernemer.* It seems that almost all languages have a reference for this position in society.

- Today, companies with fewer than 500 employees account for 99.5 percent of all U.S. businesses. These companies employ 53 percent of nongovernment, nonfarm workers and produce 50 percent of private-sector output. The same is true in Canada, where one in seven Canadians run their own business.

- Neither entrepreneurship nor the high-tech field are showing any signs of slowing down. Technology now accounts for approximately 10 percent of America's GDP, and in Canada, the information and communication technology sector is currently growing faster than the Canadian economy as a whole.

- In Silicon Valley alone, 3,575 new businesses were launched in 1997, venture capitalists poured a record $3.7 billion into these startups, and these same companies generated 53,000 new jobs, which translates into twice the national average.

- On a global level, women are making great enterprising strides. For example, 40 percent of the 23 million small businesses in the U.S. are owned by women. They employ 18.5 million people and contribute more than $2.3 trillion annually to the U.S. economy. Women-owned shares could rise to 50 percent of businesses by the year 2000. And in Canada, women-owned businesses make up approximately one-third of all Canadian businesses, providing almost one million jobs.

About 16% of Canada's workforce now work for themselves, up from 10%, as recorded in the early 1990s.

REPORT ON BUSINESS
MAGAZINE

No matter how you look at it, this kind of entrepreneurial rage is good for all of us.

the lightness of entrepreneuring

Given this matrix of growth and opportunity, it is not surprising then that according to a recent article in *Inc.* magazine, "Entrepreneurship achieved cult status in the 1980s and has become de rigueur in the 1990s." It begs the question: How does one achieve de rigueur status and become part of an optimistic vocational and lifework trend?

If you think I am talking about leaving your job and starting up a software company in Mountainview next month, you are missing the point. Starting your own venture is certainly an entrepreneurial act, but I am talking about something even more basic than that. The definition of entrepreneuring I would like to share with you begins with a willingness to shift your perspective of the world slightly to one side, learning to look at how you are currently making your living from a new viewpoint, whether you are working in an entrepreneurial company or not. The best way to describe this shift is captured in a quirky Australian movie I once saw called *Love and Other*

Catastrophes. At one point, one of the lead characters asks, "So what do you choose, weight or lightness?" The entrepreneur is the person who unhesitatingly reaches out for the latter. In career terms, this means defining your success in terms of the unusual approaches and solutions you have brought to each job you have done, rather than by the impressive titles listed on your résumé. In management, it means recognizing that the higher you rise in an organization, the more you will become dependent on those below you for information. And in personal equity terms, it is reflected in the eclectic portfolio you build as you gain experience and knowledge. The lightness of entrepreneuring will be found in the choices you make and the risks that you take. *That* is what will push you forward.

A person's reasons for adopting an entrepreneurial stance are often visceral, complex, and fickle, but the rewards are truly compelling. Most of us are looking for a sense of freedom in our lives. We want to believe in something greater than ourselves, and we want to create a better place for ourselves than the one we are in now—and we'd like to have fun along the way. The spirit of the new entrepreneur *is* about the potential to take you places you've never been before. Personally, entrepreneuring allows me to travel around the world and conduct business with people I would never have met otherwise. And as with any new adventure, it will introduce you to challenges that you never thought you would have to face. Along the way, you will struggle with new ideas about what "belonging"—to a partnership, company, and community—means. While getting to these places you have never imagined, you will dance with risk, tell stories, and find a new level of energy in all that you do. Perhaps you will even find something new to believe in.

"read the directions, even if you don't follow them"

And that's exactly what I hope you will do with this book. Why? Because true entrepreneuring begins with storytelling, study, and observation, and can often lead to insight that will motivate you to create your own set of directions. That is what I, and many other entrepreneurs before me, have done. What matters most is that creating these directions leads you to understanding your *own* set of beliefs with an insight and clarity that lasts.

This book is not another "99 essential ways to start your own company and make money." Instead, by drawing on my own experiences and the experiences of many other dynamic, inspired entrepreneurs, it provides some important guidelines and signposts to look out for in your quest to create an entrepreneurial stance in your work—and possibly even in the

Silicon Valley's 6,000 high tech companies boast total sales of more than $200 billion a year.

THE ECONOMIST

The information and communication technology sector in Canada is currently growing faster than the Canadian economy as a whole.

INDUSTRY CANADA

way that you live. This book is a collection of trigger points and stories designed to, I hope, set you off in a new direction that you were not even contemplating a week, a month, or even a year ago in pursuit of your own definition of entrepreneuring.

I have taken the small mini-revelations that I have learned on my entrepreneurial journey and organized them in a way that will hopefully serve as an experiential guide for you.

The first section of the book tells my story and sets up the major themes of the book. Section Two deals with the profile of the new entrepreneur and how to develop an entrepreneurial career path. Section Three focuses on the major issues that face entrepreneurs and intrapreneurs alike, as they determine leadership skills, build teams, look for money, and brand themselves. Finally, the last section of the book is about the personal struggles that entrepreneuring creates, and the advantages of that kind of dynamic tension.

I hope, in the end, that this book will so intrigue you that you will rise to the challenge of trying to come up with your own understanding of what it means to be a new entrepreneur. I also hope that you will eventually be able pass that understanding onto others.

Based on the results of *Inc.* magazine's latest 500 List, those companies listed generated 71,464 jobs in 1997 with a total of $12 billion in sales—a 33.3% increase over the previous year.

INC. MAGAZINE

this book is not about technology

I am a new entrepreneur, but not a technologist. The fact that I have created entrepreneurial opportunity in technology is more a sign of the times than anything else. There are many things that technology has done, and will continue to do, that will affect how people and companies succeed and fail, and how people perceive change and why. But technology will not define the art of entrepreneuring. Within the pages of this book, technology is simply a backdrop to the stages of my journey. While the world of high tech dramatically affects the mood and tone of the stories I will share with you, the knowledge and strategies are transferable to any industry.

some rules of engagement

Writing a book and engaging readers is no different than commencing any new venture or new deal. We need to make sure that we are reading off the same page, that we have a clear and compatible understanding of expectations. There aren't *too* many stipulations from my end.

■ This book is a collection of perceptions and ideas that have worked for me and for many of those who helped me talk through my initial concepts over the years. They are not absolute truths. I do not believe in absolute truths. My hope is that you will take whatever is of value to you and apply it to your own journey.

■ Jim Collins, co-author of *Built to Last: Successful Habits of Visionary Companies*, describes an emerging crowd of business people who are "hungry to think." This book is for those people. It does not matter if you are an entrepreneur, a developing entrepreneur, if you never thought of entrepreneuring as a verb, or if you simply want to sit back and feed a craving that you may never act upon. Regardless of where you are on the risk curve, the desire to understand the spirit and attitude of the new entrepreneur is the only qualifier for readership.

■ Readers may not agree with everything I say. It would be unrealistic to expect that from any book or any approach. This book was written in the true spirit of the new entrepreneur—to challenge, to break rules, to reinvent, to provoke.

■ Entrepreneuring is a verb, an active stance that requires energy and commitment. It is the most dynamic, rewarding, challenging, and effective way to create something out of nothing that I can think of.

■ Who am I, and why am I writing this book? I am, like many of you, a local hero, a person who has succeeded, and continues to succeed, as a new entrepreneur in the very real day-to-day world of business. Young and female, I have created a company on the cusp of the emerging technology wave—its revolution has been my playground. Some people know me, many do not. I wrote this book based on what I know, what I have learned and continue to learn as I "entrepreneur." This book is for my friends and colleagues, and all the other people that I have not yet met who are just like me. These people are on a path. They want to learn more and get better at what they do, and they yearn to be on the verge of greatness. They are eager and impatient, tense and tentative. And they are surrounded by opportunity just out of their reach.

Women-owned businesses make up approximately one-third of all Canadian businesses and provide almost one million jobs.

WOMEN BUSINESS
OWNERS OF CANADA

According to the National Association of Women Business Owners, each day 1,600 women start a new business.

REPORT ON BUSINESS
MAGAZINE

THE ENTREPRENEUR	*the new entrepreneur*
Local	**Global**
SNAP DECISIONS	*Consensus through confrontation*
HEART	INTUITION
Passion	Obsession
LONE RANGER	*Champion Seeker*
MASTER OF INNOVATION	MASTER OF INTERPRETATION
Specialist with an idea	Generalist with a team of specialists
SUPPLIER/PRODUCER	*Deal Maker*
KNOWS THE TRADE	LEARNS THE BUSINESS
Self-reliant	Sensitive extrovert
FEAR OF FAILURE	*Focus on quick recovery*
ORGANIZATIONALLY ORTHODOX	REBELLIOUS LEADER
Start up	Start up or whatever
TRADE ASSOCIATION MEMBER	*Web surfer*
SELF-SUFFICIENT PRAGMATIST	MAGICAL REALIST
Think product/service	Think brand/cachet
SUPPORTIVE SPOUSE AT HOME	*Spouse runs own business*
SMALL BUSINESS FOUNDER	ENTREPRENEURIAL STORYTELLER
Seat of the pants	Eternal researcher
BOSS	*Collective entrepreneurship*
MALE	Mixed
Entrepreneur as an adjective	Entrepreneur as a verb
STANCE OF THE ENTREPRENEUR	*Spirit of the New Entrepreneur*

storytelling

Creating something lasting and meaningful in the work that you do requires the adoption of a new spirit that is flexible enough to accommodate changes—technological or otherwise—and savvy enough to know how and when to perceive these shifts just long enough to create opportunity. In these evolving times, embracing ambiguity is the sure way to own one's destiny. It is the basis of the new entrepreneur's spirit.

THE NEW ENTREPRENEUR IS SOMEONE WHO KNOWS HOW TO UTILIZE THE FINE ART OF STORYTELLING AND CAN DO SO WITH BOLDNESS, IMAGINATION, CHARISMA, AND TENACITY. STORYTELLING PROVIDES A LOGICAL FORMAT FOR "CREATING SOMETHING OUT OF NOTHING."

Everybody has obsessions. Mine is storytelling, not just for the sake of telling a story or entertaining my listeners (though that in itself is worth the effort) but for the sheer pleasure of engaging others, of creating a place that simply did not exist before the story was told and only remains if the story is potent enough.

What does storytelling have to do with entrepreneurship? It has *everything* to do with it, because storytelling provides the logical format for "creating something out of nothing." And its effects are not limited just to the commercial world. A high-powered public relations person and fundraiser named Leslie went to Guatemala to take a language-immersion course. While there, she was deeply struck by the suffering and poverty of the Mayan Indians. When she returned to her U.S. home, she shared her story with everyone—her general practitioner, her eye doctor, people in her church, as well as many of her friends. Before she knew it, she had 40 volunteers who paid their own airfares to go down for two weeks and set up a medical clinic. Today, four years later, she is the head of Xela-aid, one of the largest privately owned not-for-profit organizations in the U.S. She and her team have built a school and homes for homeless villagers, inoculated hundreds of children, provided eyeglasses for hundreds of people, distributed millions of dollars worth of medical supplies, and initiated business ventures for the people in the Mayan village they work in. And it all started with her ability to tell a story and engage others.

At the heart of the new entrepreneur is the myth, the parable, the fable that, in the beginning, shapes the experience that will eventually happen. As author and consultant Geoffrey Moore says, stories are the basis for entire economies being created, for countries going to war. For the new entrepreneur, storytelling is about designing a place that, for all intents and purposes, does not yet exist. By describing it, drawing people into it, evolving a plot, and adding characters and twists to that plot line as you see them happening, you are in effect filling in the missing details of this mythical

Never before has the hunger for entrepreneurship been higher. According to Karl Vesper, a professor of management at the University of Washington, Seattle, entrepreneurship is taught at about 400 universities.

INC. MAGAZINE

location with real feedback and live interest. In marketing, this technique is called "effective messaging." In business plans, it is called your "point of differentiation." But in real day-to-day life, it is called storytelling.

Great entrepreneurs are often great storytellers. The delivery varies, but what is constant is this: Storytellers understand that people want to be part of a story and that people need someone else to take on the responsibility of creating the plot so that they can step into it. For me, the power of storytelling became crystal clear the day I made that phone call to John MacDonald, asking him to help us to save our company. I knew that if I couldn't tell my story well, if I couldn't convince him to believe in our product as much as we believed in it ourselves, I would run the risk of losing control of the company I had worked so long to build. He believed in my story because we had spent years building it, through the press, through the customers we had attracted, and by the way we had put together our unique corporate image. These are the forces that draw people in. Bulldog's ability to create elements of surprise and drama, exemplified by our bold desire to move from a design service business to a product company, was the kind of style that captivated people and made them want to be a part of what we were doing. In the telling and retelling of our story, we sometimes revealed more than we should. Sometimes, we even showed our vulnerability, then resolved the tension through our own entrepreneurial efforts. Our story linked together moments of courageous deal making and memorable image building. Our staff and customers became the heroes, and our story was believable and attractive because it combined design style with technological pioneering, carving out new ways to look at success in the infant stages of the multimedia design industry.

Storytelling is the place for the new entrepreneur to start because it provides a structure in which imagination and definition lead to the act of creating many "somethings" out of nothing.

risk

THE NEW ENTREPRENEUR UNDERSTANDS THE DYNAMICS AND REWARDS OF RISK. EMBRACING RISK IS ABOUT CREATIVITY, NOT COURAGE. IT IS ABOUT INTUITIVE CALCULATION, NOT GUT RESPONSE, AND IT DEMANDS THE MASTERY OF INTERPRETATION, NOT INVENTION.

I'll make a bet with you. Ask anyone what they think are the most important attributes for successful entrepreneurship, and nine times out of 10, they will cite "risk taker" right at the top. People do not wake up in the morning and say, "Boy, I wonder where I can find some risk to deal with today!" But the new entrepreneur understands the merits of what Bill Sahlman, associate dean at Harvard Business School, calls "the risk-reward cycle." You take

One in seven Canadians run their own business.

VANCOUVER SUN

Understand the risk and plan against it. Then focus on executing towards the reward.

DOUG KEELEY,
PRESIDENT AND CEO,
THE ICE GROUP OF
COMPANIES

risk to gain reward, and you generally cannot have one without the other in the world of entrepreneurship. To understand the new entrepreneur's relationship to risk, we need to look at three important elements.

the willingness to embrace risk is more important than where you sit on the risk curve

Not everyone is comfortable with risk. Not everyone wants to be on the far side of that curve. But everyone has the ability to embrace elements of risk within their business affairs. The new entrepreneur views risk as a creative necessity. Inherent within this definition is the understanding that you can have more creativity than courage and still be an entrepreneur. The need to determine how far out you want to go with risk is a personal choice. But keep in mind that if you embrace risk, it will necessarily allow you to be more creative about the way you go about achieving your goal.

For example, when we first started Bulldog, we did not know how we would ever be in a position to create a product. Instead of identifying the financial and structural risks involved in trying to build an engineering talent pool from scratch, we created a sister company, Empower, that would act as a separate system-integration consulting service to support our own computer setup and design-studio needs. Aside from the expert support that this company provided for us, Empower eventually attracted the right engineering talent to help us actually start up a product-development team. We incorporated risk into a creative problem-solving exercise.

The value of risk taking in the life of an entrepreneur can be seen in a conversation I had with one executive in the retail business. He described entrepreneurship in three stages: sourcing an idea, having the conviction to see the idea through to its conclusion, and the ability to not let repeated failures get in the way. He ascertained that the reason he was not a new entrepreneur per se was based on the fact that he was good at executing the first necessary step—sourcing an idea—but he did not have the ability to see an idea through the risk stage. The fact that he did not have the conviction to embrace risk limited his ability to think and implement creatively.

Over one million U.S. professionals from across all industries call themselves independent contractors.

THE WALL STREET JOURNAL

the new entrepreneur is focused on interpretation, not invention

Many people believe that to entrepreneur requires an ability to invent something new. Sometimes that is the case. However, for many of us in today's world, it is the ability to interpret trends, to read signals, and to create a model of business based on one's ability to interpret, not invent, that is the mark of the new entrepreneur. A great example of this ability to interpret is seen in a Boston-based company called Mac Temp. They recognized that there is a $50-billion-a-year temporary staffing industry in the U.S. and that many highly qualified contractors and consultants, particularly in the technology industry, require representation. As agents for software engineers, programmers, and multimedia designers, this company now generates revenue of $100 million annually based on their interpretation that these highly skilled freelancers needed representation, much like actors, authors, and sports celebrities do.

Sometimes, being able to read signals accurately cannot only create opportunity, but it can save a company. When Bulldog was still in the multimedia production business, we, like everybody else, became fascinated with CD-ROM publishing and began to seriously discuss the idea that this might be the product we should hang our hats on. At the time, we had already produced a number of one-off CD-ROMs for Apple Computers and Maclean-Hunter's *Marketing* magazine. We began working on Excel spreadsheets and conducting extensive research in the hope that we could find a viable business model in CD-ROM publishing. But it was not until we met with a potential investor who claimed interest in setting us up in the CD-ROM business that my antennae perked up. As I responded to the investor's numerous questions, I began to realize that there were two problems with CD-ROM publishing: First, having the expertise to design CD-ROMs is not the same as having the content that will make them a best-seller—we had no inherent competitive advantage or story content. Second, and perhaps more important, CD-ROM publishing was a half step in the revolution that we had been tracking. It was new technology that relied on an ancient business—the retail sales channel. It wasn't until the Web came along that we realized just how right we had been to pass on CD-ROM publishing.

calculated intuition

Recognizing the difference between calculated intuition and gut response is an important element of deal making. In my experience, taking risks and struggling with the element of risk in business is like most other skills—you get better at handling it the more you do it. To be a new entrepreneur, you have to be dedicated to learning to hone your intuitive understanding of a situation. You need to learn to embrace risk as part of a deal-making process—the means to an end, not a milestone along the way.

Risk has played an important role in the field of developing technologies, because the perception of risk is heightened with each new technology cycle we are subjected to. The stakes get higher, and the need to reevaluate where you sit on the risk curve comes around more often and in a more definitive way than ever before. In corporations, this reevaluation process can be seen in their approach to embracing the Internet and intranet as integral parts of their communications plans, rather than as "special projects" that sit in isolation from the rest of their marketing and sales channels. The new entrepreneur appreciates that the heightened risk factor involved in the technology game will necessarily create gaps in understanding between perceived risk and the intuitive calculation required to create a comfortable deal-making environment. Often, opportunity lies just around the corner from this very intersection in the form of new products or new services that were previously unknown. Dancing with risk definitely has its rewards. By playing with risk, you discover trigger points, ideas, and approaches that may become solutions to a problem itself. You cannot find these solutions, however, without going through the risk dance.

breaking boundaries
THE NEW ENTREPRENEUR UNDERSTANDS THAT BREAKING THROUGH BOUNDARIES IS A WAY OF LIFE.

Every entrepreneur whom I admire tells and retells one cherished story about the moment they understood the importance of breaking boundaries.

Why go to the trouble of breaking boundaries? Because doing so ensures that you will maintain an openness, a fluidity in the way that you go about your day-to-day, often structured, vocational activities. It will keep you open to seeing signs that may otherwise pass you by. In Bulldog's case, if we had stuck to traditional service/product boundaries, we would never have allowed ourselves to think about creating a software product from a design and multimedia background. We did not have the engineering background, we were not in the software business, and we did not have a foundation in product development. But by insisting that we would pioneer our own model of business success, we did away with those assumptions and limitations. That does not mean that we did not get advice or carefully study other examples of success and assess them for ourselves. It means that, since breaking through boundaries was Bulldog's rule of thumb, as a company, we were a lot more comfortable with the risk required to get us from point A to point B.

A continuous line flows between breaking boundaries as a way of life, embracing risk as part of the business process, and creating enticing stories. The further along the risk curve a person sits, the more open one is to breaking through boundaries. The more success one achieves by going out on a limb, the more willing one is to explore the not-so-obvious in the storyline. But, as with anything that promises great reward and return, there are always consequences. Sometimes, things do not pan out the way you intended. Sometimes, the practice of breaking boundaries can put you in a position that is not worth the risk. Unfortunately, this can be viewed only from hindsight.

> Seeing the "market white space" is about seeing something that no one else does and then filling that space with an idea. That idea takes on currency and becomes very real.
>
> HEATHER REISMAN,
> PRESIDENT AND CEO,
> INDIGO BOOKS,
> MUSIC, & CAFÉ

A recent speech I gave on investment strategies is a case in point. Four or five people in the audience told stories about entrepreneurs they knew who were determined to own 100 percent of their software companies, rather than seek outside financing, which resulted in the demise of those very companies. These entrepreneurs would have benefited by breaking the boundaries of the notion of the sole proprietor and deciding that it was better to have a smaller piece of a bigger pie than to own 100 percent of not much at all. I suspect that these individuals were mistakenly intent on proving themselves and showing the marketplace their independence. Although breaking boundaries often requires you to move beyond outwardly imposed limitations, proving yourself to others should not be the motivator. The real reason that one should commit to boundary breaking is to provide oneself with a new perspective, to move the camera lens slightly to the left to perceive something new and different. Asserting new game rules without justification almost always results in regrettable repercussions.

Breaking boundaries has a social stigma attached to it. The line between gutsy and inappropriate is not always an easy call. Pushing through boundaries often forces people to venture outside of their "comfort zones," an action that can feel alienating and isolating at times. That is why it is important to balance these challenging elements with three themes that act as antidotes to the temptation of breaking boundaries for the wrong reasons. The new entrepreneur embraces champions, cachet, and magical realism to ground them in their risk-taking activities.

championship

WITHOUT A FIERCE DEDICATION TO SEEKING OUT "CHAMPIONS" TO HELP ONE ACHIEVE ONE'S GOALS, THE ENTREPRENEURIAL DREAM WILL NEVER EVOLVE BEYOND A GREAT IDEA AND A SPREADSHEET OF NUMBERS. CHAMPIONS ARE THE LINES THAT CONNECT THE DOTS.

In the dictionary, a *champion* is defined as "someone who defends a concept or a person." Beyond networking or mentorship, championship is about creating relationships with people and groups of people who are committed to *defending* a cause—whether that be your career, your product, your business plan, or your integrity. Inherent in this relationship is a mutual exchange of value—there is a reason for the champion to defend the cause, and there is a motivation for the recipient of this championship to maintain and build the relationship. The art of championship requires active and equal participation between two or more people.

On the tactical side, championship is not just about how many business cards you collect at a trade show or how many phone calls you make in a week. It is not about who you play golf with on the weekend. Championship

The word *phoneme* means "the smallest unit of speech that distinguishes one utterance from another." Sometimes, it is this tiny level of interpretation that the new entrepreneur must focus upon when looking for a new angle that will determine their most important business decisions.

is about a dedication to creating a matrix of your business needs and goals and a matching matrix of people and skills. It is about the process of creating strategies that will ensure that you are mutually connected with the people who will be willing to defend you, your company, and your product or service every step of the way.

Building a strong web of champions across industries, across hierarchies, with partners, investors, industry associates, and friends and family provides the new entrepreneur with the confidence and the grounding necessary to take the kind of risks they need to succeed, so that they can break the necessary boundaries. Without champions, risk-taking activities can become random, and boundaries are broken based on bad habits rather than on sound business assessments of the situation. Without champions to tell one's story to, there are few reasons to tell a good one.

cachet

CACHET IS THE INTANGIBLE SIDE OF MARKETING. IF CACHET IS MISSING, THINGS STILL HAPPEN, BUT IF IT IS PRESENT, MAGIC PREVAILS. THE NEW ENTREPRENEUR WRITES IT INTO THEIR BUSINESS PLAN.

The entrepreneur, like the artist or the intellectual, is simply looking for freedom—of expression and of the spirit. Perhaps it is best to leave the mystery there.

PSYCHOLOGY TODAY

I once asked a well-known entrepreneur in the entertainment industry to define cachet. He responded by saying, "Cachet is like sex appeal—it is undefinable but completely recognizable." What I think was missing in his definition was that it is also indispensable. When Uncle Benny says to Pendel in John le Carré's novel *The Tailor of Panama*, "I've said it before, Harry boy, I'll say it again. You've got the fluence. You've got the rock of eye," he was talking about cachet. That is what Prince is referring to in his song "Style" on the *Emancipation* album. Myrna Loy in the *Thin Man* series had the corner on the glamorous version of cachet.

What does cachet mean for the new entrepreneur? When a prospective key hire is down to the wire in determining which firm to go with, or a potential hardware manufacturer is determining whether it's going to bundle your product—or the competition's—in its next sales initiative, or a large retailer is down to a shortlist of two advertising agencies to become its agency of record, cachet will often be the deciding factor. It will not be found on any checklist of haves and have-nots, but it is the one thing that can change the turn of events in your business. Cachet is the intangible element that makes people say things like, "I don't know why, but I really want to go with this agency," or "Something tells me they have what it takes."

For the new entrepreneur, creating cachet demands a methodical commitment to "branding" and "style," both as a means of engaging people in the stories they tell and in creating a sense of the intangible that automatically sets them apart. Does developing cachet mean just hiring the right person to create a solid marketing plan? That's a good start. Does it mean throwing the best parties in the industry? That is also part and parcel of cachet. But what cachet ultimately translates into for the new entrepreneur is the ability to rise above the necessary day-to-day tactics and create a presence, an aura, that people will undeniably and unquestionably identify with a specific person, company, or product.

I remember when we were only 20 people, standing up and telling my staff that Disney started with a guy and a mouse. We could be whatever we wanted if we truly believed that "impossible is a state of mind."

DOUG KEELEY

I know a young entrepreneur in Toronto who is well known for his company's culture—beer in the fridge, beanbag-chair meetings in the loft at night, and dogs everywhere. What began as a loose management style became, in essence, the symbol of this company's success. As the company grew and matured, what was talked about as much as the products and the success was the company's ability to maintain and evolve this same hip approach to management—a recognition that something which was once taken for granted had become a cornerstone of the company's image. Good marketing and advertising can enhance a company, but it cannot replace cachet. Like breaking boundaries, cachet becomes a way of life that must genuinely become a part of the entrepreneur's style for it to work. When one does not recognize the importance of cachet as a part of a business plan, the career plan, or the corporate mandate, the entrepreneur's story loses its passion, and people do not understand what they are trying to belong to. The images created do not last in the client's memory, and there is no powerful aura that can be properly associated with the product or company.

A great case in point is Apple Computers. Despite its dire straits, the upheaval, and dramatic loss of market share in 1996, Apple signaled a revitalization of its history in 1997–98 by using the campaign headline "Think different" in all its advertising efforts. The word *different* reminded people of the former cachet associated with Apple, and they picked up on this idea and talked about it because they wanted to believe in Apple's ability to reinvent itself and once again be on top. In other words, Apple's cachet was still intact.

Cachet requires an element of the whimsical. Why? Because most people do not have enough fun in their working day. Even if they do have moments of distraction or playfulness, they are always in need of more. If you can become the person or the company that becomes a symbol of style, if you can create an element of playfulness within the daily business grind, then you and your idea will be much more memorable than the others will. At Bulldog, we are constantly coming up with small things to surprise and delight the people we meet. We have a whole host of Bulldog rub-on tattoos that we hand out shamelessly wherever we go, mousepads in screaming colors, and dogtags and leashes with our WWW address embossed on them. But we don't just hand them out; we make a connection with the person we are giving them to. We tell a piece of the Bulldog lore and add to our company's cachet. And it works! People do not forget our company name, and they certainly never forget our image. They laugh at the checkered bulldog on the tattoo, and they ask for more t-shirts for their staff. They would rather be part of something that is fun or hip than not, and they will have reasons to come back for more. The new entrepreneur is a committed image builder.

magical realism
"MAGICAL REALISM" IS NOT ONLY A LITERARY TERM. IT BELONGS IN THE BUSINESS LEXICON UNDER "MINDSET."

Let's go back to November 1995, where this particular story began. Once Bulldog made the decision to raise the ante by letting go of our relationship with our original investor and started to play the wait-and-see game with our new potential investor (BCE Capital), we were in true entrepreneurial limbo. Intellectually, we knew that the only thing that mattered was securing outside investment so that we did not lose the entire company. Paradoxically, at the same time, we were determined that we maintain our ambitious product-development schedule. Despite the pressure and internal turmoil our financial crisis was causing each of the partners, we did not even hint at any issues regarding the financial uncertainty of our company. Many entrepreneurs believe in telling their employees everything that is going on within the company, but there are times when I do not think that this is the best strategy.

In 1995, when resolving our financial investment crisis, I used what I call "magical realism." It's a term applied to a particular literary method in fiction writing. For the new entrepreneur, it is the state of mind required during much of the day, but especially when one reaches a crossroads, a decision-making moment, or a time of crisis. Magical realism is a combination of allowing yourself to envision the final outcome—the place where you need to end up to successfully complete your process, the place you visualize as your point in the future—and applying *realism*—the unavoidable and ruthless pragmatism, everything you must think of and do—to ensure that you get to that magical place.

At this particular crossroad, we allowed our engineers and designers to see *only* our unbending commitment to meeting our product deadline, not our doubts. They were counting on our dedication, and they matched our commitment in their own work. The dynamic which this created within the company was one that we could hardly have done without if we wanted to reach our goals. For example, during the due-diligence process, when the BCE executives and their various consultants came around to assess our company, the product, and the team, they saw an extremely productive, committed, and talented product-development team that seemed unaffected

Magical realism describes a particular style of fiction writing. For the new entrepreneur, it is also the state of mind required during much of the day.

by the possibility of crisis. They also saw a management team that was committed to the potential of the product, regardless of the lack of value the initial investor saw on the table. We openly told our customers and the various technology partners of our pending need for outside investment, without communicating a level of panic. When they were interviewed as part of the due-diligence process, there was no hesitation in their recognition and belief in us as a company and the market potential that existed for our product.

Sometimes more magic is required, and other times pure realism is in order. The new entrepreneur recognizes that the delicate balance between these two juxtaposed activities establishes a state of mind that allows ideas to flourish but is diligent about focusing on the here and now. Both attitudes are required. One does not work without the other.

Truth: there's no such thing
Risk: everything
Intention: to be you
Curfew: suffering in silence
Knock out: any contender who wants a shot at the title
Yearn: for infinity

THE ROCK GROUP TRICKY,
POST MAGAZINE

the alchemy of entrepreneuring

Alchemy is the process of turning base elements into gold. The word has a broader concept today—a kind of miraculous change based on choosing the right proportions to allow something "better" to happen. In the universe of the new entrepreneur, no single tactical or strategic ploy has the power to create something out of nothing. Getting financing is never only about getting money but about what kind of money you can live with. Gaining market share within an industry sector is not just about how good your product is but about how you read the signals of what the customer needs ahead of your competition. As in most lifework, there is no shortcut to the art of entrepreneurship and no one formula to follow. But the ability to know how and when to combine the right proportions of all the elements—risk, dreams, realism, championship, and storytelling—suggests an endless number of possibilities. The new entrepreneur is professional in choosing the required elements and knows how to take risks with proportions, because they are aware that out of this process, a seemingly miraculous power is in full play.

chapter 2 **Relentless Convergence**

Think back to 1991. If you were like me, you were using a fax machine that worked 99 percent of the time, you were still relatively amazed at how you ever got anything done in the days before your souped-up desktop computer, and maybe you were coveting the newest Apple laptop. You read as many business magazines as possible, you watched the stock market when you could, you made sure that you were aware of the latest buzzwords in your industry, you defined yourself by your job title and maybe your nationality, and you traveled as much as possible.

Why are all these things important? Because they describe a life before "convergence" became a word that we had to come to terms with. I am positive that back in 1991, I was not spending two hours (minimum) a day "online," scanning small bits of misspelled, unrelated information from all parts of the world (in the form of email messages). I was not as concerned about all the information I could, should, would be accumulating if only I had a faster way to access it from my hotel room; and I certainly was not in a constant process of redefining myself and my business concerns as they related to a concept as esoteric as convergence.

some perspective

It is important for us to stop, take stock, and remember how far we have come since 1991. Internet years are like dog years. For every one that passes, it seems like seven. For me, 1991 represented the year that I would become part of a business revolution in which convergence would be my white knight. Back then, convergence was simply referred to as the c-word and one that caused confusion, but it also created opportunity for those brave enough to live with the ambiguity it caused.

In the early '90s, most of the world, even those directly involved in the evolution of the media industry, were in the dark as to the magnitude of the changes multimedia would bring into every aspect of our lives.

acceptance of computers in the early 1990s was hovering at 30 percent

Although it is hard for those of us who now live and breathe in a diverse digital universe to imagine, the statistics that were generated on customer acceptance of the computer in the early '90s were not very impressive. An October 1994 article in *Macworld* that I had cut out at the time reminds me of how recently technology truly began converging with our everyday lives.

It took about 70 years for 50 percent of Americans to obtain phones. Within 34 years of its introduction, television was in nearly all U.S. homes. In fact, in the early '90s, there were more homes with TVs than with indoor plumbing. VCRs in the home reached about 65 percent market penetration in just 13 years. But the personal computer was only at 30 percent market penetration 20 years after it became a mass-market product.

Without enticing and ubiquitous ways to use a computer in the home or at work, it was not seen as valuable enough to invest in. Of course, with the advent of the World Wide Web, enhanced digital content, and faster, bigger, better hardware, this has dramatically changed. By the end of 1997, 82 million personal computers were connected to the Net, which is a 71 percent increase over the previous year. By 2001, 268 million computers will be hooked up to the Net. Interestingly, in a recent survey conducted by Industry Canada, Canada was found to be number two of the G-7 countries in terms of Internet users, Internet hosts, and computers per capita. Somebody is obviously enticed.

Less than a decade after it opened for commercial activity in 1991, the Net is poised to turbo charge e-commerce into a blockbuster economic force. Market researcher Forrester Research Inc. figures that by 2002, Internet e-commerce among U.S. businesses alone will hit $327 billion, equal to 23% of the gross domestic product.

back to 1991

By the summer of 1991, I had accumulated seven years of expertise in marketing/communications and public relations. Like many of my peers, I had my list of achievements on a sheet of paper for anyone who was interested. I had helped improve the Canadian Dental Association's public relations rating dramatically in six months, and I had sold millions of dollars worth of conceptual marketing services to retailers and real estate tycoons alike. I had managed people, and I had dabbled in consulting. I had lived abroad and had love affairs go awry. I could wrap my experiences around me like liquid trophies. But what I hadn't done was decide how I was going to truly test my hand at entrepreneurship.

Nineteen ninety-one was the depth of the recession, unemployment in Canada was high, and the real estate market in Toronto had dropped dramatically. It was the age of specialization, free trade was beginning to make the headlines, and desktop publishing was allowing everyone to create their own newsletters at a frightening rate. My partner and I both had considerable expertise in marketing, design, and communications. We decided that while those around us were hunkering down to wait out the quiet before the storm, we would begin to scheme.

We spent a good few weeks congratulating ourselves for making the decision to be entrepreneurs. And then slowly it dawned on us: We knew the game plan, but we still had to figure out what exactly our business was going to be. This is where that all-important term "relentless convergence" first came into play in our lives.

When faced with unknown territory, the new entrepreneur focuses on "strategic agility" as a means of making intelligent guesstimates. The momentum created by this active state of mind creates the basis for opportunity. In our case, it led us to an entry point right in the middle of the mad, mad world of technological convergence.

Zenith and Motorola are a good case in point. They both started out as television manufacturers. Zenith decided to continue to define themselves as a television manufacturer *only*. But throughout the years, Motorola has ventured out—from building microprocessors to integrated circuitry. In the process, they have become one of the most successful and recognizable brands in the world, based on a kind of strategic ability that made assumptions about the kinds of technology that people would want to pay for and the way people would want to use technology. Perhaps they considered these as certain eventualities that were worth building their business(es) on. Interestingly enough, today at the University of Houston at Clear Lake there are courses such as Studies of the Future that help students ascertain the competencies that will make them as flexible as possible as a means of preparing for the future.

For us in 1991, strategic agility translated into trying to find the few things that were certain in a world that seemed completely uncertain. This is the unedited shortlist we came up with:

Convergence: the integration of computers, communications, and consumer electronics. With the advent of audio CDs and digital video, it has become clear that all forms of information, both for business and entertainment, can be merged together.

- Start with what you know.

- Make intelligent guesses.

- Stay flexible so that you can completely change your mind midstream.

Out of this rather simple process, we recognized that creating an entrepreneurial premise begins with trend-hopping, it requires one to be a selective historian, and it is based on an understanding that one can leverage the knowledge gained in the service business as a means of finding the right entry point into product development. Here is what we did.

the wonderful world of uncertainty, or finding the "bumping-up-against" point

TREND-HOPPING IS THE FIRST STEP TOWARD CREATING A BUSINESS PLAN THAT IS BASED ON "STRATEGIC AGILITY." IT IS THE INTELLIGENT PERSON'S VERSION OF PREDICTION.

The new entrepreneur focuses on "strategic agility" as a means of making intelligent guesstimates. The momentum created by this active state of mind creates the basis for opportunity.

In 1991, the desktop computer was rapidly becoming the vehicle of choice for most design shops. Although the cost of a high-end computer station was pricey, the time and money saved by avoiding the production of artboards, hand-drawn renderings, versioning, and revisions made up for the initial computer investment. And yet, despite this fact, many of the larger advertising agencies refused to incorporate technology into their organizations, claiming that it interfered with the quality of creativity, which, according to them, could not possibly be captured on a computer screen. Many of them stuck to their denial of the value of computers in the design process with a religious fervor.

That denial worked well for smaller boutiques looking for a point of entry into an already overcrowded industry. Convergence in the design industry resulted in a revised definition of "design excellence," which involved a combination of production efficiency and graphic impact. This was accomplished without the self-consciousness that we currently bring with us when trying to understand technological convergence today. In 1991, design shops were simply looking at new ways to compete while maintaining the integrity of their profession. As marketers, Chris and I questioned what the correlative was for us. At the time, we did not call it convergence, we called it "trend-hopping."

With a blank page in front of us, we did not map out what "the business" would be. Nor did we scope out a game plan for getting there. Instead, we took a bird's-eye view of the world we knew best—the world of graphic design and marketing—and mapped out the trends that we were seeing in the marketplace. Then we tried to find a pattern—to see if there was a point of differentiation that we could bring to the table to take advantage of these trends. After hours of heated discussion, coffee spills, and skipped meals, this is what we came up with.

Desktop publishing was getting more sophisticated every month and building momentum.

Realization: If we could attract the right talent (or train the right people), we could focus on creating a highly sophisticated digital design output studio. Eventually, we could develop an alternative to traditional design and marketing firms by offering higher value for lower cost.

The major visual computing technology players, such as Apple and SGI, were banking on the notion that the corporate and consumers' desire for more media-rich material would eventually become the standard in media creation.

Realization: Most corporations were not adept at maintaining the right in-house talent to leverage the benefit of the new software programs and upgraded computer equipment required to create media-rich content. In addition, somebody would have to assess the value of media-rich materials and make the appropriate investment in technology and human resources to support this new design paradigm. The computer companies that sold the software and hardware wanted and needed this new media guidance to be conducted by a third party. The field was wide open for someone to become this third party.

The recession and the "me trend" of the '80s had produced a glut of over-qualified, unemployed consultants in many industries, including marketing, design, and communications.

Realization: Many of these people did not really want to be entrepreneurs or freelancers but did want to be involved in a pioneering adventure. If we could provide a place for them to work, we could attract the talent we were missing.

Ironically, as computer technology was getting more sophisticated, "human communications" was increasingly becoming the benchmark for success. While companies were investing money in upgrading their computer systems, they were also spending human resources dollars on training their customer-service people how to answer the phone "with meaning," in other words, to communicate more effectively. The gap was wide between the available technology, along with its potential to improve the delivery of information and service, and the corporation's ability to utilize this powerful technology in human interface.

Realization: If the lines between technology, design, marketing, communications, and business were starting to blur, a major opportunity for new types of businesses should emerge. We sensed that this shift would be

The convergence of change that is currently upon us may be summed up in three ways: the shift from reason-based to chaos-based logic; the splintering of social, political, and economic organization; and the collapse of producer-controlled consumer markets.

JIM TAYLOR AND
WATTS WACKER,
THE 500 YEAR DELTA

dramatic. More important, we knew that we wanted to be right smack in the middle of it. If we dedicated ourselves to being at the center of what we then called "the bumping-up-against point," we were bound to be in a position to leverage our accumulated knowledge in marketing and design to create true opportunity. We had to commit to "bumping into" people, places, and trends that were signposts of this blurring of lines—what we all now refer to as the technology convergence.

Many people do not realize that the very first use of the term "multimedia" occurred in the mid-fifties. At that time, a film producer and entertainment entrepreneur named Mike Todd defined multimedia as the bringing together of wide-screen film presentation technique using a 65mm camera and 70mm prints with stereophonic sound on a magnetic track.

The last realization we had was not so much a reaction to a trend but a personal desire. Looking at our whiteboard scribbling and following the arrows we had bravely drawn between our random ideas, we thought, If we are going to sweat through the details of creating our own business, we better determine why we are doing this.

As with all good partnerships, the answer to the "why" question was one we could both agree upon instantly. We both wanted to test our ability to pioneer a new trend, leverage our knowledge from years in the service business, and ultimately create a company, an image, a myth that would offer us long-term staying power. This company would be a representation of what we believed in: risk, storytelling, and the blending of ideas. We wanted to make as much money as we could and to play an international game, and we were not afraid of living up to the saying "Better to be loved and hated, than not remembered at all."

THE NEW ENTREPRENEUR UNDERSTANDS THAT THE ACCUMULATED KNOWLEDGE GAINED BY BEING IN THE SERVICE BUSINESS IS OFTEN THE MOST DIRECT ROUTE TO TARGETED PRODUCT DEVELOPMENT. IT IS THE BEST WAY TO ALLOW FOR "CERTAIN EVENTUALITIES" AND PROVIDES THE AGILITY TO RESPOND TO THOSE EVENTUALITIES WITH SPEED AND ACCURACY.

If you asked author and consultant Geoffrey Moore (*Crossing the Chasm, Into the Tornado, Gorilla Game*) what he thinks are the three key attributes for successful entrepreneurship, he would probably put one idea at the top of his list: creating a service business that will allow you to test product concepts as a means of encapsulating true customer need. In his view, this is especially important when you are creating new products or radical ideas for new product categories in the world of high tech.

Back in 1991, we only knew the service business—the design and marketing service business. We had a hunch that if we stayed close to our customers on the service side of the equation, they, in turn, would lead us to a software product, based on a need, a gap within their business processes. Based on our trend-hopping exercise, we kept ourselves as close to the emerging trends within our customers' industries as they related to the technology they used, the design they employed for visual impact, and the marketing/communications strategies they created to disseminate their messages. In the end, it was out of the leverage we garnered from the intersection of these trends that we began to formulate the basis for building a product.

THE NEW ENTREPRENEUR IS SOMEONE WHO CREATES PERSONAL BRANDS THAT REPRESENT WHAT THEY STAND FOR, NOT WHAT BUSINESS THEY ARE IN.

A good friend of mine describes the world of convergence with one simple statement: "Just when you think it is going to zig, it zags." Now that my partner and I had completed our whiteboard exercise, we were ready to launch into a business that was somewhat foggy around the edges but was eventually going to put us right in the middle of convergence. We had finally narrowed down our objective to "being at the point of convergence of design, communications, and technology in order to productize our accumulated knowledge." (No, really! We actually said that!)

Brand is really a set of attributes that outside customers project onto a company. A brand must stand for something and *then* you put a name to it.

While finding our initial launching point, we asked ourselves many important questions: How did one name a company that would be in the business of changing, moving, and being *entre*—in between—a variety of industries? How did one choose a name that would allow one to zig while the rest of the world zagged, that could ride out the various changes that we were fairly certain were going to be a constant in the business we had chosen?

We were stuck. Every company name we came up with seemed to limit us in our ability to grow beyond a design firm or a marketing agency. We needed something that also reflected the convergence of technology, and yet we were not really in the technology business, nor did we necessarily want to be.

When in doubt, our rule of thumb had always been: Take a look around; go on a journey. So that's what we did. We went on a visual journey. We looked around and collected all the logos and company names that created a simple but powerful mood and image and in some ways told a story. We also looked at people who we felt reflected a brand, in other words, who in some ways had branded themselves as personalities and created equity in their own personal brands.

Using the trend-hopping exercise in a revised format, this is what we came up with:

- Since we were in the depths of the recession and times were tough, we needed something that would communicate strength, determination, and tenacity.

- We liked icons that had a humorous element, something that was visually whimsical, because we believe that you should never take yourself too seriously.

- We definitely did not want to brand ourselves in any one business, because ultimately, we knew that if we played our cards right, we would be moving from one business to another throughout the history of the company. Therefore, any words that represented the design world, the communications world, or hinted at technology were not in the running.

- When we thought about what we stood for and what we wanted to be remembered for, we were able to isolate one word: attitude. We liked the fact that everyone thought we were crazy to be starting a company on our own in such turbulent times. We liked the fact that our concept was ambiguous and begged a lot of questions. We also liked the fact that we were jumping off a cliff, not quite sure whether we would land safely.

- We were design hounds, visual junkies, and we wanted a name that would allow us to create beautiful, sometimes funny, but always memorable icons. We wanted to be branded from day one.

As Michael Moon says, our brand had to reflect our own version of our "moments of truth."

Once we had put all of these ideas down on a page, we were able to see that what we were after was a memorable icon that had nothing to do with anything. Ultimately, we realized that creating a brand that was associated with the attributes that would represent who we were and what we stood for, a brand that would be remembered, was only going to come about through our own entrepreneurial efforts, by our own dedication to design and visual impact. As Michael Moon says, our brand had to reflect our own version of our "moments of truth."

Bulldog is the name we came up with. It was tenacious and memorable, had a slightly funny, almost whimsical feel to it, and definitely had absolutely nothing whatsoever to do with the business we were in. Our challenge now was to foster the attributes that we wanted associated with our company name. Today, many years later, Bulldog has become the absolute icon of tough, tenacious entrepreneurial energy with a twist of humor. I still walk into boardrooms around the world and inevitably someone will say, "How did you come up with the name Bulldog? I love it." And then I launch into the telling of the Bulldog story, the retelling of our myth, the building of our metaphor—and we are remembered.

WHILE TREND-HOPPING AND IMAGE BUILDING, THE NEW ENTREPRENEUR EATS HUMBLE PIE FOR BREAKFAST, LUNCH, AND DINNER—AND REVELS IN IT.

A friend of mine who works for a major consulting firm once told me that, in the very early days of their existence, whenever a customer asked him, "How many people work here?" the magic number was always "around 20."

Somehow, this number sounds as if you have the proper quantity of people needed to get a big job done yet reflects a reasonable payroll. When I first heard this, I was astounded at what sounded like advice to engage in an outright lie, but as we started to eke out a living from Bulldog, I began to understand the thinking behind my friend's statement. In essence, saying you have 20 people working for you is a way to force yourself to start acting like a bigger company right from the beginning, when most of your energy is taken up by pure survival tactics. From the very first day, it is an important business tactic for the new entrepreneur and their organization to create business standards and rituals that are often reserved for more mature companies. To mature gracefully, you need to act older than your age. This is something that we have been doing since we started Bulldog, and we continue to maintain this notion of "bigger than we are." For example, we were creating quarterly financial reports long before we had investors to show them to; we held regular board meetings and had our lawyer take the minutes long before we had any other partners who were not related to us. In acting bigger than you are, you can step into the next phase of your company's growth with ease and grace when the time ultimately comes. The qualitative difference is that you will have had months and years of training by the time you are as grown-up as you are trying to be.

Bulldog's first year was a time of searching. Although we were lucky enough to partner with some very talented, creative people, rather than being at the point of convergence, we were in limbo between traditional design and multimedia technology. We ate humble pie for breakfast, lunch, and dinner, even though we acted as if we were running a 20-person studio. We reveled in this stance because it was absurd. We stuck to it because we were bulldogs. But the reality was that, although we knew that we really understood the concept of differentiation in the form of digitized media, we were not able to translate that knowledge into a growing customer list fast enough. Then a few things changed.

UNLIKE THE "LONER" ENTREPRENEUR OF THE PAST, THE NEW ENTRE-PRENEUR IS ONE WHO SEEKS OUT OTHERS, WHO WANTS TO BELONG. PARTNERSHIP CAN BE A WINNING FORMULA.

I left my job. I should restate this. I was offered an incredible amount of money and a promotion that I wanted, but after weeks of total indecisiveness, I realized that I just couldn't do it. I finally took the leap. I said no to my old job and yes to full-time entrepreneurship.

We decided to divide and conquer: I dedicated myself to the sales and marketing of Bulldog, Chris dedicated himself to account management, and we both dedicated ourselves to understanding the trends within the world of new media. We also found a third partner, Tom Howlett, who had worked with me as the VP of production at another company. Soon Tom was running the day-to-day operations of Bulldog, and directing the design and production. He was much better than either Chris or I in the management of creative resources.

Bringing on Tom says something important about our definition of entrepreneuring. Many entrepreneurs decide that they want to create a company and put a stake in the ground that is wholly theirs. Many of these individuals are very successful, and they certainly match the cultural stereotype of the entrepreneur as the "Lone Ranger."

Call it "collective entrepreneurship," call it "mutual trust." In the end, the ability to bounce ideas off each other is indispensable.

From our experience, and that of many of my peers, however, partnership has been the best way to ensure that you are creating a formula for success. When you are intent, as we were, to create opportunity in uncharted waters or in the midst of convergence, you are working against time. The question of whether or not you *will* be able to accumulate all of the required skills for running your company alone is not relevant. Instead, you need to create a game plan that ensures that you will have to focus only on the skills you are best at. You accomplish this by seeking out partners who are equally expert in the areas where you are lacking and who have the same investment in the life and death of your company as you do. Call it "collective entrepreneurship" or "mutual trust." In the end, the ability to bounce ideas off each other is indispensable. The story of Bulldog's early years is a case in point. By dividing our skill sets in three, we were able to identify the trends in the marketplace just ahead of the sea changes. This created our competitive advantage. As a team, we were able to extend our ability to master interpretation in three areas—technology, design and marketing—with relative speed and accuracy. Here is how we did it:

IF YOU ARE UNWILLING TO SUBJECT YOURSELF TO THE NOTION OF RELENTLESS CONVERGENCE, MANY OPPORTUNITIES WILL REMAIN IN A HOLDING PATTERN JUST OUTSIDE OF YOUR ENTREPRENEURIAL REACH.

We built backdoor relationships. We got as close as we could to companies that were leading the trend in the area of new media creation and delivery and found ways to become partners with them as opposed to suppliers. We focused our relationship-building efforts on companies such as Apple Computers, Kodak, Northern Telecom, and SGI. It would have been easy for us to offer our marketing and design services to any of these companies, but we resisted. We knew that if we did, we would only become one of many companies on their roster of suppliers, and we did not want to be viewed in that way. We needed to be on a much more intimate level with them in order to be the first to hear about trends that we had inklings of, but nothing more.

Kodak is one case in point. We did not try to be their marketing or design supplier but, instead, agreed to provide them with multimedia presentations that utilized some of their latest products in exchange for our ability to test some of their beta products within our own production environment. By working with them in this capacity, we got a glimpse of their strategic intent in the industry and how they were approaching the growing sophistication in the consumer marketplace through products such as the Kodak Photo CD. We started to see how and why they were focusing on the consumer's growing desire to create, store, and organize media. By focusing on the long-term potential of the relationship, we built a worthwhile partnership by knocking on the back door rather than walking in through the front. We applied this same kind of partnership approach to our relationships with Apple Computers and their New Media Division, SGI, and to Northern Telecom and their video-conferencing product.

As we at Bulldog started to formulate our strategy for evolving from a service company into a product company, we kept revisiting this growing business and consumer need for sophisticated visuals. We perceived that companies were developing a desire to share their intellectual property and understand how to efficiently share, store, and distribute their graphics, photos, and images as they did their documents. We still did not see how we were going to make any money from this knowledge, but we marked it with a placeholder in our minds.

Result: We began to see that our core talent consisted of the ability to combine our design and programming talent with our marketers' mindset. This enabled us to create business models that demonstrated how and when technology could be used and then to find the right wizardry to create the product that would answer that need.

Today, I look at hundreds of companies, such as Silicon Reef and Spray, that are thriving in this business. But I do not believe I am getting nostalgic when I say that, in those days, it was not usual, especially since it was so difficult to make any money doing it.

We invested in people and technology we could not sell. At Bulldog, we found as many different ways as we could to invest in computer hardware and software, even though some of it was way beyond our means. We also hired individuals who had incredible talent in multimedia design and programming, while knowing that our client base was not yet ready to pay for that kind of expertise. Our goal in doing both of these things was that eventually, the in-house equipment, knowledge, and expertise we were acquiring would leapfrog us into other new media opportunities that we could sell as part of our service business.

Result: We were in a constant state of cash crunch.

Our fancy multimedia presentations got us in the door (sometimes even the front door), even though the customer ended up buying our more traditional services, such as graphic design, collateral material, and marketing programs. For example, when we first met with the A&P company, we were keen to incorporate our multimedia design into a network of kiosks in their stores. These kiosks would be linked to what we knew was a pretty sophisticated database system they had created to track their customers' profiles and learn about their buying habits. In the end, we were hired to produce the quarterly magazine for A&P's new house brand, Master Choice. In the meantime, however, we were able to learn about their database model—later this would be invaluable to us.

We started to see and learn how digital tools affected the design process within our own studio and to formulate ideas about how to organize the ideal digital design studio of the future. We also began to understand the hurdles that we had to overcome to optimize human and technology resources. Two years later, when we finally made the leap into software development, this firsthand knowledge gave us a basis for product modeling and credibility for what turned out to be a production-intensive customer base in the entertainment and broadcast businesses. The information we were collecting in our travels was something that no research and development (R&D) lab could replace.

We kept doing what we were good at. Despite the distraction of multimedia and the lure of technology, we stuck to what we were good at while we explored where we were going next. This may be a routine exercise in a large company, but it is a difficult juggling act within a small company. In our off-hours, we dabbled in the promise of where new media design might lead us in the form of a software product. Meanwhile, we shuffled whatever funds we generated from the service business into our informal version of an R&D lab, while still maintaining a leadership position in multimedia design and marketing communications services. We held wild parties in our loft space, and we produced beautiful and surprising promotional material as often as possible. We stayed close to technology and kept increasing our client list and the scope of our portfolio.

Result: By subjecting ourselves to convergence and abandoning any notions of being a company grounded (and limited) by our roots in design, communications, and technology, we were able to create a hybrid organization. Bulldog became a brand that was synonymous with the tenacious ability to maintain a nondefinable category which sat somewhere between design, business, technology, and communications. By the end of our first year together, we were growing at a rate of 300 percent and attracting major clients (TD Bank, A&P, Second Cup, the Movie Network, CIBC) who liked our style, were impressed with our digital know-how, and felt that they were getting traditional marketing expertise with the promise of new media.

The press started to talk and write about us *(The Globe and Mail, Maclean's* magazine, the CBC), talented designers started to inquire about job openings, and we gained a new confidence in our ability to do what we were best at: mastering the interpretation of the signs of change, not inventing new ones.

SOMETIMES YOU CAN EVOLVE YOUR BUSINESS ONLY BY BUMPING UP AGAINST YOUR OWN GLASS CEILINGS. THE NEW ENTREPRENEUR ANTICIPATES THIS.

By 1993, we were by all accounts doing well. We acknowledged, however, that we were still competing in a race that we knew—delivering traditional marketing and design services to the corporate world, using the latest and greatest in software and computer technology.

I'd like to point out that there is absolutely nothing wrong with this. In fact, for many entrepreneurs, this represents a formula for success that can be played out for many years. Today, there are thousands of companies, hundreds of thousands of people, making a great living in just this arena. But when we looked back at our answer as to why we were doing all of this, we knew that this play between design and technology could not last forever, and it certainly was not going to get us into a pioneering position for establishing a product company.

More urgently, our cash requirement for our R&D was growing. It was getting harder and harder to wait until our customers' comfort level in buying large multimedia projects matched our eagerness to invest in our own pet R&D projects.

Our employees were starting to question our sanity. We were reevaluating our dedication to the notion of "masters of interpretation." And finally, the day came when we, too, looked around and said, "We need a way out of this and fast." We were starting to bump up against our own glass ceiling.

THE NEW ENTREPRENEUR DOES NOT TRY TO UNDERSTAND HOW TECHNOLOGY CONVERGENCE WORKS BUT HOW TO INCORPORATE THE CHANGES IT CREATES INTO A BUSINESS PLAN. SOMETIMES OPPORTUNITY IS FORMULATED THROUGH A DIVERGENCE.

In physics, you can choose to see the subatomic world in terms of either waves or particles. In life, you have people who see things in terms of things and others who see things in terms of energy. Physicist Werner Heisenberg

According to an Imat multimedia survey — 53% of firms reported profitable operations for the 1995 fiscal year. A survey of multimedia developers in the U.S. showed just 4% claimed profitability.

THE WALL STREET JOURNAL

said that you have to choose one perspective over the other. You can see light either as a particle or a wave, but not as both at the same time. To understand what light really is and why it behaves the way it does, however, you need to look at it both ways. When it comes to changes in technology, the same view may hold true, but looking only at the "particles" gives one, at best, a severely limited picture and, at worst, an incorrect one.

Michael Moon of Gistics believes that convergence is a word that was originally championed by "thing-oriented" people who think in ones and zeroes and see in black-and-white terms. But as Moon points out, in reality, when we look around us, we recognize that this approach is far too limited and artificial to describe the dynamics of what is actually happening. When I look at the positive disruption a new concept such as the WWW is creating, I think of metaphors such as groundswell, earthquake, tidal wave. These images imply that a momentum has been created, something that at times feels unstoppable, out of control, and beyond our ability to predict or manipulate. If anything, the coming together of these elements creates more of a divergence of the unlimited possibilities and opportunities that will become available after the occurrence of this new collision of elements.

High-tech business has created 7,000 millionaires and a few dozen billionaires in the last 25 years.

FORBES MAGAZINE

If you are a company or a person trying to cope with this kind of fluid, ambiguous, powerful force, you know that the more you swim in it and the more you ride out the wave, the more comfortable you will be with it and the more you will find ways to use its momentum to jettison you forward. Ironically, approaching convergence in this way will give you more value. Your ability to benefit from all of the diverging elements will increase, as if you moved from the belief in a flat world to a round one.

It is exactly this thinking which led to my view of the rapid changes in technology as it relates to entrepreneuring as a playground that serves as a catalyst, allowing seemingly conflicting agendas to work side by side for our mutual benefit. Whether this means telco/cable mergers, service mergers, Hollywood buying technology companies or vice versa, what's important is that in such instances, the lines have blurred to such an extent that defining which side of the business you are on is often a misnomer. In the end, confusion spells opportunity around the globe. It allows companies such as Media Asset Factory to create a 3-D rendering service bureau. It creates a market for three young doctors in Alberta to sell their interactive games worldwide under the name of BioWare Corp. It allows companies such as AutoNet to offer hassle-free connections to more than 14,000 auto dealers in North America through the Web. It creates the need for new media companies such as MouseHouse in Denmark to flourish, Australian companies such as LookSmart to redefine search tools, and Canadian companies such as NCompass and Numetrix Ltd. to succeed. Each of these players, and many like them, stepped right in the middle of the technological chaos as a means of finding their particular opportunity.

That's what the residents of Miramichi, New Brunswick, have done, and their story has stayed with me since I spoke at one of their events a few years ago. This small town was best known for its fishing, forestry, and ship-building industries. Unfortunately, since the 1970s, it has suffered a number of losses, including a decline of its natural resource-based economy, and in effect, it has experienced the highest unemployment rate in Canada. But rather than give in to this despair, the staff at the NBCC Miramichi were determined to create a self-sustaining economy that would transform the community from a resource-based community to a knowledge industry by creating the Learning Technologies Centre. Today, this center has two functions: as a school for training entrepreneurs in multimedia production, design, and programming; and as an R&D lab for beta-testing various new products in the high technology and multimedia industries. By creating this center, the people of Miramichi had managed to attract technologists, designers, and business consultants of the highest caliber from around the world, creating an incubator approach to teaching these new skills to the people of their province. An added benefit was that they had attracted the attention of outsiders who now considered their town to be part of the new technology order.

After I had delivered my speech to a group of 300 people, we listened to the local fiddlers perform. Then we all talked about the potential of what they had accomplished and how this achievement would formerly have been unthinkable in a part of the world that was about as far away from the technology convergence as you can get. The juxtaposition of worlds was not lost on any of us. The government officials and private-sector citizens of Miramichi who had committed to uniting technology and multimedia design to a part of the world that had no context for this kind of commercial activity are to be truly commended. Their achievement remains in my mind as a lasting image of the great potential that is often created at a point of divergence of ideas, cultures, and opportunities and the positive effect it has on the people who are part of that powerful force, confluence.

it is about context and content

If convergence is actually confluence, then in the midst of confluence, it is better for the new entrepreneur to build a strong, flexible, and adaptable boat that will enable them to ride the tidal wave, moving with its sudden and uncontrollable changes, than to stand looking at the wave from a distance, trying to figure out what caused it in the first place and what it is made of. As Michael Moon says about the information age, "Think of it as content and context. If you get fixated on the content, you miss the whole point. If you get fixated on the context, you have a wonderful experience, but no results. You've got to be able to swim in both worlds with the confidence that you built the right boat to sail around a round world."

Translating this imagery back into the very real world that Bulldog was experiencing back in the early '90s, our company soon realized that we were trying too hard to control the way changes were going to affect us in the ongoing technology convergence. We were, mistakenly, seeing this convergence as a set of things that we could pull apart to determine where and how we were going to stop being a service company and suddenly appear on the crest of the next wave as a product company.

What we really needed at this point was to build a boat that was going to keep us afloat for as long as each tidal wave lasted. It had to have all the right equipment, including state-of-the-art satellite global positioning and the latest safety features, to ensure that we were able to survive a storm just long enough to ride out the inevitable tidal flow that we were already in the middle of.

This was not exactly the eloquent imagery that was tossed around our boardroom. The experience was more like living with a panic-stricken screech that kept us all awake at night. Only by teaching ourselves to see convergence as confluence were we able to start moving forward again in a way that would enable our company to survive—to diverge.

We started by reevaluating the assumptions we had made in our original trend-hopping exercise and by revisiting the notion that our proximity to the customer in our service business was the key to our (as yet unborn) product. By doing so, we came to the realization that the gap was widening between what was being touted as the future and potential of media and how much the corporate world was willing to spend to enhance its marketing and sales messages at the present time due to fear. With the knowledge and experience that Bulldog had acquired, we could fit right in between that gap, acting as the catalyst for bringing the two halves together.

In doing this, we became more valuable at both ends of the food chain. Our customers could rely on our ability to interpret the technology offering (computer networks, software and hardware configurations) within their own marketing and sales departments. At the other end of the spectrum, the technology companies we worked with (such as Apple and SGI) could start to see us as the champion of their new technology mantra: new media.

Additionally, this hands-on experience would provide us with the means of seeing what new patterns and gaps would emerge—perhaps even suggest a product that we could develop and sell. We turned up the volume on the level of ambiguity we were living with: Were we a design firm? Were we a systems-integration consulting group? Were we technology wanna-be's? Were we sophisticated marketing hacks? We let go of these labels and simply told ourselves, "We are in the business of change." We added this line

Think of it as content and context. If you get fixated on the content, you miss the whole point. If you get fixated on the context, you have a wonderful experience, but no results. You've got to be able to swim in both worlds with the confidence that you built the right boat to sail around a round world.

MICHAEL MOON,
PRESIDENT, GISTICS

to the digital video we used for corporate presentations, we tattooed it on our foreheads, and we got busy building our new boat.

THE NEW ENTREPRENEUR DEALS WITH CONFLUENCE BY FOCUSING ON THREE CONCEPTS: SUBJECT YOURSELF TO CHAOS, ABANDON ALL YOUR PRECEDENTS, AND MAKE DEALS.

My particular convergence/confluence story is surrounded by developments in new media design capabilities and emerging trends in the creation of media-rich design. For other entrepreneurs, the story will take the shape of money-market fluctuations or the erratic price of coffee. Regardless of what form the signs and guideposts take, it is our ability to interpret these signals that always leads to a new juncture, an opportunity to diverge. When it comes to determining where you are in relation to technology confluence, I have found it helpful to think in terms of the following three points:

subject yourself to chaos

Understanding how to interpret trends is not about invention but about subjecting oneself to the momentum of confluence. When you subject yourself to a relentless level of change, just past your comfort level, opportunities will emerge. For example, in 1831, Cyrus McCormick was in the business of producing books for farmers to encourage them to become more mechanically minded. In his line of work, he discovered that farmers could get incredibly high yields from their land if they purchased combines. Combines were expensive, however, and the gap was too great between what the typical farmer could afford to put down on a combine and the potential of what that new technology could potentially yield. But by subjecting himself to the changes that he saw as inevitable and by putting himself smack in the middle of them, McCormick invented what we know today as "installment credit." Whatever industry you are in, find the point of chaos and subject yourself to it as a means of finding your point of opportunity.

abandon your precedents

When you subject yourself to confluence, technological or otherwise, you will need to abandon traditional business rules of thumb. Abandon your notions that you cannot be a company without a mission statement. Abandon the idea that you have to have a clearly defined relationship with all your customers. Abandon the concept that you are alone in your quest and cannot collaborate with competitors. Especially abandon any notion that there is a right way to maneuver through this jungle gym of chaos. By letting go of these ideas, you will be able to figure out your game plan a lot quicker.

I don't buy the notion that the world is organized the way universities and companies are. Ideas don't know what discipline they're in.

JERRY ZALTMAN,
FAST COMPANY MAGAZINE

make deals

In the heat of the moment, we often get lofty in our thinking and want to conquer the world. It is true that no one can predict the future and that when change is happening at a great speed, particularly in the world of technology, the unpredictable can happen. Products that have little merit suddenly become showstoppers; services that do not have a sustainable offering pull out into the lead. For the new entrepreneur, however, the operative word is survival. One vicious hit by the tidal wave, and you might go down, never to arise again. In Bulldog's case, we kept doing what we were good at while we developed our ideas about creating a product company, even though, in the beginning, we didn't have a specific product in mind. While we lived in a world of magical realism every day, we also paid homage to survival. We stuck to what we did well—making business deals in design and marketing that would enable us to pay our bills. And we were committed to maintaining the integrity of our services. There was simply no other way.

What I have found to be the most important element in surviving and benefiting from the collision course of change that we are all in the midst of (regardless of how you choose to define it) is asking the questions.

The mindset that the entrepreneur works to cultivate is similar to the description of the Buddhist temple of truth. This temple is protected by two guardians: one of paradox and one of confusion. In their quest for a point of entry, an entrepreneur thrives on this dichotomy, holding onto these two conflicting truths simultaneously without suppressing or disconnecting one from the other. Out of this struggle comes a beautiful and dynamic tension. If you persist in this battle long enough, a synthesis will appear, a third creative resolution of these two seemingly incongruent truths, perhaps a divergence.

The new entrepreneur takes hold of these solutions, these shifts, these moments of pure inspiration only if they are willing to subject themselves to paradox, to abandon any notion of what the outcome should be and to work hard to survive the challenges that this world of conflict will create. In doing this, they are cultivating the art of positive entrepreneuring.

Convergence (confluence) has truly become my white knight, and Bulldog's software reflects this dynamic. The knowledge that we had to gather together to create our product in the first place required an understanding of the confluence of all three disciplines—technology, design, and communications—in the form of new channels, such as the Web, networked distribution, and the remote work groups in the production studios we would be selling to. Even today, as Bulldog continues to work with our top customers, including Sony Pictures Entertainment, Microsoft Studios®, and General Motors, confluence still comes into daily play as the team moves through unclaimed territory. We are constantly discovering new opportunities for assisting companies and people as they seek to manage the massive amounts of digital media that the advent of the Web (as only one of many examples) has generated—and at a level no one could ever have anticipated.

THE NEW ENTREPRENEUR DOES NOT FOCUS ON GETTING THE RIGHT ANSWER, BUT ON FINDING THE QUESTION.

"Technology confluence" is not an easy concept to wrestle with and one that has been the focus of many books, much discussion, and many inaccurate conclusions. I do not propose to know any more or less than anyone else about the fast pace at which our world is changing. Like you, I listen closely to those who watch trends, and I look for predictions that make sense to me—whether that means truly embracing Charles Handy's "upside-down thinking," Peter Drucker's approach to entrepreneurship and innovation, or Peter Schwartz's writings, which provide us with a "set of organized ways for us to dream effectively about our own future." What I have found to be the most important element in surviving and benefiting from the collision course of change that we are all in the midst of (regardless of how you choose to define it) is asking the questions.

The new entrepreneur focuses on what questions to ask and does not worry whether they get the right answer. An associate of mine, Bill Buxton, chief scientist at Alias Wavefront, always uses the evolution of the wristwatch as a guide for how we should be looking at our world today. He says, "Tell me which question the watch, as we know it today, was created to answer." If you are like me, you probably said, "What time is it?" Wrong! Invented in the 1700s, the watch was originally created to answer the question, "Where am I?"—helping ships to navigate at sea. How ironic!

The world of confluence is no different from my friend's historical reference. The key to navigating through confluence can be found in developing the ability to ask the right questions. Don't get caught up in asking questions like, "Why is all this change happening?" or even, "How are these changes happening and where are they going?" Instead, ask questions that will force you to wonder, "Where am I in relation to this confluence of change, and what am I going to do about it? What boat will I build?"

chapter 3 My Trip to Mecca

If you are one of the tagalong baby boomers like me—not quite as lucky as the baby boomers a few years ahead of you but not as cynical and fearless as the "Nexers" on your heels—then you probably spent much of your childhood reading about people who lived in faraway places. You saw films, leafed through your dad's *National Geographic*, and watched videos at school. I always tried to imagine what I would do if I suddenly found myself in those countries. Would I brush my teeth in South Africa the same way I did in Canada? Would I be able to have cereal for breakfast in the Bahamas? Would I be able to talk about the same things at the dinner table in Spain? Being Canadian, I was always much more attracted to the warmer places and wanted to know what it would be like to go out on the streets in the middle of December in a place where there was no snow. When I think now about how I parachuted into Silicon Valley, this daydreaming exercise comes back to me vividly.

In my more dramatic storytelling moments, I describe the transition from Toronto to Silicon Valley as follows: I was offered the opportunity to set up an office in Cupertino by one of the most influential characters who worked out of the New Media Division at Apple Computers. On a whim, I packed the car, drove across the prairies, and began to work in sunny California, leaving my company in the hands of my partners. I never looked back.

Usually I save that story for audiences who thrive on sweeping dramatic statements but are not really interested in process or learning from the details of that particular character-building, exhilarating, and sometimes painful journey. Here is what really happened.

In the early '90s, Bulldog set up a sister company called Empower Computerware. Empower was set up as a VAR (value-added reseller) of Apple products, Macromedia software, and other peripherals. Empower also performed technical support, network setup, and consulting, focusing on the digital design studio marketplace. There were three reasons for setting up this new company:

- Our computer-equipment and software consumption was constant and often required ongoing technical support for all the designers in our studio. We could not find any company that could really support us and keep us on top of the latest and greatest products within our budget. If we became a VAR, then we could get a discount for equipment and software, which would be financially beneficial. In effect, we could become our own biggest client.

- We looked around at others in our industry and realized that they were having the same problem. If we could offer them consulting and technical-support services through an arm's-length autonomous company, we could probably do a pretty good business.

- We wanted to stay close to some of the leaders in the world of multimedia software and hardware, such as Apple, SGI, and Macromedia. VARs with good volume sales are often asked to be beta sites for new products coming onto the market. At a minimum, VARs get information regarding new product releases far ahead of the general public. This could not hurt us. And the cost for setting up a VAR, especially with the guaranteed business that Bulldog could provide, was nominal.

Apple was very influential in the visual design world. Some two-thirds of all websites are thought to have been created on Macintosh computers.

TIME MAGAZINE

At the time, this move was somewhat of a diversion from our hybrid organization of marketing/multimedia production and a technology consulting business, requiring resources and people we were unfamiliar with managing. But in the end, the evolution of this sister company became an important building block in our move from a service business to a product business, because we were able to attract engineers who were more comfortable in this type of environment than in a design environment. Empower ultimately became the home of our informal R&D lab.

In 1992–93, Apple was leading the multimedia parade. Their New Media Division out of Cupertino was quickly becoming the champion of rich digital media creation, and "new media" was becoming the war cry of all designers and production studios, print and publishing houses, and the high-end advertising agencies. In fact, there were people at Apple who had the title "evangelist" on their cards. And that is exactly what they did. They traveled around the world and evangelized the importance of new media and Apple's leadership role in this new world order.

By this time, we had developed strong relationships with many executives at Apple Computers in Canada, and working with them was exciting and kept us close to new developments. But we, like every other design firm, wanted to get to the center of activity, the hub of its decision making: Apple's New Media Division in Cupertino. For us, San Francisco and Silicon Valley comprised the Mecca of multimedia design—a place that we had read about, heard about, and daydreamed about for years. But how was Bulldog going to be noticed amid the clamor of every other multimedia design firm, including the hordes of companies in the Bay Area? As I've said before, when in doubt, take a journey. Sometimes it has to be big journey.

Through my relationships at Apple Canada and after traveling to Silicon Valley on a reconnaissance mission, I was introduced to Paul Wollaston, then market-development manager for Apple Computers' New Media Division and for Apple Pacific. As it turned out, he provided my entry point to Silicon Valley. Once again, even in the world of digital hype, it is the people you meet who connect the dots, the champions who move you forward.

When Paul and I met, we had three things in common: We both had a history in Canada, and we loved good food and wine. Most important, we both had a driving business need for the heightened integration of new media production and interactive design into the corporate world's marketing and communications activities. Paul was Apple's new media evangelist and was traveling around the world promoting Apple as a leader in the industry. In the process, he was searching for good examples of companies and people who were supporters of this message.

As it turned out, we supported his message in more ways than one. Through our sister company, Empower, we had become an Apple VAR selling lots of Apple gear. We had created beautiful multimedia designs that made their products shine, and we had a showcase video-conferencing product with Northern Telecom, which featured Apple hardware, that was getting great press. Additionally, through our service business, we were doing a good job of convincing corporate customers to invest in new media production and marketing on Apple hardware. Bulldog had become an example of converging industries, and Paul viewed our company as a perfect example of an evangelist of the "new media mantra." We had captured his interest.

Within a few months, Bulldog had begun working with the Apple head office in Cupertino in two ways. First, we became a supplier of marketing services, producing a lot of digital design and multimedia projects to support their marketing efforts. Second, we started to appear in their evangelizing presentations that toured around the world. We had become one of a handful of companies that exemplified the Apple message in action.

LIKE MOST DELICIOUS THINGS TO EAT, RARE INVITATIONS HAVE AN EXPIRATION DATE. THE NEW ENTREPRENEUR KNOWS WHEN TO DROP EVERYTHING ELSE, GRAB OPPORTUNITY OFF THE SHELF, AND RUN WITH IT. IN THIS CASE, IT CAME IN THE SHAPE OF AN APPLE.

Over the next few months, Chris and I developed a strong relationship with Paul. We often found ourselves talking about the future of new media and guesstimating where we would all be in five years. On one particular evening, Paul asked what I would do if I were given the chance to establish a presence for Bulldog in Silicon Valley. I answered, "I'd set up camp long enough to find the right technology players, the right influencers who would help us pinpoint a product—something related to new media design and production." A few weeks later, Paul left me a voicemail message. If I was interested, I was invited to set up a temporary office alongside a host of other consultants inside the New Media Division in Cupertino. Not only would this help Bulldog with the work we were already doing for Apple, but it would get our foot in the door in Silicon Valley. His offer was the sign of a true champion.

I well remember the day of his call. It was sometime in August 1994, and Chris and I were having coffee on a beautiful Saturday morning. The topic was lingering somewhere two inches above our espressos when, at the same time, we both said something like "We have no choice. This offer will definitely have a 'best before date,' and we should jump on it while it's hot." Four weeks later, we packed my car and drove across the country to California. We made the trip in three days, and I truly have not looked back since.

In retracing the steps that led to that decision, I realize now that this move to Silicon Valley was the riskiest thing I had ever done for a number of reasons:

- I was leaving my company without having put the right sales structure in place to replace me and my driving sales efforts. This decision would come back to haunt us in a traumatic way—though at the time, I was cavalier about it.

- I had not spent enough time researching the workings of Silicon Valley and learning how deals were made there. This, ironically, turned out to be a blessing. My naïveté helped me to break the rules productively without recognizing it.

- I was knowingly setting my company on a path that would require a lot more capital and resources than we could afford, and I sensed that a financial crisis would not be long in coming. This, too, became a painful reality.

- I was embarking on a personal journey that was going to create havoc in my personal relationships, setting up new rules of engagement for my husband, my friends, and my family that are still a constant struggle for me today.

But I also knew that the invitation which was being offered to me was rare—hard to turn down, despite the personal upheaval it would inevitably cause. It was the kind of opportunity that only happens when someone truly believes in you and your ideas. To an entrepreneur, that combination is hypnotic, propelling you forward with a momentum and drive that at times feels superhuman. When risk is your state of mind, it takes on a drug-like quality. When you are in the midst of its effects, you cannot imagine the world around you looking any different. When everything is over and you are back outside of it, you cannot imagine going back into that state of being that is perilously suspended between belief and imagination, slightly to the left of pragmatism. This is the mindset that I took with me when I moved to Silicon Valley. Despite the risk, I never doubted that I would succeed. I just had to figure out what it was that I was going to succeed at when I got there.

the three angels of advantage

THE NEW ENTREPRENEUR IS A TRIATHLETE, AND THREE SPORTS THEY CONSTANTLY TRAIN FOR ARE OBSESSION, INTUITION, AND SACRIFICE— NOT ALWAYS IN THAT ORDER. THESE ARE WHAT I CALL THE THREE ANGELS OF ADVANTAGE.

Although melodrama appeals to me, I do feel it is important to take a pause at this point and talk about three words that I embrace in everything I do: *obsession*, *intuition*, and *sacrifice*. These words are resting just behind my eyelids when I wake up; they are hovering above me like angels when I am in a moment of crisis. They taunt me when I am bored and remind me of why I am doing what I do every night before I fall asleep.

Can a person learn to embrace these qualities? I don't know. Does everyone have them? Yes, in varying degrees. How can you ignite them? You don't. They ignite you. What if you do not naturally take them for granted? Well, if you don't, then you had better be incredibly dedicated to learning about them and willing to work hard to make them feel natural. Without them, entrepreneurial moments are hard to come by.

obsession, not passion

In his book *The E Myth Revisited*, Michael Gerber talks about the myth of entrepreneurship. One of these myths is the fatal assumption made by many entrepreneurs that "if you understand the technical work of a business, you understand a business that does that technical work." Passion alone is not a good enough reason to go into business for yourself. For example, just because Suzie loves making sweaters does not mean that she should go into the sweater-manufacturing business. The reason behind this is that Suzie likes making sweaters more from a technician's standpoint, from the standpoint of the sweater-making expert. If she goes into the sweater business, she may get very frustrated by all the other things she is going to have to do to make her venture successful, things that have nothing to do with the art of creating sweaters.

I agree with Gerber. Repeatedly, people ask me why I never talk about passion and the importance of loving what you do as a key success factor in entrepreneurship. My answer is that passion does not an entrepreneur make. Obsession does. Some days, I feel as if I could switch to another line of business at the drop of a hat, and I probably will. I know that I will succeed at that too, eventually. Why? Because I am obsessed with selling new concepts that will change the way people work and think. I am in the business of creating my own industries wherever I go.

The point is, to entrepreneur successfully, one must have a total commitment to a concept at the visceral level. When I asked a friend of mine in the investment community whether he thought entrepreneurship was a profession, he replied by saying that it is a professional disease—the E-disease. This may sound a little dramatic to some of us, but his point is well taken. When you allow what you are passionately interested in to take you over, then obsession, like a disease, quickly sets in. This is not a popular idea; it flies in the face of the myth of the "ultimate balanced life." But, in my experience it is a lot closer to the truth. This E-disease is not just reserved for the entrepreneur. Look at Maria Callas. No one ever said, "That Maria Callas is so obsessed with opera. How terrible." Or "Georgia O'Keeffe was terribly consumed by her art until a ripe old age. How awful." Ten years ago, my own mother, because of her age (63 years old at the time), had to apply four times to the Ph.D. program at a major university before she was accepted. What caused her to prevail in the end was her obsession with furthering her education. For these women and many like them, their work was their life, their happiness. As their stories demonstrate, obsessions can be joyous as well as challenging and difficult. Just as everyone has the ability to take risks, everyone has the ability to be constructively obsessive to some extent. And that is a wonderful thing. Moses Znaimer of Citytv sees the entrepreneur as "the artist of business," and as an artist, one is constantly struggling to push the envelope.

intuition

I will admit to you that when I first arrived in California, I, like many eastern skeptics, broke down and went to see a psychic. It was the thing to do. And the gentleman I went to see had impressive credentials. He coached money tycoons in New York every morning before the markets opened and had been hired by police forces in several cities to solve murder cases. And, the truth is, he was fantastic. But why? Because he was the embodiment of intuition, a man with a tremendous natural aptitude for tuning into and listening to the cues suspended in the air around him, just waiting to be picked up.

When I went to see him, he spent five minutes chatting. And then, without a flicker of an eye or a change in his tone of voice, he started to tell me about myself, my childhood, what I was doing, and where I was heading. He was incredibly accurate. Later, when I asked him how he "read" someone, he said that it was as if he were sitting in front of a 3-D screen, letting all the elements of someone's life fly by all around him—a true virtual experience. Then he just described out loud what he was seeing.

This man was able to tap into a layer of intuition that, for him, was innate. But he also said that as he worked with this intuitive skill, his ability to watch the 3-D screen and interpret to the listener what he was seeing had heightened. As time went on, he learned to perceive more information, faster, and with more accuracy.

When I left his office, I came away with a lot more than just some useful and fascinating information about my own life. I took away with me a key realization. Although intuition, in some form or another, is innate and resides in each of us to some degree, I believe that this skill can be honed and improved with careful practice. The more you allow yourself to sit back and observe what is going on around you on the 3-D screen of your life, the more you will be able to improve your ability to be intuitive. Interestingly enough, when I asked Moses Znaimer, the founder of Citytv in Toronto, what he thought he was best at, he said that it was his ability to "see ahead and envision how things would turn out." Many entrepreneurs talk about being able to envision where their version of the world is going to take them long before they get there. These are finely tuned, intuitive people.

Moses Znaimer of Citytv sees the entrepreneur as "the artist of business," and as an artist, one is constantly struggling to push the envelope.

Why should we bother with intuition? Because our best decisions are always made through a combination of logical analysis, fact gathering, experience, *and* intuition. Be aware that intuition is not an exact science and that on its own, it can be deceiving. Know that sometimes your intuition will lead you astray; but ultimately, it is advantageous to think expansively, to try to let intuition seep into your thinking alongside analysis and research, rational thinking, and experience.

When I was offered an invitation to set up camp in Silicon Valley, I intuitively knew two things: The first was that I would have to say yes to this invitation; the second was that this decision would change the course of our company forever. I took my intuitive response for granted. Most new entrepreneurs do.

sacrifice

I am not a martyr, and anyone who knows me will vouch for this, but I do depend on my ability to sacrifice what others take for granted as a necessary part of my entrepreneurial journey. Why? Because I have stopped seeing what I do as a sacrifice. It has simply amalgamated itself into my life.

In the movie *The Big Night*, two brothers are trying to make it as restaurateurs in America. Despite the beauty and depth of their culinary capabilities, the restaurant is failing. As a last resort, they hold a final dinner, based on a promise from a richer, well-connected mentor to deliver a famous singer in an attempt to save the restaurant. As the evening progresses, however, it becomes evident that the guest of honor was never actually going to show up. The two brothers turn their hurt and disappointment onto each other. On a moonlit beach, in a great scene where they are questioning their future, the older brother Primo turns to Secondo and yells, "I sacrifice my work, and I die!"

This is the temperamental chef's version of sacrifice. For others, it might mean the sacrifice of money for a cause, of family for a job, or of one's home for a once-in-a-lifetime business opportunity. In my experience, sacrifice does not usually follow the simple formula "One sacrifice begets one advantage." It is usually a lot more heartrending and dramatic than that. One female entrepreneur I met talks about her and her husband's early years as entrepreneurs. During that time, their kids had to wear ski jackets to bed for months on end because they could not afford to pay the heating bills during the winter, all part of their sacrifice for the business's success. Today, this same woman is a major shareholder in one of the most successful public companies in the U.S. She is not sure what her children remember most about those early years of struggle, and she is not sure that she wants to ask them.

The invitation that Paul offered me, to uproot and take a flier in Silicon Valley, involved additional issues for me, both as a woman and as a Canadian. As a woman, I knew that, at least temporarily, I was going to have to sacrifice everything that I cared about: my marriage, my company, my status, my security. I also knew that I would have to deal with certain social pressures: "Why are you leaving? Aren't you married? Where are you going to live? How are you going to deal with being on your own, and for how long? Aren't you worried?" These and many more questions came at me in volume.

The Swedes have an expression: *logum*. There is no exact translation for this word in English, but it means something like "just enough." This is exactly the kind of concept I had to fight against as a Canadian who decided to temporarily leave Canada. "Isn't it enough that you guys are doing well and pioneering multimedia design in Toronto?" *Logum*. "Why do you need to uproot yourself and your company by moving, when you are already on a path of success?" *Logum*.

My answer was, No, it is not enough. Yes, I need to do this, despite the sacrifices, because this is what it means to be on the entrepreneurial quest. My company, my husband, my life were all part of the same continuum, and therefore, we did not see sacrifice as outside the equation but as part of the inevitable entrepreneurial journey that we had willingly signed up for. Anyone who tells you that you can adeptly sidestep sacrifice, and big ones at that, is not being truthful.

There is no magic formula here. The confidence you need to make these kinds of decisions will be directly proportionate to the building blocks that you have worked long and hard to put into place. In my case, these elements were:

In my experience, sacrifice does not usually follow the simple formula "One sacrifice begets one advantage." It is usually a lot more heartrending and dramatic than that.

- **Partnership:** I had two partners who were behind me 100 percent.

- **Mission:** We had worked for three years to figure out what it was that we really wanted. I had a mission.

- **Quest:** We had asked ourselves, "Why are we doing this?" long enough to know that we wanted to play it big, to try and pioneer something that would change the way people think and work.

Anyone who tells you that you can adeptly sidestep sacrifice, and big ones at that, is not being truthful.

Finally, my angels of advantage are always tempered by two important qualifiers: (1) When it comes right down to the line with sacrifice, you always have a choice, and (2) Risk comes on a sliding scale.

You can always choose to say no to one sacrifice and yes to another, knowing that you may be losing out on a particular opportunity that you are simply not ready for, sliding yourself back on the risk scale to a place of greater comfort. For example, if I had not had two partners who believed that my decision to move was the right one, I might have chosen to say no to the offer. Or if I did not think that Bulldog had accumulated enough expertise in multimedia, I might have held off trying to compete in Silicon Valley, where multimedia design and software were light-years ahead of many other places. Your decision-making powers combine the pieces you have put into place with your desire to move forward. How do you find the confidence? Through the three angels of advantage that you work to develop and keep highly trained every day of your entrepreneurial life: obsession, intuition, and sacrifice.

navigating silicon valley
THE NEW ENTREPRENEUR NEEDS A CERTAIN LEVEL OF NAÏVETÉ AND WELL-DISGUISED FEAR WHEN ENTERING BRAND-NEW TERRITORY.

The people I spoke with when I first moved to California always asked me, "But what do you do all day?" Obviously, Bulldog did not yet have any customers in San Francisco or its environs, and I had no office or staff to manage. When it came down to it, I had only one goal, albeit a pretty daunting one at that: to meet the people and companies within Silicon Valley who would show us where our accumulated knowledge as new media designers, producers, and consultants could be leveraged into a potential software product. To that end, my time was divided into the following activities:

- **I "mapped out":** I created a master military map that outlined who the key technology players were in Silicon Valley, what the key trends to watch for were, who the hottest new companies were, and who were the key influencers to meet.

- **I conducted tests:** From the information I collected, I began to formulate what Bulldog would become, how it would be defined in the context of this new space that I was learning about. I tried on a lot of positioning lines for our company at dinners and lunches with people I hardly knew. By meeting with the directors of industry associations, I tested the water to see how far I could stretch our service business model into something that was moving toward a product model. I chatted with press people to find out who was who in the industry, and I talked with fellow horseback riders who worked in the heart of Silicon Valley. Each person I met had many opinions and pieces of information, and I tried each and every one of these ideas on for size. Eventually, one would have the right fit.

- **I looked for new customers:** As we were still in the customized multimedia production business, I needed to generate revenue to offset the costs of keeping me alive and well in California. Using my mapping-out exercises, I was able to focus in on several key potential customers to support our service business.

- **I contacted home base:** Afraid that I would lose my momentum or my nerve (or whichever came first), I did not allow myself to return to Toronto for six months. Unfortunately, the strain and pressure of running the day-to-day business of Bulldog in Toronto, combined with our tight cash situation based on this bold foray into Silicon Valley, did not permit Chris to come and visit me for weeks on end. At times, I felt very isolated. To counter this isolation, I became religious about holding regular telephone meetings with my partners at home base every few days, feeding them the information I was learning so that they could begin to incubate those ideas and turn them into something we could sell, and soon. I also received much-needed pats on the back over the phone line.

My angels of advantage are always tempered by two important qualities: (1) When it comes right down to the line with sacrifice, you always have a choice, and (2) Risk comes on a sliding scale.

SUCCESS USUALLY FOLLOWS IN THE FOOTSTEPS OF FAILURE. THE NEW ENTREPRENEUR DEPENDS ON THIS WINNING COMBINATION.

Everyone has stories of failure and success. Everyone knows that you cannot have one without the other. But the new entrepreneur sees their failures in a positive light and depends on them to provide them with clues for accessing the next success, the next breakthrough. This concept of success became key for me in my dealings in Silicon Valley.

When I first started working at the Apple offices, I invested a lot of energy into drumming up more multimedia design work for our company and in understanding how to network effectively within the Apple organization. I wanted to leverage my much-coveted office space within Apple's New

Media Division into revenue-generating projects. Ironically, the more hours I spent at the Apple offices, the less progress I seemed to make. I realized that I had to figure out a way to leave Apple headquarters, or I was going to go into a downward spiral.

In essence, that decision became my point of entry. I suddenly realized that if I stopped using Apple headquarters as my office, I could no longer feign involvement in their New Media Division. I would have to create a whole new network of people and champions. Once again, I pushed up my risk level by knocking away the last crutch that I had brought with me.

As it turned out, my angels were right. Within a month of leaving the Apple offices, my sales efforts started to pay off. With our portfolio in hand, I began to attract new customers in California, including Wells Fargo and the American Film Institute. For us as outsiders, this was a real milestone, especially given the number of high-caliber multimedia consultants and design firms in the Bay Area alone. But more important, in working with these customers to establish an effective strategy for integrating the Web with the rest of their more traditional marketing programs (i.e., print and broadcast), the original ideas we had formulated back in Toronto when we first worked with Kodak, Apple, and Northern Telecom began to solidify.

We all agreed that if we were ever going to determine whether there was a product buried in this model of digital bedlam, we needed someone who could lead us through the product-development process. It was time to find another partner—a specialist—in this case, a technologist. And so I began my search.

Through my championship efforts, I met a young man named Peter DeVries. As one of the original members of IBM's Object Technology Group, his credentials as a facilitator for adopting technology into corporations from all over the world were impressive. The way he described his view of how technological capabilities should work to support various business processes seemed to fit with what we were struggling to articulate on the business/content side. We began to compare notes and started to see complementary ideas and skill sets—his on the technology side, ours on the content-creation side.

But that was only the beginning. As the months went by, we realized that Peter was not only one of the most technologically lucid people around but someone whose vision was in line with our own. Whatever boardroom we brought him into, his ability to bring process and technological capabilities together in a structure that made sense both to the technologists and the nontechnologists in the room was unrivaled. As entrepreneurs, we had drawn him into our company because we had fostered an attitude, created a place that he was attracted to—built on a desire to test new, untried ideas as a means of finding our leverage point centered around new media. Today, Peter is our chief technology officer (CTO) and the author of our

The new entrepreneur is someone who plans for the worst but behaves as if only the best outcome were an option.

software. Back then, he was my leverage into a deeper understanding of how technology and business processes necessarily merged.

So, while we consulted and designed award-winning multimedia projects, we began to put every penny we made into building a software prototype that represented our vision of the convergence of technology, design, and business processes. And we based this model on what we knew best—the banking industry.

Our prototype was based on this premise: If we could provide a link between the customer profile information and the media required to advertise to a particular target audience, a marketing manager at a bank would be able to create an ongoing series of special offers that would have a much higher rate of success because they were based on the matching of profiles and marketing concepts. By digitally collecting pieces of media (such as current mortgage rates, the latest marketing blurb on a given product, the visuals used in the latest brochures that were in the bank branches) from a datawarehouse (where the customer profile information was stored), the marketing manager could author marketing programs by choosing relevant pieces of media from the central media library or repository. The same manager could then publish this new information on the Web to a select number of customers who would be prime targets for that particular product. Imagine the cost and time saved by creating a direct link between the customer and the products! Imagine the competitive advantage of creating marketing campaigns that your competitors would not know about and could not match in price or features! Imagine the power of marketing messages and visuals when applied to an audience that was truly in the business of looking for that very product or service.

At the same time we began building this model in our minds and on our boardroom whiteboard, we were coming up against a real efficiency issue in our own studio. The more we worked on complex and interesting multimedia projects, the worse we seemed to be at organizing, filing, and sharing the media files amongst the team. When we worked on a multitiered project for a customer, whereby we had to produce a printed brochure for marketing purposes, create a CD-ROM for sales training, and design and update the intranet site, we had all sorts of logistical nightmares. It became difficult to keep track of all the digital versions of photos, video clips, graphics, and text that we needed to create, search for, and reuse.

The business model we envisioned, based on the combination of the hands-on experience we had working with large corporations in the multimedia design process and our own studio experience, was a compelling one to us. Of course, this sort of model sounds familiar today, because now there are many authoring tools that create wealth and opportunity based on this thinking. But at the time, we were ahead of our market. The initial reaction to our concept was a mixture of marketing intrigue and technological hesitation.

Object relational databases: databases that store and manipulate vast troves of corporate data and make that information available across computer networks; allow users to create, store, manage, and analyze complex data types, such as images, audio, video and World Wide Web documents.

FORTUNE MAGAZINE

**IN REAL ESTATE, THERE ARE THREE MAXIMS: LOCATION, LOCATION, LOCA-
TION. FOR THE NEW ENTREPRENEUR, THE KEY IDEA IS LEVERAGE, LEVER-
AGE, LEVERAGE, OR HOW TO BE IN THE RIGHT PLACE AT THE RIGHT TIME.**

On a gorgeous spring morning in 1995, I walked into a boardroom at
Tandem Computers. Little did I know that, rather than the opportunity to
work with a potential new customer, kismet was about to strike—I had
arrived at the right place at just the right time.

Here is what happened. Within a few months of arriving in Silicon
Valley, I managed, through my evangelizing activities, to get an introduction
to the VP of multimedia at Tandem Computers' head office. This VP's
mandate was to find ways to integrate new media into Tandem as a means
of creating a competitive advantage for their core businesses—which were
in the financial services sector. Despite the fact that I could have pitched
Bulldog as the ideal developer for their own Internet and intranet sites, I
resisted. Intuitively, I sensed that this person might be more interested in the
product model that Peter DeVries and his engineering team had been
refining based on our model of how we saw digital media moving through
a financial services organization. And I was right.

After several conceptual meetings and some due diligence on her part,
this VP came back to me with an offer. She was willing to create a think
tank to assist us in further developing our financial services model. As it
turned out, two of the members of the Tandem committee she set up to
work with Bulldog were from a start-up company called Illustra
Technologies. Illustra, at that time, was one of the only object relational
databases in the world, developed by Michael Stonebreaker, a professor at
the University of California at Berkeley, and his team. When I met the
Illustra folks, they were fast becoming one of the hottest companies in
Silicon Valley. This visibility was based on their attempts to redefine the
database industry with their concept of media management. They defined
media management as the efficient organization of various digital media
files throughout a company, enabling its employees to easily engage in all
the activities that were being bandied about in the world of media, from e-
commerce to just-in-time publishing to customized Web design. For me,
their object technology capabilities and their desire to define a new niche
category encapsulated what Bulldog had been grappling with for the past
three years. At the same time, other companies we knew in visual computing reinforced the innovation of their technology. Meeting the Illustra
people was truly one of those eureka moments. We listened to their
description of a media-rich world, we tested their database product, and we
knew that we had finally found our leverage point into the product world.
They were a technology company that wanted to establish a niche category; we were media-creation experts with enough technology know-how

**Media asset management,
in its simplest terms, is the
ability to store, search
and distribute complex
media, such as video,
audio, image, HTML and
any other form of digital
media, across the
enterprise.**

to create a front-end product that would integrate media management into the studio and corporate environment.

The deal I had made with Tandem resulted in more than just a mutually advantageous prototyping exercise for our companies. It created a chain reaction. By focusing my efforts on the long-term goal of finding a leverage point for my company into the product world, I had found a true champion. This champion, to her credit, not only trusted in our ability to deliver value to her company based on our expertise in new media production but also recognized our desire to cross over into a product category, and she made the connection for me with another company with similar beliefs, ideas and complementary skills. She pointed me in the direction of leverage, leverage, leverage.

THE NEW ENTREPRENEUR UNDERSTANDS THAT BEING IN THE RIGHT PLACE AT THE RIGHT TIME IS ONLY HALF THE EQUATION. KNOWING HOW TO DELIVER AGAINST THAT LEVERAGE POINT IS THE SECOND HALF.

Over the next several months, we spent a lot of time familiarizing ourselves with the Illustra product, meeting with the key players within the organization and their key partners, and trying to understand exactly where our point of intersection might be. Throughout these meetings, we not only focused on the very tangible elements of building a product spec and prototype from an engineering standpoint, but I also took the time to communicate who we were as a company, the intangible side of Bulldog, and the evolution of our company based on embracing convergence.

A perfect opportunity to display Bulldog's cachet as a point of tangible differentiation soon presented itself. Illustra had four key international customers who wanted a customized application to be built on top of their object relational database. Illustra knew that they were not in the application business. They also knew that these four customers were important to them. So they put out an RFP (request for proposal) to eight companies, including Bulldog. As luck would have it, a few of their key team members were going to be in Toronto and agreed to visit our offices.

Here is where our cachet came into full play. When the Illustra people walked into our offices in Toronto, they were struck by the juxtaposition of a dynamic atmosphere that was punctuated by a seriousness and commitment that did not match what I later learned they would have expected from a marketing-driven organization. The range of work digitally displayed in our boardroom was right in line with the kind of customers they were currently dealing with. Our CTO was able to map out his version of an object-oriented software application, which he had been working on for years. His pointed questions about the Illustra architecture reflected a level of understanding that took them by surprise. They were left with the best

The growing-pain threshold of media asset management: a global studio of over 500 users can see a 10.2 ROI (return on investment) within a three-year period, based on incremental revenue from licensing and increased business valuation.

possible combination of two complementary worlds, the intangible and the tangible, a powerful zeitgeist that can beat the tangible alone any day.

Three weeks later, we heard back from Illustra. In the RFP process, we were the only non-systems integrators and the only Canadian company to compete. And we won the contract.

I do not want to minimize our excitement or the immediate impact this win had in my ongoing efforts to integrate our company into Silicon Valley. Within weeks, we were inundated with visits and phone calls from various third-party software companies and Illustra customers from all over the world who wanted to understand our thinking. To all of these companies, we were seen as a new media company that had both a knowledge of production and the technological sophistication to create a prototype that mimicked a production environment. This was exactly the leverage that we had been working toward on the long road from service to product.

Studies show that an average worldwide brand has between 20,000 and 50,000 images associated with it, at a creation cost of over $20 million.

When the excitement had died down, we turned our attention back to the contract we had just won. In the final analysis, we were being asked to create a product that required a detailed and expert understanding of the process of digital media creation and to turn it into an application, a product. That was perfect. But we wanted this to be our *own* product, not just a well-paid contract for application development. To accomplish this, we needed to change our relationship with Illustra from that of supplier to that of partner. Our angels of advantage would simply not have it any other way.

Despite the fact that we had been depending on this money to enable us to hire the additional engineering staff for the project, we knew that we had to forfeit the substantial paid contract that we were being offered for our work in exchange for product ownership. This was a very painful decision for us because our core multimedia design business was starting to falter. The three risks that I had taken in moving to Silicon Valley were starting to come back to haunt me. Even though I had met the right people in Silicon Valley, putting us in a place of great opportunity, I had also created a need for new resources that we could not financially support.

We also knew that we had a talented hot property on our hands in the form of our CTO. Now that he was turned on and ready to invest in a product that we knew he had the ability to create, we could not let him down. We could not afford to lose him.

We looked at our books, talked to our board, hashed things out internally, and finally agreed that whatever happened, we had to figure out a way to own this application. This was the leverage we had trained ourselves to recognize, and we had to take the risk.

From that day on, we were definitely in a state of *entre*—between being at the top of the multimedia production and marketing services business and segueing over to the software product business. We did not give ourselves a choice.

In December 1995, we signed the last of many papers and became the sole owners of the media asset management system to be built on the Illustra database. Three weeks later, to our total surprise and delight, Informix bought Illustra for approximately US$400 million—one of the biggest deals of the year! Within months, we had gone from a potential supplier of a front-end application to the owner of an application to be built on a product that was valued at 40 times its annual earnings. That is what you call leverage, being at the right place at the right time.

For us, the Informix buyout signified the leverage we were looking for and has been the turning point for our service/product model. But, ironically, as I write these paragraphs, Informix has suffered through a year of tumbling revenues and plummeting stock price. For us, Illustra was a major stepping-stone in our evolution. Because of our work with them, we were able to jump into a brand-new product niche that is now the focus of many companies. Today, our media asset management system is a stand-alone product that works on several platforms for customers worldwide. According to Frost and Sullivan, an international marketing and consulting firm, the total revenue for media asset management systems will grow from $152 million in 1998 to $2.58 billion in 2004. That's a 68.2 percent compound annual growth over a six-year period. Already this software niche is catching the interest of some of the most influential companies in the world, as evidenced by our strategic partnerships with Sun Microsystems and Oracle and by Sony's announcement to become a minority investor in our company in 1998. We will always tell and retell this episode of leverage, of timing, and of success as part of the Bulldog myth.

Aleatory: of or depending on luck or chance in regard to either profit or loss. Unpredictable.

"luck favors the prepared"

One often hears that you have to have a lot of luck in business. While I believe there is great truth in that statement, luck is not something you can really either control or count on. My dad has a joke that he likes to tell: There is this old man who goes to the Wailing Wall in Jerusalem two times a day and prays to God that he wins the lottery. After 20 years, he still has not won, and his very distraught rabbi says to God, "Why can't you let him win the lottery just once? He has been praying to you for 20 years." And God says, "I would consider letting him win, but first he has to buy a ticket."

So it is in business. You cannot count on luck, but you can certainly set yourself up so that if luck should happen to fall your way, you are prepared to walk through that open door.

Some readers might want to neatly wrap up our story and attribute it to good fortune. I prefer to subscribe to what John le Carré says in *The Tailor of Panama:* "Luck favors the prepared." A good friend of mine describes the new entrepreneur as someone who plans for the worst but behaves as if only the best outcome were an option.

Each step of the way, Bulldog planned for the worst. I could have left Silicon Valley in a flash without any leases or outstanding debts to worry about. We could have placed the greater part of our focus on the consulting side of our business and made more money if we needed to. We could have ultimately said yes to letting Illustra pay us for the application, rather than trying to own it. But we acted as though we were destined to get into the product business, and luck favored us along the way.

we are always "becoming"

When people ask whether I am involved with the creative or the business side, I am often stumped about how to answer. In my mind, entrepreneur-ship *is* the creative side of business, the most creative activity I can conceive of. To me, the new entrepreneur truly is "the artist of business." A painter begins with a blank canvas, a writer needs a blank page, but the new entre-preneur does not even know whether the paper or the paintbrush is actu-ally the best tool to invest in.

In the process of entrepreneuring, a million nuances will abound. Knowing how and what to look for is part of the creative process. The entrepreneur depends on angels of advantage and embraces concepts of sacrifice, intuition, and obsession. They do away with worrying about how long something will take and adjust their comfort level to a state of "hurry up and wait." They welcome ambiguity, depending on the fact that what they have set out to do may never materialize in quite the way they imag-ined it, but that along the way, they will find their point of entry. To shape something out of this murky backdrop requires a creative energy that is hard to rival. The new entrepreneur recognizes that their opportunities will arise from unexpected places and that it is only their ability to connect the dots that will allow them to take the next step. We live in a risk-for-reward kind of world today, one that requires, as a way of life, our full attention, not just in our actions but in our attitudes.

THE NEW ENTREPRENEUR RECOGNIZES THAT THEY WILL TAKE MANY TRIPS TO MECCA. EACH ONE WILL RESULT IN A BETTER UNDERSTANDING OF THEIR STRENGTHS AND SKILLS.

My move to Silicon Valley was a trip to Mecca, a pilgrimage in every sense of the word.

- I was going to a place I had not been to before, in the hope and promise of what it would bring to me and my clan in the form of knowledge, experience, and confidence.

- As with any journey, I had set out not knowing how long it would take, who I would meet along the way, or what skills I would need to survive the trip. One thing I did know: my goal was to get to Mecca, and the conviction with which I traveled that road never swayed.

- Many pilgrims make the trip to Mecca with ideas and visions of what it will be like when they get there, with expectations based on the stories they have heard from those who have been there. Often, what they find when they get there is not at all what they have imagined. My trip to Silicon Valley started in one place and ended up in quite another. I immediately realized that this was the point of the journey.

- A trip to Mecca transforms our view of everything. My experience changed what I thought were my strengths and taught me more about my weaknesses. It changed the direction of my company forever. This was what I had come there for.

Many pilgrims and their children and their children's children make the trip to Mecca each year. I know that I will have to go on many journeys and seek out many different kinds of Meccas. The point of my search will not be to discover what a place has to offer but what I will become when I get there.

the professional eclectic

the
professional
eclectic

chapter 4 Profile of the Sensitive Extrovert

Think about ducks swimming in a pond. They seem to move quietly across the water, but really they are madly paddling just below the surface. That is the image I have of myself as an entrepreneur, but only on those days when I am able to see the humor and absurdity of it all. This chapter is dedicated to refining that image and to understanding the seeming paradox of the image of the duck and the reality of what keeps it moving that lies just below the surface of the water.

a question of conflicting demands.

Marketers map out the demographics of consumers, governments divide populations into various socioeconomic groups, and investors rate companies by potential revenue and market-share figures. But how does one categorize the entrepreneur? Is such a thing possible? And if so, what do we learn from this exercise? Many studies of entrepreneurs focus on finding definitive answers for certain basic questions about entrepreneurship: What makes the entrepreneur different from others? What are their identifying traits? Are there patterns that evolve in such individuals? What qualities are required for successful entrepreneurship?

Although this kind of psychological assessment is fascinating, this book is not about what makes or does not make the perfect entrepreneur. In fact, after much reading and research, I determined that a good deal of what I found did not provide me with the answers I was looking for but simply helped me to ask the right questions. The question is not, What traits must an entrepreneur have? but, What personality profiles support the person who says, "I entrepreneur"? My own observations have led me to some very important insights:

- The profile of the new entrepreneur is one that requires *conflicting* traits and qualities.

- By building the right kinds of partnerships, entrepreneurial teams can cover these diverse layers of opposing qualities and traits much better than any one highly flexible and responsive entrepreneur could.

- A winning team is made up of competent people whose default setting of skills and talents are diverse, opposite, and complementary.

- Most companies do not spend enough time profiling but focus instead on building skills. This is a mistake when it comes to successful team building.

"ENTREPRENEURSHIP IS MORE LIKE A ROLLER COASTER THAN A ROCKET SHIP," SAYS BILL SAHLMAN. MY BELIEF IS THAT THE PARADOXICAL PROFILE OF THE ENTREPRENEUR ENSURES THAT THEY RIDE THE ROLLER COASTER AS IF IT WERE A ROCKET SHIP.

Bill Sahlman describes the entrepreneur's quest as one that is analogous to a ride on a roller coaster, not a rocket ship. Few experiences can equal that of an astronaut, when you come down to it. But the proverbial entrepreneurial roller–coaster ride comprises:

- A world that demands that you receive and analyze information faster than the rate that it is coming in.

- A job that requires you to communicate and humanize your organization while you maintain a leading-edge understanding of how to integrate the latest technology into your environment.

- An era where the rate of failure is worn like a badge, where competition and partnership are often murmured in the same breath.

- A business landscape where market opportunities shrink and companies need to amalgamate forces in order to survive.

- A work environment where cynicism and idealism are combined in a new generation of employees who toggle between the two with a finesse that is the mark of their reality.

- A media-oriented world where performance is the sign of a leader.

- A sense of timing that is marked by a constant rush up to an endless waiting queue.

To successfully cope with these elements at play requires an acceptance of the contradictory.

profiles of paradox

The following list of 11 profiles is by no means exhaustive. My intention is to provide you with the beginnings of a list of some of the more interesting and common profiles—each one a study in paradox—for those who entrepreneur. Examining the stance required to toggle between each of the opposing qualities contained within each profile has helped me to understand how to face the challenges of entrepreneuring on my own rocket ship-cum-roller coaster.

the long-term doer

One evening, I was talking on the phone with my sister, a Crown prosecutor who lives in Vancouver. I respect her, more than anyone else I know, for her analytical powers, and yet I often found myself agitated and impatient as I tried to explain to her (for the umpteenth time) what it was that I did all day—what made me seem so busy, so crazed. When I thought about it, I realized that my sister was not the only person I knew who was puzzled. Most of my family and friends had the same difficulty in imagining my life.

On this particular evening, my sister had an idea: "Why don't you pretend that I am a villager from some remote South American tribe. Write me a letter and explain to me what you do."

"Sure," I thought, "in my spare time." But the next time I was on a plane from Toronto to San Francisco, I actually put pen to paper and wrote a 15-page letter that detailed what I did all day, using the previous few days as my sample agenda. I sent it off to my sister. She called me back a week later and told me that she finally understood what I did. With her unique gift for the perfect analysis, she said, "You are a long-term doer." And she was right. Let me explain.

Often you read books that tell you that the leader of the company should never be in the "do" mode but, rather, the "coaching" mode. I generally agree. Unfortunately, entrepreneurs, especially at the beginning of their careers, do not have the luxury not to *do*. "To know, to go, to do, to be" is a closer assessment of the entrepreneur's activity list—and not necessarily in that order. When I reread my letter and thought about what my sister had said, it suddenly struck me that my day was based upon a long-term vision, a feeling that I had in the pit of my stomach, in the tips of my toes when they hit the carpet running each morning. In general, I almost always knew where I was going, but I also needed to make sure that I was peppering my day with activities that moved me along toward achieving my vision, not just talking about it. This was true in my dealings with my customers, my employees, and my partners. Here is the sample agenda that I sent my sister, exemplifying my own balance between knowing, going, doing, and being:

To know,
to go,
to do,
to be.

CHARLES HANDY,
THE AGE OF UNREASON

Sunday, November 22, 1996

- Wake up late (night before, hosted dinner at our place for new client).

- Chris and I both need to spend four hours in the office organizing materials for the next few days. Check emails: 148 in in-basket. Check vmails at San Fran and Toronto offices: 14 in total. Clear them all out.

- Car picks up Chris from office to go to airport: London, U.K., bound.

- 4 p.m.–6 p.m. ER practices for radio interview, grabs a bite on the road.

- 9 p.m.–11 p.m. Arrive at radio station; conduct live interview with three other guests.

Monday, November 23

- 9:00 a.m.–10:00 a.m. Magazine interview on the topic of women in technology.

- 10:15 a.m. Check messages and emails (38 new emails since yesterday afternoon, nine more voicemails).

- 10:30 a.m.–12:00 p.m. Cancel originally scheduled meeting due to required emergency marketing meeting with marketing, design, engineering, legal. Legal issues discussed regarding the name we chose for the software product as well as design clarity and impact for customers. Agree that we need to talk to a number of key champions, influencers, and clients and get direct feedback. Deadline for final design approval is Tuesday a.m.

- 12:00 p.m. Phone conference with U.S. PR firm.

- 12:30 p.m. Phone meeting with Canadian PR firm.

- 12:45 p.m. Check messages, emails: 14 new emails, eight new messages.

- 1:00 p.m.–2:00 p.m. Cancel monthly status meeting with COO. Get on the phone with influencers re. name issues.

- 2:00 p.m.–3:30 p.m. Meet with marketing director to review outline for CEO report and marketing overview for quarterly report to the board. Discuss employee issues re. reorganization of department from last week.

- 3:30 p.m. Meet with writer regarding speech for CATA conference next month (I'm late).

- 4:30 p.m. (actually 5:00) Meeting with key board member at his offices (I'm late).

- 6:00 p.m. Return to office. Check vmail and email: 25 new emails, four new vmails. Ignore them.

- 6:30 p.m. Final copy approval for press kits arrives on my desk—42 pages. Due next day.

- 7:30 p.m. Receive urgent message from marketing director reminding me that the decision re. name of product required by a.m. Tuesday.

- 9:00 p.m. Complete review of most of the package. Review responses from influencers and customers regarding name. Determine that I will sleep on it.

- 10:30 p.m. Crash. Get ready for tomorrow.

Many would question my involvement in some of the details of the public relations campaign, of the naming of the product, and of the direct work with the speech writer. But I see this as part of the need to be doing. Each of these elements—from meeting with customers to talking to the press to meeting with the whole marketing team to reviewing the public relations for our upcoming press tour—gives me direct access to information, nuances, and firsthand communication, all of which provide me with material that I can incorporate into my long-term thinking. This does not suggest that I am not allowing time in my schedule to think and reflect, to allow for the ongoing growth of my vision. These activities are simply a part of the "doing" part of the exercise.

I am mostly a long-term doer who thinks and plans, whether doing, going, knowing, or being.

Inherent in this description of my day is a portrait of the "multitasker extraordinaire." There is an innate contradiction, another kind of paradox, in being a successful multitasker. While you must be able to do many activities all at the same time, if you do not focus your attention on a *limited number* of these activities and bring to each task a tenacity that is unwavering, you merely become an adept juggler of many things, not a visionary who is unafraid "to do." In this sense, my "doing" and my "going" allow me "to know" and motivate others on my team to continue doing the same. The energy I bring to each of my varied activities allows me "to be" throughout the process, as opposed to an absentee landlord who is never around, never involved in the details of the issues at hand. Some days, I am a short-term thinker, other days, a long-term thinker, and still other days a multitasker. But regardless, I am mostly a long-term doer who thinks and plans, whether doing, going, knowing, or being.

the sensitive extrovert

I am often frustrated when I scan through the best-seller bookshelves and find yet another book devoted to shy, introverted people—not because I don't think this is a worthy cause. All of us can benefit from a new method to boost our confidence. Often, however, these books are aimed at the "highly sensitive." I am still waiting for the book to come out that will be dedicated to helping those of us who are cursed with being what I call "sensitive extroverts." For that matter, this book should be shelved in the business section, not the self-help section, because that is where it will do the most good. It should be pondered by the entrepreneurs among us who have to hop between these two extremes, who are good at one side of the equation precisely because of the other.

When I was first faced with the challenge of raising money for Bulldog, I was able to secure a meeting with one of the partners at a well-known venture capital firm on Sand Hill Road, home to many of the biggest venture capital firms in Silicon Valley. At this point in time, our ideas were well formed, but our preparation for the meeting was lacking. I nervously walked into the office of this particular senior partner of the firm, and within 30 seconds, I realized that I was way over my head. I knew that the five-page outline I had so proudly put together as a discussion paper was not going to be appropriate. But being the extrovert that I am, I pushed forward and began my pitch—of our product, of our understanding of the reasons why new media was not being incorporated into organizations at the rate it could be, of the market potential, and of the companies we were working with, such as Illustra Technologies and Tandem. The faster I talked, the more I realized I was losing him.

And then my highly sensitive nature kicked in. I recognized that I was wasting my time and his. If I was going to leave his office with any value, I needed to put my extroverted, performance self aside and move on to the sensitive profile within. "Listen," I said, "I am not properly prepared for this meeting and would be wasting your time if I continued with my pitch. I know your time is limited. Let's forget about the beginning of the meeting. Assume that I am not looking to you for financing. Instead, I would be very grateful to you if you could take the remainder of the half hour and help me to understand the variables at hand, anything and everything you are willing to share with me so that I can move forward to properly secure financing for my company." There was a change in his face, a relaxation in his posture, and a complete turnaround in the meeting. Grateful to be able to give advice with no expectation of anything in return, he spent over an hour with me. I learned more than I had ever intended or hoped regarding financing and how to go about preparing for it effectively. We shook hands, I sent him a thank-you note, and that was that. When we eventually did secure our financing, I sent him an announcement card and was delighted to get a voicemail of congratulations. In the end, I had been able to find the right person to talk to, to secure the initial meeting, and to walk into the room because I am an extrovert; and yet the success of the meeting was a result of my sensitivity.

New entrepreneurs strive to be sensitive extroverts as a means of ensuring that they are (a) keeping their intuition as finely tuned as possible so that they do not make decisions based on a lack of sensitivity to the environment around them, and (b) making sure that they are including people in their activities and not leaving anyone in the wake of the "performances"

Many centuries ago, a Chinese poet wrote that being able to describe something in words was like living twice.

they are required to conduct on a daily basis. A sensitive extrovert can adeptly motivate employees because they have a keen sensitivity to their resistances. The sensitive extrovert is someone who can walk into a formal business gathering and be an extrovert first and a sensitive listener second. The sensitive extrovert is the "being" part of the doing-going-knowing-being equation. Sensitivity allows space for intuition to have some breathing room, and in the end, it creates a performance that has already accounted for the incoming desires, goals, and interest of the audience at hand, be they employees, investors, or competitors.

the lone coach

My friend Jonas Svensson runs an incredible company out of Stockholm called Spray. At 29 years of age, he has five offices and 250 employees, and his company is growing by leaps and bounds. He describes his role as "the coach who brings water to the team members." He knows that he has spent a lot of energy finding the right players, practicing with them on a regular basis, but often what he simply needs to do is continue bringing them water when they need it. I love this image, but it also contains a paradox, as do each of these profiles.

As a coach, you both set the rules and nurture the talent that is there. You can't always make the play yourself, but you can help the players strategize properly to set up for it. Inherent in that role is a certain level of authority. You set the rules: If they do not make practice on time, they are off the team. What is less obvious in the entrepreneurial setting is that as the center of the team's attention, all eyes are on you, and yet you are not really a member of the team. Although individual team members might complain about some of your rules and regulations, for the most part, they will have been supported and encouraged by you and their teammates. As a coach, you cannot always rely on that same kind of support; in fact, you are often lacking it. As an entrepreneur, you are not necessarily able to get support and nurturing from your investors, board members, or the press.

The paradox of this profile lies in the fact that you are completely alone despite the fact that you are the leader of the pack, the center of attention. You need to move in the world as a completely self-reliant entity, in the way you speak, in the way you approach a meeting, and in your body language. And yet, ironically, you are interconnected to your partners and your team in a very symbiotic way—you can be self-reliant *because of* the team that you work with. Your team achieves the goals *because of* your input. You need the distance of being alone so that you can maintain a certain level of perspective, and yet you need the team atmosphere in order to fully realize the role of each member of the team.

My partner Chris sums it up best. When we are at a crossroads, when we need to move the company forward and know that this decision will require aggravation, turmoil, and resistance, he always says, "I do not want to relate to 'engineering' ('sales,' 'marketing'), I just want to understand enough about what they need, to know how to deal with the variables." He is bringing water to the team.

the chameleon

When we first started selling our software product in Hollywood, we discovered, as had many before us, that it is truly a strange place. In her book *Hello, He Lied*, Lynda Obst depicts the absurd and yet frighteningly true mode of understanding required of producers in order to sell scripts to the studios in Hollywood: "Every studio has a flavor. A personality. A mood. Clearly it derives from the flavor, mood, and personality of the boss, so it changes with personnel and the season. Many lunches are spent speculating about the nature of these moods, and these are profitable discussions." As a world unto its own, Hollywood has a unique business atmosphere that is as enigmatic as it sounds.

I distinctly remember one encounter that took place in West Hollywood at some swank café. I was meeting with a particularly hot young entrepreneur who was in the post-production business. With his extremely tiny phone ringing constantly throughout our conversation (Could he not have turned it off for a little while? We all know where the off switch is on our cell phones), he told me all about himself for more than an hour. He delivered this autobiography pretty well nonstop and pretty well at the same volume, with the same emphatic intonation. Rather than wonder when he was going to ask about me and my company, I simply kept asking him questions, one after the other. In that one hour, my head ached, my ego was down around my ankles, and I was seriously questioning whether the cumbersome new cell phone that I favored was going to cut it in Hollywood.

When I reflected on the dynamics of this meeting, I realized that I had completely disappeared against the backdrop of the café and allowed this person to dominate the meeting. It was not my first encounter with this kind of arm-waving ego, nor would it be my last. Suffice to say, I was not happy about how things had gone. But out of this absurd encounter, something had crystallized for me. I walked away with a new and useful image of how we should do business in Hollywood—as chameleons. Ironically, as Canadians, we know how to utilize that tactic and do it well. By adopting the image of the chameleon, we could walk into any meeting, any café, and take on an unassuming pose. And that is exactly what we did.

By playing the underdog, the highly researched, well-prepared, but relatively low-keyed player at the table, we would often be able to identify the decision maker in the room and hone in on the process for installing a beta site with relative speed. We would also be able to figure out who would be our champions, who would be willing to defend our cause and our

When is the age of the CEO of a start-up company 46? When you combine the age of the two founders.

company. In Lynda Obst terms, we could pick up on the flavor, the mood of the team at hand. As chameleons, we were not seen as the loud easterners, the techies from Silicon Valley, or even as "the Canadians." We simply blended in, and in the process, we were able to gain a comfort level with our key customers. We learned how to "ride the horse in the direction it is going."

There is an important caveat to remember here, however: Do not try to be something to everyone. Know when your chameleon stance is not working for you. No matter how eclectic and well-rounded your skills and staff are, no one company can appeal to all customers, nor can they answer all their demands. Recognize the times when you are out of your realm of expertise and simply cannot deliver what the customer is expecting of you.

Rob Ryan of Entrepreneur America (a boot camp for entrepreneurs) describes his training process as finding the strength of the core business you are in, not focusing on the product you sell. The chameleon profile demands that you blend your talent, your team, and the input you get from your surroundings, and camouflage yourself until you gain the trust and acceptance of the customer you are dealing with. Chameleon strategies are based on long-term growth, not short-term bravado. When you decide to change profiles, this approach affords you a flexibility and a sense of surprise that the competition will not know how to anticipate. In fact, they may not even be able to find you in your camouflaged state.

the experienced hipster

When is the age of the CEO of a start-up company 46? When you combine the age of the two founders. The mean age of today's founding partners, particularly in the high-tech field, is substantially lower than it used to be. Twenty-three-year-olds are starting up semiconductor chip companies and getting funding for it. Millionaires are made at 29 and younger. Many of the entrepreneurs I talk to find that their age and immaturity as businesspeople are either extreme advantages or disadvantages. I would be remiss not to talk about the issue of age and maturity within the context of the profile of the new entrepreneur.

Being a young entrepreneur can be an advantage, particularly if your level of knowledge and understanding is surprising despite your age and lack of experience. In fact, as a rule, people within the high-tech and software world experience a definite comfort level around young entrepreneurs, especially since young, talented people proliferate in this industry in such great numbers. The time when a young entrepreneur is at a disadvantage is when they are dealing with the specific corporate cultures of larger establishments outside of technology—companies where, for some individuals, age is an issue and maturity is a requirement. If the CEO is lacking in both, this can often inadvertently create a level of threat or mistrust that may really have no basis in reality.

Since Bulldog is basically a company run by young entrepreneurs and staffed by young and talented people, I have learned three important things about youth over the years.

The anonymity of technology helps us to a large extent. At Bulldog, the speed with which we work demands that we often form relationships on the phone and via email before actually meeting the customer face to face. Because of these modes of communication, we are able to convey our level of knowledge and our ability to communicate and respond to the customer without encountering any bias toward our ages or the few gray hairs we have.

Even a paranoid has some real enemies.

HENRY KISSINGER

Image still counts. Once when one of our investors was conducting the due diligence, our CTO Peter DeVries had bleached his hair blond and was shaved to the scalp—not your typical CTO hairdo. Rather than becoming a disadvantage, his youthful style actually helped us in establishing our credentials. The surprise element of a hip image combined with an exceptional level of knowledge and experience is a potent combination. I call this the profile of the "experienced hipster."

Maturity is not something you can add to your image. Business maturity cannot be taught and cannot be bought. Rather, it is a quality that gradually builds. The more issues you have to deal with, the better you become at navigating yourself and your team through them. If a customer or a business associate is not comfortable with your level of maturity or immaturity, find someone else on your management team whom they can relate to. Never push youth on someone. By maintaining the profile of the experienced hipster, you are focusing on the high level of knowledge that you have, despite your age, not trying to assume a mature image that will only come with time.

the successful failure

"Entrepreneurs never fail, they just have learning experiences." Bull. When you spend over half a million putting together your product and find yourself 10 days away from bankruptcy, it is only by facing the hard, cold word *failure* that you can motivate yourself to pull through and, in the end, succeed. The difference is the new entrepreneur knows that 55 out of 100 times they are going to fail. But that is not what they think about 55 percent of their day. What they focus on is the "boomerang effect," learning how to take that potential failure and use its momentum to turn it into a success.

Some people claim that entrepreneurs are not "bowled over by the same insecurities as the rest of us. . . . The world can be falling in around them, and they don't run for cover."

Some studies call this reaction "rejection insensitivity"; others relate it to the need to prove oneself against a rejecting father figure. The real question we should be asking ourselves in such cases is not Why? but How? How does a person keep from running for cover when the world is falling apart and failure looks inevitable? The answer is by focusing on what Jim Collins calls the "big idea." The big idea is an expression of what the company (and, by inference, the new entrepreneur) stands for, rather than the products they sell. In Walt Disney's case, this means "making people happy." In Merck's world, it is "to preserve and improve human life." In Bulldog's case, it is "to improve the way people think about the media they create." By focusing on the big idea, what you and your company stand for, not what you do, you will always be able to focus on success—through, around, despite, and because of the failures that you will invariably meet along the way. By focusing on the big idea, you can learn how to develop strategies and ways of working that define who you are and what your company stands for—much in the same way that "long-term doing" propels you into a constant refining of your long-term vision. The big idea lasts much longer than any particular product, and it means more to the health of your company than anything else. For example, at Bulldog, we failed to maintain our number-one position within the world of multimedia design in Canada, but we successfully turned this failure into a reflection of our long-term goal: to productize our knowledge in media creation and distribution. By embracing our big idea, we turned each failure into a boomerang that propelled us to the next stage of our company's growth. This is what it takes to truly embrace the profile of a "successful failure." Call a failure a failure, and be proud of it.

fool's gold

If we look back at my arrival in Silicon Valley, it is clear that one of my most valuable assets in this venture was that I was not quite sure what I was there for. It was this very uncertainty, the refusal to lock myself in, that allowed me to push the boundaries and discover "it." I call this kind of activity "looking for fool's gold." Repeatedly, over the years, Bulldog has found itself in situations where we were moving along with very little knowledge, refusing to stop at any easy answers, exhaustively searching for the long-term solution. This strategy ensured that we would not allow ourselves to settle for the obvious, to stop at a point that did not provide us with knowledge or added value but simply seemed like an easy concept for us to rally around.

The quest for knowledge cannot be done in isolation. The new entrepreneur needs the help of their partners to give them the courage to step out a little further along the ridge of "not knowing." Partners help the new entrepreneur to hold to the conviction of the big idea, focusing on what they and the company stand for, not what they sell. They remind the new entrepreneur that only by staring failure honestly in the face can one boomerang back. With that kind of support and experience in hand, the new entrepreneur is able to go to any lengths to add to the knowledge "pie." They will take journeys, dance with risk, and welcome surprise. Most of all, they will compare notes with their partners and turn initial foolish thinking into a pot of gold.

Inherent in this process is a balance between discovery and execution. Constantly gathering knowledge is not the goal of the exercise. In a world where easy access to more and more information is an ongoing temptation, the challenge is knowing when to stop—when to recognize that you now have about as much information as you need and should stop gathering and begin to synthesize. That is when you are truly mining fool's gold, all the while knowing that you are about to strike the real 18-carat mother lode.

**Trust everybody,
but cut the cards.**

FINLEY PETER DUNNE,
MR. DOOLEY'S PHILOSOPHY

the trusting paranoid

A strange thing happens at the onset of a business relationship. Whether you are hiring a key employee or considering a strategic partnership with an important industry influencer, an unusual level of optimism sets in, and that is not always a good thing.

At Bulldog we learned the importance of the "trusting paranoid" profile when dealing with one potential software partner who was working in a related, but noncompeting, software category. After a number of initial meetings, we all felt that there was real synergy and a reason to move forward on some joint-selling scenarios. Despite the fact that the company seemed resistant to nailing down a contract, we liked what we saw. We got caught up in the rush we felt when we thought about the relationship's potential. We put our faith in their intentions and their goals with an openness and generosity that we usually held in reserve. We agreed to conduct joint client presentations and even offered to share our space at a major trade show. But we had not allowed ourselves the time to sift through worst-case scenarios. Had we properly analyzed the situation, we would have realized that we were not going to be working with a company that would be complementary to our goals. Rather, they were a group that was hungrily looking to take a big bite out of our own client list and expand their product line to include aspects of what our own product already did.

What began as a mutually beneficial relationship turned into one of competition for the customers that we had so trustingly brought to the table. In the end, we did not actually lose any customers to this particular company, but we lost a lot of time and energy retracing our steps and evaluating what went wrong. In the heat of the moment, perspective is a very difficult thing to maintain. It is best to be paranoid in the coolness of time, before you get into bed with anyone, and save the trust for afterwards, when you are sure that this is who you want to be with. Then, once committed, you trustingly never look back.

the harried bencher

This profile is simple and familiar to everyone. Whether you are in a large corporation waiting for approval on your revised marketing plans for your division or you are sitting on pins and needles waiting for the results of your due-diligence process to be completed, many of us are in a constant mode of "hurry up and wait." The image this brings to mind is that of the harried bench warmer on the basketball team. You feel as if you are in a crisis mode, in the thick of things, and yet you are actually sitting on the sidelines waiting for others to determine the outcome of the game.

As a new entrepreneur, you will face this unusual scenario many times—not just with outside parties, but with employees and team members as well. The natural urge is to do something, anything, to create a flurry of activity to avoid the growing sense of lack of control. When you feel the overwhelming need to create some action coming over you, I offer you two pieces of advice:

It is an equal failing to trust everybody, and to trust nobody.

ENGLISH PROVERB

- Resist the temptation to do anything. If you have just gotten a sales process moving but it is not moving fast enough, try not to jump in right away. Let it move forward for a while, and let the other team members catch up to where you, the pioneer of the process, already are.

- Remember that things take longer than you think—almost always. By forcing action or activity at a time when you really need to be taking a pause, you often interrupt the natural flow of things, not allowing the team to be able to function efficiently or customers to come to a decision that is wholly theirs.

When you feel that you are warming the bench, use this time to carry out much-needed self-reflection. Often this period of waiting comes directly after a particularly harried period of "long-term doing." Take the opportunity to get away, to gain some perspective. Know and trust that you will eventually be in the thick of things again. Take the time in between activities to reevaluate, to reshape your thinking for the next challenge ahead.

dangerous diffidence

John le Carré's spy character in the book *The Tailor of Panama* is encouraged to maintain a level of dangerous diffidence in order to conduct his line of business efficiently. He maintains interest in his contacts and in his geographic region, but he never allows himself to get too close to any one thing or place, creating a sense of being once removed.

The world of espionage has its own peculiar rituals, and not that many apply to the new entrepreneur, but when I read the term "dangerous diffidence," I knew it had relevance to the entrepreneur. Because of the obsession that we often have, because of our drive and need to push forward with a rush of ideas through a maze of people and places—and a strong focus on the goal at hand—we all too often let ourselves, our ideas, or those of our team members sweep us off our feet. The new entrepreneur knows how to stay slightly removed from this overwhelming desire to be in the thick of things, even though that is precisely where they need to be much of the time. Dangerous diffidence provides the new entrepreneur with:

Individuals don't do much. High-performance teams do a lot.

BILL SAHLMAN,
ASSOCIATE DEAN
OF BUSINESS
ADMINISTRATION,
HARVARD BUSINESS
SCHOOL

Perspective. For a leader, perspective is the hardest thing to get and keep. You are usually the first one to lose it, and once lost, it is very hard to regain. By removing yourself slightly from the fray, you are able to reflect about what is going on around you with a coolness that is in direct contrast to the "in-your-face" demands of your day-to-day world. As Roger Shattuck says, learning how to gain perspective is much like looking at the night stars: "Don't look directly at [a situation]; look slightly to one side of it."

Ability to improve. By placing yourself slightly to the side of the issue at hand, you have just enough detachment and perspective to be emotionally able to say, "I made a mistake." More important, as a leader, you need to be able to hear others' observations. When you are too close to any one activity in your company, you risk becoming defensive in your reaction to what could be valuable advice. Diffidence helps foster a team of nurturing critics, not finger-pointing demolition derbies.

Flexibility. Cultivating dangerous diffidence enables you to move between roles on the turn of a dime. This is a skill you often have to exercise, especially at the beginning of any start-up company. If you are leading a sales team and it is not doing well, learn not to take it personally. When you are dealing with investors and there is a problem with the financial results, you do not have to defend these results blindly. When you are challenged by the press, you can learn to take it in stride and dedicate yourself to telling the truth, as painful as that truth might be. You have the ability to do all of these things with a slight gesture of "once removed," enabling you to move through the various roles you must assume more seamlessly.

Crisis. With diffidence, you can jump into action with greater speed and accuracy when you are *really* needed. By removing yourself and standing slightly to the side in your thinking, you will be able to perceive when it is time to stop focusing on one activity and dive into the next. You can prioritize with precision.

One of my closest friends, Michael Levine, is a world-renowned production designer for film, theater and opera. When I asked him how he approaches the design of a new opera, he said, "The key is not to be too 'precious' with any one of my ideas. I try to immerse myself fully in the information surrounding the piece I am working on, but then I pull back, get distance, and try to stay one step removed. In that way, I am always open to better ideas; and when I bring the concepts I have been working on to my collaborators, I can accept feedback from them with an open mind because I haven't bought into any one of my ideas too fiercely, despite my unbending obsession with the project at hand."

That is what I mean by dangerous diffidence. Your customers recognize it as maturity—your willingness to talk about the weaknesses of your product as well as its strengths. Press people respond to this attitude too; they believe in what you are saying, because you give them a sense of objectivity. Your team members feel more willing to discuss new ideas and approaches to the business, knowing that you are bringing a larger perspective to the meeting. This kind of diffidence is a potent tool.

freedom fighter

In 1983, my father's real estate company was in a very difficult position. Having secured all the required buyers for a particular residential building, they were able to construct it on schedule. Although 90 percent of the building was completed, at the last minute, for no apparent reason, one of the largest North American banks decided to request that a second bank (financing this same real estate deal) guarantee the second mortgage on his building.

The result was that my father and his partner (his brother) spent one and a half years fighting the bank. There are a lot of nuances to the story and details that would give you goose bumps. What stayed in my mind, however, was what my father described to me as the root of their strategy: "We focused on the fight. Not just for the sake of fighting and not just so that we could get in their way, which we definitely did, but we fought for our freedom. We fought in order to free ourselves from thinking that they could ruin us with one decision." In the end, after 18 months of battle, my father and his brother won. Not only were they able to save their firm and the building in question, as well as avoid going to court, but the bank that opposed them ended up losing $7 million, as opposed to the potential $2 million risk factor they were worried about in the first place. While they fought the bank, these entrepreneurs had been anything but free; when they reached their goal, they saw themselves as freedom fighters.

This is just one of the many stories that my father has in his back pocket and tells with drama and a twinkle in his eyes. The moral of this story and the focus of this profile are twofold. As a new entrepreneur, you fight because you have to, just as your relationship with risk is not about loving risk or looking for it or even wanting it but, rather, about dancing with risk to reap the rewards. You sometimes go to battle not because you want to or enjoy it but because you are focused on the freedom to make your own

**Teach us to care
and not to care.**

T.S. ELIOT,
ASH WEDNESDAY

decisions and to form outcomes that others cannot take away from you. You fight to reach a place that provides you with the choice to make new decisions, to determine new meaning in your business and in your life. Ironically, the obsession and focus on freedom is what actually frees you although, along the way, it can feel anything but freeing.

finding your kindred spirit

A team of kindred spirits creates winning companies.

Partnership is so crucial. It provides the indispensable balance that is required for exceptional entrepreneuring.

In the book *Hyperspace*, author Michio Kaku describes the difference between a theoretical and an experimental physicist. Citing the work of Victor Weisskopf, a theoretical physicist at MIT, Kaku describes the theoretical physicist as the one who draws diagrams, sees patterns, and predicts the outcome of a certain dynamic. The experimental physicist creates the tools, builds the structure, and tests the dynamic changes in the lab. Weisskopf uses Christopher Columbus and his voyage to the New World as an analogy.

In the time of Columbus, the theoretician would be the person who figured all the equations and charted all the maps and weather patterns that would create a relatively accurate estimate of where Columbus would land at the end of his voyage and how long it would take him to get there. This kind of physicist would conduct all of his research back in Europe, only able to dream about the faraway places that Columbus would eventually arrive at. The experimentalist would be the person who would build the ship that Columbus would sail in, install the right navigation tools to ensure that he would get to India, and perhaps even join him on the journey. Of course in the end, Columbus sailed a lot longer than expected, did not take the route that he was meant to take, and arrived on the shores of North America. Because of this, a whole new world opened up to the theoretician and the experimentalist alike—something that would never have occurred without the random changes in the course of the journey. But both skills were required to make the journey happen; both approaches were valuable in dealing with the challenges at hand that led to a New World.

In my own case, the theoretician within me said, "We need to go down to Silicon Valley because that is the epicenter of multimedia." The experimentalist within traveled there and began to create a whole number of interactions and reactions that both sides—my theoretician and my experimentalist—could review and assess according to the reactions that were created. As it turned out, Bulldog did not end up doing much business with Apple Computers, which had originally been the reason we went down there. We did not create a lot of long-term wealth and opportunity through our multimedia design and consulting business. What did happen was that we met people we could never even have imagined at companies such as Illustra, Tandem, Sun, Microsoft, SGI, and Sony. We met people who talked about multimedia in a completely different way that eventually led us to understand which product we were destined to create.

Today, Bulldog moves in a world of databases, client servers, and object technology that is very far removed from the multimedia epicenter that we aimed at with our charts and maps before the journey began. In a sense, the theoreticians and experimentalists of the team are really just different sides of the same boomerang.

In the New World of business, the entrepreneur must embrace the qualities of both the theorist and the experimentalist in all that they do. Often this task is extremely difficult to accomplish alone. Very few people can theorize accurately, build the boats, sail the ship, and know what to do when they land. Only a team can bridge these two opposing approaches and create the kind of flexibility that allows for the random course adjustments which must occur over time.

Sometimes the new entrepreneur is a lone coach, sometimes an anti-hero, and often a freedom fighter. Paradoxically, however, what underlies the various profiles listed above is the reality that no one person can possibly contain all of these contradictory traits at any one time—nor should anyone want to. By finding what I call "kindred spirits," the new entrepreneur can balance various opposing qualities, catch their breath between performances, take stock of whatever needs to be focused on next, and assume the appropriate profile. The best way to achieve this completely paradoxical stance is to create a team or a partnership that covers as many bases as possible.

Business associates make good business decisions. Kindred spirits work to create long-term "big ideas" that last.

what is a kindred spirit?

A kindred spirit is not just someone who equally shoulders the responsibilities of leadership. In addition to the particular engineering, sales, or operational skills of any one person, kindred spirits are the people who are headed to the exact same spot on the horizon as you are, with the same boomerang in hand. They are just taking a slightly different route to get there. In Charles Handy's terms, they are "knowing" and "going" the same way you are, but they are "doing" and "being" in a completely different fashion.

Bill Sahlman describes this dynamic as follows: "Individuals don't do much. High-performance teams do a lot." Rob Ryan of Entrepreneur America will not accept anyone into his entrepreneurial boot camp who does not have a team in place. Jim Collins suggests that "almost by definition, an enduring great company has to be built not to depend on an individual leader."

A successful partnership based on a notion of kindred spirits is focused on a collective contribution for the betterment of the company whereby what each of the partners contributes, the mechanisms they put in place, will increase the possibility for future opportunities for the company in the long run. Remember: Business associates make good business decisions. Kindred spirits work to create long-term "big ideas" that last.

Looking for and finding kindred spirits takes a lot of work and often requires a lot of time. There is no magic formula. The best way to start this process is to assess what your skills are, what your biases are, and where you are lacking in the ability to deal with the contradictions at play in business, long before you determine what product or service you will offer. Then look for those whose default qualities complement and pick up where your own leave off.

Understanding the dynamic combination of the contradictory and complementary elements found in both our own profiles and the profiles of those with whom we work should be our ultimate goal. With a kindred spirit, over time and with experience you will begin to work together with a fluidity and efficiency that is hard to beat. The process of looking for and finding a kindred spirit reinforces the fact that entrepreneurship is as much about partnership as it is about self-sufficiency.

chapter 5 The Developing Entrepreneur

No matter where you go, no matter what job you take on, no matter what company you join, entering into new, unknown territory always involves an exploration and assessment of the rules of engagement. By widening your range of experiences, you will inevitably come to know those rules of engagement you can live with and those you cannot. This is an important notion. Despite the disappointment in certain jobs, the seeming divergence in a career, the new entrepreneur seeks to add a wide range of projects and jobs to their portfolio of experience. They know that it is what you take with you from each episode, an understanding of which rules of engagement you can and cannot live with, or a newly discovered passion for a topic that you would otherwise have missed out on, that provides you with the necessary tools of the trade. In entrepreneurial terms, it is what sets you up to cope with the profiles of paradox.

circle of learning

A friend of mine told me that his golf teacher does not allow his students to say that they are "not really golfers." Instead, they must tell people that they are "developing golfers." By calling themselves "developing golfers," they are already actively involved in the pursuit of their end goal—to be golfers. This exact reasoning applies to entrepreneuring. Whether owning a company is your ultimate goal or creating a position within an organization that is focused on creating change or simply testing the waters to see where you sit on the scale of entrepreneuring, your journey starts with the clear knowledge that you are "a developing entrepreneur." By thinking of yourself in this manner, you will maximize your inherent traits and skills, and you will bump up against the paradoxical nature of the pursuit you have chosen. This will help you to build your own profile as an entrepreneur, one that captures and crystallizes your abilities in a very tangible way. There are three essential concepts and five strategies required in developing an entrepreneur's training program.

the developing entrepreneur begins by embracing the "circle of learning"

If the original investors of the railroad had determined that they were in the transportation business and not in the business of laying, maintaining, and extending thousands of miles of steel rails, they would probably have evolved into some of the most powerful industry leaders today. But they didn't. Instead, they focused on the business they were in only in the most immediate sense and did not foresee the evolution of what they were experiencing and what they were learning. They did not understand what they could take away from the existing business to propel them into the next round of opportunity.

I consider myself a struggling, burgeoning, and learning-on-the-job entrepreneur.

PAMELA WALLIN,
PRESIDENT,
THE CURRENT AFFAIRS
GROUP

It is the same with entrepreneurship. When you are building up your portfolio of experience, the goal is to focus on a circle of learning that will be indispensable as you continue to move forward toward the bigger picture. The jobs you get along the way deserve your full attention and your absolute professionalism, but they are not the defining factor of your career. Jonas Svensson of Spray talks about his developing entrepreneurship as follows: His first job after attending the School of Economics in Stockholm was with a major Swedish media conglomerate. When this company determined that it would be worthwhile to explore the World Wide Web as a potential communications channel that could generate revenue, Jonas and his friend Johann saw an opportunity. They put together a white paper that explored the potential of the WWW and identified where business opportunities might lie in the near and distant future.

The best way to look at their approach to recognizing opportunity is through what Charles Handy calls the "circle of learning": question—theory—test—reflect. His theory is that by cycling through these four activities, the potential for improving one's original idea, for bringing on constructive change, is more attainable. And it is this circle of activities that the entrepreneur in training needs to subscribe to.

In Jonas's case, he began to question how the power of interactive communication might translate into a viable business opportunity while he was still at school in Stockholm **(Stage 1: Question)**. He began formulating a concept for a company based on a worldwide collective of entrepreneurial multimedia production houses working together to create content for the Web. After traveling around North America for several months, he met with many experts in the area of digital media and was able to test out some of his ideas and assess the validity of his concept **(Stage 2: Theory)**. It wasn't until he began working for the media conglomerate that he was able to publish a white paper that reflected the information he had been collecting and actually open and manage an Internet service provider called

Everyday, where he could further test out his ideas. Unfortunately (or fortunately), the parent company sponsoring him was not willing to support the venture long enough for it to turn a profit, and the company folded **(Stage 3: Test)**. At this point, Jonas was able to truly reflect on the path of learning and experience that made up his portfolio to date and to come up with the idea that became the basis of his company today **(Stage 4: Reflect)**. Together, he and his partner Johann are now the founders of Spray, an international new media design and training organization. This company represents a circle of learning in action. By focusing his efforts on the business he was poised for, entrepreneurship, Jonas was able to question, test, theorize, and reflect in a manner that allowed him to recognize where his strengths and weaknesses lay. These activities also supported the notion that he was assembling a portfolio of experience in the spirit of entrepreneuring—not for the next possible job but with the goal of adopting an entrepreneurial stance in everything he did along the way.

The learning you gain through the process is exactly the point of entrepreneurial training. By subscribing to this long-term approach to learning, you will inevitably ask questions of yourself and of those around you that will help you create a customized paint-by-numbers version of your model of entrepreneuring. In doing so, each experience, each job that you undertake, will be more clearly defined and will work to support a more specific notion of the kind of entrepreneur you want to be. Those of us who want to hone our skills and maximize our entrepreneurial opportunities need to commit to this idea of the "developing entrepreneur" (entrepreneur in training) with zeal and tenacity. And we need to take the cuts and bruises we inevitably receive along the way with a twist of sweet courage.

Circle of learning: question— theory— test— reflect.

CHARLES HANDY, *THE AGE OF UNREASON*

the professional eclectic: a way of life, not a job

One day, I was sitting in the office of the president of one of the largest advertising agencies in Canada, closing in on the final round of interviews for an upcoming job. Having spent most of my life focused on what I call peripheral (i.e., not mainstream) companies, I had determined that I should try my hand at a job on the other side of the fence. This was the final interview. The president turned to me and said, "Overall, how would you describe your skill set in one or two sentences?" Without missing a heartbeat, I answered, "I am a professional eclectic." Proud of my ability to cleverly package the experience and skills I had been honing throughout my working life into two words, I left the office convinced that I would get the plum job. The next day, I was called back in to see the president. Smiles, handshakes, and then a very succinct description of why I did not, in the end, get the job.

The professional eclectic is an individual with "transportable" skills.

"Everything you have done is very interesting, of course, and your presentation skills are flawless, and you do have relevant experience. But, well, frankly, we do not know where to put you in the organization. You don't really fit into any one category, and we cannot really make an exception for you or we would have to do that for everyone. As you said, you are a professional eclectic. And we do not hire professional eclectics. They are simply too difficult to categorize. I'm sorry." (Smile, smile, with a sickly feeling in my stomach as I left.)

In that moment, my disappointment was coupled with insight and learning. When I thought about it, he was right. His company could not and did not accommodate professional eclectics—and probably never would. But I could not imagine that there were not many companies out there, and many situations, that would benefit from my lack of categorization, from the combination of skills and the breadth of experience that I had accumulated. There must be companies, I thought, that *would* value someone who had taken chances with jobs and projects rather than maintained a narrow path along a well-traveled line. All I had to do was figure out what I meant *exactly* by "professional eclectic."

I sat down and described the profile of a professional eclectic to myself. It was, I decided, someone who was devoted to pushing the envelope of knowledge and experience as far as possible and yet was professional in pursuit of this goal. In doing so, one could seamlessly move from one task to another, could adapt to any situation with finesse and flexibility. In addition, the professional eclectic could build relationships based on an ability to adjust quickly to the topic at hand and continuously add information, ideas, and concepts to their "portfolio of expertise" in a manner that created a lasting image. In short, the Renaissance model revisited. For instance, the professional eclectic is reflected in the person who has a law degree and then decides to take on a job in a small town in eastern Canada teaching law in French rather than working for a large, substantial legal firm. They do this not because teaching law in French is better than working for a reputable law firm but because this choice is representative of a person who is focused on developing an eclectic approach to his chosen profession that has merit in its diversity and unpredictability.

Charles Handy differentiates between these approaches to learning by borrowing a term from E.M. Forster called "flat people"—those who have only one dimension to their lives. In my books, the professional eclectic is the antithesis to this one-dimensional profile, in that they are focused on building up what I call "transportable" skill sets. Furthermore, they accumulate a unique set of choices in their career that are often valued for the person they represent, regardless of the milestones achieved. In Hollywood terms, Lynda Obst might refer to professional eclectics as people who are of "whole cloth," self-created individuals collecting portfolios of eclecticism.

The word *eclectic* originated with the eclectic philosophers of the 1st and 2nd centuries B.C. Rather than confine themselves to the precepts of a single school of thought, they held themselves free to choose such elements from the various schools as suited their personal preferences. Eclectic came to mean "selective, freely choosing, or borrowing."

As business moved from the 1980s into the 1990s, my instincts told me that the profile of the professional eclectic was going to become more and more important. And it has. Nowhere is this more evident than in the merging world of high tech, where lines are blurring, where definitions are sliding into one another. In the case of one of my Hollywood pals, does it really matter if he is defined as a new media digital expert, as an entertainment consultant with technical know-how, or as an educator who is the catalyst for the merging of educational content with entertainment models in the field of technology? No. What gives him creditability, what allows him to shine at what he does, is what I call his level of professional eclecticism. As he puts it, "I am in the business of creating structures that allow lots of people from a variety of fields to realize their dreams."

By focusing on professional eclecticism, one is also creating a profile of transferable pieces, experiences that are the precursor for understanding and embracing the paradoxical nature of the entrepreneur's profile. With professional eclecticism in your side pocket, you will not be stupefied by redefinitions of business rules, and you will not see the business landscape in categories. You will be able to slide, hop, jump, and mostly swim between the tidal waves of change that you cannot control. You will become a master navigator.

Leonardo da Vinci integrated his knowledge and understanding of fine arts, science, and, in some ways, his entrepreneurial spirit to create his livelihood. He supported himself by adapting his drawing skills to the more lucrative fields of weapons design and military engineering, and yet the thing we remember him for is the art he did in his spare time. In my mind, he is a great example of a professional eclectic. Today, the same agility is required to bring together opposing skills and sometimes move through a series of contradictory professional experiences. It is just accomplished with a different set of tools.

The difference between a generalist and a specialist is that a successful specialist does best talking to and comparing notes with other successful specialists. The successful generalist knows how to put together a top-notch team of successful specialists.

the developing entrepreneur is a generalist in their approach to business. their specialty is entrepreneuring.

When asked what kind of people she looks for in candidates for her much sought-after New Media School in New York, Red Burns always responds, "Bring me clowns!" She is more interested in those who can perform many tasks than those who arrive with a preset notion of how they are going to approach learning new media. In other words, she would rather see people who would focus on building an infrastructure for transportation than on building a railroad. The person who merely builds the railroad has inherent value for what they do and is essential to pave the way for the other to exist.

But their focus will always be limited in its transferability and in its flexibility and therefore cannot necessarily move with the times.

Rob Ryan of Entrepreneur America believes that a successful entrepreneur must have a combination of both generalist and specialist in their makeup. At Harvard Business School, student candidates are examined for strong leadership potential, focusing on an ability to manage the risk/reward cycle. I take this concept a step further. I suggest that being a generalist by training enables developing entrepreneurs to focus on engaging in many professional scenarios that will force them to increase their level of eclectic information, understanding, and experience. As they gain experience, properly dedicating themselves to eclecticism, they will eventually discover the area of specialty they are most suited for. The same student of law whom I mentioned earlier took law in university as a stepping-stone to assist him in understanding what he could do with his skills outside of the area he was trained in. Today, this same person has a list of experiences that has led him to be executive producer of one of the hottest television and film production houses in Canada and then executive producer of MSN Canada (Microsoft Network). Each milestone he achieved was the result of his approach to specializing in developing his entrepreneurial spirit and generalizing his approach to business in everything else he chose to do.

In the world of technology, there is often a misconception that the idea itself is what carries the success of a software company, a new product, or a service offering. But Geoffrey Moore has a different take on the generalist/specialist profile: "Specialists at their *worst* tend to believe that the value of the company is pretty much the value of their idea. What the marketplace will tell you is that the value of an idea is less than 5 percent of the value of a company. That comes as a shock. For example, venture capitalists are not *just* looking at the technology, they are looking to find something that can create what we call a discontinuous innovation that can create a long-term competitive advantage."

As one entrepreneur succinctly put it to me, "You might be a good chemist, but you're not necessarily a good entrepreneur. I have a good chemical formula, but can I find financing for it? Can I motivate people to work for me? Can I negotiate a good deal? Can I keep all the balls in the air at the same time? Often this same brilliant chemist will do best if he or she hooks up with someone who can do all of these things and he has to focus only on the brilliant chemistry formula."

Once again, we are back to the concept of paradoxical profiles—in this case, of the need to specialize and the need to generalize simultaneously. I believe that the majority of us need to make a choice between training ourselves in an area of specialty versus gaining experiences as a generalist who will be trained in applying a wide berth of understanding to various areas of specialty. As a developing entrepreneur, one should focus on being

You've got to know enough about something to change it radically.

MOSES ZNAIMER,
PRESIDENT,
CITYTV

Specialists? They tend to think in terms of things, not in terms of means.

MICHAEL MOON

a generalist first, because that is the best means of training for the kind of flexibility required in today's world, where the emphasis is on lateral movement within industries and within companies, within trends and within the global economy. Entrepreneurship, unlike other professions, is not a discipline, though being *disciplined* is a requirement. By maintaining some distance as a generalist, the developing entrepreneur approaches a new challenge by seeing the larger picture more clearly and is therefore able to maximize their particular expertise much faster than if they started in a particular area of specialty and kept narrowing it down from there.

Let me give you an example. A friend of mine studied graphic design and architecture in university. He had all the degrees required to practice in either discipline, and he did for a while. But then, like many of us, he got the entrepreneurial bug. He wanted to create a company of his own that would take him to new places, that would challenge his skill sets in a new way. He began by asking himself what talents he had. He met people and listened to what they had to teach him, thereby testing out his notion that he could leapfrog into a new industry and leverage his accumulated skills in a new context, and he theorized and reflected on the information that he gathered.

Ultimately, because of his generalist approach, he was able to take his capabilities and transport them to Hollywood. At that time, in 1992, music-video production was in full swing. Production companies were finding that what they needed was not only an art director with good ideas and a strong visual sense but someone who could also direct the building of the often complicated sets required, someone who could draft blueprints accurately. Thinking as a generalist, my friend let go of his ideas about his profession and began to build a business based on this niche—art direction with a focus on production requiring architectural capabilities. Today, he is one of the hottest art directors in this niche market, with credits for videos by Madonna, Michael Jackson, and Nine Inch Nails in his portfolio.

Do not get me wrong. There are thousands of highly trained and highly successful entrepreneurs who come from one particular area of specialty and swiftly and adeptly move into an entrepreneurial venture built on a product they create. We hear about these successes every day. For example, there is a company called Rambus, a highly successful example of entrepreneurship, whose stock soared 600 percent in 14 weeks after its IPO (initial public offering). The company's success is based on a very specialized idea—a different way to handle computer memory based on a complex mathematical construct. It was an act of pure specialty and introspection. As Geoffrey Moore says, in this case "generalists need not apply."

But more and more, many of us are recognizing both the need for and the benefit of a generalist approach to entrepreneurship as well as the power of partnership. Today, some of the top universities that have entrepreneurship programs are focusing on this very issue. "Unlike many universities, the

I can live within contradiction. I have no problem with the notion of infinity, when things are so small they become huge, and vice versa. It is an inherent conflict within the entrepreneurial mix—you have to be a specialist at being an entrepreneur, but you have to be a generalist in how you get there.

PAUL WOLLASTON,
EXECUTIVE PRODUCER,
NIMM NEW MEDIA

Massachusetts Institute of Technology encourages business and engineering students to work together on plans. Many of the teams are composed of an amalgam of MBAs with marketing and finance skills and engineers who thoroughly know technology," says Kenneth P. Morse, managing director of the MIT Entrepreneurship Center. At Stanford, there is a program called the Technology Ventures Co-op Program, "which is a nine-month curriculum to teach engineering students to become entrepreneurs. Two or three students apply for every spot in the program. Those who are brilliant and lucky enough to make it can look forward to a dose of real-world experience." Other universities have similar programs. The University of Washington has a program called the Hatchery, which allows students to write their own business plans and have them evaluated by outside entrepreneurs from the business community.

I personally feel that if I had to choose, I would focus on the model of a generalist and find a specialist rather than the other way around. The difference between a generalist and a specialist is that a successful specialist does best talking to and comparing notes with other successful specialists. The successful generalist knows how to put together a top-notch team of successful specialists. And it is the top-notch teams that are best suited to create opportunity. Rob Ryan talks about this when he coaches entrepreneurs in training. Bill Sahlman looks for it when he reviews the candidates for the Harvard MBA program, and most entrepreneurs I talk to swear allegiance to it. In the case of Intel, Arthur Rock was a generalist who was really good at picking the right people to do the job—in this case, Andy Groves and Gordon Moore. And he did this in a variety of industries.

In a world where the lines keep blurring, where intellectual property is the currency and people view their accumulated experience as a stock, I would suggest that honing one's skills as a generalist, with a focus on broadening the eclectic portfolio, has the kind of elasticity required for a much larger pool of entrepreneurial opportunities. Approach the circle of learning as a generalist. Along the way, you will discover an area of specialty that turns you on, and you will seek out the specialists required to help build an opportunity.

There are five key strategies to developing and honing one's professional eclecticism.

a university degree in speaking, writing, and performing

Regardless of what undergraduate university degree you have or decide to take, the criteria are as follows: You are forced to analyze a lot of incoming and seemingly unconnected information; you can succeed only by producing well-written, well-structured research papers (arguments); you are asked

In Canada there are many entrepreneurial programs being offered, including McGill — the Dobson Centre for Entrepreneurial Studies; the University of Manitoba — the Asper Centre for Entrepreneurship; the University of British Columbia — an MBA program that specializes in entrepreneurship; Brock University — the Burgoyne Centre for Entrepreneurship; Ryerson — the Centre for Entrepreneurship; the University of Toronto — the Centre for Management of Technology and Entrepreneurship; and York University — an MBA program specializing in entrepreneurial studies.

These and other educational programs are an important step in introducing the notion of entrepreneurship to a wide range of students.

to present information verbally on a regular basis; and you learn how to perform on stage with many others. In my experience, that provides the developing entrepreneur with a basis for conducting business with ease and grace, regardless of what industry they choose to focus on in the end. In short: speaking, writing, and performing.

musical intelligence

In his book *The Age of Unreason*, Charles Handy talks about the seven categories of intelligence: analytical intelligence, pattern intelligence, musical intelligence, physical intelligence, practical intelligence, intrapersonal intelligence, and interpersonal intelligence. Each of these categories includes specific talents. For example, pattern intelligence is exhibited most often by mathematicians and scientists, who have the ability to see and recognize patterns. Interpersonal intelligence is often seen in managers and leaders within companies and in a politician's ability to get along with many kinds of people. Obviously, it is rare for one person to possess all of these categories of intelligence. Often, though, we are strong in one or more of these categories and can, over time, train and improve in the areas where we may not necessarily be naturally talented.

Among the Renaissance intelligentsia it was somewhat of a social embarrassment to be unable to read music, sing, or play an instrument.

Musical intelligence is a particular bias of mine. Perhaps because one of the *only* rules that my parents were absolutely uncompromising about was the need to develop musical ability. In fact, there are studies that indicate that studying music from a young age actually increases levels of intelligence. That in itself sounds like a good enough reason to learn to play an instrument.

More important, I do think there is a certain model, paradoxical in nature, that is part of your musical training that sets you up for the entrepreneurial environment. (a) Music requires an incredible discipline, even if you are naturally talented. Disciplined training, especially based on long-term reward, is more easily learned when you are young. Practicing music requires this. That sense of long-term commitment in the world of entrepreneuring, and in life in general, is essential. (b) At the same time, you need to find balance between the discipline of practice and the fluid, loose, visceral mindset that will actually allow you to improve faster than you normally would through sheer discipline. The need to find the balance between discipline and a particular mindset is very personal and not something that you can teach someone. Rather, this balance is found in the experience of actually performing a particular task. As with entrepreneuring, it is the best way to move through the testing portion of the learning cycle.

Another paradoxical profile of the new entrepreneur comes to mind here. (c) Learning music is a complex activity that requires skill, discipline, the reading of a language, the use of a tool, and an emotional commitment to the music. Over time, this kind of complex combination of elements will provide an acquired skill and a sense of reward that you will never lose. In the process, you are training yourself for the many complex activities, the layering of skill, mindset, and training that is the hallmark of entrepreneurship. What creates real greatness is the combination of long-term complexities, not any one element on its own.

(d) Music is often most rewarding when played in groups. The concept of partnership begins to take shape when you are in a musical group. This group participation allows you to understand that it is the combination of various dynamic elements that in the end creates great moments. It is at the completion of an ensemble work—the pause before instruments are lowered, before hands are removed from the keyboard, when the resonance of the sound bounces off the floor and gently settles into the air before it disappears—when the group effort is truly realized, beautiful and precise. This kind of group dynamic is what gets entrepreneurial ventures started. Returning to those moments of perfection is what keeps entrepreneurs coming back for more.

Interestingly enough, many of the people I have met over the years often have either a musical background or are currently involved in music. Bill Buxton of SGI and Alias Wavefront has colorful stories about his stint as a jazz musician in Amsterdam. Paul Hoffert, executive director of Intercom Ontario, was the founder of the rock band Lighthouse long before he was involved in the worlds of high tech, telecommunications, and authorship that he is known in today. He sees the musician as someone who has had to come to terms with the interaction between creativity and technology by having to express oneself using an instrument. Now, the tools of technology are more complicated than this, but the interactivity between creativity and the tools required to create is the same. All of these musicians-cum-technologists/entrepreneurs talk about moments in music, which they have experienced either alone or in a group, that have required this magical combination.

Others find this kind of training in sports or in other group activities. Joanna Lau, president and CEO of Lau Technologies, is determined that her daughter play team sports, because she believes that by being in a collective team environment, her daughter will experience these indescribable moments, which will be good training for the "coming together" that is essential in business.

"beside-the-point" companies

As opposed to "flat people," the developing entrepreneur looks for jobs and career moves that will propel them forward and provide them with leverage and breadth of experience where transferability is the operative word. When Pamela Wallin is asked about the slim opportunities that exist within the television broadcast industry, her advice is to broaden one's notion of an

The seven categories of intelligence are analytical intelligence, pattern intelligence, musical intelligence, physical intelligence, practical intelligence, intrapersonal intelligence, and interpersonal intelligence.

CHARLES HANDY,
THE AGE OF UNREASON

opportunity. "If you look at the traditional broadcast pyramid, it looks steep. But in fact, 46 percent of viewers in the United States, for example, now watch cable television, so forget about the major networks as a starting point. Go work for one of the specialty channels. Go start at the bottom in a cable company and learn the ropes. You may find you hit your stride there. And if you don't, the experience will be invaluable. You will be able to gain leverage from these places from which to build your own version of programming."

The person who learns sign language will have honed their skills of intuitive listening and observing, which will bode well in any job that requires a fine sense of communication. The person who decides to take a job abroad, regardless of what the job is, will definitely discover their strengths and weaknesses of character by putting themselves in a completely foreign environment.

**Peripheral:
"beside the point."**

What do each of these approaches have in common? It is a strategy that I call focusing on "peripheral companies." This is by no means a derogatory term but, rather, a term to enable you to transform the way in which you view *any* job in the development of your eclectic portfolio. In my thesaurus, *peripheral* is described as "beside the point," and that is exactly what I mean. As part of their strategy, the professional eclectic focuses their job-searching efforts on companies that are privately owned, smaller rather than larger, and companies that are not necessarily mainstream in their approach to business. For example, if you are interested in software related to the Web, work for a small multimedia design firm rather than attempt to join the ranks of one of the key visual computing companies. If you are in the retail business, try working for a company that is promoting private-label goods in a new market rather than working for a well-established household brand. By working within these kinds of environments, by focusing on "beside the point," you will learn a few key lessons that will serve you well in entrepreneuring.

Better Fish—Better Pond

You've heard it many times: Be a bigger fish in a smaller pond. But sometimes, being a bigger fish in a smaller pond is really about being a better fish in a better kind of pond. The benefit of this scenario is not just more responsibility or room for faster promotion but also the opportunity to challenge your circle of learning in a way that would not be afforded to you in a larger company. In a smaller company, you can often create a job that simply did not previously exist. For example, one receptionist I knew, who worked at a systems-integration company, spent the first two months assessing where the biggest source of confusion and frustration lay within the company as a whole. She discovered that it was in the trafficking of sales information, from customer inquiries to managing the volume of information coming in to each of the sales reps to the collating and delivery of packages back out to the customers. Although it was not part of her job description as a receptionist, in addition to her daily duties, she focused her attention on improving the process for trafficking sales inquiries. Within six months, she was promoted to sales administration manager and was managing a staff of three.

Close to the Skin

Smaller organizations work closer to the skin. There are fewer buffers between people, processes, and structure, which allow you to participate and gain an "in-your-face" experience that you cannot get elsewhere. In this kind of environment, you will be able to watch the inner workings of how people manage teams, how partnerships work or do not work, in a way that is often denied to you in larger companies. In beside-the-point companies, a sence of urgency permeates most business activities with an immediacy that is often buffered in a larger organization. This allows you to begin to entrepreneur in small ways that will allow you to test your own comfort level with self-initiation, with confrontation, with a lack of precedence. Not only can you take these experiences with you when you move on, but your accumulated observations of what make entrepreneurial enterprises work, or not work, will assist you in creating a model of entrepreneurship that you may eventually want to actualize.

I look at my résumé as a reflection of my career wanderings, en route to becoming a new entrepreneur.

AN ENTREPRENEUR

The Rule of Indispensability and Levels of "Bounce Back"

The rule of indispensability is best described as follows: The employee (developing entrepreneur) never comes forward with a question or a comment about a current problem but begins each meeting with their boss with a proposed solution to a problem that their superior did not even know existed. By creating this model as the basis for your interaction with superiors, you are learning how to see the world as a series of solutions rather than problems.

In addition to ensuring that you become indispensable, working in beside-the-point companies allows you to test your resilience, or what I call your level of "bounce back." A well-known entrepreneur in the telecommunications business described her first experience of bounce back as follows: "I was an account manager for a telecommunications and networking consulting firm in the '80s. I detected that our company was losing market share within the real estate market, which was in a real slump. I sensed that the company was going to start laying people off, so I took the matter into my own hands. I approached my boss and made him a deal. I would agree to go on a 100 percent commission plan for six months. In return for forfeiting my secure salary, he would allow me to venture into the healthcare market. If I met my projected sales targets, he would seriously consider promoting me to manage this new sales area. Not only did he agree to this arrangement, but in changing the rules for both me and the company, I learned the power of deal making."

Small companies thrive on self-sufficient and self-motivated team players. These team players are more highly valued in their solution approach, because in a smaller company, there is rarely enough time to set up structures to help them handle transitions or improve a set process. Become the solution provider, and you will be indispensable. That is a very good place to be and a great way to test and leverage the skills you are learning on the job.

Learn How To Be an Employee

Many entrepreneurs claim that the most time-consuming and often difficult part of their job is dealing with human resources issues. The entrepreneurs who tend to have an easier time of it in these situations are those who have actually been employees themselves, particularly employees for other entrepreneurs. By participating as a team member in an entrepreneurial enterprise, you learn the concerns, the areas of frustration and confusion, on a firsthand basis. Should you decide to create your own entrepreneurial opportunity or manage your own entrepreneurial team down the road, you will have a heightened awareness of what it takes to motivate, manage, and lead employees. You will also have credibility with them, having been one yourself.

sell, sell, sell

There is an organization called the Holden Corporation whose mandate is to create a training process that elevates sales into the category of a profession. A very successful outfit, and one worth exploring, this company was created in reaction to the misconceptions about selling that were circulating in the 1980s. At that time, the focus seemed to be on closing a deal rather than on providing a solution to someone's problem. A badge of glory was not based on the level of knowledge or service that someone brought to their customers but on the size of the sale, the amount of revenue brought in.

The Holden method taught you how to build a long-term sales plan professionally, not just as a means of selling more product or improving a quarterly quota (though this inevitably happened) but to enable you to maintain the long-term sustained selling that is required as a means of succeeding in almost any job.

I have always said that when I was in pure sales for various companies in my career, I was truly in my element. And it's a good thing, because as an entrepreneur, you are constantly in selling mode. You are always selling the concept of your company to prospective employees, you are selling the perceived value of the concept of your product to potential investors, you are selling the story of your company to the press, and you are always selling your product or service to your customers. Sometimes you call this

Is a generalist really just a dilettante of vocations?

The developing entrepreneur has long-term goals, but not short-term expectations. Expectations like perfectionism are oppressive and often thwart motivation.

pitching, sometimes team leadership, and other times storytelling. The bottom line is that it is *selling*.

If I had to give a graduating student one piece of advice, it would be this: Find a sales job and excel at it. In assessing the psychology of entrepreneurs, Jerry Mitchell of the MIT Enterprise Forum notes the importance of sales in a start-up. He "is amazed by how many entrepreneurs spend their time seeking financing while they have a product which they could be out selling. Selling requires a certain emotional makeup and a willingness to face the music, which is why it is easier to avoid."

FIND A SALES JOB WHERE YOU CAN OPEN DOORS AS A GENERALIST AND CLOSE THE SALE AS A SPECIALIST.

A specialist is someone who does everything else worse.

RUGGIERO RICCI

I would take Mitchell's statement a step further: Find a sales job where you can open doors as a generalist and close the sale as a specialist. Diane McGarry, CEO and president of Xerox Canada, began her career as a sales rep based in Fort Wayne. She took the tough jobs, the line assignments, where, I suspect, her ability to get in the door had more to do with her generalist approach to listening. Her ability to turn that entry point into a sale probably had to do with her determination to learn everything she had to to close the deal—as a specialist. Every developing entrepreneur, every professional eclectic, needs to have a sales position somewhere in their portfolio as a means of understanding the role of both the generalist and the specialist within the cycle of success. It is often helpful to find a job that allows you to sell in teams, further reinforcing the concept of the generalist who leads (opens the doors) and the specialist who closes (provides the particular expertise required).

Chris Strachan, when he was first in commercial real estate, was able to turn his youth and inexperience into a real asset by immediately hooking up with a partner. The senior sales partner had all the contacts and was able to open doors as a generalist. Chris, through hands-on experience, became the expert contract negotiator and was able to close deals quickly by understanding the legal issues in commercial leasing situations. Eventually, Chris was able to take what he had learned from his generalist partner and his own specialty in contracts and become a sales entity on his own. Ultimately he learned a transportable skill that has tremendous value today when, for example, he's faced with a roomful of lawyers in a financing situation.

I will go even further and suggest that you should try your hand at sales by beginning with conceptual selling. This would include tasks such as selling a service or a product that requires long-term consulting, which could include marketing, telecommunications call-center installations, or outsourcing contracts. Then move on to product sales, selling software, hardware, consumer goods, etc.

Here is what you will learn from a sales position:

You will learn the balance between the generalist approach to telling a story and the specialist approach to expertise. In selling, you will quickly find your comfort level in these two opposing approaches to selling, because you have to; otherwise, you do not get paid.

You will learn to be extremely resourceful by thinking out of the box. In any competitive industry, it is the person who is able to come up with new ways to view the same people or opportunities who will be able to open doors (that were always there in the first place). I know a broker who has come up with a formula for selling that is flawless. She focuses all her attention on the up-and-coming female market and hosts "salons," whereby women are invited for dinner and are entertained by a guest speaker. Rather than inviting a lecturer to discuss investment options, she invites speakers to talk about issues relating to independence and self-confidence. Through association, these speakers are then able to weave in the notion of financial independence and financial investment as another piece of the independent woman's profile.

This broker found a way to capture the attention of a growing target market—working women. She represents the model of interpretation that we talked about earlier. She is not inventing a new product, in that she did not come up with any proprietary financial instrument or special investment opportunity that she has an exclusive on. But she is a master of interpretation of the topics and issues that she knows will trigger a response in her target market. She then sells based on this interpretation.

You will understand the notion of the outsider. The salesperson spends most of their day on the outside of all the organizations and groups of people that they must sell to. This is a great training arena for concepts such as the "lone coach"—the center of attention, but not quite part of the team. Your ability to toggle between these two areas will be indispensable in helping you to understand the specifics of this paradoxical profile of the new entrepreneur.

You will learn how to fail. When I was selling for a corporate communications company, I had a rule that I was going to sell only through referrals. By this time, I had enough of a track record that I did not have to sell by cold-calling. One day, my assistant revealed to me that she thought she had what it took to do sales but was absolutely petrified of the potential rejection she might have to face. I decided it was time to change her mind. I looked through my list of prospects that I had generated from months gone by and chose the one on my list with a star beside his name, indicating that he was never to be called back again because of his particular lack of telephone etiquette. I put the phone on conference and called the number. Luckily, he was in. I began my introduction as calmly as I possibly could, knowing the eruption that would ensue. Within seven seconds of my introduction, he began his tirade: "I am so sick of getting hounded by every marketing hack in this city with your fancy communications processes. I do not need to improve my communications processes, and if I did, I certainly would not choose someone who has to cold-call me for that kind of expertise."

The irony was obviously lost on him. I tried to counter his argument. Halfway through my sentence, he swore under his breath and hung up the phone. My assistant was dumbfounded and slightly terrified. "See," I said, "I am still here. I am still relatively intact. I did not enjoy the last few minutes, but I certainly am not going to take it personally. You need to learn how to do that if you are ever going to go places, and not just in sales."

Arriviste: someone who will use any means to achieve success.

I still believe this. Every salesperson goes through a period of failure. Every salesperson has had someone hang up on them midsentence and has had to commit to an air of success despite the losing streak they are on. And every salesperson will tell you that while rejection is ruthless, it is not fatal. This kind of rough-and-tumble experience is important to have. You will get plenty of bruises during your entrepreneuring expeditions. You will need the calluses.

You will learn to listen. Great salespeople do not talk very much. They mostly listen. As soon as you learn this rule, your sales will begin to soar, your ability to attract the right kind of decision makers will quadruple, and you will deduce that listening is the most important element of any sales presentation. In his book *Selling the Invisible*, Harry Beckwith explains that the most compelling sales message is prefaced with "I understand what you need." The selling message "I have (this or that product)" is about you. The message "I understand" is about the prospect. You cannot master this selling technique without listening. And training to listen sets you up for the profile of the chameleon. Listening improves your ability to improvise, to adapt, to bounce back, to transfer your ideas into different kinds of languages and different kinds of presentation styles. It is, in fact, the first step in adopting the stance of the "sensitive extrovert."

In her book *Hello, He Lied*, Lynda Obst talks about the particular skills and strategies required in pitching movie scripts in Hollywood. Her "know thy buyer" concept is as much about tapping into the personal tastes, the passions, favorite writers, movies, restaurants, and hobbies of the executive you will be pitching to as it is about having the right script, the right team. Of course, if you have been developing a portfolio of eclecticism, your ability to find common ground with these personalities—in terms of their tastes, hobbies, and interests—will be extended and heightened. The qualifier here? That you listen. Without listening, in Lynda Obst's world, you cannot catch the particular mood swings that a studio may be in the middle of, you might miss the nuance that reveals a bias or a particular taste of a key executive—and you could ruin your chances at the pitch due to bad timing.

When I tried to pitch to a top venture capital firm on Sand Hill Road in Silicon Valley, I was trained to listen so that I could adeptly move from "pitching" mode to "teach-me" mode in three minutes flat. As a developing entrepreneur, you will find that selling is one of the best ways to train yourself to listen. Without it, you cannot understand the customer's needs. Without the customer, entrepreneuring is not possible.

portfolio building

When I was in university, I volunteered for a program called ACTRA, a literacy program for maximum-security inmates in Archambault, Quebec. Every week, six of us were driven out to a desolate prison compound north of Montreal. It was strange and surreal; it was frightening and exciting.

One particular session sticks in my mind. After a few months of participating in this program, I found that teaching within the constraints of a prison became familiar to the point where I often lost sight of the reality of the situation when I was in the middle of a class. One day, I was leading an improvisational drama session. Everyone seemed to be engaged except for one inmate at the back of the room. Without thinking twice, I said, "Excuse me, but if you are not interested in this class, you might want to leave, because your talking is disrupting the others." In a flash, this man came tearing up toward the front of the room in a pent-up rage like nothing I had ever witnessed in my life. Before I knew it, I was down on the floor in some kind of bear hold without a chance of getting away. The guards rushed in and very quickly took this man away, and he was never allowed back in the class again.

I was shaken, but not scared. After that, I never viewed the sessions at Archambault with the same cavalier familiarity as I had foolishly done on that one day. I simply filed it away in my portfolio of experiences, under "C" for "character building."

Whether one files these types of experiences under "C" for character building or under "G" for "get up and try again," by building a portfolio with breadth of experience, the professional eclectic is also creating a great means for establishing a wide range of relationships and connections to people. This is invaluable in the exercise of creating circles of champions as part of the entrepreneur's network. Throughout my career, I chose not to take a straight path. When I was in public relations, I chose to test my hand at social marketing, working with various government and not-for-profit organizations. When I was an aspiring account director in advertising, I decided that I wanted to go into full-time sales, even though there was no job with that title available. In each case, I was dedicating myself to incorporating eclectic experiences into my developing entrepreneurial portfolio. And this approach paid

So you just want to look like an entrepreneur, eh?

CONVERSATION
OVERHEARD

off. At every job interview, I got more questions about the ACTRA program than I did about any one job I had ever had. It was a great way to break the ice and get the conversation going smoothly. When I was in communications sales, I was able to use stories from my varied experiences as a means of finding common ground with a very wide range of customers. The professional eclectic finds ways to weave elements of "beside the point" into her portfolio. Like learning how to dance with risk, portfolio building is a never-ending exercise that is essential for the developing entrepreneur.

An intrapreneur is someone with an entrepreneur's attitude and approach, but whose playing field is within the boundary of an established company.

THE WALL STREET JOURNAL

a word about the corporate hound

I have never worked for a megacorporation (surprised?) and probably never will, and therefore, I am not an expert on how to entrepreneur in that kind of large setting. But in talking to many entrepreneurs as well as intrapreneurs, I am struck by the fact that most people fall into one of two categories: those who are in complete favor of the notion that intrapreneurship is a relevant term and a worthwhile career path; and those who are diametrically opposed to the idea that working for a large company allows one to nurture and develop the entrepreneurial spirit successfully.

For example, when you talk to an entrepreneur such as Katrina Garnett, founder and CEO of CrossRoads Software in California, she attributes her ability to raise more than $15 million in investment, create a new product category of enterprise communications software, and manage a start-up to her experiences at large technology companies including Oracle and Sybase. In fact, she encourages young women to find intrapreneurial opportunities as a training ground for entrepreneurship. Garnet strongly feels that many of the skills required for running CrossRoads Software came out of her job as VP General Manager of the Distributed Objects and Connectivity Group, a 300-person development organization for Sybase.

Others I have spoken to in the field of high tech strongly suggest spending some time working within a highly secretive development branch, or the research and development division of a large company. Their feeling is that often these "skunk works" groups are focused on pioneering products and services within an industry sector and therefore are able to function to some extent as autonomous units. A friend of mine in retail packaging was able to move from the head office of her company to start up their new California division from scratch. To her, this experience provided her with entrepreneurial challenges in the context of a large company that she feels are indispensable.

On the other side of the coin, many corporate hounds (as I like to call them) have either tried to assert an entrepreneurial spirit within their area of responsibility as they move up the corporate ladder or are parachuted into a corporation to introduce an entrepreneurial flavor. Many of these people have not had such great experiences. Others such as Geoffrey Moore question whether one can "institutionalize" something like entrepreneurial energy within a larger, more bureaucratic setting. "There is an important dark side to entrepreneurship. It is an act of rebellion. Many large institutions tend to celebrate a culture of risk aversion. What ends up happening is that you create incubators that in some ways become a way of cocooning would-be entrepreneurs from taking the initial risks that are so essential for defining their future. . . . In some ways, it is like approaching entrepreneurship with training wheels." Although Moore agrees that large corporations may be good training grounds, he feels that ultimately, they have to be jumping-off places, not settings that one gets used to being in.

the intrapreneur redefined

Entrepreneuring can happen within a number of organizations, big or small, public or private, wildly successful or only intermittently so. The qualifier is that (a) the company must aggressively encourage people to pursue new opportunities, with the recognition that a certain amount of risk taking comes with the turf; (b) it must be committed to the continuous refinement of what an opportunity is; and (c) most important, the leader of the pack must truly foster an environment that accepts others' failures as a necessary part of success, while encouraging the concept of difference and interpretation as valuable business precepts at all levels of the company. At that point, it does not matter whether the company takes the shape of a larger company like General Electric or an entrepreneurial enterprise like Yahoo. The difficulty is that larger, more structured corporations have been built on a different set of constructs. They are like large, unwieldy boats. It is not that these boats cannot turn around or head in another direction but that it takes much longer to change direction and often requires superhuman effort. In spite of this, today we are seeing more and more companies trying to infuse an entrepreneurial approach into the work that they do.

The Upside Factor

Despite the challenges and barriers that do exist, it would be inaccurate to reflect only doom and gloom in the profile of the corporate hound. In fact, right at this very moment, most of the business world is thriving on, building careers in, and making a lot more money in these megacorporations than either I or many of the entrepreneurs out there. I have spoken to many intrapreneurial spirits who derive a lot of learning and success and meaning within the structure of corporations. They suggest that, as with any organization, there are a few rules you must get around. Once you've managed that, however, with the right mix of people within your division and your spheres

Many companies foster a truly entrepreneurial spirit. 3M founder Bill McKnight says, "Listen to anyone with an original idea, no matter how absurd it might sound at first. Encourage." 3M introduced 500 new products in 1996.

FORTUNE MAGAZINE

of influence, change and improvements and even waves of entrepreneurial activity *do* occur. Here are the few words of advice that I have picked up from the experts, people who have successfully built their careers and honed a sense of entrepreneurship through the megacorporations of the world.

One Vision at a Time

In the words of a senior executive who led many initiatives at Tandem and IBM, "The hardest part of entrepreneuring in a large corporation is figuring out the best way for you (the business venture, the unit) to accomplish your goals while matching what the corporation also needs." If you are focused on change within a megacorporation (or anywhere, for that matter), the number-one rule is that you do not begin to set a new vision for your division or your project that is separate from the company's overall vision. If you are setting out on a new venture, you may feel the temptation to do a reset on the company's vision that will justify your ideas but might be in direct conflict with the company. This will result only in confusion. Ultimately, the company vision will win, and you will lose.

This idea of conflicting visions was driven home to me by an entrepreneur (let's call him Bob) in the Web design business. The manager of a division of a bank (let's call him John) that Bob was doing some work for wanted to create an entirely new Web architecture for his particular division. Through various meetings that Bob attended with VPs from other divisions, he perceived that his direct client was really creating a whole new approach to a communications channel (the Web) that was in conflict with what the rest of the bank was comfortable with. Although Bob realized that John's idea was far more progressive than those of VPs in the other divisions, he tried to persuade him to minimize the differences in design and some of the interactive elements he was determined to introduce. John decided *not* to take Bob's advice, convinced that once the Web site was up and running, the other VPs would see the value of his approach to the information architecture.

As it turned out, they didn't. Not only did John have to pay Bob for all his work to date, but he was suddenly faced with such a reduced budget that he was barely able to create a Web presence that properly reflected his division's products and services with any sense of the design or interactivity elements that it deserved. The company's understanding of the Web, not surprisingly, won out.

The Duplication Factor

The foremost complaint I have heard from entrepreneurial mavericks is that you often find that you are championing a new idea at the same time as someone else is in a completely different division. This sounds to me like convergence of similar ideas. Often, however, the "happy coincidence" of this synergy is not what is perceived. Instead what ensues is a turf war in

ENRON was voted the most innovative company in the U.S. in the *Fortune* poll in 1996. Their universal stock option plan promises to pay employees twice their annual salaries after eight years.

FORTUNE MAGAZINE

which much time and energy is spent on lobbying ideas rather than moving forward in unison. One associate of mine was shocked at the amount of time spent on what he called "protecting your territory." Here is his advice: Know that these sorts of situations will exist, and simply ensure that you are better at lobbying than the next person.

The Random Factor

Time after time, I hear stories of executives within a corporation who are moving along with their project. Everything is intact, budgets are in control, resources have been hired, and then, suddenly, the project is pulled. For no reason. Or so it appears.

If you are involved in an entrepreneurial venture within a large corporation, there is more potential for what I call the "random factor." Randomness exists, of course, in every company, entrepreneurial or not. In purely entrepreneurial companies, however, where there are few layers between you and the ultimate decision makers, you can often see the signs of randomness ahead of time and you may even get warning signals. In larger companies, decisions get made for particular reasons that are often out of your control. Because your entrepreneurial project is not "core business," it often falls victim to getting cut out of a quarterly or yearly business plan.

Ensure that you are in a situation that allows you to practice "bounce back," and start to lobby for a revised version of your project with urgency and conviction. Using the "rule of indispensability," ensure that you can present a solution to a problem that your superior did not even know existed. Just make sure that your solution can be achieved *only* through this improved version of the original idea.

The Suggestion of Formality

In talking to a number of senior VPs within large corporations, I have been told that there is a formality in megacorporations but that it is only the *suggestion* of one. This means that you need to pay homage to the processes that are put into place, but if you really need to get a decision made in your favor, the same rule of "whatever it takes" applies. The more seasoned players in these scenarios know how to work around this formality of meetings, agendas, waiting times, hierarchy, structure, and process. After they have gone through the rounds, they begin to lobby their efforts the informal way. If you have trained yourself to be a "chameleon," you are going to be able to adapt to many more personalities at the top. If you have been dedicated to championship throughout your career, you are going to have a network in place that will defend you and your ideas. The rest of the antics are just formalities.

Entrepreneur Is a Verb

Does this mean that I view intrapreneurship as less valuable than entrepreneurship for the developing entrepreneur? I sometimes wish the world were that black and white, that simple. But it is not. What is true and simple is that we each need to view our career as an entrepreneurial venture and take on the task of creating a portfolio of professional eclecticism as a way of life that will add to our own personal branding. And it begins by seeing entrepreneuring as a verb. There are ways to look for entrepreneurial opportunities by seeking out companies that recognize risk and failure as a necessary part of the corporate learning curve, and there are particular areas within any company or organization that lend themselves to more entrepreneurial activities than not. Project management of a new product team is absolutely entrepreneurial—it involves creating something out of nothing. Starting a new division, leading a team to explore partnerships with other companies, mergers—all of these and many more are entrepreneurial activities.

I am convinced that entrepreneuring can occur at various levels along the "e-spectrum" (entrepreneurial spectrum), from a long-term corporate company player to a pioneering microbiologist. Anything is possible; I live by that rule. But I also believe that some company cultures lend themselves to sustaining the entrepreneurial spirit. The kind of entrepreneuring that wakes you up in the middle of the night and stays with you when you are in deep REM mode requires a training ground that will build the necessary confidence to initiate changes. You need the type of training that will set the stage for navigating through a series of successes and failures that are "beside the point" rather than the only point of the exercise. The entrepreneur-in-training recognizes entrepreneuring as a verb, and through their actions, they learn what it means to find the spirit of the entrepreneur in all that they do.

a few words of wisdom for the professional eclectic

on job searching

When you first start out, take a job because of the opportunities it affords you, not because of the salary you can make—and never for a title. No one pays attention to titles these days. An indispensable person can always leapfrog their salary level with the right experiences in their back pocket. The reverse is rarely true.

on job prepping

The developing entrepreneur takes looking for a job very seriously. In fact, they treat it like a business in itself. They hire people to help them research the field, design their résumé, and help to write up their letters, if need be. They get an unappealing job in the meantime to pay the bills. Don't stop short of this kind of thorough approach. Read books, talk to experts. Building your portfolio is a job in itself. It deserves professionalism right from the start.

on token entrepreneurship training

Some of you may disagree with my take on intrapreneurship based on your own experiences. I simply suggest that you revisit the experiences that others have had when looking for a job in the corporate world. And remember to consider these ideas: Regardless of the size of the company or the recognizable logo it boasts, make sure that (a) if possible, your direct superior recognizes your entrepreneurial hankering and accepts it for what it is; (b) you do enough research and reconnaissance to determine whether the company truly is dedicated to an environment that allows for failures and encourages constant refinement of opportunities as a way of life; and (c) you have a plan in place to balance your chosen path by filling your portfolio with enough eclectic extracurricular activities. Further down the road, should you decide to venture forward into other more purely entrepreneurial environments, you will have already honed a host of other skills and interests for future use.

Entrepreneur **is a verb.**

on goal setting

The developing entrepreneur has long-term goals, but not short-term expectations. Expectations like perfectionism are oppressive and often thwart motivation. The goal is to collect as many qualified diverse and relevant experiences as possible that can set you up for entrepreneuring. What happens along the way that is not perfect, or does not meet your expectations, is simply part of the reality package. You evaluate the experience, then just move it to the back of your portfolio.

on balanced portfolios

The developing entrepreneur recognizes that diversity has to be balanced with stability. The idea is not to jump from job to job but to set out on a journey that will allow you to hone skills which may be "beside the point" of the job you are doing at the time but provide you with long-term rewards. I like to call it "career wanderings." For example, you may fail miserably at cold-calling, but you will gain a comfort level in rejection that will stay with you forever. A well-known entertainment lawyer I know spends his spare time creating historical documentaries, not because he has to or because it is a side business. He does it because it keeps him in the loop of processes, which allows him to maintain a connection to a world outside of his day-to-day constructs and in a sense balances his very well-formed portfolio.

from victorian corsets to suede chaps—try it on for size

In my second year of university, I was accepted into an intensive theater program at Stanford University. For one term, 40 of us worked as a team, putting on eight productions in nine weeks, rehearsing and training our bodies, voices, and minds for 14 hours a day. One day, on a break during a particularly hectic rehearsal period, the director of props and costumes allowed all of us to go into the costume shop to try on as many of the costumes as we wanted, as long as we put them back where we had found them. The scene resembled a circus, with Victorian corsets and cowboy chaps all mixed into one pile. But what I remember most about that afternoon was that each of us eventually gravitated to the one costume that suited us best. And when all was said and done, we looked around the room and, truly, everyone seemed comfortable in the costume of their choice. What allowed us all to find the right costume was the fact that we had the run of the costume shop. We could pick and choose, revisit, and then change our images, our costumes, and our choices many times before we found the one we really wanted.

Developing entrepreneurs are really maneuvering through this same kind of exercise, though often it does not feel like that much fun. By allowing yourself to try on various opportunities, by ensuring that you are providing yourself with choices that have more breadth and depth than you ever imagined possible, you are actually able to hone in with confidence and understanding on what suits you best.

From corsets to chaps, dedication to a career of professional eclecticism trains the developing entrepreneur to zero in on the paradoxical realities of the new entrepreneur.

tools for the developing entrepreneur

Circle of Learning: It provides for a wide array of opportunities and circumstances to question, theorize, test, and reflect.

Generalist and Specialist: A level of general interest can become professional in its breadth of experience and suggest ways to work with specialists.

Championship Preparation: It provides for a portfolio of stories and experiences that will allow points of entry with a far greater number of people on the road to developing essential championship networks.

Transportability: It necessitates an attitude of flexibility and provides you with an opportunity to gain transportable skills, which are necessary in today's world of blurring definitions, roles, and responsibilities built on paradox.

Bounce Back: It teaches the indispensability of resilience to change and ambiguity that the new entrepreneur must demonstrate throughout their career.

Listen, Fail, and Sell: Without listening, you will fail. You'll learn that failing is not so bad. Selling successfully is better. Professional eclecticism will require that you face each one of these life skills every day.

Long-Term Doing: It requires long-term discipline, a variety of tasks, and a recognition that it is rarely one person who makes or breaks success but rather the combination of a dynamic group in tune with each other's particular contributions.

An entrepreneur should train to be a short-order cook—too much to do and too little time.

AN ENTREPRENEUR

personal branding

In the final analysis, a dedication to professional eclecticism is the beginning of creating a personal brand that will grow in complexity through time. Just as Jim Collins talks about the big ideas of companies, rather than the products they create, the professional eclectic is building a portfolio of interests, skills, and discipline based on their big idea, what they stand for, not the specific skills they have acquired or been graced with. In separate pieces, the contents of this portfolio are merely a list of things, unrelated and varied. But together, they paint a unique picture of the professional eclectic, a memorable icon, a differentiated character who will evolve into their own personal version of the new entrepreneur.

As the developing entrepreneur builds their portfolio of eclecticism, they are building an image, a story, and a personal brand. As they move forward into more active entrepreneuring—into a world that is built on stories that are told and retold—they will have a personal brand that will far outlast a trend, that will have more staying power than a particular specialty, and that will always have merit and relevance. The professional eclectic's brand is based on a big idea, on a portfolio of combined experience that will outlast cycles of change and adapt to the rough spots along the way. After all, they have been in training.

chapter 6

The F(Email) Factor

My grandmother is one of the most ferocious entrepreneurs I have ever met. Knowing of her lifelong ability to create anything out of absolutely nothing, and seeing her strong self-image that sometimes borders on the hyperbolic, I was not surprised when she first recounted to me that one of the best days of her life was the day she was run over by a truck in western Canada.

It was February 1934, in Edmonton, Alberta, and the wind was howling. The Depression had hit western Canada as badly, if not worse, than it had hit other parts of the country. Only 34 years old and a recent immigrant to Canada, my grandmother was able to make a bare living for her three children and ailing husband by running a grocery store and delivering eggs and milk door to door. Determined to send her children to university, she kept the store open seven days a week, 16 hours a day, in an attempt to put away some money for the future. But her savings were not adding up fast enough.

And then, one day, while crossing a busy street, she was hit by a truck on an icy, wintry road. Both her legs were broken. I assume that the agony was intense, though she never talks about that part of the story. Instead, she jumps to the fact that mitigating circumstances resulted in her getting paid $3,000 insurance compensation by the company that owned the truck. In those days, receiving $3,000 was like winning the lottery. My grandmother was ecstatic. Despite the advice of those around her to put the money away, she chose to use this handsome sum to get a loan at the bank and begin to invest in real estate. She had been watching how the population of the town was growing and knew that this trend was going to continue. When the Depression ended (which she knew had to happen eventually), she forecast the need for housing and that prices would jump. In the months that followed, she met with bankers, lawyers, and accountants to ensure that she was doing everything possible to maximize her investment. The rest of her energy was spent investigating and buying properties. Meanwhile, she left the management of the grocery store to her eldest son (my father), who was then only 12. The decision to act in this way did not come without a sacrifice. She was ostracized in her community because she was venturing out and ostensibly doing a man's job, and she was accused of neglecting her children because she was away for hours at a time. Furthermore, she was criticized for taking a big chance with money that had been miraculously dropped into her lap.

If you ask her today, at age 98, what she thought she was doing at the time, she will likely tell you that this was the day she began to "do business"—her version of female entrepreneuring. She will also tell you how, for years, a day did not go by that she was not tempted to try and get run over again so that she could perhaps get another insurance claim and add to her growing real estate business! But luckily, she didn't. Not because she did not have the guts but because, by that time, she was starting to succeed or, as she likes to say, "I was in good business."

I think about this story often, because in some ways, it has the overtones of a modern parable: a woman caring for her family alone, trying to make ends meet. And yet it is about a desire for more that just survival. It speaks of acquiring the taste for doing something of one's own, while still recognizing that such choices do not come without a price, without sacrifice. This was true back then, and even today, many of these same dilemmas still exist. To be an entrepreneur in this day and age is challenging to begin with. But when you are continuously asked by those around you to redefine yourself as a "female entrepreneur," it is difficult not to question why this qualifier exists in the first place.

Like my grandmother, I do not think of myself as a "female entrepreneur." In an attempt to understand my role as an entrepreneur and as a woman, I look to whatever strong and inspiring role models I can. Some are male and some are female. Often, however, I come back to the model of my grandmother, who, out of necessity, became an entrepreneur—and, out of desire and choice, remained an entrepreneur for more than 76 years. Her stories focus on the successes and failures she experienced and what she made of them—as an entrepreneur first and as a woman second. I wonder what stories I will tell my granddaughter when I, too, have had many years of entrepreneuring under my belt. Will I tell her about my adventures being a female entrepreneur? Or will I paint the profile of an entrepreneur who happened to be female, focusing on the things that I accomplished because of who I am?

In the several years that I have been busy entrepreneuring, I am sure that I have sometimes been singled out simply because I am a woman. Being in the field of new media and technology has only heightened my "specialness" in a business world where women are only now beginning to take on leadership positions within corporations, and as entrepreneurs in their own right.

I am aware that my experience may be unlike that of many of the women I read about who are fighting a battle on the corporate battleground to be paid equally, to be heard, and to be included alongside their male counterparts in policy discussions and power plays. But I can write only about my personal experience.

Wealth usually comes from doing what other people find insufferably boring.

GEORGE GILDER,
RECAPTURING THE SPIRIT OF ENTERPRISE

I have found that being an entrepreneur who happens to be female has only been advantageous for me, though some may think this an anomaly. What I choose to do with this specialness is use it as a catalyst for changing the ground rules when it comes to entrepreneurship and gender differences. In my view, female entrepreneurship is not special but, rather, part of the norm. I tend to agree with Sheelagh Whittaker, president and chief executive of EDS Canada Ltd., when she says, "I've always said that we'll have true equality when we have as many incompetent women in positions as we have incompetent men."

Personally, I'd like to continue the process of building the equality equation and pave the way for competence and confidence by citing examples of successful entrepreneurs who happen to be female. In doing this, like millions of women around the world, I, too, am grappling with my identity within a business context and searching for professionalism by being a successful entrepreneur who happens to be female. And, most important, I wonder what I can pass on to others in the way of useful experience, ideas that will entice and motivate them to pursue an entrepreneurial path as a means of defining their contribution to the world at large. I cannot provide a concise and conclusive "to-do" list for women that will ensure smooth successful female entrepreneurship. Nor do I believe that such a list exists. I cannot debate the nuances of gender-inequity issues within corporate North America with insight and perspective, since this has not been my realm of experience—nor do I choose to. But what I can do is provide a few modern-day insights that have helped me to come to terms with being a woman who has chosen to be an entrepreneur.

I have discussed these ideas with my grandmother, curious to see whether she thought they were sound. In her words, she has told me that they make "good business." I pass them on to you.

THE NEW ENTREPRENEUR DOES NOT TRY TO DEFINE FEMALE ENTREPRE-NEURSHIP BUT LEARNS HOW TO EMBRACE THE NECESSARY BALANCE OF WHAT MIGHT BE CONSIDERED FEMALE AND MALE TRAITS WITH ONE GOAL IN MIND: TO WIN.

The profiles of paradox that are required of the new entrepreneur—"the harried bencher," "the lone coach," and "the sensitive extrovert"—extend into the arena of gender. The female entrepreneur requires a chameleon-like stance in relation to what are traditionally considered male and female traits. Rather than being trapped by studies which espouse that women manage through consensus and that men are more assertive in the language that they choose, the new female entrepreneur learns to lead with confidence, to act as aggressively as need be while maintaining her own unique style, be it feminine or otherwise. I call this profile "the sidesaddle jockey."

The number of women business owners in Canada increased by about 150% just in the years from 1979 to 1996, a period in which male business ownership grew by a third that proportion. Almost a third of businesses in Canada today are owned by women.

THE GLOBE AND MAIL

the sidesaddle jockey

Often I hear women debating the merits of exploiting one's femininity in their approach to business or who question whether or not female characteristics, such as nurturing, team building, and consensus building, dictate the approach they must use to manage their employees effectively. In my mind, they are toying with secondary concepts, asking the wrong questions. The real question is, What is the mix of traits and characteristics required to move a business forward, to extend one's career, regardless of traditional gender issues? In my experience, the choice to throw off the yoke of gender stereotypes and push the envelope of one's ability to incorporate and play out what are considered male and female traits is the key to successful entrepreneuring. Here is how the profile works.

Results of an America Online poll indicate 94% of the girls who participated are interested in pursuing a career when they grow up. While 43% consider actors, musicians, and athletes their mentors, 77% would consider pursuing a career involving computers.

SAN FRANCISCO CHRONICLE

Having been in sales within corporate communications and advertising for many years, dealing with both men and women in the corporate and marketing world, I was used to my fair share of learning to read the atmospheric influences in any given scenario. In sales, one runs into all kinds of people. Most often, great relationships evolve. But sometimes you have to deal with underlying agendas that are difficult to navigate. There are the territorial-minded midlevel managers who are fighting to maintain autonomy and budget control. There are the women executives who need to appear smarter and prettier than you but need you to win the job because they know that you have what it takes to make them heroes. There are the young hotshot males who need to simultaneously flirt with you and assert their expertise. And there are the masochistic types who string you along until you think you are going to lose the deal and then give it to you so that you will be forever indebted to them.

Again, having to learn to deal with this diversity of personalities is why sales training is the best preparation for entrepreneuring. As Diane McGarry, president and CEO of Xerox Canada Inc., claims, a career in sales is key. "It doesn't matter what you look like or who you know. All that matters is that you sell." In my experience, sales teaches you how to win the day with people and characters whom you would otherwise not have to play ball with. It teaches you how to play to win.

In each sales situation I approached, I would read the personality barometer and determine how aggressive or how placating I needed to be to close the deal. I had a matrix in my mind of the characteristics that would best suit the situation. In some cases, my ability to be open and personable was far more of an asset than my knowledge of the market research I had conducted. In other situations, my ability to maintain a less flexible persona was required as a means of establishing my power.

But when I first began conducting deals in the technology sector, I had to up the ante on the barometer reading. Ironically, since I was fairly new to the industry, I found myself having to ride sidesaddle more and more often. In many of the meetings I attended, I was immediately overwhelmed by the obvious competition at play within a given boardroom. Regardless of gender, regardless of industry sector, and despite personality types, there was a direct correlation between technological savvy and personal power. In Hollywood terms, "Who's got the juice?" I was suddenly thrust into meeting after meeting where the size of one's pull-down menu was a ritualistic way of testing out a secret pecking order. I had to revisit both my intuitive personality readings and my chameleonlike approach to winning. Here are the strategies I found most helpful in these situations:

the one-goal meeting: the deal

When you are in situations that are heavily loaded with egos and where depth of knowledge is used as a measuring stick to weed out the nonplayers, the key to successful navigation is to focus only on the deal at hand. I would prepare for each meeting with what I called my personal meeting mantra: "Close the deal, nothing else matters." With this firmly in mind, I found that I was able to ignore any attempts to lure me into the game of "who knows more." I resisted my competitive nature and refused to test my aptitude at arguing with the smartest person in the room, and I refused to spend energy on cleverly finding holes in someone else's ideas. Instead, every time the meeting began to swerve away from my goal (closing the deal), I would use whatever means necessary to redirect the conversation.

Many times, I would walk into a room and immediately intuit that the fact of my gender was going to result in a meeting that was going to be confrontational at best and disastrous at worst. In those cases, I would be very specific about my goal for the meeting and refuse to engage in any other charades. In one particular meeting, I could tell that I was not going to win a sale, probably because I was a woman, but I had already determined that I was not going to leave the room until I had successfully obtained one qualified referral from this person. Knowing ahead of time that I was willing and able to lose any other contests that were at play (who knows more? who has done more?), I was able to focus on my job, not my gender advantage or disadvantage. In this particular case, I was able to turn the qualified referral into one of my largest sales. With my personal meeting mantra tucked into my back pocket, I rarely walk out of a room disappointed.

Power in the entertainment business is about more than money. It's about the deal, about who you can call and who you can convince. For the first time in history, women hold that kind of power.

WORKING WOMAN MAGAZINE

"you are the expert—tell me everything you know"

In Lynda Obst's book *Hello, He Lied*, she talks about how it is important for a film producer to go in the direction the horse is already going in. In this way, a person can take the momentum created by an industry, a studio, or an executive and utilize it to move their own agenda forward. I suspect that the notion of going with the momentum already in play holds true with deal making in many industries. In the meetings I have attended in the high-tech industry, the fierce momentum already in play requires a constant reevaluation of the question, How does one ride the horse in the direction it is going in these scenarios? How does one go with the flow when you are simultaneously trying to sidestep it? The best way to ride this momentum to your advantage is to leave your ego at the front door and allow the experts to be the experts, because that is the direction they are all headed in anyhow. I ask as many questions as possible and take on the stance of "You are the expert. Tell me everything you know." If you have a normal, healthy ego, this is not easy to do at first. But I have found that, with practice, it gets easier, and the results are almost always worthwhile.

you gain an ally when you most need one

If you allow those who have a need to exert their authority and knowledge to get this out of the way at the beginning of the meeting, you will often notice that they relax. In more than one case, I have started a meeting by asking the "experts" in the crowd to tell me about the accomplishment that they are most proud of. In doing so, I know that they will be able to demonstrate their technological expertise immediately. With this out of the way, we can move on to the agenda at hand. By the time you have wound the meeting down to deal-making agendas, these same experts are often silent at worst and even supportive at best. You have allowed them to be experts; now they can allow you to close the deal. You are allies.

your surprise tactic of playing second fiddle is disarming

By admitting that others in the room are the experts, teaching you something you do not know, you are creating an atmosphere that they are not used to, whereby they are actually allowed to shine in the undeniable number-one position. This usually unnerves them, taking them by surprise. While they are trying to adjust, you gain some much-needed time to gauge the general atmosphere in the room. You can read the personality barometer of the other, perhaps less assertive, members of a meeting scenario and plan the strategy that will help you to segue away from the glut of expertise being tossed around and into the deal-making conversation. As

The media should place more emphasis on the expertise and the business savvy of women, rather than emphasizing stereotypes by focusing only on stories about balancing career and family.

THE WITI REPORT, BUSINESS IMPACT BY WOMEN IN SCIENCE AND TECHNOLOGY

a second fiddle, you are not in the spotlight and can more easily read the signs. If you are in a meeting like this with someone from your team, one of you can play the leader and direct the conversation, while the other can play second fiddle and watch for signs of disharmony.

you become a professional quick study on the job

As a new entrepreneur, you are always in learning mode. This is especially true when you are venturing into a new industry and need to learn the lingo, understand the elements at play, and recognize the nuances that are not always apparent in the books and reports that you study. By asking the experts to exert their expertise, you are not only allowing them to establish their prowess but making it possible for you to gain knowledge and enhance your ability to be a quick study in a new field. What you learn from one expert in one boardroom will inevitably assist you in your dealings at the next meeting.

remember: every idea is their idea

If the object of the meeting is to close a deal, then who generates the ideas during the meeting is inconsequential. I will always forfeit ownership of any idea for the sake of a deal. In the end, if the other team owns the idea, they will be more committed to the concept, which will allow for smoother deal making. In heated boardrooms, where the knowledge competition is still in full throttle, I have been known to say, "You know, that is a great idea you just came up with. I love it. Can I take your idea now and turn it into a plan, a deal?" I know then that we will all be happy. They own the idea. I close the deal.

the genderless war

I approach each meeting as an entrepreneur—only. I am not a woman trying to prove how smart I am, I am not a female entrepreneur trying to assert my authority, and I am not crushed by attempts to destroy my sense of self. I was in a situation once where we were conducting a five-way conference call with three other technology companies with whom we were partnering for an upcoming trade show. It was *my* conference call, *my* gig. I was feeling fully in control until, halfway through the meeting, I realized that one of the most senior executives participating in the call was criticizing every idea I had, saying that they were "invalid," "too expensive," or "not well communicated." But I took three deep breaths and remembered my meeting mantra: "Close the deal. Nothing else matters." My partner Chris was in the same room on the conference call. I quickly scribbled a note to him, asking him to suggest the exact same idea that I had been trying to put forward for group consensus for the past 10 minutes. With a

I was suddenly thrust into meeting after meeting where the size of one's pull-down menu was a ritualistic way of testing out a secret pecking order.

slight variation on my original idea, Chris succinctly put forward the same concept. "Great idea. I love it," said the senior executive who had spent the past half hour rejecting this very idea. "Then are we all in agreement to move forward on our plans for the trade show?" I asked. Done deal.

As a woman, I was going to be denied entry and acceptance. I would not be given credit for my idea. But as an entrepreneur, I had won. I found a way to accomplish my goal, gender issues aside.

I am a laissez-faire manager. I expect people to learn, work hard, and perform. I give people the freedom to take steps to nurture (i.e., learn) themselves. Those that accept the responsibility and take action, excel. Those that don't, quit.

CATHY DEVLIN,
PRESIDENT,
DEVLIN APPLIED DESIGN

traits of choice

Do not mistake the above-mentioned tactics for a list of ways to humiliate yourself or deny yourself the ability to compete on equal footing with other men and women, exerting your own capabilities and expertise. Remember that freedom of choice is the entrepreneur's secret weapon. Ultimately, you always have the choice to turn down a deal, to decide not to work with a client or another company, because, in the end, you do not believe that the upside of the deal is worth the trying charades required to win. I have spent as many meetings exerting my expertise as I have found ways to "move in the direction the horse is going." It is only after years of fine-tuning my meeting mannerisms that I have determined my ultimate goal: the deal. In doing so, I have recognized the benefit and limitations of my obsession with winning and have found a style that provides me the odds required to win—both within my company and outside. For some, this approach may resonate. For others, this may not sit well. When you read the profiles of Canadian CEOs, from Bobbie Gaunt of Ford Motor Corporation of Canada to Joy Calkin of Extendicare Inc. or Heather Reisman, CEO of Indigo Books and Café, each one has her own way of winning that reflects her own style. I think they would agree that everyone has to find their comfort level within the game of business and within the context of winning.

Katrina Garnett of CrossRoads Software says that she is intent on creating a company that is built on her ability to interact in a more personal way with her employees. For example, she likes to walk around the office, engaging her engineers in conversation and providing her staff with a sense of nurturing in all that she does. Some, perhaps, may see this as a feminine trait, but for her, it creates a nurturing company atmosphere that people are attracted to. Charlotte Beers of Ogilvy and Mather believes in what she calls "provocative disruption" as a means of leading her team. This type of strategy, which was initially undervalued by the existing management as "too personal," eventually proved to be a winning style and has attracted many top accounts, such as American Express and Jaguar.

I suggest that what makes all these women successful is their ability to toggle their female and male traits, as dictated by their commitment to their professional goals. They will do whatever is required of them to achieve their set of objectives.

THE SIX SISTERS OF SUCCESS ARE: CHOICE, DESIRE, STYLE, TIMING, FEAR, AND POWER. THE NEW ENTREPRENEUR WHO HAPPENS TO BE A WOMAN RECOGNIZES THESE ELEMENTS AT PLAY AND EMBRACES THEM IN HER ATTEMPT TO CREATE ROLE MODELS FOR OTHER WOMEN TO THINK ABOUT.

moments of choice

I am sure that when my grandmother was pounding the pavement of Edmonton, Alberta, issues of choice or achieving her own unique approach in conducting business did not even enter into her world. Hers was the pursuit of necessity. But today, women and men often have the luxury of *some* element of choice in what style they use to pursue their careers and make decisions about their personal lives.

Choice is an important word for entrepreneur Barbara Mowat, president of Impact Communications. Several years ago she was a faculty member at a college in British Columbia and realized that, although she had some reservations about leaving her secure tenured job, she was what she calls a closet entrepreneur. Based on her background, she decided to start her own human resource training firm. Everyone told her that in order to maintain credibility she would need to work out of Vancouver, which she did. But as she built up her consulting business, Barbara found that the 67-mile daily commute to Vancouver was wearing her down. Out of her tenacious research efforts, Barbara discovered that the U.S. was much further ahead than Canada in advancing the home-based business sector, and she began to focus her energies on finding a way to support a home-based business sector for herself and her fellow Canadians. Today, based on a proposal she wrote for the British Columbia government, Barbara is not only the publisher of the *B.C. Home Business Report*, she is also responsible for helping British Columbia become the leader in providing programs and services for the home-based business sector worldwide. By recognizing her moment of choice, Barbara was able to create her own multifaceted firm which includes a national publication, seminars and training for the micro entrepreneur. And she chooses to conduct her business from her home.

When Joy Mountford of Interval Research first launched her career, it was the desire to test her ability within a field that she knew nothing about—aviation engineering—and to be the one woman within an extremely male-dominated world that led her to an understanding of the intersection of technology and research.

What keeps others going, such as Jill Elikann Barad of Mattel, is "never giving up her femininity." Some claim it is her style and approach that has

With unemployment among women around 20% in eastern Germany, female entrepreneurship is surging. More than half of self-employed professionals such as doctors, architects, and lawyers are female. Nearly a third of all businesses launched in eastern Germany since 1990 were founded by women.

BUSINESS WEEK

made Barbie the world's most popular toy. The first part of the equality equation, in my mind, is choice. The new entrepreneur acknowledges that there is choice and then decides how they want to go about utilizing their options. You, as a woman, must hold onto your moments of choice until you fully understand what you can do and *choose* to do with the options available to you. One of the most powerful reasons for pursuing a life of entrepreneuring is that it allows you to fully realize your moments of choice, and in that sense, you can truly be a "freedom fighter."

In this role, you not only have the choice for what kind of business you want to build, what kind of something you want to create out of nothing, but you also have the opportunity to assert your version of the world into the form of a company or a career that reflects your values. As an entrepreneur, you are putting yourself into a situation whereby you have choices that are wholly your own. It is only through that process that you are able to create change that is meaningful, providing other women with models of success that they can point to and understand. Choice means that you can create companies that require equality in gender and race and that you can determine the rules by which you want to play.

desire, desire, desire

When I asked Harriet Rubin, founder and former executive editor of Doubleday Currency, what she thinks are the three most important attributes for successful entrepreneurship, she replied, "Desire, desire, desire." As reflected in her book *The Princessa: Machiavelli for Women,* if you want something and embody that desire, no one can stand in your way. "Princessas don't hold back. They don't doubt their desire; they feel entitled to their wishes, and they use the potency of them." In my view, entrepreneurship is the most straightforward means of accessing desire and allowing yourself to express this quality without having to make excuses for yourself, for your gender, or for your level of commitment to your goals.

Women such as Charlotte Beers, Martha Stewart, and Darla Moore have few things in common. They are what they refer to as "strange, courageous, irreverent, and not so comfortable friends." But all have an unbridled desire to achieve their goals in their respective professions. Regardless of whether one subscribes to their approach or their style of doing business, their desire to succeed is what drives them. They do not make excuses for it. Many times, I have been accused of being too aggressive, too assertive in my desire to succeed. Never has that stopped me from paying tribute to a quality that any one of my male counterparts would not even think twice about. And neither do I. Desire is what leads you to understand where your strengths and weaknesses are. Entrepreneurship provides a platform for allowing you to test your desires by daring yourself to make your own rules, rather than try to follow someone else's. Following my attitude toward calling a spade a spade when it

Personal growth and self-determination—not attaining great wealth and building large operations—ranked high as motivating factors among women who have started their own businesses, according to Holly Buttner, a business faculty member at the University of North Carolina at Greensboro, who has spent four years in a study of female entrepreneurs.

USA TODAY

comes to failure. I propose that women call a desire a desire and not try to mask it with anything less straightforward or less visceral. I tend to agree with Harriet Rubin when she says, "Desire is key; it reframes reality."

easy on the eyes

Regardless of what one's style is, the new entrepreneur understands that being true to yourself is much more important than how that style is defined. As with the gender issue, the desire of the outside world to categorize one's style as sexy, feminine, masculine, or conservative is always going to be a challenge. As long as you are truly reflecting who you are and how you want to be seen, classifications are irrelevant.

How do you know what your style is? By testing it out. Find out what works for you and what does not. Listen to what others tell you about their experience, and then determine your comfort level for yourself. As my grandmother says, "Don't worry whether you are wearing the right color gloves or not. Just be easy on the eyes." That's her way of saying be true to your own self.

timing, or "independent percolation"

Recently, I was reading an article about Microsoft's R&D lab. One of the experiments that was being conducted by two of the statistical physicists was testing "a model that describes problems ranging from that of distribution of oil in a porous medium to the distribution of matter in the galaxy." What the model was describing was less interesting to me than the term used to describe the process: "independent percolation."

It suddenly struck me that the notion of independent percolation is a good way to describe the internal clock that quietly ticks away in each of us. The moment when percolation, or readiness to act, occurs is different for everyone. And yet it is this very notion of finding the correct timing, the right moment of percolation, that is important for the entrepreneur who happens to be a woman. This sense is all-important to how she leverages the Six Sisters of Success to her advantage. The right timing, like luck, is a concept that cannot be controlled, nor is there a secret formula for understanding how to bring it on. But understanding its role within the path to successful entrepreneurship is a goal worth pursuing. Roberta Williams, co-founder and chief designer of one of the most successful computer game companies, Sierra On-line, claims that she knew deep down inside that someday she'd do something really extraordinary or different. That time came about when she was a discontented housewife in search of something to do, something to create. Her independent percolation came when her level of dissatisfaction with her life drew her to the computer games that her husband brought home for her to see. This was

I tend to agree with Harriet Rubin when she says "Desire is key; it reframes reality."

It is said that desire is a product of the will, but the converse is in fact true: will is a product of desire.

DENIS DIDEROT,
ELEMENTS OF PHYSIOLOGY

an idea that she would never otherwise have glommed onto, but for her the timing was right. Her initial interest in computer game design inspired her to come up with her own ideas, and she finally convinced her husband to go into business with her. That idea formed the nucleus of a company that now boasts 23 computer games in the market and was bought in 1996 by CUC International for $1 billion in stock.

Independent percolation describes that moment when you realize what you really want and when you are ready to try and juggle whatever you must (family, work, freedom) as a means of reflecting your values. For some, this moment may occur at age 35, when the level of your experiences has provided you with the confidence to test your hand at entrepreneurship. For others, discontent or frustration with an existing job may bring it on. For still others, it may come as the result of accepting your calling, of acknowledging that you have a deep-seated and urgent desire to create a place that is a reflection of your values and beliefs. Suddenly, you are ready to begin your journey as a freedom fighter.

How you watch for and act upon these signals are as different and diverse for each individual as the opportunities that present themselves. In an interview with some of the "top powerbroker women to watch in America," Jill Elikann Barad of Mattel talked about starting down her career path based on what interested her rather than following a logical step-by-step process. After trying her hand at medical school, acting, and cosmetics advertising, then succeeding in the toy industry, she feels that it was her lack of knowing what she wanted that ultimately allowed her to discover what she was really good at. In her words, "I think diversity, the idea of trying everything, is important. Somehow all your experiences come together and make you multidimensional." Others, like Katrina Garnett, believe that it is essential to plan out your career as diligently as you would run your own business. "I literally would track my raises, my position. I don't believe it can be a random, casual thing. You have to be extremely deliberate about what you want."

Although it sounds as if these women are coming at the situation from completely different angles, I see them both finding their independent percolation points—the point in time when they knew they were ready to move on to the next challenge. For some, it may feel like a random event, for others a well-scripted plan. But in both cases, finding the trigger point for their next success and choosing to accept this self-created role come as the result of trusting your own individual sense of timing. This quality is key to gaining the confidence to know what to do when an opportunity presents itself. How to ensure that you are looking for the right signs of independent percolation depends on a concept that is rarely discussed in career planning: fear.

My "fear" is my substance, and probably the best part of me.

FRANZ KAFKA

More Singaporean women than ever are starting businesses. As of mid-1996, nearly 42,000 women headed companies, up from 33,000 in 1991. That put women entrepreneurs at 22% of the total.

BUSINESS WEEK

fear

When I was in university, I got it into my head that I wanted to join the McGill Hiking Club on their annual hike in the mountains of Vermont. As I was already far too preoccupied with theater and music to attend any of the preparation meetings prior to the hike, I simply signed up for Team #1 (who wants to be on Team #6?) and committed to meeting the group at 5 a.m. on the following Saturday morning. Of course, the fact that I was going to be hiking for three days did not deter me from dancing all night the Friday before. I figured I would simply pull an all-nighter since the departure time was so early. Armed with my $5 hot pink Keds from Woolworth's and a few hardcover psychology books stuffed into my knapsack (I figured we would have time for some reading once we got to the top of the mountain), I was ready for my hiking adventure.

When I arrived at the prearranged meeting place, I surveyed my team members in dismay. It appeared that Team #1 consisted of five burly guys and an even burlier woman who was our team leader. Within minutes of listening to my teammates' stories of hiking feats, I suspected that I had signed up for something that I was not quite prepared for, but in my fatigued and slightly hungover condition, I was low on alternative plans. To make an incredibly long story slightly shorter, here is what happened:

Within 10 minutes of climbing, I was completely out of breath and close to tears. The first day consisted of 14 hours of hiking and fatigue and muscle aches (thanks to my fashionable but useless Keds) such as I had never before experienced. Somehow I made it through the first day, with little support from my teammates, who, I assumed, were annoyed by having to constantly wait for someone who should not have been on their team in the first place.

The second day the team leader had an idea: a few of the guys would begin to hike. After an hour, I would follow on my own, and then the rest of the team would wait for an hour and follow behind. The thinking was that I would not slow up the rest of the team members but instead be sandwiched between them. Anyone who has ever done any hiking knows that the last thing you do, especially with an inexperienced hiker, is to let someone go off by themselves. I was only too happy to be on my own, however, and avoid having to suffer the dirty looks of my teammates. The day began well (by this time, one of the more generous team members had offered to carry my three hardcover books to alleviate the weight of my pack). All I had to do was follow the blue markers and meet the team at what was called "the nose" at the end of the day.

I had been hiking for about three hours, and the incline was quite reasonable. Having not heard anyone for a while, I called out to see how far away the other team members were. There was no answer. I called several times and heard only a rustle in the leaves. I then looked around for the blue markers. There were none.

"How will I further reflect who I am today?" Those who are entrepreneurs can act on that question in real time, and there is nothing more exciting or fulfilling than that. My advice? Read stories about others who have embraced entrepreneurship, find mentors who can guide you, and then learn to take enough risks to do it yourself.

AN ENTREPRENEUR

It was at that moment that I knew that I was completely and utterly alone and definitely not on the trail. When you are lost in unknown territory, panic sets in pretty quickly. I began to jog, then run along what seemed like a path, but I still could not find any markers. Another hour went by. At this point, I was in a full sprint, figuring that the path would eventually lead to something. It did. Out of nowhere there appeared a huge red warning sign: BEWARE. BEAR DENS. My heart stopped, and the adrenaline kicked in.

In that one moment, I realized that I was facing my worst possible fear—I was alone, lost, and in unknown territory. After I hyperventilated for what felt like a half hour, a strange calm came over me. I recognized that I did not have a choice, that I was going to get through this crisis only by recognizing my fear and asking myself the question, What am I so afraid of? I went through the obvious list of fight or flight scenarios: encounter with a bear, injury in the mountains, lost for days. But then I realized that what I was most afraid of was at a much deeper level than that. What I was most afraid of was the lack of others whom I could rely on. And here it was right in front of me. Harriet Rubin believes that "fear takes you into new frontiers. If you follow your fear, you also learn about how strong you are." At some visceral level, I tried to take myself out of the immediacy of the situation and use this experience as a way of moving right up close to my biggest fear and finding my best source of strength.

At the end of that fateful day, I had jogged right through bear-den territory and made it out alive. I came across a cabin of strange people in the hills and was denied food and water. I had to walk through dense woods, avoiding the shots of the hunters, and I had to hitchhike on the side of a deserted road and determine whether the guy in the souped-up car would be a safe bet to ride with. In the end, this journey had definitely taken me places I had never been before. I had sprinted full out up and down a mountain range for 24 miles with no previous training, and I was able to survive alone and lost in the hills of Vermont for 16 hours with no food, no compass, and little water until the mountain patrol team finally rescued me. But, most important, I walked away with an understanding that I had replaced my biggest fear, abandonment, with my biggest strength, self-sufficiency.

I believe that my ongoing determination to create a life that is based on my own ability, my own resourcefulness, comes from the recognition of my fear.

A new entrepreneur who is a woman is usually able to find her independent percolation by facing her fear and turning it into her biggest asset. For Katrina Garnett, her fear of never really knowing what else she could accomplish on her own triggered a need and desire to test the waters in a start-up software company, in a new product niche. For me, it was a desire

The flip side of fear is opportunity.

HARRIET RUBIN

Do something every day that scares you.

ATTRIBUTED TO
KURT VONNEGUT

to manifest my self-sufficiency, my resourcefulness, by creating a company that had a momentum and force of its own. The best way to face your fear is to do something every day that scares you. Like the dance of risk, fear is something you must face at close range if you want to reap the rewards. In doing so, you will certainly uncover your greatest strength, leading you to your own version of independent percolation. As Harriet Rubin says, "If you're just a little bit scared, you are always on alert, sharp, deliberate, appreciative. To put yourself in this frame of mind, ask yourself, What am I most afraid of? The answer will help you determine your contribution to the world. The flip side of fear is opportunity."

Choice, desire, style, timing, and fear. I suggest that any woman who wants to test her ability to entrepreneur successfully needs to address these concepts, using them as stepping-stones to finding her own unique version of making a contribution, of creating a place that is truly her own. But, as with risk, it is the angels of advantage that balance the scale.

THE THREE ANGELS OF ADVANTAGE—INTUITION, SACRIFICE, AND OBSESSION—GUIDE THE SISTERS OF SUCCESS. IN AN ATTEMPT TO FIND YOUR ENTREPRENEURIAL SPIRIT, YOU WILL INEVITABLY BUMP INTO ANOTHER CONCEPT THAT IS HARD TO RECKON WITH. IT'S CALLED *POWER*.

Intuition is essential for the new entrepreneur because you are constantly making decisions with incomplete facts.

intuition

Although risk is usually cited as the number-one attribute for successful entrepreneurship, the women I have met with and spoken with from around the world cite intuition as the most common advantage for women in business. Whether or not this belief is universal is hard for me to guesstimate, but almost every woman I know attributes her ability to navigate relationships at all levels of business to this quality. As a senior executive at both Apple Computers and Interval Research, Joy Mountford attributes her ability to manage people and keep them happy to an intuitive understanding that people are attracted to leaders who value teaching, not grandstanding. Katrina Garnett also believes that an entrepreneur who happens to be a woman is able to manage people and relationships at a deeper level, fostering personal connections that assist in group and team bonding and sanctions an environment of belonging.

From my perspective, the importance of intuition as it relates to the Sisters of Success is that it allows for a deeper relationship with *oneself*. Not only will that necessarily help you to intuit the desires and ambitions of others, but it will inevitably lead to a better understanding of how choice, desire, and style assist in determining your path to success. If you focus on honing your intuition, you will begin to understand what your true desires are. You will not succumb to what others determine are appropriate roles

Intuitively, I have always wanted to do things slightly ahead of the curve. Entrepreneuring is about recognizing the consistent themes in your career, accumulating experience and then building something based on what you are best at.

HEATHER REISMAN

for women to take on, nor will you give in to notions of femininity versus masculinity. Lisa Anderson, recipient of the 1997 Young Entrepreneurs Award for Manitoba, has certainly learned this as the founder of Anderson Body Ltd. "I was faced with the challenge of proving myself competent and knowledgeable in an industry where not only the majority of customers are male, but 80 percent of my colleagues are male. I quickly learned that a whimpy handshake won't do. With a strong, firm grasp, I let my customers know I'm here to do business." Like Lisa Anderson, understand how to broker both kinds of traits within yourself as a means of matching your desires with your abilities.

In a world where we are constantly faced with rules that others have created, trusting one's intuition will always lead you to choice. For example, you can choose to work for corporate North America and subject yourself to the rules of others, or you can choose to create your own company as did Barbara Mowat, Lisa Anderson, Heather Reisman, and many others. Their companies reflect the values of their choices. One path is not better than the other but tapping into your true desire based on intuition will allow you to recognize what is best for you. Relying on your intuition flies in the face of relying on studies about what and how women do business and whether or not they should succeed at it. Look around, ask questions, listen to the stories of others. But in the end, remember that trusting your intuition reflects a reliance on individuality. That is the starting point for any entrepreneur.

sacrifice

Sacrifice takes on a new meaning when you revisit the first Sister of Success: choice. By viewing your choices, by scrolling through your options, the new entrepreneur who is a woman does not view sacrifice for sacrifice's sake but understands that it is part and parcel of the choices she will make based on her desire, her own timing, and her sense of self. When Darla Moore, Martha Stewart, and Charlotte Beers were asked what they had to sacrifice for success, each one answered differently. Moore did not have children; Stewart went solo, and Beers lost time. But none of these women regrets her choice. They face them. Intellectually and emotionally, they have accepted that with choice comes sacrifice.

Recognizing what sacrifices you are willing to make, especially in the context of the universal issue of family versus work, will keep you from making decisions based purely on desire. Accepting that sacrifice is the flip side of freedom of choice will alleviate false illusions that success can occur without any cost. There is always a price. When I moved to Silicon Valley, I knew that I would sacrifice security and the sense of a home, things that I still battle with today. My grandmother sacrificed friends and community, belonging, and comfort to achieve her goals. But like these modern-day women, she regrets nothing. The new entrepreneur who is a woman accepts sacrifice and focuses on choice.

obsession

Harriet Rubin has heard this story many times. A young, dynamic woman works diligently to rise within a corporation or to break out on her own and create a business for herself. She has all the right pieces in place, and finally her timing is right. But rather than grab the opportunity by the shoulders and shake it loose, she begins to falter. She gets migraines, she becomes indecisive, and she wavers in her most important decisions. Ultimately, she does not follow her dream.

Upon closer inspection, many of the versions of this sad, modern-day tale may actually be a reflection of the fact that women have not been trained to deal with one very important concept: *power.* Often these women are afraid of the potential power they will have when they finally get to the place they have worked hard to reach. In some ways, their own special talents and capabilities are too powerful to accept. In the realm of the unknown, which is the entrepreneurs' playground, it is in facing your fears that you actually gain power.

For the new entrepreneur who is a woman, finding and accepting one's power is not just about individual female prowess. It is about being part of a bigger cultural force that has the power to reestablish guidelines and remove boundaries based on gender-specific stereotypes, among others.

Power can be taken, but not given.

GLORIA STEINEM,
MS. MAGAZINE

THE EFFICIENCY OF THE TECHNOLOGY INDUSTRY ALLOWS ENTREPRE-NEURSHIP TO THRIVE, REGARDLESS OF GENDER. ROLE MODELS EMERGE, AND THE POWER OF THE NEW ENTREPRENEUR IS PLAYED OUT IN AN ARENA THAT BEGINS TO HAVE OVERTONES OF A LEVEL PLAYING FIELD.

The technology industry represents a great example of a backdrop that will allow for this gender-bending exercise to take place. As Katrina Garnett says: "I think the technology industry is very efficient. Whether it is a male or female at the helm is not an issue. If you are smart and you know what you want and you deliver, there is always a need for great people, great entrepreneurs. The venture capitalists are looking for a great return on investment — they do not ask what gender you are." So far this statement has been true for Katrina, as seen by her ability to raise over $15 million in capital for CrossRoads Software. Likewise for Donna Dubinsky of Palm Computing. Gender certainly has not gotten in the way of Canadian women such as Gerri Sinclair of NCompass Labs in Vancouver or Isabel Hoffman of Hoffman and Associates of Toronto, and it has not stopped well known icons such as Esther Dyson or Kimberley Polese of Marimba or Carol Bartz of Autodesk.

I would even go a step further by suggesting that the new entrepreneur who happens to be a woman refuse to define herself as a female entrepreneur, a term that only continues to point to difference rather than capability. By embracing the concept of power on an individual and societal level, we are furthering the possibility of demystifying the ongoing issues of male versus female and creating the potential for being part of a gender convergence that is willing to adopt the best of both sexes. In this way, we can foster role models that reflect a better world, a place where gender is a side bar, not the focus of the success at hand.

That does not mean to say that the various programs and associations dedicated to specifically helping women are not extremely important. Educational and motivational courses such as the Canadian mentoring program called Step Ahead, the Mentorship Program run by the Canadian Association of Women Executives and Entrepreneurs, and courses offered at the Women's World Banking are just a few of the many programs that represent a great jumping off point for creating awareness and building skills that will prepare our women (and men) to succeed based on their own dreams and goals.

Alongside these programs, it is in an emerging industry, such as technology, where a whole new set of rules are just now being shaped, creating a window of opportunity whereby entrepreneurial men and women can compete and succeed on equal footing. In this way, entrepreneurship is a catalyst for setting these ground rules. By focusing on successful entrepreneuring, regardless of gender, a new precedent is established for the generations that follow.

For me the potential to reshape the guidelines for defining individual success and promoting differences is a motivating factor in my desire to test a model of life that reflects my values, my style, and my choices. As a new entrepreneur, like my grandmother did before me, I can pass on a meaningful role model to my granddaughter that has the power to affect change, is a celebration of difference, and a testament to individuality.

I think women can be rational and less obsessively growth-oriented in their management style. They are more likely to focus on letting someone else come out feeling good versus steamrolled in a situation, which can be very healthy. But I really apply both consensus and directive styles in my work, depending on the situation.

JOY COVEY,
CFO, AMAZON.COM

we remember stories, not facts

We need more women who are willing to tell their stories. We need to hear that some women will be able to juggle it all and others will not, but that they will still succeed. We don't have enough women who are willing to openly discuss, without leaving out any details, why they cut out of a corporation. We need to hear the stories of the women who started out independently wealthy and the women who began with nothing.

This need for diversified stories of trial and error, of success and failure, is only going to increase with time. According to the U.S. Department of Labor, by the year 2000, about half of America's businesses will have a female owner. The more role models we have who exemplify diversity in their definition of successful entrepreneuring, the more choices we will be able to show young women as they fill these important entrepreneurial roles themselves. As an entrepreneur who is female, it is essential to tell your story with as much honesty as possible and to show the results, good and bad, with pride. Whether this is done in an organized format through an association such as Girl Power or in the privacy of your office with peers and associates, it is essential to pass on your particular experience, as a local hero, an accessible version of the entrepreneur, not as a mythological icon or a superwoman. Storytelling provides a place for people to belong, and the new entrepreneur who is a woman needs to remember this. Without stories of the here and now, where will the young women who look up to us belong? And when their time comes, how will they know how to pass on their knowledge to others?

I am in the world to change the world.

MURIEL RUKEYSER

mythical role model or a story to believe in?

Four kids had to be bundled up against the winter cold that had set in. She had to prepare food for the day, set aside clothes for the next day, clean the house, and arrange for the money to pay the woman for her work. After rousing, dressing, and finally delivering the children to the other side of town, she returned home. She had to get dressed for work and ensure she got there before the real hustle and bustle of the day began. She admired the articles of clothes she had carefully chosen the night before. She had everything she needed: her outfit, her money, her lists, her materials, and her determination. She hoped that her husband would not return home early today due to the bad weather. She would have to take that chance. She took one final look around the room and left the house. She was ready to face her real working day.

Does this sound familiar? Could it be one of many working women preparing for the day ahead? Or does this story sound a bit clandestine? If you detected a little of both, you were close to the mark. Although this morning routine has elements that are familiar to all of us, the difference is that this was a woman named Zelda, living in a small *schettle* in Poland in the year 1865. And for all intents and purposes, she was an entrepreneur, though she did not think of herself as such and probably never would for her whole life. Her reality revolved around the fact that she could not live without the hustle and bustle of the marketplace, and she would do whatever was necessary to ensure that she could add to the household income based on her own ability to earn money. In those days, this was no easy feat. Three days a week, when her husband traveled to the countryside, this 22-year-old woman shuttled her kids off to a woman who minded them for the day. She had to pay the woman extra, not because of the quality of her work but because of her willingness not to tell. The secret she was paid to keep was that on those particular days, Zelda dressed up as a man. In this disguise, she would walk the extra five miles to the market just outside of town, where she would not be recognized. She would sell what she could—trinkets, fruit and vegetables, and baked goods that she would make late at night when everyone was asleep. The trick was that no one could know that she was actually engaging in these commercial efforts—not her husband, not her parents, and not her community. If they ever found out, all of them would look down upon this kind of activity with a ferocity that sometimes even scared her. But this was not enough to stop her, to make her resist the thrill of being part of the marketplace three times a week, to make her give up the power of having a choice.

My grandmother claimed that this woman may have been a distant relative, though the names and dates are a bit vague. Of course, when she told this story, I always knew that there was an element of fantasy mixed in with the truth, but I did not care. I understood that this woman represented a mythical role model for my grandmother, one that embodied the Six Sisters of Success, someone who celebrated turning nothing into something in her own way. As a new entrepreneur, I recognized that, just like me, my grandmother had also wanted a role model to look toward for guidance. She, too, needed a story to believe in.

the chaos pilot

the chaos pilot

chapter 7

Secret Recipes for a Disordered World

When I was a developing entrepreneur, the term "professional eclectic" best described the portfolio that I was building. But once I started a company of my own, one of my favorite words, my own personal "call of the wild," became *chaos*. There are four different definitions of chaos in the dictionary, but this one appeals to me most: "A pattern or state of order existing within apparent disorder, as in the irregularities of a coastline or a snowflake." When I saw that definition, I recognized an exact description of my day-to-day world. As in any start-up company or entrepreneurial setting, there seems to be little order and few routines to fall back on. Despite this fact, through effective entrepreneuring during my early days at Bulldog, I always managed to create a certain order out of all the existing variables. And like a snowflake or a coastline, it made perfect sense.

Surrounded by chaos in my day-to-day world, I found insight, not surprisingly, by looking more closely at the Chaos Theory, which shows us that a little inspired effort backed by a whole lot of knowledge has a huge effect on our environment. This is the famous Butterfly Effect: "The flapping of a single butterfly's wing today produces a tiny change in the state of the atmosphere. Over a period of time, what the atmosphere actually does diverges from what it would have done. So, in a month's time, a tornado that would have devastated the Indonesian coast doesn't happen. Or maybe something that wasn't going to happen does."

What I found even more relevant to my entrepreneurial notion of chaos were the ideas of a meteorologist named Edward Lorenz, who began working on equations for weather prediction and convection in the early 1960s. Lorenz's findings were as follows: "There were only two kinds of order previously known: a steady state, in which the variables never change, and periodic behavior, in which the system goes into a loop, repeating itself indefinitely. Lorenz's equations are definitely ordered—they always followed a spiral. They never settled down to a single point, but since they never repeated the same thing, they weren't periodic either."

Anyone who works within the area of new media is essentially living in a steady state of unpredictability in which the element of chaos is always present. Doug Humphreys, president and CEO of Skyrocket and Red Sky Films, has managed to create an "ordered chaos" by leveraging the chaotic world of new media to help him spin off a number of entrepreneurial ventures. These projects include a digital production company, a digital advertising and design agency, and a children's video production facility. Through each growth phase of his entrepreneurial ventures, Doug used a spiral approach to leadership—"never settling down to a single point"— and with the addition of each new company, Doug found, as many entrepreneurs do, that the issues he had to face, from the start-up of a film production house to the initial concept for a new media training and design company, definitely did not repeat themselves in any predictable manner.

Evan Solomon, co-founder of *Shift* magazine, a publication devoted to new media technology, targeted to hip, smart, media-savvy 30-somethings, talks about his relentless commitment to flexibility, claiming that it has been the determining factor in his success in the publication's early years. Solomon navigated through his own maelstrom of chaos by deciding that it would be most effective not to try and create a set pattern of how a publication should be successfully developed too early on in the company's existence. Instead, he maintained an openness to all the possible ways that his company could evolve into a combined print and digital voice for the media culture. In a sense, this notion of chaotic navigation is the entrepreneur's version of the Chaos Theory. The most essential role of the new entrepreneur is the ability to navigate through and despite the chaos, not only as a means of survival but also as a means of actively shaping and imagining where and how one needs to lead the organization forward.

If we think of the new entrepreneur as a pilot, then finding a form that accommodates the chaos, "the mess" as it were, is as important as navigating effectively. For Evan, finding the right form for meaningful editorial content involved steering his team into the uncharted waters of digital online publication, then recognizing that he needed to refine this plan further to ensure its viability for his particular company. His flexibility and relentless determination allowed him to redirect his efforts. Today it is not surpising that *Shift*'s website is an integral part of its overall package. For Bulldog, finding "the right form" meant pushing the financial envelope and the risk curve as far over as possible so that we could accommodate the research and development we wanted to do during the time when we were essentially a service operation.

In all chaos there is a cosmos, in all disorder a secret order.

CARL JUNG

I dream, therefore I exist.

AUGUST STRINDBERG

In searching for the right form, in guesstimating the right route, you inevitably create more chaos along the way—employees who do not believe in a new direction that you are leading them toward; initial concepts of a product that do not pan out; naysayers who try to destroy your confidence by not believing in your conviction that you will succeed. As a "chaos pilot," your job is to steer right through these tumultuous weather patterns, riding the waves (of confluence, for example) as best you can. As with any profession, being a pilot requires that one develop certain attributes and tools that will improve your chances of successfully navigating through many meaningful journeys time and time again.

Here are the key characteristics of successful chaos piloting:

- Chaos is random. There is no reason or rhyme to the events that occur.

- Only by envisioning, by actively assessing and imagining the outcome, can a chaos pilot determine what tools are required for a successful journey. It is the focus on action, not perception, that is the key to creating the future.

- The chaos pilot is a navigator, watching for the best conditions within which to move forward.

- The chaos pilot is a performer, knowing that others are watching and that they are depending on a grand finale.

To find a form that accommodates the mess, that is the task of the artist now.

SAMUEL BECKETT

navigating the chaos

Throughout my entrepreneuring career, I have revisited this notion of chaos navigation many times. Let me tell you what I have learned.

A GOOD CHAOS PILOT KNOWS THAT TO NAVIGATE THROUGH CHAOS INVOLVES THE INTIMATE UNDERSTANDING OF THREE NAUTICAL TERMS: "DEAD RECKONING," "THE RIGHTING MOMENT," AND "THE ZERO-MOMENT POINT." IN ENTREPRENEURIAL TERMS, THESE ARE KEY TO SUCCESSFUL JOURNEYS, TO ACTUALIZING A VISION.

dead reckoning

In the 1800s, there were no lighthouses, Coast Guard stations, or meteorological stations around Sable Island, off the coast of Nova Scotia, and many sailors and ships went down there. The reason for this was that in a storm, without sophisticated electronic equipment, it was nearly impossible to anticipate the random curves of the 60-foot shoal that surrounds Sable Island. "Often shipwrecks occurred because of errors in navigation: the westerly current was so strong that it could throw boats off by 60 to 100 miles." Today, when a boat has lost its electronics (GPS, radar, and loran) due to a storm, the captain of that boat is effectively back in the old days, charting the Grand Banks on his chart table and estimating his position based on the compass heading, forward speed, and wind conditions. This is a very dangerous and often fatal position to be in, and the life or death of the crew depends on the captain's freefalling abilities to "dead reckon."

This same skill is required of the chaos pilot. Often an entrepreneur cannot overcome the random biases of a customer, the sudden changes within an industry, and the fickleness of market perception, despite thorough research, study, and observation. Having all the latest equipment and technology does not always guarantee survival. Sometimes, success is based on nothing more than the chaos pilot's skill at dead reckoning.

Never be afraid to be afraid.

ANONYMOUS

In reality, plans just don't "go wrong," they erupt, they collapse and they disappear. The chaos pilot is well prepared for plans that go, as the French say, "bouleversés."

Dead reckoning reflects a combination of intuition and skill. The accumulated experiences of navigating through many storms is what provides the navigator with the necessary portfolio of piloting experience. A developing entrepreneur accumulates these experiences by working within entrepreneurial organizations (or beside-the-point organizations), where they are asked to take on a wide range of tasks, forced to watch for changes in conditions, and made to focus on indispensability. Pamela Wallin attributes her newly found entrepreneurial capabilities in the broadcast industry to her intuitive sense of knowing when and how to ask the right questions: What do I believe is the model for effective journalism? What do I think my audience wants to hear? What are meaningful issues to them? What is an entertaining format? These very questions led her to understand how she could actually turn her ideas of a news show into an entrepreneurial production company that reflected this very concept. For the chaos pilot, dead reckoning is based on a more finely tuned understanding of where intuition and acquired skill intersect. It is a life skill worth investing in.

the righting moment

In a storm, a ship at sea is dependent on a concept called "the righting moment." To greatly simplify, the lateral distance between the two forces (buoyancy and gravity) is called the righting arm, and the torque they generate is called the righting moment. Boats want a big righting moment. They want something that will "right them from extreme angles of heel." When my father and his partner were facing a bank that was making impossible requests on their real estate property by demanding a second guarantee, through distractionary maneuvers and diversionary tactics they were able to introduce enough torque to give them a great righting moment. They did this so well that they were eventually able to take the company from an extreme heel (bankruptcy) to survival and then on to unexpected profit, even through the tumultuous real estate market of the late 1980s.

If we go back to our developing entrepreneur, the notion of righting moments is not that far off from the concept of "bounce back." The ability to contain and correct a completely life-threatening situation is not new to the chaos pilot, because they have been practicing, in calmer waters, their ability to bounce back from situations that are unexpectedly thrown at them.

the zero-moment point

"Finally, there always comes a point where the boat can no longer right herself . . . the zero-moment point." As any pilot or sea captain knows, there may come a time when there is no solution to the problem, and survival is the issue. In Hollywood terms, as Lynda Obst says, "No single movie or event makes or breaks your career. Everything can be undone, including success."

As a chaos pilot, looking out for trouble as far ahead as possible is crucial to successful navigating. At 82, William Ungar, president and founder of the National Envelope Company, is still running his company based on a notion of looking out for what lies ahead as he incorporates technological advances into his plant, uses email, and gains knowledge through the Internet. When he first got into business with a partner in 1952, he had a sense that he was going to have to grow and expand and take risks that would propel him to be the largest privately owned supplier of envelopes and stationery in North America. But when he detected that his partner wanted to build the company based on greater restraint and caution, he knew that unless he bought him out, he would reach a point where his company, in the metaphor of a boat, reached the zero-moment point. To right his ship, he had to be able to freely take the required risks. As the recipient of an Ernst & Young Entrepreneur of the Year Award, that is exactly what he went on to do.

Chaos pilots such as William Ungar recognize that on any adventurous journey, the potential for the point of no return (the zero-moment point) exists. Acting as if failure or surrender is not an option—enduring through the process of re-imagining the way out—is the chaos pilot's only navigational choice.

tools for navigation

So what are the tools, the navigational equipment, that the chaos pilot can rely on? Because entrepreneuring is such a personal journey, every chaos pilot will tell you something different that reflects their secret recipe for maneuvering through chaos. In my view, two things are required for successful piloting: active envisioning and performing.

They were like secret rules. Every business has them. In most fields of endeavor there are no easy jobs, there are only graceful ways of performing difficulties.

LYNDA OBST,
HELLO, HE LIED

active envisioning

THE CHAOS PILOT BEGINS WITH A SET OF WELL-DEFINED BELIEFS AND THEN MOVES "FROM THE DREAM OUTWARD." BELIEFS ARE THE BASIS FOR BELONGING. ENVISIONING IS THE ACTIVE FORM OF PERCEPTION, BUILT ON BELIEFS.

To run a company, division, or a group of people requires a set of beliefs. This might sound simple and obvious, but I have met many an entrepreneur who does not reflect a clearly defined belief system. They reflect ideas, guts, and smarts, and they often succeed. But in my mind, to navigate a group of people or even one other person, a partner, through the chaotic world around us requires a firm set of beliefs and values. Why? Two reasons:

You see things, and you say "why?" But I dream things that never were; and I say "why not?"

GEORGE BERNARD SHAW,
BACK TO METHUSELAH

- Beliefs represent a lasting notion and become the basis for the vision of a company. In essence, they become the story that attracts people, that entices them to want to belong. Without an underlying belief system, it is difficult for a chaos pilot to set the course of the journey ahead, and it is difficult for the crew to commit to the company with conviction.

- Beliefs and values are long-term propositions that do not change. By committing to a belief structure that lasts, the new entrepreneur has the flexibility to change the strategy, change the mode of envisioning the future of their company, as often as required, and as the company matures.

Bulldog was built on a belief that anything is possible with hard work and open-mindedness, seasoned with attitude and cachet for good luck. But our company philosophy extends further than that. We believe in giving to others as much as possible, recognizing that what goes around comes around, and I truly do subscribe to these values.

We at Bulldog strengthen our desire to maintain and act upon our beliefs as a basis for building a company worth belonging to. Whether providing office space to a business associate in need or agreeing to support students in our offices, our ability to bring our beliefs to life through our actions makes them tangible and real and adds to our cachet. It has become the basis for envisioning the who and the what of our entrepreneurial enterprise.

THE CHAOS PILOT IS COMMITTED TO ACTIVE ENVISIONING. IN DOING SO, THEY ARE CONTINUALLY RE-IMAGINING THE POTENTIAL GOAL OR OUTCOME BASED ON THE CHANGING REALITY AROUND THEM. BUT THEY ARE ALSO AWARE THAT BY ACTIVELY ENVISIONING, THEY WILL FIND WAYS TO ACCUMULATE THE COLLECTIVE SKILLS REQUIRED TO ACHIEVE THAT VERY VISION ALONG THE WAY.

There is much discussion about the term *vision*. Political leaders have vision, spiritual leaders are graced with visions, and many believe that entrepreneurial success depends on vision. I have read books that give vision specific qualities, saying that it must be realistic, inclusive, and transformative. How could one disagree with any of these notions? To be a successful entrepreneur, you need all of this and more. But as a navigator, the chaos pilot benefits most by focusing on the verb *to envision*, actively seeking ways and means to ensure that they are constantly exercising their ability to imagine what does not yet exist.

My notion of envisioning is more about action than about perception. For example, when we first started Bulldog, we did not have a vision of how we were going to create a multimedia design company and then segue into the software business. Instead, we kept asking our customers and employees questions that created a picture in our minds of what kind of product they thought it would be worthwhile for us to create, one that would have market value. By actively engaging in a circle of learning and pushing the boundaries of a service model in our minds, we were able to envision a product. We then continued to push our circle of learning (question—theory—test—reflect) further and further, creating bigger and bigger circles, until we were able to see a clearer picture of a product and begin moving toward it.

Envision: to imagine (something not yet in existence); picture in the mind.

This sequence of events reflects a process of envisioning that kept changing as we learned more and more about the new media model from a service and a product standpoint. Along the way, by abandoning the notion of a single vision, we were able to recognize the skill sets we did not have (engineering, product development) and built a team of specialists who would actively envision with us.

Envisioning is not an easy concept to describe in 10 easy steps. It is like many artistic endeavors—cooking, dancing, music—where the magic combination of ingredients is as much about how you mix the elements together as it is about what elements you choose. Though in some ways magical, it is not a magic trick. Instead, it is a very focused effort on figuring out the models of business that you need to build and the envisioning required to get there. It is about asking enough questions until a product concept begins to take shape in your mind; tuning into your viewers until you have a notion of the kind of news show for which there is a market demand. The qualifiers for effective envisioning are:

- A complete focus on the act of envisioning, with an understanding that one's vision will evolve and change.

- A recognition that envisioning requires time and space. Sometimes not committing to the notion of attaining a single vision is what allows for a stronger direction for the company.

■ A recognition that through active envisioning, the missing skills and team members required to achieve one's goals will become obvious.

Sometimes, as an entrepreneur, you need to envision a very large picture, a change in the company's direction, or a change from a service to a product company. Other times, the envisioning exercise is much more focused, such as the need to envision how the company will be perceived in the press in advance of a product release. Moses Znaimer's ability to "see how things will turn out" in any given situation is his particular entrepreneurial skill set. Evan Solomon is relentless about re-imagining his way out of one vision and into another, changing the focus but not the conviction for finding a way to re-imagine along the way. Katrina Garnett, on the other hand, is more methodical in her approach to envisioning the plans for her company's future.

Envisioning where and how your company will move forward needs to be a trained skill like anything else. Here are four concepts that I have found extremely helpful in envisioning effectively.

The Postcard Theory

When we first started Bulldog, I had to build up our sales with speed and accuracy. I had accumulated enough sales experience to know how to sell, but somehow, the fact that I was suddenly selling multimedia design services for my own company added a pressure that I had never felt before. To achieve sales results, I used what I call my postcard theory. When you get a postcard in the mail from a friend in a far-off place, it makes you pause. You can't help but look at the photo of some remote island or some charming country farmhouse for just a few more seconds, long enough to imagine yourself standing there. And then reality beckons you, the phone rings, someone steps into your office, and you drop the postcard on your desk. But over the next few days, you return to the photo every once in a while and imagine yourself there. My postcard theory is based on this very notion. There are three steps involved in this exercise:

Creating a timed image

In my early days at Bulldog, I would create a postcard in my mind with as much detail as I could muster. This postcard was a visual representation of the place I wanted to be within six months. In this case, it was a photo of employees (more than we currently had) and a new office space (to accommodate them) and examples of our design work on the wall behind them. I then built in the appropriate audio and 3-D elements, imagining the conversations of the employees as they rushed to complete one of the new projects that I had just brought in for a new highly coveted client. I imagined the meetings that had led up to solidifying that client, and I imagined

**Magic is good.
No, magic is necessary.**

FROM THE MOVIE
ONLY LOVE

**Life will bring what
you attract with your
thoughts.**

AN ENTREPRENEUR

the board meeting where I would announce the new client to my associate board members.

Real-time image revisiting

I kept this 3-D postcard alive and well in my mind. I visualized it sitting on my desk, and I revisited it as often as I needed to when things were not going according to plan. Sometimes I allowed myself to alter small details of the postcard based on real happenings. For example, I saw the exact face of a new employee that we had just hired, I added in a particular project that we were working on and placed an award beside it, knowing that we were a nominee in an upcoming design competition. In this sense, I was constantly improving upon the postcard image, blending my original fictitious visual with elements of reality as they occurred.

Moving towards the image

The most important element of this exercise is the act of moving toward the image on the postcard. Every day I envisioned myself walking toward my postcard image, getting closer and closer to the picture I had imagined. By actively engaging in this exercise, I was able to attract long-term clients and close deals faster than ever before. Within a year, I had increased our sales by a factor of 10. Whether you create a three-month, six-month, or a year-timed image, the key is to keep actively moving toward your image until you are actually standing in the postcard itself. In the final analysis, the postcard theory allows you, the chaos pilot, to navigate toward the end goal until you have arrived. At that point, it is time to take a pause, congratulate yourself, reflect on what worked and did not work in your creation and movement toward the image. Then it is time to begin creating your new postcard and move toward it.

When I first began using this exercise, I kept the parameters of my image loose. For example, I did not specify what kind of client I would add to our roster or what the dollar value would be. But after I used this envisioning exercise a few times, I found myself getting more and more specific about what I wanted in my postcard—the size of the contract, the profile of the new board member I was interested in soliciting. The postcard theory has become one of the most powerful goal-setting tools I have ever discovered and has made the notion of envisioning a real part of my entrepreneuring.

The 1001-Day Plan

Envisioning is not to be mistaken for unrealistic goal setting taken a step too far. The second part of my envisioning exercise is what I call the 1001-Day Plan. For example, one day I called a friend I had not spoken to in more than a year. After a few minutes of catching up, I found out that he was a father, had changed cities twice, and now was in the process of getting a divorce. In

Hope was transubstantiated into belief incarnate. I believe you call it "the power of positive thinking."

DIANE JOHNSON,
LE DIVORCE

Being an entrepreneur is not within the realm of rational discussion. It is a burning, sometimes pathological, need.

MOSES ZNAIMER

addition, he was contemplating a complete change in career direction—from medicine to playwriting! I thought I was a glutton for change and chaos, but this sounded extreme. When I asked him about this, he said, "I know it sounds like a lot at once, and it has been, but I never do anything without setting realistic expectations. I plan my life changes within 1001 days—about three years. Changing jobs, and potentially moving to another city within three years is not that unrealistic, especially if I work toward it methodically." And ever since then, I have used this same thinking. When I am contemplating major changes, I put together a plan that spans 1001 days—giving myself the time and space to re-imagine a new vision. At Bulldog, we started contemplating going into the software business in earnest back in 1992, the second year of our business. By 1995, three years later, I had created a presence for us in Silicon Valley, we had secured financing, and we were close to completing a beta version of our product. One thousand and one days is a good reality barometer for major envisioning.

You cannot unknow something, but you can act upon your refined perception so as to entrepreneur more effectively in the future.

The Four See's of Nebraska

A few months ago, while hiking through Marin County, a friend and I were talking about the different idiosyncrasies that various cultures and various geographical locations create. I was telling her about a French-Canadian designer with whom I had worked who always used to use French sayings in translation. I would ask her how a client meeting went, and she would say, "Ah, Ellie, it was like budder [butter] in da pan!" I loved that expression, though it was always comical in the context of any client dealings. Then my friend told me about the time she and her parents were traveling through Nebraska and had become lost, despite the flat vista in all directions. When they stopped to ask for directions to their destination, the local farmer said, "You take a right and then your first left and, well, it's about four see's from here." It was not until later that day that they found out what this meant. In Nebraska, "four see's" is four times as far as you can see from where you currently are standing. This image stuck in my mind, because I use a similar concept in envisioning. When I am envisioning a more immediate goal, I usually try to focus on my own version of four see's, which is about as far out as I can see from where I am standing, realistically. When I moved to Silicon Valley, I used this notion of four see's in hooking up with the right influencers. I would focus on the person I wanted to meet and then allow myself to engage in as many as four means and ways to connect with that person. If none of these tactics worked out, I would pull the plug, change my strategy, and begin again with another four see's. This element of setting limits, of knowing when I'd expended enough effort and it was time to start again with a better prospect, was what helped me to reach my goal.

Sometimes, we are so busy envisioning where we want to get to, we forget to look around and notice that we are actually exactly where we are supposed to be. Part of envisioning requires a goal-setting mindset, part of the exercise requires a visual representation, but a dose of present-tense reality always helps. Envisioning should never deter the chaos pilot from being able to look around in the midst of the journey and acknowledge that they are actually doing exactly what they are supposed to be doing.

performing
THE CHAOS PILOT UNDERSTANDS THAT IF THEY THINK OF THEMSELVES AS A PERFORMER, THEY WILL GAIN A SENSE OF TIMING AND DEXTERITY NOT ONLY ON STAGE BUT IN THE TIME AND SPACE IN BETWEEN PERFORMANCES, WHICH OFTEN MATTER MOST.

Many of life's failures are people who did not realize how close they were to success when they gave up.

THOMAS EDISON

As in hiking, don't look where you don't want to go.

JOY COVEY

The chaos pilot, in the final analysis, needs to understand that they are a performer. Geoffrey Moore points out that today in our culture there is a heightened awareness and celebration of the performer, whether that be the athlete, the movie star, or the musician. Along with this celebration of performance come opportunities in business to create the same promise of achievement. The trend toward giving employees extra compensation based upon their performance is one example of how companies tap into that same reservoir of personal energy. The ongoing profiles of celebrity entrepreneurs and corporate tycoons are examples of personal performance on another kind of stage—people searching for a way to leave their mark, to do their personal best in the same sense as Olympic athletes do.

When I was little, I had to play tennis. When I first started taking lessons, I spent hours endlessly picking up balls at the back of the court or hitting them way over the fence time after time.

In the midst of my greatest feelings of frustration, my teachers assured me that one day my rhythm would come to me and my timing would kick in. In spite of this encouragement, I continued to be frustrated by the time spent in between the misplaced shots. Then one day, my mother (a great tennis player) told me to think of my time on the court as a performance. All of it, from the minute I got onto the court to how I picked up the balls to how I concentrated in the moment before I made contact with the ball to how I walked off the court. She told me a little secret, "Just remember, Ellie, it is the moments in between the shots that count just as much on the tennis court as the actual shot itself. If you can focus on timing, confidence, and positive thinking while you are walking back to the base line, between points, then when the time comes to perform, you will ace it. Try it."

I did, and it worked. By viewing the entire process as a performance, I could redirect my interest toward doing my best, toward making a difference on the court. Suddenly, I was hitting the ball time after time, my feet, my arms, and my brain in perfect unison, discovering a dexterity that I had never had before in this particular sport. Although I am sure that I was picking up as many balls as I was before, I now saw those moments as part of my performance.

This same concept of performance is brought home to me every day of my entrepreneurial life. In sales, it is not just the presentation that you make but how you perform in between the time when you initially make contact with a customer and the many phone calls, emails, meetings, and chance encounters you have with them. When you are trying to find an investor, it is not just how well written your business plan is or how cleverly you can justify the numbers on your spreadsheet. It is also the confidence with which you answer a certain question during a presentation. It is the way your office looks when an investor surprises you on a Friday afternoon and the way you leave the room when you have been turned down.

It takes a different skill to build a business than it does to keep it going once it matures.

BUSINESS PLUS

As with luck, I believe that timing and dexterity favors those who are prepared. Performers focus on their art form, their sport, their métier with perseverance and dedication. In the process, they gain an intuitive sense of timing and dexterity of skill. The same is true for the chaos pilot. As a developing entrepreneur, a portfolio filled with a wide range of close-to-the-skin experiences will prepare you for intuiting the right time to bring up a touchy topic with a client. You will know when to move into a new position or to take the chance and start up your own company. The nuance of timing in a sport or in a performance allows you to recognize when it is the right moment to be assertive and take center stage and when it is the time to sit back and observe or let your partner or employees take over.

In the early stages of starting an entrepreneurial venture, it often feels as if you are spending most of your time picking up balls at the back of the court and hitting your fair share over the fence. But if you think of the entire process as a performance, recognizing that those who matter to you are watching, then you will learn how to take those in-between moments and incorporate them into your performance. With this in mind, you will start to do your best in areas that you did not think were part of the entrepreneurial game. For example, you will be able to handle administrative issues with grace until you can afford to delegate this to someone more suited to the task. You will discover new ways to motivate and negotiate with employees, even though you never thought that was your strong suit. You will keep practicing, until one day, you will find your timing and your rhythm. You will realize that you have finally developed the dexterity required to perform in a number of new situations.

THE CHAOS PILOT STRIVES TO DEVELOP A MATURITY THAT WILL ALLOW FOR EFFECTIVE LEADERSHIP, KNOWING THAT IT IS THE ONLY WAY TO TRULY RE-IMAGINE A VISION AND ULTIMATELY TO GROW A COMPANY.

In December 1997, *Wired* magazine announced the appointment of a new editor-in-chief and a publisher. This was a big step for founders Jane Metcalfe and Louis Rossetto, who had happily played this role since the inception of the organization. But it was a necessary one for both the growth of the magazine and the maturity of the overall entity—Wired Ventures. This decision was particularly important based on the diverse nature of the holding company, which was not only responsible for publishing a magazine but had branched out into different areas, from book publishing to software tool creation to online publishing. Jane recalls: "We finally realized that we needed to let others run the day-to-day operations, because the reality is that we have a very diverse company with a lot of different activities. . . . And ultimately, we realized that the magazine deserved full-time people who are there every day." Letting go of the branding of the magazine, as well as the hands-on editorial direction, was no easy exercise for these two entrepreneurs. And yet, this is what is required of all entrepreneurs at some stage in their growth curve. It is the moment when you recognize that it is time to allow someone else to take center stage. As a performer, it is the equivalent of knowing when it is time to forfeit a solo for a dramatic chorus interlude.

When I think about the notion of the chaos pilot, I am struck by the image of someone who needs to navigate through tumultuous and unforeseen situations, who needs to perform their best for those around them, but also someone who is reflective enough to take the time to nurture these same attributes in others.

Sometimes maturity means recognizing when it is time to bring someone else's ideas forward, allowing them to be a chaos-pilot-in-training, making room for their need to perform and their desire to envision, alongside yours. Other times, it simply means understanding when it is time to move over and see what will come of those who step into the limelight.

Bulldog's evolution as a company is a dramatic example of this process. After seven years as president of the company, I chose to evolve from my day-to-day operational role into a coaching role as an advisor to the board. Why have I chosen to do this? Because after many years of entrepreneuring, I have come to understand that the real chaos pilots among us have the intuitive ability to tap into the essential needs of their company while possessing the maturity to know when it is time to allow others to take center stage and simply guide from the wings. Ultimately, what truly drives the new entrepreneur is seeing others invest in your vision and watching others take ownership of the ideas you pioneered. Every organization begins its life by taking its cues from the leaders and founders. But winning organizations take on lifeforms of their own that are based on a long line of new entrepreneurs dedicated to the successful re-imagining of the entrepreneurial spirit. Knowing when to move on, to allow your company to move forward, is the true sign of a chaos pilot.

The most cherished moments for entrepreneurs are when others—your customers, your employees, your investors—take ownership of your ideas. Then you have truly created something of value.

HEATHER REISMAN

in the final analysis, secret recipes do exist

Throughout this chapter, I have revealed many elements of what it means to be a chaos pilot, but I cannot deny that there also exists a certain mystery in the requirements for navigating through chaos. Just as the horse whisperer can magically calm down a wild horse that is otherwise unmanageable, and just as a dancer has a grace that is indescribable, the chaos pilot, who is the artist of the business world, has a technique for navigating through chaos that is their own secret recipe.

In the fall of 1997, en route from a speaking engagement in the Netherlands, I was visiting my friend Michael Levine, who was working in Amsterdam. At the time, he was designing a production of *Rigoletto* by Verdi and was in search of a particular kind of 17th-century fabric for his set design. One rainy day, I accompanied him to the house of one of the top suppliers of 17th-century fabrics in Europe. From the minute we stepped into her house along the canal I was in visual heaven, surrounded by the most luxurious fabrics I had ever seen. They were draped over chairs, hanging on walls, and falling out of drawers and off shelves. Each fabric had a history that she shared with a wide-eyed fascination as if it were the first time she had ever told anyone that piece of history. But the story that stayed with me the most was about a particular kind of fabric called Fortuny, a unique Italian-printed velvet that has been produced by the Fortuny family in Italy for generations. When we asked her how they made the intricate patterns and were able to create such vivid colors, she looked slightly abashed and said, "I can only tell you what I know. Even though I have worked with, studied, and conducted business with the makers of this exquisite material for 15 years, I have never been allowed into their studio to see exactly how the process is done. It is a family secret, the secret recipe that cannot be described. But that adds to the allure of its beauty, no?" Yes, it did, and it still does when I think about it today.

Just like the secret recipe of the Fortuny fabric studio, the chaos pilot, too, has their secrets, what Moses Znaimer refers to as "a mysterious impulse that cannot be analyzed beyond a certain point." Each chaos pilot has a different way of going about chaos navigation. But that adds to the allure of its beauty, no? Yes.

chapter 8 # Exceptional Emblems

The scene repeats itself over and over again: an informal cocktail hour in a swank club on the last night of an industry trade show in a foreign city. The aluminum bulldog dogtag hangs from my neck with a certain conviction, matching my bulldog belt and alluding to the bulldog tattoo that has slightly worn off my arm from the day before. Someone is walking toward me with a big grin on his face. In the wake of cynicism that sometimes occurs at the end of a three-day conference, I quickly try to determine if I know him, should know him, or even want to know him. He is shaking my hand. "You're Bulldog, right? That is so cool. I know you guys. You are *the* best in multimedia design. Truly one of the hottest shops around."

"Thank you. I am flattered," I reply. And as I make my way to the bar, I *am* flattered, but also slightly stupefied. How could we possibly be perceived as the hottest shop around when we have not been in the multimedia design business for years?

I take a sip of my drink and allow my mind to wander as I scan the room for a familiar face, and then, before I can segue into another conversation, realize that of course I know the answer to my question. I simply missed it in its simplicity. It's called creating exceptional emblems, or brand building.

As a new entrepreneur, I discovered that the traditional concept of marketing (price, product, place, and promotion) is only part of the necessary business equation. But as an early-day entrepreneur, the one thing that is absolutely necessary to know about marketing is branding. Branding is the essence of building equity—in terms of value, money, potential, ideas, and belonging. It is the monopoly money that you cannot do without.

This may sound audacious, but it is closer to the truth than anything else I could possibly communicate to you about marketing in the early days of building a company. These guidelines will not necessarily carry over once you are past your initial start-up phase. Once you are beyond that point, there are many books and experts that can truly help you through the dos and don'ts of advertising and how to use digital marketing and the WWW to enhance your message. They can tell you how to run an effective trade show, how to hire the right people, and how to do the planning required to market effectively. What I am talking about in this chapter is a lot closer to the notion of branding as the cornerstone of identity in the game of entrepreneuring.

IN THE EARLY DAYS OF ENTREPRENEURING, WHEN PRODUCT, PRICE, PLACE, AND PROMOTION DO NOT EXIST, BRANDING IS YOUR SECRET WEAPON.

Early-day entrepreneuring is about living in a fluid world that is defined by its dependence on ambiguity. As Geoffrey Moore says, "In the early market, there are no facts. So the only way you can create coherence is through mythology. It's like saying, How do you handle the world before you have a telescope or before you can mathematically describe the calculus of orbits? You make up stories about Venus and Mars and Jupiter, and then you begin moving toward an understanding of that very unknown place."

At every stage of Bulldog's segue from service to product, we were able to move our notion of our company forward only because we were so closely tied to our brand. To a large extent, our investors were buying into this brand, since we did not yet have a finished product. Likewise, our technology partners around the world (SGI, Sun Microsystems, Informix, Oracle, etc.), at the initial stages of our software product evolution, were buying into our brand as both a company and a product, recognizing that we would create a distribution channel and a price structure that would be viable, *as* we built the brand. Therefore, in many ways, notions of product, price, promotion, and place took a backseat to brand.

Jane Metcalfe, president of *Wired* magazine, believes that branding was the element that kickstarted their idea of a magazine for and by digital revolutionaries. "Branding is about being able to sell your idea and get a bunch of people to sign on to your hallucination. It is consensual hallucination, because at the early stages, we were talking about a magazine that did not yet exist, but we could all see it and feel it and taste it."

In his evolution to the style of naturalistic art, David Nash describes the moment when he recognized that shape and form are inseparable: "It seemed so simple that I did not trust it—thinking that art needs to be more intellectual."

The same held true for me when I first said, "In your early days, branding is all you need" out loud. To me, a marketer by nature, the truth of this was too obvious to have meaning. It was like saying that it is important to breathe or eat or sleep for survival. But as La Rochefoucauld states in the culinary realm, "To eat is a necessity, but to eat intelligently is an art." Like David Nash, I realized that in my art form, entrepreneuring, the simplicity of branding does not have to be some kind of distanced intellectual exercise but, rather, a very intimate and visceral one, one that the entrepreneur and

You have an idea, and you build it up, and you find that you are not just releasing a product, you are building a business, you are creating a momentum. You are always in the process of creating a brand.

It seemed so simple that I did not trust it—thinking that art needs to be more intellectual.

DAVID NASH, ARTIST

those who want to belong to their venture live and breathe every day. Jane Metcalfe found that people wanted to belong to *Wired* not for the money, not for the opportunity, but for the intellectual challenge and the sense of purpose it gave them—to be able to change people's attitudes about the digital revolution that we were all facing.

six essential e's of branding

So how does one create a visceral, intimate, and powerful brand that people gravitate toward in big and small circles? It begins by temporarily putting aside the four P's of marketing and focusing on what I call the "Six Essential E's of Branding": existential branding, extensive relationships, the essence of branding, experimental branding, emotional branding, and eclipsed branding.

existential branding

THE NEW ENTREPRENEUR RECOGNIZES THAT BRANDING IS A TWO-ACT PLAY. IT BEGINS WITH THE NOTION OF WHO YOU ARE AND YOUR PERSONAL BRAND, AND THEN TELEGRAPHS A SIMPLE BUT POWERFUL MOOD, IMAGE, OR STORY THAT ADDS VALUE.

I once read a magazine article directed to entrepreneurs that said, "Whatever you do, do not take your company personally." I was stopped in my tracks by that statement. Entrepreneuring is only personal. You have to come up with tactics that will assist you to make decisions to move through crisis and to keep the momentum going, but they are also very personal tactics, intrinsically based upon who you are and what you stand for. That is where branding actually begins for the entrepreneur. As a professional eclectic, you have been building a personal brand for years, as in the case of my mentor, who said, "Ellie, you are your own industry." What he meant by this was that I had been honing my notion of identity, expanding my image of self, and assessing my belief system to see what elements would ultimately formulate the basis for my ability to envision actively. For example, Jonas Svensson of Spray has been extending his brand ever since he opened his doors in the early '90s. What started as a new media and Web design company (Act I), evolved into a company that now includes Internet training, information technology consulting, and information architecture services. In addition, through the process of looking for and solidifying investors, Spray now has evolved a model for financing that they have incorporated into their services—to help finance other companies (Act II). Without a strong existential brand based on beliefs and ideas of new media

Branding is about being able to sell your idea and get a bunch of people to sign on to your hallucination. It is consensual hallucination.

JANE METCALFE,
CO-FOUNDER,
WIRED VENTURES

to start with, notions of how to extend the original service or product offering would be limited to the product or service brand that they originally committed to.

THE SOONER YOU RECOGNIZE THAT BRAND IS ABOUT PEOPLE NOT PRODUCTS, THE SOONER YOU REALIZE THAT THE EVOLUTION OF AN ENTREPRENEURIAL VENTURE AND THE BRANDING OF THIS VENTURE ARE ONE AND THE SAME. IF YOU COMMIT TO ACTIVELY OWNING YOUR BRAND, YOU WILL PAVE THE WAY FOR THE REQUIRED MATURING AND ESCALATED EQUITY IN YOUR COMPANY.

Today, *Wired* is one of the most influential publications in the business world. What started as a very personal and real notion of the digital revolution became the basis for creating a brand for a magazine that was "by and for digital revolutionaries."

Existential branding begins with the notion that branding is about people and not products, and that is where the entrepreneur must begin. When you talk to Jane Metcalfe, she will tell you that *Wired* is about the people who "were working and toiling in obscurity, who were influencing the way we work and live and needed a voice. They found it in *Wired*." *Wired* began as a personal quest and extended into the notion of showing and telling people how to approach the digital revolution that is upon us. In this case, branding is larger than a product.

Wired started out as a magazine reflecting a belief in digital media, and in fact, that was the only business plan they had for investors to look at. But as the years went by, it became obvious to the founders and to the employees that *Wired* was about much more than a magazine; it was about how to apply the notion of a digital revolution to our lives. As *Wired* has continued to search for the right vehicles to carry their messages, they have extended their brand to include a whole host of communication channels, such as television, book publishing, and software products. How well they succeed in these new areas is part of the exercise of redefinition that every brand struggles with. That is the game of equity. You need to build equity into your brand and then struggle to find the right home for it as you and your company grow.

Particularly in the new media realm, you are often selling a product or service that the customer does not even know they need yet. Three years ago, media asset management was not even a term that people were familiar with. In a recent survey of information technology (IT) and management information systems (MIS) professionals, media asset management was one of the priorities for many of the vice-presidents and directors of IT and MIS within the large entertainment and broadcast organizations that Bulldog works with. In fact, total revenue for media asset management systems will grow from $152 million this year to $2.58 billion in 2004, a 68.2 percent compound annual growth over a six year period. Regardless of what products and services you create to support Brand E, you are focused on building equity that is transferable, that transcends the customer's knowledge or understanding. You are building value even before the other variables are all in place.

Owning the brand wholly is directly related to the notion of active envisioning that we talked about in the last chapter. In fact, active envisioning and existential branding are so tightly woven together, one depends on the other. For example, existential branding built on a set of beliefs is what allows the new entrepreneur to truly benefit from the postcard theory and actively grow their company by moving toward a very well-defined image or vision, based on their own brand. Spray and *Wired* are good examples of this process. Conversely, as the new entrepreneur learns their employees' and customers' perceptions of the brand they initially envisioned, this, in turn, allows the new entrepreneur to revisit the brand and improve on its relevance to them. As Geoffrey Moore says, a good brand is built on a story or a myth, a fable whereby the storyteller keeps adding new chapters and new twists to the same tale. Existential branding is about taking your personal brand, beliefs, and ideas and extending them to create a place for others to belong. You build value based on the new twists and turns that you add to each new chapter.

The sooner the new entrepreneur recognizes the absolute necessity of branding within both their business plan and their ability to create equity through reflecting a point of differentiation, the sooner they will begin to recognize how to utilize branding as the catalyst for growth. For Moses Znaimer, the branding of Citytv was a distinct representation of attributes that he wanted people to associate with the medium of television, creating a new notion of belonging: "There was an absence of character in the medium at the time. Television channels were nothing more than electronic addresses where you could find different programs at different times, reflecting every gender, demographic, and taste on the half hour. In my mind, this wasn't an attribute of the medium; it was an attribute of the way in which the medium had been organized up to that point in time. I wanted to create a consistent kind of presentation which could then take on the attributes of character. Then the electronic address itself would mean something, because the channel would do a more limited number of things consistently well. It would have a brand."

As Andy Cunningham, who runs one of the top public relations firms in Silicon Valley, puts it, "PR isn't public relations—it's personal reinvention." The fact that we at Bulldog had transferred our multimedia, packaging, and print design capabilities to support the branding of *our* product is a good example of personal reinvention. It only further enhanced the versatility of the Bulldog brand. In a sense, our ambition was expressed in the creation of the Bulldog brand, and we never once stopped creating, directing, and owning that brand existentially.

Existential branding begins with the notion that branding is about people and not products.

PR isn't public relations— it's personal reinvention.

ANDY CUNNINGHAM

extensive relationships
JOY COVEY, KATRINA GARNETT, JOHN MACDONALD, GEOFFREY MOORE, BILL SAHLMAN, EVAN SOLOMON, PAMELA WALLIN, PAUL WOLLASTON, MOSES ZNAIMER . . .

I suggest that any new entrepreneur must spend 30% of their time finding, developing, and evolving champions.

There is one common thread among these people. They are all part of somebody's network of champions, or what I call a place of enlightened belonging. We already know that championship is part of what grounds the new entrepreneur in their risk-taking notions. If existential branding begins with a well-defined relationship between you, your ideas, and your beliefs, then the next phase of branding logically extends to the relationships you build with others.

When Pamela Wallin needed to figure out how to create her own version of a news show, she realized that she was used to being in the power seat, answering her audiences' questions. Suddenly, she needed someone *she* could ask questions of, someone who could truly become a champion for her ideas. She found that champion in Adam Zimmerman and has been building her brand ever since.

When the founders of Roots Canada first started in the negative heel shoe business, it was by focusing on the notion of influencers that they were able to set their shoes apart from all the contemporary competitors. By sending free pairs of shoes to famous feet around the world, such as Paul McCartney, Cher, Elton John and Pierre Trudeau, Roots shoes were dubbed the "Gucci shoe of the crunchy granola set" by *People* magazine. This was the beginning of a retail story that has been in the black ever since.

The champions you gather around you will, in effect, become the sounding board for your ideas. They will extend your branding in a way that you could never do by yourself, ultimately helping you to evolve your branding in a way that will ensure its relevance and timeliness as you cycle through new products and services.

three types of champions
THERE ARE THREE KINDS OF CHAMPIONS THAT THE NEW ENTREPRENEUR NEEDS AND NURTURES: CHEERLEADERS, INFLUENCERS, AND DOERS. BY BUILDING CIRCLES OF COINCIDENCE, LOOKING FOR PURPOSEFUL COLLISIONS, AND ENSURING THAT THEY HAVE A METHOD TO THEIR MADNESS, THEY CAN CREATE ENLIGHTENED BELONGING.

Geoffrey Moore suggests that the very first act of an entrepreneur is "to go and get customers." I agree with this, but I also know that what the new entrepreneur is really involved in is a "chicken-and-egg syndrome." You are in the process of maturing your product while you're actively pursuing input from customers to help you define your product. Going out and getting customers begins by finding champions. As with many things in entrepreneuring, this is a game of leverage, a fight against time. The faster and more effectively you can scale and build your brand through a meaningful network of champions, the faster and more effectively you will be able to mature your product notions, accurately determining where the need is highest within the marketplace. If you have focused on your existential brand just long enough to create an emblem of difference that rises above the noise of all the other new entrepreneurs, then you will find a powerful network of champions. Initially, they will be attracted to you because of this brand. Once they are part of your network, they will work with you to leverage that brand in ways that you could never do yourself.

Champions can be found in all kinds of places, in all kinds of industries, at all levels of organizations. You can have champions who are strategic partners, champions who work in the press, and champions who are investors. Champions can be the business partner you are able to do a deal with; they can be your employees, a parent, or someone you have nothing in common with. In my world, regardless of what vocation or what industry is represented, the new entrepreneurs' champions fall into three key categories: cheerleaders, influencers, and doers. Let me give you a quick synopsis of each.

**To eat is a necessity,
but to eat intelligently
is an art.**

LA ROCHEFOUCAULD, IN
THE ART OF EATING

Cheerleaders

Cheerleaders provide you with the required moral support. In 1994, one of the largest publishing houses launched a magazine called *Profit Home Business*, which was targeted to home-based businesses in Canada. Barbara Mowat, president of Impact Communications, claims that she never would have had the courage to compete with this publication without her network of cheerleaders—friends, colleagues, and family members. Today, the *B.C. Home Business Report* is published by Mowat's company and is a national publication that has been in existence and thriving for ten years.

Influencers

An influencer is anyone within the spheres of influence that directly relate to your business. They can influence other relationships, on the sale of your product, or they can help you improve the messages you communicate about your company to your major stakeholders. Business influencers do not have to be the most senior executives within large organizations, but they need to have the ear of the senior executives and be highly respected by many within a given community. Sometimes they are press people; sometimes they are academic figures. Often they are strategic planners within influential companies whose main focus is to watch for new trends, companies, and ideas that larger companies need to understand and sometimes even incorporate into their plans.

In technology, influencers are crucial. As a software entrepreneur, you are often challenged to find ways to describe your solution in terms that relate to the agenda of much larger technology giants, almost as if you were the bird that sits on the elephant. Influencers can help you to get the attention of the elephant in such a way that it cannot help but take notice. These people will know how and when to get attention and how to push your agenda forward effectively. For example, by focusing their attention on important technology influencers such as Richard Saul Wurman and Nicholas Negroponte, the founders of *Wired* magazine were able to associate themselves with *spheres* of influence, with people who would, in turn, spread the word faster than any marketing campaign alone could have done.

If cheerleaders provide the backbone that helps you determine your brand, influencers have the power to help you move that brand forward.

By itself, reality isn't worth a damn. It's perception that promotes reality to meaning.

JOSEPH BRODSKY

Doers

Doers are people and companies in action mode. Often, but not always, their actions are directly related to sales. They are going to make money because of you, and vice versa. The key qualifier here is that there is usually one person (or a few people) within the company you are dealing with who is closest to the revenue line. Don't be fooled by thinking that it is always the most senior person. Doers are often very strategic in their actions. They are often someone in a sales role. They often have their finger on the pulse of your mutual potential customer and/or have the ability to change the course of a deal midstream.

In Bulldog's case, Todd Kirkpatrick is someone who will always hold a special place for us. When we first started out in the multimedia design business, Todd was the one who kept us up to speed on the changes going on in the industry. As he moved up the ladder and across various technology organizations (Apple, SGI), he made certain that we understood the trends that he was seeing in his sales and, later, in the teams he was managing on the hardware side. It was Todd who got us hooked up with the right people at Apple, ensuring that we had their endorsement in our initial evangelizing efforts in Canada. Todd got the first meeting for us at SGI in Mountainview, when we were barely a software company. His intentions were strategic and supported his sales mission. But his actions had our best intentions in mind.

Doers are important because:

- They tend to be out in front and on the lookout for people and companies that will provide them with immediate results.

- They are action oriented and are a great complement to your other two categories of champions.

- They can make your bottom line if you have enough of them, and if they're good.

a word about partnerships in the context of championship

In the world of new media and software, partnership is one of those jargon words that has maintained significance. Partnership is also a key element in the building of one's Brand E, in the context of creating enlightened belonging. There are people and divisions within large technology companies whose sole purpose is partner relations (i.e., who create strategic alliances with smaller, nimble software companies). Regardless of whether you are dealing with a doer, an influencer, or a cheerleader, when you are working to establish partnerships with large technology companies, there is one important thing to remember as an early-day entrepreneur: You often have only the beginnings of a product or price. Therefore, it is your ability to lead with your brand and follow through that will allow you to build strong and meaningful champions within a partner company.

For software companies, a large hardware company will provide you with a lot—a channel, a sphere of influence, money, and resources. How good you are at negotiating for these elements within a partnership varies greatly. But one thing is certain: With a well-defined brand, it is the newness of your ideas, the vigor of your conviction, and the swiftness with which you can maneuver in an industry that is most attractive to people, especially those within larger corporations. Why? Because by the very nature of their size, they find it harder to renew their original entrepreneurial spirit, to be agile enough to rekindle their brand with the freshness that a young entrepreneurial company can.

Prospective partners are looking for brands and products that are easily recognizable as new and different from whatever else is out there. In the process, through brand association coupled with customer input, the partner company will renew its own ability to sell, to differentiate itself from its competitors, and to change perception in the marketplace. You gain a partner that will heighten your chances of succeeding in wider and larger circles. The partner company gains a distinct version of branding that is relevant to its core business. Together, you create enlightened belonging that is mutually beneficial.

building circles of coincidence and purposeful collision

I was asked to be on a think-tank committee for an interactive new media installation in Hollywood. This represented a great opportunity for me to extend my championship network, particularly in a new arena of importance for us—Hollywood. Fifteen of us assembled for a full-day meeting and batted around many ideas about how to communicate the importance of digital media to a select star-studded constituency who were (except for a few) paying lip service to technology that only mildly interested them.

That evening, we all assembled at a cigar bar. Some of us were from the software industry, some were talent agents, some were producers, and some were technology executives from large hardware companies. At one point, while I was talking to three or four of the committee members, a newcomer joined our circle. I was describing the Bulldog product and why our customers in Hollywood were endorsing it. Suddenly, out of nowhere, this guy took a step forward and said, "Who are you? And how come I don't know you?" I was stunned. How does one answer such questions? Later, after I had gotten over the arrogance of his question, I realized *exactly* what he had meant. As it turned out, he was the top sales director for one of the most important technology companies in Hollywood. That evening, as he listened to my description of the Bulldog product and my list of partnering organizations, he was probably thinking, We move in the same circles, why don't I know this person? He simply needed help to rephrase his inquiry elegantly.

Meeting that individual was an example of what I call circles of coincidence. Through him, I was able to set up one of the most important meetings that our company would have that year at the upcoming visual graphics trade show, Siggraph. Out of that meeting, a partnership would evolve, and a whole new set of champions would be added to help promote the Bulldog brand and solidify three of our most important customers.

And so the circles within circles within championship networks continue to grow. For Dan Dadalt, circles of coincidence allowed him to find the right investors, who bought into his notion of an "irreverent" new alcohol called Redrum.

Through the creation of these circles, deals are made, new champions are found, and connections between existing champions are reinforced. To this day, when I am meeting someone for the first time, I can often sense whether or not they will become an important champion. I smile, and with my tongue firmly pasted against my cheek, I whisper to myself, "Who are you? And why don't I know you?" And then I set out to make the connection by building circles of coincidence around them through my existing network of champions.

purposeful collision

Purposeful collision describes the methodical means through which you meet and foster relationships that have purpose. Its goal is to extend your net as wide and far as possible and create circles of coincidence that will further generate collision with the influencers, cheerleaders, and doers who will buy into and help you build your brand.

Always begin the process by creating what I call a "reality matrix" of your goals and needs. Create short-term goals ("I need to meet customer x at company y within three months") and medium- to long-term goals ("Within four years, I want our product to be the number-one recognizable brand in its niche for producers in Hollywood"). Then create a list of all the people you know and want to know and all those who you think can lead you to the right people to help you achieve your goals. Choose about 5 to 10 champions for each goal. Ensure that you have "evolve our brand" as one of the goals on your list. Match 20 champions against this goal. Ensure that you have a balance between the cheerleaders, influences, and doers—you need them all. Carry this matrix with you and update it weekly.

Categories of the reality matrix

- Your goals: List your goals within three-month, six-month, and one-year time frames, then three-year and five-year time frames.

- Your attributes: List your three top attributes that will support each of the goals you have set out within each time period.

- Champion profile per goal: Identify the profile of the champion (i.e., cheerleader, influencer, doer) who you think will best help you achieve this goal—don't worry about who specifically, just the kind of champion.

- Desired action, per champion per goal: What do you want this champion to do to help you achieve the goal?

- Potential candidates: Go through everyone you knew or know, starting with the names on your profile chart.

- Means of gaining access to this person: Where you are missing people, list anyone who can help you get to the appointed champion.

- Time lines: Realistically assess how much time you are going to require to get to this person and how long you will give yourself to achieve the goal.

Guidelines for the reality matrix

- The guidelines for each of your goals need to be as specific as possible.

- Limit yourself to one goal per time period to start. Later you can add another two or three.

- Limit yourself to only one attribute required per goal.

- List your potential champions per goal in order of your ability to access them.

- Do not edit anyone out if you don't know how to get to them.

- The desired action per champion per goal should be extremely specific. For example, "They will assist me in getting a 500-word blurb highlighting our product printed in *New Media* by the next Siggraph Design Expo."

- When you are going through your potential champion list, be bold. Think of people you have heard of or people you wish you could meet. You will be amazed at what you can achieve once they appear on your matrix.

- In identifying a way to gain access to the champion you are interested in, think out of the box.

- In creating your time lines, be realistic. Assume that it takes a minimum of three months to access anyone who is more than one person away from you.

- Add a column to your chart that is titled "Accomplished," and check it off each time you achieve any step along the way.

- Leave the "Accomplished" list on your chart for at least three months to motivate you when you are having a particularly unproductive spell in your championship endeavors.

- Don't be afraid to edit and redo parts of your matrixes as you gain information.

- Don't give up after three months.

method to your madness

There are two key elements to the tactical side of building your circles of coincidence: (a) You will need a database that can be cross-referenced, and (b) you will need to build championship into your business plan; it needs an expense line.

Create a Champion Database

Whether you use your standard company database and/or you create your own personal database that will house your champions, the key is that this database be built to accommodate the following information:

- Name, title, address, telephone, fax, email, cell numbers, web site, etc., of your champions.

- Categories listing your champions as cheerleaders, influencers, or doers.

- A prioritization of your champions alphabetically, according to which ones you are working on currently and who have the most immediacy attached to them because of either who they are or how crucial they are to one of your goals.

- The capability to bring forward the next date you need to communicate with them.

- The ability to cross-reference your lists by date, priority, category, etc.

- The ability to track the information you send to them (i.e., marketing materials, notes, copies of articles, etc.).

Write Championship into Your Business Plan to Ensure That:

- you take the notion seriously

■ you plan for the resources required to accomplish these activities (i.e., you may need to hire someone to help you update the database, or to conduct research on some of the champions that you are focused on adding to your circle).

The bottom line is that, as you can see, a methodical process will create coincidence, just as luck favors the prepared.

Sounds like a lot of work, doesn't it? Yes, it is. But it is the method behind your championship program that is going to be the tool that will differentiate you from others.

developing your relationships

Ensure that You are Crossing Hierarchies and Industries

Abandon any notion that you need only focus on building relationships within the industry that you are in. That is shortsighted. The trick to creating circles of coincidence is to create relationships within many different industries that you feel are related to yours, places where you have a hunch there might be investment opportunity. Connect with people and companies that have contacts which may lead to attaining champions who you have on your list. Don't be unduly concerned with hierarchy. Particularly in a world of confluence, one never knows where someone might end up. Remember the Pepsi executive who became the president of Apple Computers, the television producer who moved into software, the marketing manager from a major bank who now is VP of an e-commerce software company.

As with sales, you will have good championship cycles and not so good championship cycles. If you are not making any headway with the champions on your list, expand your horizons. Try going to a trade show with a friend who is in a completely different industry, and test your branding notions on a fresh audience. You may meet someone, or you may simply discover a new perception of your brand that you were not getting through your existing champions. The operative word is *expand*. When you have the choice of champions, you can begin to focus your attention on which ones you wish to make your priority.

Keep your Champions Happy

The new entrepreneur is fighting against time, scale, and resources. Assume that your champions are also lacking in all of these areas, and respect that. The best way to begin a championship is to set out the terms of engagement. Explain what you are looking for, find out what they want out of the championship relationship, and constantly communicate with them so that you are both building the image of who you are, enhancing the brand of you and your company, and establishing what everyone's needs and interests are. If you commit to this idea, you will build not only strong championships but ones that will introduce you into new circles of coincidence that you never thought imaginable.

Clarity, Cachet, and the Fun Quotient

The art of championship should be perceived as a business process. Like any process, it requires clarity, guidelines, and a mutually understood plan of action—otherwise, confusion reigns, and the process will be bogged down. The point here is that you approach this as a transaction. Here are some guidelines to follow:

- When the time is right to address the champion, position the discussion within the context of mutual benefits of the relationship—starting with what you can bring the other person.

- When talking about what you hope to get from them, address this issue by asking them first. For example, you could approach it by saying, "Assuming that you have time to meet . . ."

- Define the role of each champion in your own mind before communicating expectations to them directly. If you have been diligent about revisiting and editing your matrix charts, this should be an easy task. Define the role in one sentence that is easy to understand and easy to buy into.

- Don't be afraid to ask questions. Find out how they like to be communicated with. Some people prefer email, others like voicemail, others want paper. Some like to receive constant communications, others just want a top-line précis. Whatever their bias, they need to know that you are not wasting their time (or yours).

- Do not underestimate the "fun" quotient in your dealings with champions. This is especially true when dealing with doers and influencers whose time is always at a premium. If you can be the most fun part of their day, they are going to put your requested action point at the top of the priority list. Focus on cachet when dealing with these people. Influencers especially like to be part of something that is intangible, that simply has a feel that appeals to them.

Evolve Championships

Just as a company needs to have the room to mature and evolve, so do championships. You will find that some champions are simply not able to evolve with you. For example, when I first started Bulldog, I had a champion within a large retail environment. For years, his support and insight into our brand and positioning in the marketplace was invaluable. He was also a great cheerleader. However, as we began to move away from service to product, he became less comfortable with our notions of entrepreneuring. It was harder and harder for him to see us in a new light, and he was constantly referring back to a Bulldog that was no longer relevant. After a while, this looking backwards was actually detrimental to my ability to create an evolving brand, one that was more relevant to the software industry. Recognize when it is time to redefine the relationships and move on. Do not be afraid to let go when it is time to leave a championship behind and find one that is more relevant.

Become a Champion for Others

I will go out of my way to become a champion for someone else for two reasons: First and foremost, I believe in giving back to the community of entrepreneurs everywhere. Second, I believe that the relationship itself often provides me with insight and ideas or poses questions that I would never otherwise have thought of. By creating circles of coincidence for others, you will see what works in the development of a championship, in the communications tactics used, and in your own ability to help someone else create and recreate their Brand E. Whether you create an email relationship with someone you meet within the industry or simply find someone less experienced or younger than you and take them to lunch once a quarter, it is a highly rewarding experience. But remember, being a champion takes time and energy. Do not agree to be someone's champion if you cannot commit the necessary attention to the task. Otherwise, you will both be disappointed. If you can find the time, it will be an invaluable step toward your goal of understanding how enlightened belonging occurs within circles of coincidence.

Today, brand is the most important thing because the marketplace is so crowded and one can easily be elbowed out. Be sure your brand has true value and is perceived as "different."

HEATHER REISMAN

the essence of branding

In 1993, I was standing in a large *souk* (market) in the town of Aswan, in Egypt. Despite the distraction of the many herbs and spices in huge canvas sacks lining the narrow, dark twisting alleyways, I was drawn to a small perfumery off to the side. For the next three hours, I listened while the owner described, in broken English, the process he used to create the perfect perfumed oil that would respond to each person's particular kind of skin. I am sure he was practiced at this preamble, and inevitably, I walked out of the store with many more bottles of sweet, musky, and unusual oils than I would ever need. But the aromas that he let me test on my skin were unlike anything I had ever smelled before. What stayed with me was the notion that it was the infinitesimal amounts of the many kinds of herbs and flowers, mixed together and constantly condensed, which created a particular smell that lit up the olfactory sense. The slightest difference in quantity of one kind of flower versus another could create a completely different aroma. And, of course, what smelled heavenly on one type of skin might be too pungent on another.

Like the perfumer's subtle proportions, the careful mixing together of risk, storytelling, and realism are what creates one's brand. The essence of branding does not come from one particular element but, rather, from the blending of many infinitesimal pieces that create an aroma that lingers in the most potent way. To create what I call "eau de branding" requires a constant condensing of the key tactical elements. Together they create a brand that is memorable and unforgettable.

Creating an Enigmatic Emblem through Elevated Design and Exceptional Articulation

Branding begins as an exercise in existentialism but is complemented and filled out by creating what I call an enigmatic emblem. The making of an enigmatic emblem involves:

- The ability to articulate who you are and what your company stands for.

- The commitment to elevating that articulation to an aesthetic, a design, or a visual that will be memorable.

Moses Znaimer of Citytv had a notion of how to turn a television station from an electronic address to a place to belong. As someone who has always had a strong sense of design, he describes his need for exceptional articulation coupled with elevated design as follows: "A really great slogan is, in its way, a work of art—not a copy line or a cute turn of phrase that you change or roll over every week or month, but some brilliant reduction of the essence of your organization and your ideas that, once you achieve it, gets elevated to high art."

How do you create this enigmatic emblem? How do you ensure that it will be powerful and memorable? The initial existential branding consists of answering three primary questions:

- What do I believe is essential in creating a place where people want to belong?

- What do I want my company to be remembered for in 100 years?

- Where is the intersection between my collected skill sets, a product or service, and a hunch for what people may want or need?

If you can answer each of these questions honestly, then you are well on your way to creating a brand that will be a memorable icon of who and what you stand for. Hiring outside experts to help you—to coach or edit and refine your answers or visually reflect your image—is completely acceptable and usually very helpful, though sometimes costly. The right person is worth it.

Extra Oomph

Memorable icons, emblems, and brands come from an ability to articulate attitude through words and visuals and the spaces in between. Although branding is a lifelong pursuit, making a splash, making enough noise to rise above the others, particularly in a relatively fast-paced industry such as technology, requires more than a good logo and a meaningful tag line. When Illustra first came out with their object relational database, they came up with what I think was a great event that added extra oomph to their positioning against other database companies in the industry. They created "24 hours in cyberspace," a collaborative effort to document how cyberspace affects our lives, which connected information and Web sites from around the world for simultaneous distribution, all out of one database. It was an event that reflected the brand they wanted to be remembered for.

Similarly, Dan Dadalt recognized the importance of attitude when he decided to start up his own company in the highly competitive, highly monopolized spirits industry. His company Redrum reflects an irreverence that is typical of his target market, 20- to 30-year-olds, who are young and slightly cynical and want to create their own brands, not just accept those that have been handed down to them by the generations that came before. They buy different cars, they read different magazines, and they want to drink different alcohol. Everything the company does reflects extra oomph, from the unusually designed red bottle to the fact that Redrum is a takeoff on the movie *The Shining*, where murder is spelled backwards in one very dramatic scene. And it works. Redrum is becoming an emblem of a kind of attitude that people want to belong to.

Extra oomph might take the form of the checkered bulldog that dashes across the computer screen as part of our screen savers sent to customers. Extra oomph at Citytv is in the open-space concept, where passersby can watch shows being produced as they walk by the ground floor of the Citytv building in downtown Toronto. Extra oomph helps to maintain the fun quotient in the new entrepreneur's circles of coincidence and gives employees an emblem to be proud of.

Fantasy—that is, good acceptable fantasy—is really only fact with a whimsical twist.

WALT DISNEY

experimental branding

Branding, like so many of the new entrepreneur's decisions, must include risk. Let's make no bones about it. Risk can involve losing money, or it can involve potential damage to a brand; if an idea gets misinterpreted, it can involve alienation. But risk is a necessary part of creating a lasting brand. One of the best examples of branding risk that I have heard comes again from *Wired* magazine. When Jane and Louis first launched their magazine in January 1993, they had a total of $70,000 to spend for everything— advertising, launch party, marketing, public relations, etc. As Jane describes it, "Because we had no reputation for editorial integrity at that point, we had to prove the journalistic quality of what we were producing through packaging and personality. Particularly since the magazine would be racked with many other computer publications, we wanted to make sure that our magazine stood out and almost felt more like a lifestyle or general-interest magazine, though in 1993, that would probably have been pushing it. And so, despite all the naysayers, we created a very grassroots launch. Because Louis and I had lived in Europe for many years, we were intrigued by the kind of underground outdoor advertising that is used as street-level communication. We wanted to recreate the notion of billboard advertising, to create more of a happening, close to the street, on the sidewalks, not on huge billboards in the distance. We focused on New York, Boston, Chicago, San Francisco, San Jose, and Los Angeles as our target markets. We did postering everywhere: We would put them up on construction sites and dumpsters and everywhere. Because we were launching in January, the vibrancy of our branding provided a streak of color in the gray mornings in cities like New York and Boston. We then decided that we could leverage the dollars we had available much more effectively by postering along the bus routes and the subway routes (up and down Madison Avenue, for example, in New York), where many of the media people and the advertisers work. They would come out of the subway on the way to work and see our posters, they would get off the bus and see our posters. And then to top it off, we branded the buses that went along the key routes of our potential champions of the brand. Of course the final result was that we acted like a much bigger company than we really were. These audiences soon felt as if there was this major force, with a presence everywhere, launching a magazine. We took a chance and it paid off in spades."

This is just one of many stories about companies that took a chance with their means of communicating their brand and it paid off. The key here is to experiment—with the visuals you use, the media you choose, the slogans you create, and the intensity with which you deliver your message. One Silicon Valley marketing consultant told me that she encourages her clients to think of marketing and branding as a set of experiments, which requires constant qualitative and quantitative assessment. When it comes to digital branding (i.e., buying banners on a Web site for advertising purposes, setting up an online customer-comments forum on a Web site, etc), she warns her clients that they should not assume that their first two digital branding attempts will succeed but rather will provide the clients with the information necessary to come up with the right mix on the third attempt.

But I do leave you with one word of advice: Sometimes the ideas for branding overtake the initial goal—to build and extend a memorable and meaningful brand that people want to belong to. For example, although one year our marketing department was able to convince the marketing team at Bulldog to produce dog leashes with our WWW address on it, the idea of

The image is more than an idea. It is a vortex or cluster of fused ideas and is endowed with energy.

EZRA POUND

dog collars that the booth attendees would wear at Siggraph was shot down—and for good reason. It was taking the experiment one step too far. Coco Chanel was known to say, "When you have finished dressing, look in the mirror and take one thing off. Then your outfit will be perfect." So will your brand.

emotional branding

The last element within the mixture of the essence of branding is the emotional element, which is directly tied to belonging. Why do people want to associate themselves with a brand? Image, fun, and exceptional articulation are all part of the answer, but these do not have weight and power without the element of emotion. We see this use of emotional branding all the time—phone companies use it to advertise service that is really about rates, and yet we associate their service offerings with phone calls from grandchildren and friends from far away. At the very beginning, when cellular phones were rare and expensive, the cellular phone companies figured out that executives could be persuaded to buy cellular phones for the image. Soon, having a cell phone became a convenience for a wider range of people who needed to make calls on the road, in airports, etc. The sales of cellular phones really took off, however, when the telecom companies created an emotional reason to have one. This reason was directly tied into the notion of having a phone in the car in case you were stuck or in trouble. People's fear became the emotional element of the sell, and one that many consumers bought into.

The biggest error I see in the technology industry today is the belief that emotion does not play a role in the purchasing decision. That defies the way people function. In every purchase, whether it is the back-end database, a palm pilot, or a Web design for a new division of a company, there is both a rational and an emotional or instinctive element to the purchase decision. The new entrepreneur in the technology industry recognizes this and builds a brand that begins with a visceral reason to buy and ends with a list of features and functions, not the other way around.

Bo Peabody is someone who certainly understands emotional branding. This 27-year-old CEO of a start-up company called Tripod, in Williamstown, Massachusetts, is creating a new breed of virtual communities for the twenty-something crowd by inviting free membership in exchange for personal information. Having tapped into the emotional understanding that twenty-somethings like nothing better than to talk about themselves, Tripod expects to keep members happy and interested by exchanging information and attracting advertisers—based on the wealth of knowledge Tripod houses about this target market. Peabody has found a way to package his lumberjack image with a strong business model, attracting outside investment to the tune of $13 million. With 40 twenty-something employees and a model for how

[A brand] is not only a gorgeous graphic twisting in the ether, a kind of empty gesture which many companies engage in; [it is] a matter of developing a presence in the community that was genuine and [delivering] against that promise.

MOSES ZNAIMER

to create a twenty-something media conglomerate, Peabody is committed to extending his brand to include TV programming for CNN and a Tripod magazine shrink-wrapped with Prentice Hall college textbooks. But regardless of what new ventures he focuses on next, his brand begins with the notion of his company's image—a surprising combination of lumberjack and entrepreneur—that will propel him forward first, followed by a host of products and services that will reflect a brand of virtual communities for the twenty-somethings.

The elements of exceptional articulation, elevated design, extra oomph, experimental notions, and emotional lure need to be continuously blended together to create essence. The beauty of the fragrances that the man in the *shuk* in Aswan was creating came from his constant combining and distilling of the herbs and flowers until there was a seamlessness about the various elements that made up each particular aroma. It is the same with branding. By continuously combining and distilling the branding ingredients, the new entrepreneur will evolve a brand that truly is the essence of who you are and what you represent. The subtlety of the reaction of people who get a whiff of your brand should be similar to the subtleties required in wine preparation. As Cyrus Pine (a character in *Chasing Cezanne*) says to the unsuspecting stewardess en route to Europe, "Could you make sure the wine doesn't get too cold? It should be chilled but not startled." So should your enigmatic emblem.

Could you make sure the wine doesn't get too cold? It should be chilled but not startled.

PETER MAYLE,
CHASING CEZANNE

eclipsed branding

Eugene Sue in the book *Mysteries of Paris* describes how the idea of gossip columns first came to be. According to this source, characters in Paris called *auteurs* would spend the majority of their days in the French bistros, paid by the locals who were entertained by their exceptional storytelling abilities. Slowly but surely, however, they found that people were more interested in their stories and paid more money for them when they would weave in elements of what was really going on in the neighborhood (the butcher who had a grudge against the shoemaker, the wife of the banker who had an affair with the tailor, etc.). In essence, this was the first time that society was supporting the notion of self-reflection. People began by merely liking it but soon found themselves addicted to the notion of myth and reality mixed into one, told by a master storyteller.

The concept of the *auteur* reinforces the notion of the new entrepreneur as a master of interpretation more than as a master of invention. The ability to evolve stories and weave aspects of reality into the initial allegory is crucial to successful brand building. As a master of interpretation, the new entrepreneur is able to mix these opposing elements beautifully, beginning with the "creation myth," in telling how the idea for a company got started. As a company grows, the need to revisit and retell the creation myth is an essential element to building a strong brand for the newest members of the team and the newer customers who were not there when you first started, when your myth and your reality were intertwined. The founders of *Wired*, of Citytv, and a host of other entrepreneurial companies, discovered that as they grew in size, without committing to telling and retelling the creation story, they risked diluting the original spirit or impulse on which the company was based.

While the new entrepreneur must dedicate themselves to creating and directing their brand at the very early stages of their company's existence, they must also recognize when to let the brand evolve, when it is time to let it mature and grow as it should. As with the *auteur*'s storytelling, the key to brand maturation is the ability to let the outside world's perception of the brand penetrate just enough to ensure that the brand evolves.

Look for Inflection Points

Your salespeople are the best monitors for helping you recognize when your brand is starting to falter, when your positioning needs to be tweaked. At AFI (American Film Institute), the notion that they would have to revisit their brand only became clear to them when they truly began to ask for input from all of their constituents. As they consulted with their customers, their champions, and their industry associates, it became obvious that AFI's brand was completely dependent on the activities that each particular individual engaged in. If they attended a film festival, then AFI was an exhibition organization; if someone knew about their work in saving lost films or publishing the AFI catalog, they might reasonably think of AFI as a champion of film preservation; if they attended one of the technology training classes, they might think of them as cutting-edge digital media educators in Hollywood. Even though each of these descriptions was accurate, these splintered perceptions did not lead to a powerful evolved branding that incorporated the full scope of AFI's activities or paid homage to its original impulse. By studying the confusion that surrounded their brand, AFI was able to eclipse their brand and to renew the essence of their organization. Their new positioning does this very well: "AFI: advancing and preserving the art of the moving image."

The Virus Thought Form

Michael Moon of Gistics has a great term that he uses, called the "virus thought form." The more you open the door to the perspective of others, the more your brand has the potential to evolve effectively. When Canadian novelist Douglas Cooper was introduced to the Web in 1994, he immediately recognized the significance of the medium and made a deal to publish his second novel, *Delirium*, online. The virus that occupied his thoughts went like this: "I saw the Web, and I thought, this is exactly what I am looking for.

The company leader sets the culture of a company, and the culture sets the brand.

HEATHER REISMAN

Because the novel was looking for a medium that had a labyrinthine structure and the Web was already a labyrinth."

To evolve a brand effectively, the new entrepreneur must simultaneously keep the past alive and let it go. They have to both own the brand and give up its ownership at the same time. By blending the myth and reality, present day with the past, they will create an audience that will be dedicated, if not addicted, to their stories. As George Orwell says, "Myths which are believed in tend to become true."

Myths which are believed in tend to become true.

GEORGE ORWELL

Exquisite Silence

Silence for entrepreneurs is no easy concept to grab hold of, but it is an important element of branding. Just as on the tennis courts, the moments in between shots are as important as the shot itself, so the moments of silence, the definition of the spaces in between activities, words, and visuals, are important in branding. The power of exquisite silence is best described in the context of reaction and reflection.

When you are reflecting on your brand in an attempt to evolve it but are not sure what to do, you fall into exquisite silence. When a competitor is trying to make comparisons between your brand and theirs, and you know you are being baited publicly, maintain an exquisite silence until you can recreate your brand with a renewed notion of differentiation, not as a reaction to others' attempts to distract you. When your company is in the midst of change and the pressure is on for the new logo, the new slogan, or the new positioning, and you do not feel that you are there yet, convince your team that exquisite silence followed by accurate and powerful messaging is their best strategy for success.

In the early 1990s, around the same time that we were contemplating getting outside investment for a software company, Molson came out with a new beer called Red Dog, featuring none other than a bulldog as its icon. In Canada, the beer company launched a multimillion-dollar teaser campaign that was based on the image of the bulldog only—no product name or tag line was revealed. Graphic, tenacious, and memorable, it appeared on television and billboards and buses. We had no idea what the campaign was all about, but rather than worry about its proximity to our name and image, we maintained an exquisite silence. In the interim, our clients and industry associates were certain that this was our ad campaign and kept asking us about it. "It's a teaser campaign, right?" "Can't say," we'd answer. Impressed by its scope, they spent a lot of time speculating as to how we could possibly afford such an extensive ad campaign. Our silence added to the mystery. In the meantime, we stayed "top of mind," and their notion of the Bulldog brand was extended. Eight weeks later, the name of the beer was launched, and any confusion about Bulldog the software company and Red Dog the beer was clarified. In the meantime, our silence allowed for a kind of covert branding activity which only added to the notion that, as Paul de Mann says, "Metaphors are much more tenacious than facts."

Beautiful Death is a book of photographs of statuary fragments in European graveyards by a man named David Robinson. When I first leafed through the book, I was acutely aware of how this photographer's perception of graveyard statues left a lasting notion of his brand as a photographer and a storyteller in my mind. It was not only the stark black-and-white photos that stayed with me but the silence that surrounded each image long after I had turned the page. Like this photographer playing with the silence that surrounds his photos, the new entrepreneur carefully chooses their moments of "exquisite silence" and weaves them into their active branding as a means of creating a lasting image in the spaces in between.

Euphoric Propaganda

"That Jack Nicholson, he is one strange-looking guy. I don't know why every girl is crazy about him. If he was pressing pants, no one would pay attention." Recounted with the perfect New York accent, this is just one of the many funny, but often true, insights that my friend's mother has been known to espouse. What is it about Jack Nicholson that people want to be part of? Why does he exude such a magnetic image when others don't? The answer can be found in what I think of as "euphoric propaganda," which has a lot more to do with a notion of non-belonging than anything else. Let me explain.

Moses Znaimer sees branding as a kind of evolutionary propaganda. The original impulse that attracts people to you and your entrepreneurial venture in the beginning is, to a large extent, the desire to find a place where a non-belonger can belong. "You attract all the other oddballs . . . people who feel alienated in the larger existing companies, who ultimately are there because of a variation on the same impulse that got the entrepreneur going in the first place. And it's a powerful influence that can last for a very long time. . . . When I first started calling my on-air promo publicity and advertising 'group propaganda,' everybody was a little horrified, because they interpreted the words negatively. But I was very interested in what moved groups of people, what icons reflected their beliefs. I wanted to create a video personality that people would identify with because I was able to most perfectly articulate their world view, their tastes in music." Mac Cosmetics was born of a need to accommodate a much wider range of skin tones; *Wired* was started by people on the periphery of traditional business.

In all cases, the notion of the non-belonger is crucial to the people and personalities who help the new entrepreneur extend "the original impulse."

Metaphors are much more tenacious than facts.

PAUL DE MAN,
ALLEGORIES OF READING

erroneous branding notions

As in all aspects of entrepreneuring, there are many do's and don'ts that are sure to help you in your pursuit of the creation of a meaningful brand. In my experience, these are the most common erroneous notions about branding that I have encountered.

Excessive storytelling as a means of branding. Storytelling can be overdone. The best description I have ever heard of bad storytelling is by Geoffrey Moore: "Bad stories are stories where fantasy overwhelms reality, and then the only thing that's holding the story in place is the willfulness of the storyteller." Here is the rule of thumb for storytelling as a means of building your brand: Add chapters, and renew and blend reality and fantasy while you're building toward an eclipsed brand, at which time, you will begin a new chapter in your storytelling.

When **we have a product we will need branding.** So often I have heard people from technology start-up companies make excuses to me as they hand me a corner-store copy-center, generic version of a business card. And they usually end with, "Well anyway, until we have our product ready, we don't really need to worry about our brand." *Wrong.* You are already setting yourself up for a negative brand in the absence of anything worth belonging to. In the world of technology, where it is so hard to create a memorable brand around a product that is a list of features and functions, the only thing a new entrepreneur can do is create a branded company. As their product matures, they will be able to bring the best aspects of their brand with them, removing them from the vast wasteland of the anonymous, easy-to-forget names of technology companies with the word media, info, tech, or Web on the masthead. Do not underestimate the power of a brand that lives above and beyond a product, regardless of how great your product is or will be.

Hire a marketing type to figure out what our brand is. In early-day entrepreneuring, no one but the new entrepreneur can own the branding. Handing this job off to someone else, or worse, to a new hire, is a recipe for disaster. Once you have evolved your brand, released your products, and have a semblance of a customer base, you can consider handing off parts of the marketing job to someone else. But do not be fooled into thinking that you can be responsible for active envisioning while handing off your company's branding to someone else. The two go hand in hand in early-day entrepreneuring.

Let's watch the trends for an idea for our branding. If you are watching trends as a means of looking for styles, design, or icons, you will lose out. If you are reading about it, someone else already owns that brand. Be careful not to mistake trend watching for being a master of interpretation. A master of interpretation is someone who can take two or more seemingly unrelated elements and put them together in a way that creates a memorable brand. It is closer to trend setting than it is to trend watching.

It's not whom you know, but what you are able to do with them. Whether on corporate mainstreet, idiosyncratic Hollywood parking lots, or on Silicon Valley turnoffs, it is never just whom you know but what you are able to do with those contacts. Do not mistake networking for building circles of coincidence. One is about collecting business cards, the other is about strategically planning a way to build and extend a brand through an influential campaign called "word of mouth."

Let's only brand ourselves digitally. In the hype that is generated by the WWW, I have seen companies that create incredible images on the Web, but when you finally meet them at a trade show or at a meeting, they have not extended their branding to the analog world. Just because you are digitally connected, it does not follow that you can create a brand by merely surrounding people with digital visuals and icons that represent you and your company. Branding requires commitment at all levels of communication. Create a brand, extend it into your print materials, your office space, your trade show presence, and your personal cachet. Account for digital branding and marketing in your plans, but do not let the digital realm replace the notion of a complete brand identity.

I **am the brand.** Megalomania and entrepreneurship are two notions often seen in one icon, person, or image. There are many examples of megalomaniacs who are also the most successful and glorified entrepreneurs of our modern age. However, there are many more entrepreneurs who have assumed that they have the same level of charisma, luck, and skill that can enable them to mimic these icons of power. And they have suffered the consequences of their own storytelling gone bad. For the majority of us new entrepreneurs, it is better if we do not mistake our image, our persona, for the brand of our company. The new entrepreneur is simply the owner, the director, and the champion of the brand. Yes, the brand has to reflect your beliefs and ideas, but if you are a true new entrepreneur, you already know that your brand will evolve until it eventually eclipses part of your ability, then others will influence the brand and move it out of the realm of "I" and into the notion of "us." Branding is about belonging. If you are the brand, there is no room for others to be part of it.

You are nothing; your knowledge is everything.

PETER DRUCKER,
INC. MAGAZINE

the ecstatic landscape

When I asked Sarah Diamond, the executive producer and artistic director of Television & New Media & Visual Arts at the Banff Centre, what she thought was the most important aspect to consider when searching for a brand in technology, she responded by saying, "Creating an ecstatic landscape for your staff, your customers, your investors, and yourself—a place that people truly want to move toward." She is right. So often, the new entrepreneur takes people to places they do not know about yet, to an existence that is in the making. As such, it is best if it can be a beautiful, even ecstatic landscape when they finally arrive—a place they did not know existed before you provided them with a reason to belong.

chapter 9 The To-do List of Architects and Heroes

the era of knowledge deal makers

In the fourth year of Bulldog's existence, we held our Christmas party at a funky pool hall in downtown Toronto. We served martinis, played pool, danced until 4 a.m., and made sure everyone received taxi chits so that they could make their way home safely. When I looked around the room of more than 100 people, I was struck by the fact that Chris and I were one of only three married couples and one of maybe five people who owned homes. We were two of a handful of people over 30, and the average age at our company was 23. Nobody had children. When I compared notes with other entrepreneurs managing start-up companies in the high-tech field, the statistics were similar.

Attempting to gain insight into how to manage and motivate our employees, I first looked for convenient labels that described the working and living styles of various groups of people. Armed with the knowledge that I was dealing with a group of people called Generation X, I probed deeper, reading, "Self-mockery is the mark of Xer sophistication." "Xers prefer to get their information unembellished." "Generation X actively pursues the deflation of the ideal." This all seemed relatively useful. But I found out, to my chagrin, that I was in the category called trailing baby boomers, characterized as a group of people who were never going to really attain the success of the baby boomers but lacked the confidence of the Generation Xers at their heels. Therefore, I began to look for an alternative mode of analyzing and assessing groups of people, looking for patterns of behavior and characteristics that crossed generational boundaries but had thematic relevance. I am not an expert in psycho-demographic trends, but I have, over the years, been able to boil down the key common elements among the emerging employable. I have added the input from many of my fellow entrepreneurs and intrapreneurs alike who have had experience dealing with people in their twenties and thirties. This is what we have discovered about effective team management and creating a sustainable culture that attracts the right kind of team players.

Whether or not you choose to subscribe to the notion of Generation X, what is true is that we are all living in a world that is built on change, on evolution, and on a sense of insecurity—in our politics, in our technological advances, and in our definition of value, style, and success. What this translates into is a group of people who are used to uncertainty but who are still looking for something to hold onto. They want to find ways to belong somewhere to counteract their feeling of a nomadic existence, they want to believe in something they can feel good about being a part of, and they want to have some level of immediate gratification, because there is no guarantee that tomorrow they will wake up and have the same kinds of opportunities that were available to those generations before them. Hence, the mantra "Life is uncertain, eat dessert first." So what does this leave them with? What are they able to have some control over, and what is transferable, above and beyond the ever-changing landscape?

on knowledge, leverage, and dreams

Peter Drucker pioneered what it means to be an intellectual capitalist, defining this term as someone who puts a price on the knowledge they have accumulated and then finds ways to repackage this knowledge for a world of possible buyers beyond their organization. Drucker points out, "Your knowledge and experience are your new wealth." For any new entrepreneur today, it is essential to recognize that the combination of knowledge and accumulated experience that each and every one of your team members has is the only thing that is wholly their own, and not surprisingly, it is what they value most. And so they should, because it is their ticket to realizing their own dreams. In a world that is uncertain, your knowledge is the only thing that you can be sure to control, to build, to strategize about, and to use as a means of bettering your situation.

When interviewing potential employees, Doug Humphreys is distinctly aware that the interview process is a two-way street. Not only is Doug assessing potential candidates from the sample projects in their portfolio and the kinds of clients that they have worked with, but the candidates are also assessing what kind of leverage they can get within this particular company as a means of getting closer to their dreams. And that leverage is not just about salary. Leverage is about the kinds of projects they get to work on, the kinds of talent they are exposed to within the company, and how close they are to the front edge (or, as some call it, the bleeding edge) of the industry.

In a survey done by Yankelovich Partners, 87 percent of those polled who were in their twenties said they would rather own their own business than

**Life is uncertain.
Eat dessert first.**

J. WALKER SMITH AND
ANN CLURMAN,
ROCKING THE AGES

**Permanence used to
be the quality of greatest
value. Today, people
collect skills and work
experiences with an
emphasis on self-
improvement and self-
advancement, which
means that they no longer
bond permanently with a
single organization.
This also means that
companies get workers
who are more eclectic and
experienced, more focused
on learning than security.**

MARIAN SALZMAN,
DIRECTOR,
BRAND FUTURES GROUP

work for someone else. What does age skew mean to the new entrepreneur? It means a recognition that many of the people on your team today may themselves be aspiring entrepreneurs. They are merely stopping off at your company as a means of helping them leverage what they wholly own—their knowledge—on the road to realizing their own entrepreneurial dreams. As Doug Humphreys says, "The entrepreneur and his staff members are sizing each other up, wondering if their respective dreams map against each other. If they do, you have both gained a leveraged position."

These employees, then, are the Knowledge Deal Makers—leveraging their desire for knowledge with a desire to help you make your dream come true. Some entrepreneurs compare the process of creating high-powered entrepreneurial teams to professional sports, in that if you are going to put the best young talent on your team, you're going to expect to lose some of them, because they are powerful, and they have their own destinies to fulfill. Given this scenario of wandering careerists, of free agents, your job as an entrepreneur is to create a sustainable culture worth belonging to, which will provide the leverage that both you and your talented team players will benefit from. Achieving this is based on an understanding of three basic tenets that are crucial to Knowledge Deal Makers: deal making, communications, and culture. These three tenets may manifest themselves differently as you move through the cycles of your company's growth, but their significance never falters.

the fallacy of the stand-alone vision

In my experience, Knowledge Deal Makers do not buy into "vision" as a stand-alone concept. How many times have I witnessed entrepreneurs stand at the front of a roomful of employees and espouse the new vision of the company while people feigned belief and understanding—or worse, lost interest halfway through the speech? How many times have I mistaken someone's desire to work toward a goal of the company for a more intimate understanding of my vision only to watch them practically fall asleep in their chair? Many times. This is not because these are not dedicated, smart, and engaged team players. Nor is it because they do not believe in the company and where it is going. The real reason is that vision alone is a very difficult thing to try to hand off in large bite-size chunks to anyone who is not in charge of creating it, owning it, and actualizing it. Actively reflecting the vision of a company is your job, not theirs. No matter how badly I want to believe that employees buy into the vision of a company first and foremost, my experience tells me that if they cannot touch it or see it, it is hard for them to be motivated to believe in it. To

Today, knowledge and talent are seen as a stock, not a commodity.

FAST COMPANY MAGAZINE

In a survey done by Yankelovich Partners, 87% of those polled who were in their twenties said they would rather own their own business than work for someone else.

THE WALL STREET JOURNAL

"If you were talking to somebody just starting to grow a company, how high on the list of attributes or philosophical commitments would you put the idea of loyalty between a company and its employees?" Bloomberg: "Number two would be so far down that it would be hard to find."

MICHAEL BLOOMBERG, *INC.* MAGAZINE

establish a sustainable entrepreneurial climate that motivates Knowledge Deal Makers, remember the following.

Alignment Comes from Active Envisioning

Creating a vision statement is an exercise that is much more important to you, the entrepreneur, as a means of helping you define your mission at hand than it will ever be for any of your employees. Your investors will ask for it, various people will probably reprint it incorrectly, and you will sweat over the 32 words that make it up for longer than you can imagine. Write your vision statement and put it away. Instead, learn how to communicate vision in everything you do. Find tangible ways to turn a vision in your mind into something that resonates for your team players in their day-to-day responsibilities. The best example I have heard of this tactic was when *Shift* magazine relaunched their publication. Management took everybody to the country for a long weekend as a means of coming up with ideas about how to design the new office space. Of course, in reality, they were really trying to redefine and reexamine where the company was going, what kind of culture they wanted to foster within the new space, and what were important elements of a place where people wanted to belong. A year later, when the magazine did relaunch, everybody recognized that, months ago in the countryside, they had really been part of an active envisioning exercise. As Jim Collins says, "Building a visionary company requires 1 percent vision and 99 percent alignment." Alignment comes from doing, not saying.

Find a Way to Intersect Your Vision with that of Your Knowledge Deal Makers

Knowledge Deal Makers have their own personal vision of where they want to be one day on the entrepreneurial curve. If you can engage them in understanding how their vision can and will intersect with your vision, you will both move toward a more leveraged position of strength. Finding and nurturing this point of intersection is best done by recognizing the element of deal making in your mode of managing. Knowledge Deal Makers understand the rules of deal making.

Do Not Mistake Your Entrepreneurial Fervor, Passion, and Conviction for the Basis for Creating a Sustainable Business Culture

Do not fool yourself into thinking that vision alone motivates. Recognize that a company's culture is as much about the players who buy into the culture as it is about your ability to translate the beliefs and ideas that suggested a meaningful starting point in the first place.

A recent year-long study of 6,000 managers and executives from 77 companies showed that the most important corporate resource over the next 20 years will be talent: smart, sophisticated businesspeople who are technologically literate, globally astute, and operationally agile.

FAST COMPANY MAGAZINE

the cycles of chaotic growth

I once asked a well-known entrepreneur how she would describe the cycles of growth that her entrepreneurial organization went through. "Well, let's see—when you have six people or less, everyone still washes their own dishes. When you get to 15 people, no one takes responsibility for changing the toilet paper and you start to question whether you need to introduce titles on the business cards. When you get to 35 people, everyone becomes hypersensitive as to why they were not included in a particular meeting. Over 50 people, and you start to wonder who everyone is and who hired them—you look around one day and feel disconnected, and all of a sudden, you begin to wonder who *really* is in charge."

For a long time, I thought about what my friend had said, because, despite the banality of the examples she used, what she described is absolutely reflective of the kinds of changes that do occur in entrepreneurial organizations. I know she is right, both from my own experience and from the experiences of those I have talked to. As I thought back to the cycles Bulldog has gone through, I often wished that I had been able to consult a kind of revitalized Doctor Spock's explanation of the growing pains that an entrepreneur and their company have to go through as it moves from infant to child to adolescent and maybe even to grown-up.

Here is a sketch of the cycles that an entrepreneurial organization spirals through during its inevitable growing pains. With care, these cycles can be used as a means of integrating the elements of the entrepreneurial spirit into a healthy, sustainable culture.

cycle one: the days of rebellious leadership

The Rebellious Leader

If obsession is the ticket of entry for the new entrepreneur, it is not surprising that they also have a sense of rebelliousness in how they choose to pursue their dreams. Geoffrey Moore talks about "an entrepreneurial spirit attached to a very willful ego." Furthermore, he sees the entrepreneur as someone who often needs to go against received opinions of wisdom in order to pursue an opportunity that demands a particular kind of interpretation of the situation. More than that, the entrepreneur has an element of the *enfant terrible* who is constantly wondering, What would happen if . . . ? and then goes on to experiment accordingly. Rebellious leaders are the ones who in the past defied those who said that no one would watch television and ignored those who said that the phone would not be a useful

53% of U.S. workers expect to leave their jobs within five years and 18.2% of industry turnover was reported in software.

INC. MAGAZINE

Today's truly ambitious people see themselves not as entrepreneurs but as "independent professionals."

PETER DRUCKER,
INC. MAGAZINE

In a study conducted by the Boston-based Young Entrepreneurs Network, almost half of the businesses started in 1996 were started by people under 35.

THE WALL STREET JOURNAL

invention. In modern-day terms, it is the entrepreneur who says, "I know this sounds crazy, but this concept is going to fly."

In the world of entrepreneuring, the need to be able to recognize a trend before it happens, to detect a competitor's new strategy with enough time to react to it, and to put together, manage, and motivate a team of high achievers requires the ability to navigate and lead with a certain amount of rebelliousness.

Michael Budman and Don Green, the co-founders of Roots Canada, are masters at branding. But they are also in some ways rebellious leaders. What started as an attempt at acquiring the Canadian franchise rights to the Earth Shoe from Ray Jacobs in New York soon led them to determine that they could do better by designing their own more user-friendly version of the negative heel. Rather than trying to compete with the original Kalso Earth Shoe, which was promoted on "dubious therapeutic claims," Roots promised only tops in quality and comfort. Today that initial calculation that the marketplace was ready to embrace comfort as a style statement has laid the groundwork for building an extensive line of high quality, stylish, and comfortable leather goods, casual clothing, and accessories that has captured the loyalty of millions of buyers in and outside of Canada.

If you're fearsomely part of some collective, you are going to be one of those maybe happier people who find life more comfortable. It's those who find life uncomfortable and need to scratch that itch who actually become entrepreneurs.

MOSES ZNAIMER

Rebels with a Cause

The rebellious leader knows that during the first stages of a start-up organization, the team members will be following your every move. As Knowledge Deal Makers, they are looking for you to make the kinds of decisions that will carve out a new path and help them to survive in a world that has no certainty. They are watching you to help them learn the ropes so that when they strike out on their own, they will have the know-how to make the same bold decisions. Implicit in this relationship is an acknowledged symbiosis—the entrepreneur will take these Knowledge Deal Makers to places they could not get to otherwise, and, in return, they will work with the rebel to validate the rebel's cause, to create a place that has value and staying power. In the end, this creates a place of belonging for those who built it and for those who follow in their footsteps.

Keith Kocho of Digital Renaissance was told time and time again that he should not manage both a digital media service organization and a product-development group focused on creating Web television products, because investors tend to be wary of the service/product combination. And yet he was able to find investors who believed in his ability to grow this combined business model successfully. They recognized his cause—to grow his entrepreneurial organization based on his interpretation of the marketplace—and, in a sense, signed up for his rebellious leadership.

Katrina Garnett puts a copy of the company business plan on the desk of every new employee to ensure that they know exactly where the company is heading. Though more traditional thinking suggests that the company's financial and business plans are for management only, Katrina's leadership reflects her notion of trust between herself, the entrepreneur, and her team members.

Just as the element of moving along the risk curve was balanced by the three angels of advantage, rebellious leadership is offset by a well-defined belief system (as outlined in Chapter 8), which maintains honesty and values at its core to ensure that your interpretation of "whatever it takes" does not cross the integrity line.

Making History

In the beginning, when you are struggling with your notion of what your company is going to be and you have little material to work with in terms of active envisioning, then you must focus on becoming a master of interpretation. Digital Renaissance has been helping corporate, telecom and entertainment clients extend their stories by developing content and enabling technologies to transact, educate, entertain and inform across multiple media.

Regardless of what you are interpreting in the marketplace, it is your ability to take these ideas and begin to articulate them in a manner that attracts and aligns a group of talented team members that will build your company. In the first cycle of chaos, finding ways to align your interpretation of market trends with the desires and wishes of your team members is all the vision they will want and need. You build from there.

Tradition without a history

In the early days of an entrepreneurial organization, the one thing you do not have is a history, and the thing you need to begin to create as soon as possible is your own private set of traditions. Sound traditions serve as the basis of a good corporate culture, which creates a place that people want to belong to. Doug Humphreys has a huge open space on the ground floor of his loft-like office, where there are couches, a kitchen, and a fabulous pool table. At any time during the day, you will find programmers and producers and art directors in heated snooker competitions. Snooker is a tradition, and it is very much a part of who they are. You may also find them all still working at 11 p.m. at night to meet a deadline for the next day. At Narrowline, a leading transaction and media research company, on the day before Christmas, they hold Pyjama Day. At first, everyone balked at this corny idea. But eventually, it became a tradition that no one wanted to miss.

Creating and maintaining a corporate culture begins with taking the time to come up with ideas and committing to maintaining their importance as part of the creation myth of who you are, how you began, and who you are on the road to becoming.

Passion, emotion, and conviction are essential parts of the vivid description. Some managers are uncomfortable expressing emotion about their dreams, but that's what motivates others.

JIM COLLINS,
HARVARD BUSINESS
REVIEW

All human knowledge takes the form of interpretation.

WALTER BENJAMIN

Look for Low Cost, High Involvement

Every year, MondoMedia, a computer-generated game design and anima-tion studio, holds a picnic in the middle of the week for the entire staff. They all bring food and play Frisbee and baseball, rent paddleboats, and go swimming off the island on Lake Chabot. The fact that they are out in the sunshine together playing like kids, rather than working inside on a Wednesday afternoon, is not lost on anyone.

In Bulldog's second year of business, we decided to hold a contest for all the designers, asking them to create the wackiest design they could think of using the bulldog as an icon. When all was said and done, we took these visuals and created a little desktop calendar that was packaged in a computer hard disk case and gave it to all of our clients for Christmas. Each year, we create a new version of a Christmas card or gift that is a takeoff on the bull-dog, created by all of our designers. This has become a tradition loved by customers and staff alike.

All of these things are examples of relatively low-cost, high-involvement activities that can help give your team a greater sense of belonging. This is the history of your company in the making. Once you get the ideas or activ-ities started, be sure to let the staff take over the organizing of these activi-ties, and they'll be more likely to buy in and participate enthusiastically.

Show the Immediacy of Your Actions

At Spray, the extra oomph that their company's brand gained from the publication *Darling* actually began as a lark, when a few of the staff members wrote a column in their internal newsletter about dating, sex, drugs, and rock 'n' roll. Over time, this column soon became a part of the company's communications program and something that the staff looked forward to. When one of the staff members suggested that they try to turn this into a publication, their chairman Jonas Svensson responded immedi-ately. He gave them a mandate to explore the possibilities of creating a magazine, the costs, the format, and the human resources required, as well as an understanding of the market potential for this kind of publication. By putting the onus on those staff members with the most investment in this column, he showed an immediate response to their request, took the required action, and then handed off the responsibility to a few staff members who had a desire to see this idea come to fruition. In the end, this email column became the basis for the magazine called *Darling*, which has a healthy circulation of and is wholly managed by the staff members who originally came up with the idea. That is definitely a great way to segue from creating a tradition to having a history.

Well, let's see—when you have six people or less, everyone still washes their own dishes. When you get to 15 people, no one takes responsibility for changing the toilet paper, and you start to question whether you need to introduce titles on the business cards. When you get to 35 people, everyone becomes hypersensitive as to why they were not included in a particular meeting. Over 50 people, and you start to wonder who everyone is and who hired them— you look around one day and feel disconnected, and all of a sudden, you begin to wonder who *really* is in charge.

AN ENTREPRENEUR

The Submarine Environment

There is a lot of talk today about the nomadic approach to career building. Kids right out of school are moving from city to city, trying to build their career paths not only in terms of money and opportunity but, I believe, in a search for a place to belong. The lack of community in today's culture, the decreasing sense of connections to one's immediate family, either geographically or otherwise, creates a large hole in the lives of the young up-and-coming generations. And here is another reason for an entrepreneurial organization to create a history and a place where people can feel that they belong.

Especially in the early days of your company, there is a real sense of community among the whole team as you struggle to carve out a niche, to establish a track record as you build your revenue line. The camaraderie of struggle and the intimacy of all-nighters and weekend workdays are attractive and somewhat addictive. My associate David Leventhal refers to this early stage of the entrepreneurial organization as the "submarine environment," which he accurately describes as follows: "The scene is probably repeated in start-up companies all over the world: in this case, it is a Web design company. There is a 20-square-foot room in which far too many people are crammed in, practically on top of each other. The phone rings, and the boyfriend of the programmer answers the phone, posing as the receptionist. He passes it on to the salesperson, indicating that *this* is the call the whole team has been waiting for all day. While the sales guy is on the phone with the much sought-after customer, he is already scribbling a note to the designer who shares a desk with him, telling her to stop working on whatever she is currently working on, because it looks as if the client is going to agree to a contract and will need some immediate visual concepts by tomorrow. The programmer is giving hand signals to the sales guy about the changes he made since the client last saw the job. It is too hot in the room. But as far as they are concerned, they are one big engaged family in their self-made submarine, headed in the right direction.

As cozy as this submarine family environment sounds, at some point, euphoria begins to wane and, like all families, the elements of dysfunction begin to seep in. These elements come in many shapes and sizes, from a lack of communication to confusion as to who has the final say on a project, to an inability to reconcile personalities who cannot see eye to eye but who, for better or for worse, are both a part of the family.

How does the leader resolve these family squabbles? Ironically, by divesting the office of the notion of family as soon as possible. It sounds harsh, but it is a lot easier to fix a dysfunctional company than it is a dysfunctional family, and in the end, you are running a business, not serving as the head of a household. As Doug Humphreys of Skyrocket says, "It is a lot easier to be candid with criticism, to be able to negotiate employment deals, and to be able to direct human resources when you are friendly but not friends

It's not that any of us actually knows what's going to happen in the future. It's that some of us are allowing for certain eventualities that could happen and some of us are not. The more of these eventualities that you can allow for in your strategy, the more likely you are to be successful.

DOUG HUMPHREYS

Culture is what people fall back on when there are no instructions. It gives you rules for when there are no rules. It provides a common language for moving forward.

FAST COMPANY MAGAZINE

with those who work for you." I agree. In fact, I would go a step further and say that your staff, although they want to be friendly with you, are actually more comfortable with a relationship that is well defined and has a built-in space between you.

The family culture is particularly difficult to resist when the founders of the company are married. And not everyone chooses to resist it. John Evershed of MondoMedia *does* consider his business a family business. He believes that the people who work for him and his co-founder and wife, Deirdre O'Malley, are attracted to a place that has a sense of family, that cares about its employees as a family would care about its various members. MondoMedia has found a way to balance the notion of a family business with the reality of generating revenue and a growing animation business. They have done so by finding the kind of Knowledge Deal Makers whose dreams complement those of its founders. Likewise, Andrea and Jim Southcott, who are the managing directors of Bryan, Fulton and Shee, one of the largest advertising agencies in western Canada, are very specific about the kind of family culture they have fostered. "The world is tough out there—you have to struggle with customers and suppliers in selling your advertising concepts. You are often shot down, and you can feel bruised and war weary. We think it is really important to build a family-like feeling at the office, a place that is safe and comfortable for the troops when they come home."

Of course, the beauty of entrepreneuring is that the level of "family" you want to hold onto as you grow is entirely your own choice. As a rebellious leader, it is your prerogative to determine that there is no right or wrong amount of family ties within your entrepreneurial organization.

My rules of thumb: I never hire friends, my partner and I have always used different last names, and we never refer to our company as a family business. I take Doug Humphreys's advice and am friendly but not friends with those who work for me. I also remind myself that although employees may want to belong to a community, to a family, to a place, they are often coming to you, the entrepreneur, because you have given them respect for being the Knowledge Deal Makers that they are. In return, you are agreeing to create a business environment for them that has a sustainable sense of belonging built on what they can and will contribute, not based on the notion that they are a member of your family. This is an important distinction.

Creating Ambassadors in Your Organization

Communications is a major issue for entrepreneurs and non-entrepreneurs alike. To run a company effectively, leaders need to understand people's communication needs, to be good listeners and communicators, and to keep their customers happy. But there is a very specific qualifier on the type of communication required in the first "cycle of chaos" that the entrepreneur

All companies are highly dysfunctional families. You just have to find the one that matches your sensibilities.

TARA LEMMEY, FOUNDER, NARROWLINE

A new Statistics Canada study of 3,000 Canadian firms finds that faster-growing companies are almost twice as likely to innovate as slower-growing firms.

INSTITUTE FOR ENTREPRENEURSHIP, INNOVATION AND GROWTH

faces when starting up a company. This idea was best captured by a concept that I heard about at a conference called Seek in San Francisco. In discussing the elements for creating a sustainable business environment, the emcee introduced the notion of "esergy rates." The term esergy rate refers to the rate of information flowing between individuals within a company. For example, people who work on constructing a bridge need to have an esergy rate that is both high and broad in terms of the kind of information that must be passed between team members to complete their project successfully, whereas those who are tracking packages in a courier company require an esergy rate that is high but much narrower. The esergy rates of the employees you hire in the early days of your business, regardless of their function within the organization, is very high. Why? Because as the company grows, they will become your ambassadors, carrying information about the company history, traditions, quirks, rules or lack thereof, vision, and processes on to others. You will especially need to depend on the initial staff members to pass on information to the newer members of the company, because although you will make every effort to continue to have one-on-one relationships with everyone in the company, inevitably, you will have to begin relying on others to help you do this.

In my mind, there are three great ways to ensure that you are determining the esergy rate required to run your company successfully.

Opt for one-on-one meetings versus company-wide discussions. When a group of people meets, no matter how intimately they work together, something eventually happens in the chemistry of the room and everyone's brain shuts down. I have witnessed this both as an employee at other companies and firsthand in my own company. One-on-one meetings are a lot more productive. Why? Because all the participants participate, and you get an unabridged version of everyone's opinions that you can later piece together. Jonas Svensson of Spray tries to keep the communication flowing in his organization by having a half-hour chat with a different employee every week. This is his informal way of staying on top of the information that may or may not be flowing throughout his organization. Although one-on-one meetings are time-consuming and not always a viable option, try to engage in as many as possible as a means of gauging the flow of information within the company as a whole.

Give your team a forum for communications. During a period of particularly high growth, the staff at a digital news magazine were often heard saying, "Nobody tells me what's going on around here." To counter-act the feeling of being left out, the staff started a tradition whereby one interesting quotation by an employee was circulated to the rest of the staff weekly. Each quotation had something to do with the experience of

Culture is the only sustainable advantage—everything else can be copied.

HEATHER REISMAN

I look for four qualities from employees: initiative, integrity, cooperativeness, and talent.

DEIRDRE O'MALLEY,
DIRECTOR OF MARKETING,
MONDOMEDIA

coming into the company or of grappling with the transitions in structure. It became a way for employees to share their understanding of the changes going on around them. What started out as a quotation soon turned into an employee newsletter called "Page of the Future." At different points, there were attempts to kill the newsletter or to make it more formal by asking some of the executives to contribute to it. But these ideas were so vehemently opposed that eventually they were nixed.

Especially when you are in the beginning stages of the company, when you have high growth rates and/or during transition periods (which are happening all the time in an entrepreneurial organization), it is important to provide a forum for your team members to communicate among themselves. Venting concerns, talking about ideas, and having a regular vehicle for communication owned by the staff is a good way to maintain levels of energy.

Remember when you worked for an entrepreneur. When you are running your own show, periodically take yourself back to a time when you were working for an entrepreneur and remember what you liked and did not like about the experience. When I thought long and hard about it, I found that when the information was flowing between the leaders of the company and me, I felt part of a process. At the same time, when I was given too much information without enough direction, I became slightly overwhelmed by the job I was supposed to accomplish within the given scenario. As an entrepreneur, experiment with esergy levels. In doing so, you will understand how much information, what kind of information, and what mode of communication works best for the individual members of your team.

the trouble with unrules

In *The 500 Year Delta*, the term *unrules* refers to "a form of corporate discipline built on the premise that in a chaos world, the company with the fewest rules wins." It seems that every entrepreneur originally decides that they want to have a flat organization with very few rules. In the beginning when you are still a small nuclear family, this provides sufficient structure. But at some point, you look around and realize that even if you are comfortable with a loose reporting structure, as you get bigger in size, others are confused by this notion of authority. Likewise, the philosophy of unrules worked when you had contact with everyone in your company on a daily or weekly basis. But as you move into a company that is larger than a handful of people, you discover, as did Keith Kocho of Digital Renaissance, that "at the root of most people, there's a desire for some aspect of nondisclosure, and they want guidance. They don't always want to participate but want you to make decisions for them."

Pat Kelly, the CEO of PSS World Medical, is committed to "stoking the campfire."

FAST COMPANY MAGAZINE

John Chambers, the CEO of Cisco Systems, holds company picnics and birthday breakfasts, but he is also sure that employees have 1.7 million pages of information on their intranet site. He keeps the information flowing.

FAST COMPANY MAGAZINE

Some unrules will always stay in place, because they work better than other, more conservative structures. Many companies do not care what hours employees keep as long as they get the job done. Others have done away with a dress code as long as it does not offend customers. But there are two signs that indicate when it is time to begin thinking of moving from unrules to rules, of introducing more formalized processes into the organization.

Intelligent disobedience. In terms of *The 500 Year Delta*, intelligent disobedience is "what Seeing Eye dogs are taught—essentially, that they are to obey unless they have a better idea." In my experience, intelligent disobedience begins when employees are suddenly questioning everything you and the company do and ask them to do, but do not necessarily have a better idea in mind. When you start to hear team members asking "How come?" without following this up with "and I recommend," it is probably time for you to begin creating a process that will clearly identify the rules of conduct for your team members.

Fascination with titles. There comes a time in every company when the title on people's business cards suddenly becomes extremely important to them. This is often a sign that people are looking for ways to differentiate each other in terms of ability, seniority, and their responsibility to make decisions about money and resources. Consider the fact that your company is made up of many kinds of Knowledge Deal Makers. On the day that titles become an issue, you may need to delineate roles based on the different core competencies within your team.

Some Rules to Help the Rebellious Leader in the Early Days

Ask for collective thinking, and you will build an intelligent organization. When we were in the multimedia design business, we would often refuse to get involved in the creative process until the account managers, the designers, and programmers had already hashed it out and come up with their own collective solution. Although this way of working often took longer and there were more bruised egos along the way, it ultimately fostered a sense of responsibility within the team that was not dependent on our input. In the end, we built stronger teams that were committed to making *their* ideas work. If you step into the process of collective thinking too often, then your staff will begin relying on you to guide them through the decision-making process. Charles Handy suggests that "intelligent organizations have to be run by persuasion and by consent. It is hard work, and frustrating, particularly when the persuasion does not work and the consent is not forthcoming." But if you focus on fostering

If only people weren't so human!

AN ENTREPRENEUR

Fault tolerance: the capacity of any organization to tolerate calamitous events. Fault tolerance increases in direct relation to an organization's ability to say "thank you" and "I'm sorry."

JIM TAYLOR AND
WATTS WACKER,
THE 500 YEAR DELTA

collective thinking in the earliest stages of your growth, then you are creating an intelligent organization that will be able to handle changes better in future cycles of growth.

Rebels make mistakes, too. An entrepreneur I know who runs a new media company in Connecticut gave me some interesting insights into how to handle the mistakes one makes in running a business. Although his company was doing very well, one month, due to a few customer cancellations, this entrepreneur found himself unable to meet payroll for the upcoming month. After much debate with his management staff, they decided to talk to the team and explain the situation. "I began the meeting by saying that I had made a mistake. I reminded them that I did not make many mistakes and that I had steered them right for many years, but that this month, I had miscalculated our customer billings and was concerned about making payroll. I offered to give a double bonus the following month to anyone who was willing to hold off getting their paycheck for three weeks. The result was amazing. Ninety-five percent of the staff agreed to the bonus plan, and a number of my staff members told me later how refreshing it was that I was totally honest and admitted to making mistakes." Rebels make mistakes. Tell your staff that, but also show them how you can work to turn mistakes into an opportunity. And, just like them, you cannot always guarantee success. It will keep their expectations of you as a leader within the realm of reality. It will also remind you to give your team members permission to fail occasionally. These values will be added to the history of your company in the making.

Our special tree fort. When I asked Deirdre O'Malley how she would describe her company's culture, she said, "Well, remember when you were a kid and you had a tree fort? You would find bits of wood out on the street, in the back of the house, and drag them into the fort. Because everyone contributed to the tree fort, everyone felt they owned a little piece of it, and everytime someone brought something new in, it added to the excitement of the place. It is the same with our company culture. Everyone brings things in from the world around them—games, ideas, toys, posters, comics, and most of all, their creativity—adding them to our office. In the end, this tree fort belongs to everyone." When I heard this description, it reminded me how often we forget that people are so affected by their surroundings and their input into the territory they work in. When Spray opened its satellite office in Helsinki, the four young guys who went to work there wanted to create a truly unique space. Together they worked on the weekends to build a circular fish tank in the boardroom, breaking down one wall to replace it with a spherical tank that was contained within the wall itself. I have seen this office, and it is whimsical and well designed, truly reflecting the spirit of those who work there—a unique Finnish tree house.

We try to maintain a culture that gives permission to fail.

ANDREA SOUTHCOTT, MANAGING DIRECTOR OF BRYAN, FULTON AND SHEE

The new entrepreneur creates a place that has magic or a whimsical element to it and allows their team members to make it their own. As Geoffrey Moore says, "I think there is a real connection between fun and entrepreneurial success. It's not just important that the entrepreneur have fun but that their customers, partners, and employees have *more* fun. That translates into better quality of service and product and more imaginative strategies that become hard to replicate." Whether it is a pool table in the lobby or a fish tank in the boardroom, let your employees build a tree fort and let everyone have a bit of fun. You will get a lot more work done along the way.

cycle two: the adolescent years

When I think about moving from the initial cycle of start-up chaos to the second cycle of growth, I think about the day my dad taught me to ride a bike. As an entrepreneur, you will know that you are in the second cycle of growth when one day, after many days of holding onto the bicycle seat and running alongside your team, you realize that you are simply standing there applauding and your team is off riding the bike on their own. It is a delirious feeling and a milestone well worth celebrating. The president of a large advertising agency in Europe described that moment to me beautifully. He knew it had come when he was sitting in one of his company's most important client presentations and realized that all he had done was make the introductions at the start of the meeting. From then on, it was his team that presented the ideas for the new campaign and answered questions about the market research they had conducted. In the end, it was his team that won the job.

For us at Bulldog, the second cycle of growth, or what I refer to as our "adolescent years," occurred in conjunction with our eclipsed brand— moving from service to product. In the process, we experienced the pains of adolescent self-doubt and the inevitable identity crisis that is simply a part of moving on and growing up. Here is what I have learned about the syndromes that occur within this cycle and the elements that help you mature through it.

the truth about endotruths

The 500 Year Delta describes endotruths as follows: "Endotruths usually begin with the nature of the founder of the organization, and they explain why two companies in the same business often have startlingly different corporate cultures." In my experience, when we began to eclipse the Bulldog brand by beginning to invest heavily in creating a software product, I found

Strive for perfection; settle for excellence.

DON SHULA,
FORMER COACH OF THE
MIAMI DOLPHINS

I create spaces and places for people to soar within. That is an art and the job of a leader.

JOY MOUNTFORD,
INTERVAL RESEARCH
CORPORATION

a different meaning to the word endotruth: that it was possible for two people within the *same* company to have startlingly different corporate cultures. In maintaining two completely different businesses, we unwittingly created a chasm between the creative side of the company (the multimedia design studio) and the engineering side of the company (the R&D lab working on media asset management models).

Other entrepreneurs I talk to tell me that this kind of great divide is very common; nevertheless, it is not a problem that should be taken lightly. As we struggled to maintain the multimedia design company while investing our attention and money in product development, we inadvertently created a world of mistrust and jealousies. We temporarily forgot to monitor our esergy levels. Along the way, we alienated people who meant a lot to us. We wasted a lot of time later on trying to repair our corporate culture, but we learned some important lessons about moving from the infant stage to the adolescent stage of entrepreneurship.

On Vision: "I Ask You Only for a Notion of Respect for the Future"

When you choose to shift your company's focus in any way, as a new entrepreneur you can see the future so clearly that you forget that those working behind you do not have the same view. To me and my partners, it was so clear that the path toward software development would require a shift away from customized applications. We did have an inkling that we might eventually have to give up our multimedia design business if we could not sustain both businesses at once. But we did not communicate this idea clearly enough to our staff.

We finally found a means for establishing clear communication when we asked our team to simply have "respect for the future." By talking in these terms, we were able to do two things: We reminded the staff that we had a proven track record of our ability to interpret the signs and trends that would lead the company to a worthwhile future for the whole team. Second, we were able to inject the notion of the unknown into the future of the company. We reminded our staff that there is always an element of risk in an entrepreneurial company, always an element of the unknown. We were simply asking that they respect *our* vision of the future based on our leadership in the past. "Respect the future" is a great way to align everyone's vision when the company is going through a transition. But asking people to trust in this promise only works for so long. At some point, you need to actively re-envision the company to them and move toward those goals.

Vision in the Context of Projects

Doug Humphreys talked to me about how he changed the direction of his company from one of 2-D design to one of 3-D design to one of interactive

Endotruths usually begin with the nature of the founder of the organization, and they explain why two companies in the same business often have startlingly different corporate cultures.

JIM TAYLOR AND WATTS WACKER, *THE 500 YEAR DELTA*

design and, finally, to a company that specialized in technology assessment, training, and consultation. Although the nature of the work was changing, he was able at each stage to maintain a strong vision of each of the companies in the context of the projects that were brought on. The owners of MondoMedia, Digital Renaissance, and hundreds of other entrepreneurial organizations going through change have also described this process. As soon as possible, move from the notion of "respect for the future" to one of specific articulation of your active envisioning through the projects you are bringing on.

The Notion of Nietzsche

"From all the management gurus in the world, the best advice I ever took was from Nietzsche, of all things:'If you give people a why, they will endure any how.'"This philosophy is what helped Evan Solomon as he moved from the first stage of his company into the second stage. "We couldn't understand it. We started out with this magazine that gave meaning to people. We had people working 12 and 15 hours a day in a small cramped office, but no one complained. In fact, we couldn't keep them out of there. And then, suddenly, we started to make money, we had a new office space, computers, new desks, and everyone was complaining: This desk is too small for me, how come he gets a better chair than I do, I need more space. We realized that the company had attained a certain vision that had run away without us. We hadn't pushed the vision further ahead, so in a sense, the team had reached its own ceiling. Once there, they began to question everything. Somehow, along the way, we had forgotten to give these people a why, and without a redefined why there is no forgiving of the haves and have-nots."

Always inject a "why" when you are asking someone to do what they are doing, and they will find the best way, the "how," to do it.

Humanity and a Little Awe

The other day, I was struck by a headline I read in one of the quarterly magazines of Teaching Tolerance, a volunteer organization focused on encouraging tolerance among the various races in America. "The Teacher should encounter the child—every child—with humanity and a little awe." The same holds true for your team members. When you yourself are going through a redefining of your company's future, remember that your staff members are in need of more attention and encouragement than ever before. Many entrepreneurs look around on any given day and see 20 things that could be done better, and sometimes they make the mistake of focusing only on what is not working. Often you can more effectively manage and motivate your Knowledge Deal Makers by supporting the things that *are* done well. These people have come to you because of who you are and what you represent, and, in return, you need to encounter them with

From all the management gurus in the world, the best advice I ever took was from Friedrich Nietzsche: "if you give people a why, they will endure any how."

EVAN SOLOMON,
CO-FOUNDER,
SHIFT MAGAZINE

The teacher should encounter the child—every child—with humanity and a little awe.

TEACHING TOLERANCE

humanity and awe. You chose these individuals because of the talents they have and the skill sets they bring to round out your vision. They deserve your respect.

Never Fall in Love

Ask any employer what is the hardest part of the job, and they will tell you it is letting people go. With change comes more change. As you begin to articulate your company's redefined vision, through projects, through new customers, and through practice, you will begin to reevaluate your team members with a more critical eye. This is not an easy thing to do. The staff member who was the first to join the company might no longer be crucial to your operation. If you have found a way to evolve from a family to a company, it will be a lot easier to determine objectively whether these individuals can be retrained within another area of the company or if you will ultimately have to let them go. But do not assume that your ability to make sound business decisions will make up for the raw human emotions that are part of the package. Aside from your feelings of guilt or compassion, you will also find yourself getting nostalgic at such times, reminiscing about a time when your company was smaller and things were easier. The biggest danger for entrepreneurs during this cycle of growth is the notion of falling in love with who they used to be, with the kind of work they used to do, and, by definition, with the people who support an old notion of the company they have created.

For example, if Doug Humphreys had allowed himself to fall in love with the 2-D side of the design business, he may not have seen the potential of 3-D design. That was the vision that led him to create the digital design, consulting, and training opportunities that are now the core of his business. The new entrepreneur should avoid nostalgia. Falling in love with a part of your company will only deter you from making the business decisions that will define how your company moves forward. Falling in love with the people who support a notion of your company that it has outgrown will restrict it from maturing as a business.

As always, this is a two-way street. If you resist falling in love with past notions of who you were, you will be able to provide direction and assistance to your employees so that they too can determine what is best for *their* career paths. In many cases, leaving your company will allow them to mature faster than if they had remained with you, forcing themselves to proceed in a direction they are no longer cut out for. As Rob Ryan says to his students at Entrepreneur America, "Sometimes chasing someone out is as valuable as keeping them in."

Sometimes chasing someone out is as valuable as keeping them in.

ROB RYAN,
FOUNDER AND PRINCIPAL,
ENTREPRENEUR AMERICA

Three Exercises to Help You Through

Bi-directional spies. One great way to reduce jealousies among staff members and to imbue a sense of respect and shared culture between team members is to have a job-sharing exercise. Have a programmer sit in on a sales presentation and recognize how tough it is to sell a concept to a client. Have a multimedia designer spend a day with an account manager. It is a great way to introduce humanity and a little awe all the way through your organization.

Saying no will cost you. When we at Bulldog began working on projects that involved both the engineering and the multimedia design teams, we found that meetings were becoming a forum for one-upmanship. It sounds cruel, but it happens all the time in meeting rooms and companies around the world. To counteract this, we introduced a rule: Every time you begin your sentence with "no," you pay $1 to the kitty. At the end of a month, we took the money and bought beer or chocolate and took a few minutes to enjoy the fruits of our negative notions. Very quickly, the cost of "no" became too high and the desire to say "yes" increased dramatically. Try it.

"The smallest moment of inattention turns out to be the most disastrous—is that a universal truth?" I have found this quote to be a universal truth in managing people. Do not underestimate the importance of small details, especially as the company grows. As Evan Solomon found, the size of desks, the size of windows, are partly an indication of the lack of "why" that the entrepreneur must reignite for his team. But they are also part of the reality of what happens in groups of people when they get together. My advice? Focus on the why, redefine your vision through active envisioning; but while you are doing that, do not ignore the small moments in between—the skirmish over who gets what office, the expense accounts of one team member that far outweigh another, the halogen lighting in both the women's *and* the men's rest rooms. In doing so, you will avoid a series of meaningless crises that are simply a symptom of a company in the midst of the second cycle of chaos. These times of change bring an irrationality of adolescence that cannot be ignored.

from flat organization to "almost" vertical?

It wasn't until we began to work in the software business that customers first began to really challenge me about the nondescript title on my business card: "What does the title 'partner' actually mean?" Well, it didn't mean anything. In fact, it was an attempt to stay away from hierarchy and maintain a notion of a flat organization at Bulldog. In Cycle One, during the early days, the flat organization worked for us. Being a partner meant that I could move between sales and management and marketing and operations,

I try and talk to everybody every day. I try to know a little more about them. And with this knowledge, my admiration for them grows.

DEIRDRE O'MALLEY

A well-known theater producer once said, "My job is mostly about the act of nurturing talent."

as required. But as we grew in size and as we increased the breadth of our offering from multimedia service to consulting and product development, the pressure to create levels within the company and titles that reflected our responsibilities increased. And I do not think it is necessarily a bad thing.

While it is true that a more hierarchical organization is in danger of introducing bureaucracies, it also has its advantages for two reasons: It helps the new entrepreneur establish where they should be spending their time doing what they are best at; and it helps them to determine what skill sets are missing in their task of leading their company through growth. Though it takes time and commitment to effectively cajole the organization's culture away from one of open (family-like) consensus, in the end, the new structure creates a sleeker, more effective business environment, where people spend less energy trying to figure out where they fit in. When you map out a path that matches people's complementary skill sets and identifies lines of decision making within your company, you can spend more time and energy on the business itself. So, like many flat, non-hierarchical companies before us, we at Bulldog arrived at the day when we had to sit down and begin sketching out an organizational chart. In the process, here are some crucial things that I learned about building relatively productive hierarchies.

The collective brainpower of your company can be allocated among three basic baskets of intellectual assets: human capital, codified knowledge, and customer capital.

FORTUNE MAGAZINE

the management team (or, your knowledge brokers)

Jim Collins suggests that articulating a company's vision begins with identifying the core values of an organization. To do this, he recommends the creation of what he calls the Mars Group. Here is how it works: "Imagine that you've been asked to re-create the very best attributes of your organization on another planet but you have seats on the rocket ship for only five to seven people. Who should you send? Most likely, you'll choose the people who have a gut-level understanding of your core values, the highest level of credibility with their peers, and the highest levels of competence."

This same criteria is a good starting point for choosing your management team members. As you grow as an organization and as you mature as an entrepreneur, a few things inevitably happen: You will begin to see where your weaknesses are, and you will realize that active envisioning requires participation. You will want to extend yourself through a team of people you trust and respect. As you begin to recognize where your default ends and someone else's skill set begins, you will want to add to your abilities through what I call "a well art-directed management team." A well art-directed team is similar to a great set design. If you take the pieces apart, you will find that it is made up of unique individual elements that stand out on their own. But when you put them together and art-direct them into place, they create a powerful image.

Similarly, a well art-directed team creates a much more potent version of a vision in the making. As Evan Solomon discovered, "I realized early on that I am not a numbers guy. I understand accounting, but I don't like it, and by constantly focusing on it, it was taking away from what I could truly contribute to the company. Entrepreneurs are often dishonest and convince themselves that they can perform every element of building their vision better than anyone else can. The sooner you recognize your weaknesses and find complementary skill sets to actualize your goals, the faster your company will help you reach them."

I have always said that behind every great entrepreneur is an even better management team. In a world of Knowledge Deal Makers, you should be most concerned with finding what I call Knowledge Brokers to make up your team. These are the people who will be closest to understanding your active envisioning as you move to define your company and who will be the most adept at actualizing your goals in areas where you are not as skilled or that you recognize are taking you away from your core competency. Here are a few rules of thumb:

The role of the organizational chart. Once the partners or leaders have all tracked *their* strengths and weaknesses, then you are ready to look for the management team members to fill in the missing pieces. Make sure that you have mapped out where these individuals sit within your organizational chart so that there is a good balance of representation from across the company and a sound basis for growth as the company matures. The most important part of creating an organizational chart is not only that you delegate responsibility effectively but that you build in a plan for ongoing, incremental changes that matches your projected growth cycles.

Know your team members. Wherever possible, try to build a management team out of people who have been with you for a while, people you have built a rapport with. Ease of communication and comfort levels are important in building a strong core team. Particularly when you are in a high-growth stage and will need to be communicating to new employees who have no history with you, you will need to rely on your Knowledge Brokers for communication out into the company at large.

Do not distance yourself from the rest of the company. Never stop walking the halls. As with all your entrepreneurial challenges, building a management team does not come without its own paradoxical quirks. While you are working toward a company that is efficient and effectively run through a delegated management team, you are also in danger of losing your perspective if you constantly rely on your management team for all incoming information. Yes, they are your Knowledge Brokers, but you need to maintain a firsthand understanding of how the rest of the company is

As you begin to recognize where your default ends and someone else's skill set begins, you will want to add to your abilities through what I call "a well art-directed management team."

I have always said that behind every great entrepreneur is an even better management team.

reacting to your direction, particularly when you are making the transition from a flat organization to one that is more hierarchical.

Never stop walking the halls.

Ensure that you own the agenda for the management team. The role of the management team is to continuously align the strategic direction of the company with tactical spin-off. It is not an operations committee. Its meetings are not the place for project updates. Ensure that you take charge of the agenda of each meeting and delegate to a subcommittee those specific issues that are not directly related to strategic alignment of the company. For example, the management team can make a decision as to how to structure the salary scale once the director of finance presents all the required cash-flow projections and pro forma for the upcoming year. But once this scale is set and everyone votes on it, a subcommittee should be set up for dealing with one-on-one issues that are outside the usual. Do not let your management meetings turn into detailed meetings. Always write up management team meeting notes. I suggest that you need majority votes on all major items and that the chairperson of the team (usually yourself) has executive overrule, to be used in exceptional cases only.

Let your management team members present to the board. Many entrepreneurs buffer the management team from the board. The best way to build and foster a strong management team environment is to invite the various members of your team, together with you, to present their reports on particular issues directly to the board. Let the VP of sales present and defend his sales figures for the quarter. Let your CTO provide an overview of the change-in-product development schedules directly. Not only does this approach foster team spirit and allow others to see how the board operates firsthand, but it also helps to create a team that can function without your input at the most senior levels.

Remind team members that they are Knowledge Brokers. Aside from the individual responsibilities each management team member has within the company, ensure that they are also fulfilling their responsibility as conduit between you, the board, and the rest of the company. The first time our director of finance did not have the detailed notes to accompany his revised pro forma ready for the management team, it was not the partners who were most concerned but the other members of the management team. When the head of sales did not receive buy-in from the management team on his first proposed bonus structure for the sales team, he made sure that the next time he would meet with each of the individual members of the team ahead of time and get their input before re-presenting to the management team.

Knowledge Brokers need to have a good rapport with their staff members and to be able to effectively communicate the messages and directions agreed upon by the management team to the rest of the company. You are depending on them for this.

the deal-making environment

One day, it became apparent to me that one of our most valued senior employees was losing his dedication and motivation in a way that we had never seen before. When I was finally able to coordinate my travel schedule with his, I asked him about this. Assuming that the problem was the long hours he was working or his heavy travel schedule, I was very surprised when he said, "The job is fine. I love the work, and I am pleased with what I am contributing. But as we have grown in size, it just does not seem as if you are treating us like individuals anymore, viewing each of us as the deal makers you recognized in each of us when I first joined. I guess it comes down to the fact that I just do not want to be thought of collectively!"

And he was right. As you build your management team and become infatuated with the upside of structure and organization, you can often lose sight of the fact that each team and division represented on your beautifully laser-printed organizational chart is made up of individuals. And just like you, they want to be thought of as unique. It made me think back to the time when I approached one of the entrepreneurs I had worked with years before, and he had agreed to strike a deal with me by letting me try my hand at sales, even though this job description was not written into my contract and even though it did not fit into any preset notion of what an account manager was supposed to do in an advertising firm. It was incumbent on me to maintain this same kind of deal-making environment for my employees.

Remember, each of your team members wants to be treated as an individual on the road to their own entrepreneurial dream. It is part of the deal. Make minor adjustments along the way—not by setting policy for a collective group but by negotiating small deals with the individuals. This will remind them that, although your company is pursuing a goal collectively, you have no misconceptions about recognizing the individuality of each member of the team.

"oh no, we almost forgot who we were!"

As you move from a state of rebellious leadership to one of a more structured remake of the original company, it is very important to continue to reflect your reinvented structure through cultural activities. Not only will this help you in redefining yourself as an eclipsed brand, but it will communicate your commitment to evolve the company culturally, in spite of—or because of—its growth in size. Many companies, including MondoMedia

Your CTO may be someone who is just never going to color between the lines.

GEOFFREY MOORE

I guess it comes down to the fact that I just do not want to be thought of collectively!

and Vivid, have tried to turn the size of the company into an advantage by introducing an informal but well-organized learning program. At MondoMedia, their "Mondo University" includes bringing in actors to give acting classes to the animators. They'll have live models come in for a series of sketching and posing sessions with the designers to help them understand how to mimic human movements in the games they are designing. They also offer specific training sessions on new software design programs. Regardless of the content of the session, the tree-fort culture is extended through learning and an exchange of ideas. These classes are well attended and are always followed by a social event, such as a movie screened in the main boardroom.

encountering adolescent attitudes

Once a month during the summer, Chris puts on his chef's hat and barbecues for the entire Bulldog staff. Other companies, such as Silicon Reef, have a happy hour every Friday at the end of the day. But regardless of what you do, there will always be those who begin to whisper quietly and then not so quietly, "But it's just not the same around here." And unfortunately, or fortunately, they are right. No matter how well planned the evolution of your company is or how hard you have worked at trying to seamlessly encourage your team to a new and better place, there will always be resistance to change and growth, always those who want to return to what they know. In my experience, this backward-looking attitude can have devastating effects on the morale of the company. It can begin to create uneasy divisions in the staff between those who knew the company "when" and those who are not a member of that club. In either case, everyone starts to focus on "how" and begins to forget the "why." This kind of negative attitude only gets in the way of building a group of people who will be ready for inevitable change.

Soul Centers

There is a special group of people who help pilot your organization in times of change. John Evershed of MondoMedia talks about these people in his company, whom he refers to as "soul centers." These individuals are not necessarily the most productive or the most senior members of the team, but if you yanked them out of the company, you would be tearing off a little part of the company's soul. Every organization has "soul centers," players who are essential because they reflect a sense of identity that many of the staff members associate with and look up to. When your company is in flux or in transition, or when there is a sudden rash of new employees, it is the soul centers who will help you through the worst of times, sustaining your brand and your culture, because they are a positive reminder of who you

Perhaps the most common catalyst that creates whining is change. Uncomfortable, unpredictable, inevitable change.

SAN FRANCISCO EXAMINER

Soul centers? Hold on to those people. They will remind you that you have a soul on days when the business world demands that you temporarily give it up.

were and an interpreter of who you are on the way to becoming. My advice? Hold on to these people. They will remind you that you have a soul on days when the business world demands that you temporarily give it up.

"Can Your Ego Cash that Check?"

Many entrepreneurs find that as their companies grow, it becomes harder and harder to monitor each individual's interpretation of their brand, especially when the company is riding a wave of success and growth. As they get further away from dealing with each of their employees on a daily or weekly basis, they are inevitably told by a customer or a friend or even a friendly competitor that someone in their company is taking their vision a step too far. As Keith Kocho of Digital Renaissance has found, "It is hard to remind everyone all the time that we are growing a company based on customer service. You build a great culture, a great reputation, you get positive press, and suddenly it goes to people's heads. Sometimes this is out of immaturity, sometimes it is out of inexperience. What do I do when this happens? I say, 'Yeah, but can your ego cash that check?'" The bottom line is, you are running a business, and once in a while, as with all adolescents, you may have to remind them who pays the rent.

"You Can Stay Out Until the Streetlights Go On"

A friend of mine was complaining about being the youngest of four boys growing up. All his other brothers could stay out playing in the streets way past dinner time, but he had to come home "when the streetlights would go on." This was a set limitation that had little leeway. In a start-up company, you are often burning the midnight oil on more than one occasion per week. You get used to seeing a bunch of people eating pizza at 11 p.m. before going back to work for another few hours.

Most people are pretty good regulators of their own energy levels, but some are not. As entrepreneurs, we are not always very good at setting limitations for ourselves and therefore find it hard to do so for others. If you are not good at setting limits, find someone on your management team who is, and ensure that they set limits for those team members who are not very good at monitoring their work hours. You do not want a team full of completely burned-out, slightly resentful people who give dirty looks to anyone leaving the office at 7 p.m.

What are the signs that someone on your staff is in need of some schedule restraints? One indication is when you find out that they have moved to the city, started working for you, and have been sleeping on the couch in the back office because they have not had time to look for an apartment. When people let their personal lives go to this degree, it is time to tell them that they can work until the streetlights go on and then they need to head home.

At Narrowline, Tara Lemmey has seven questions she asks herself about any potential employees: Are they innovative? Do they have the "get it" factor? Are they hands on? Are they self-starters? Do they get the big picture? Do they laugh? Will they fit within our culture?

SEEK CONFERENCE

As your company grows, the entrepreneur recognizes that he, in the end, must be an architect of people, places, and patterns. He knows that it is his job to turn his team members into the heroes who make connections between those people, places and patterns.

TOM HOWLETT,
CREATIVE DIRECTOR,
THE FARM, INC.

cycle three: the sudden slowness of maturity

When I do speaking gigs on the subject of the cycles of growth that entrepreneurial start-ups go through, inevitably someone asks me how a person knows when your company is out of Cycle Two and into the next stage. The short answer is, "You don't. Because if you did, you probably wouldn't need to name it and study it so closely; you would just ease into it." But the best description of how you know you have entered Cycle Three came from my friend Steve Horowitz of Palladium, a family entertainment software company. He sent me an email one day that said, "I knew I was reaching that 'next stage' when:

- I no longer knew the name of each and every employee
- The elevator opened right in front of our reception desk
- I had to fold the phone list in order to fit it into my appointment book
- I couldn't schmooze with everyone at our company holiday party
- We hired our first senior VP
- Our executive staff formed subcommittees
- We weren't afraid to talk about profitability
- We salivated at the sound of the terms IPO and M&A
- We doubled our revenues for our last fiscal year and
- We have to do it again for next year!"

The first important point about Cycle Three is that it is not the last in a series of cycles. Entrepreneurial organizations are organic, and as such, there is no end to the possibilities and variations that can occur as each company evolves and reinvents itself again and again. Therefore, moving into the next phase of growth is as much about the mindset with which you approach your maturing organization as it is about the tactics you apply.

The second important point about Cycle Three has as much to do with the new entrepreneur's perception of themselves as it does with the teams they are building. My former partner, Tom Howlett, said it best: "As your company grows, the entrepreneur recognizes that he, in the end, must be an architect of people, places, and patterns. He knows that it is his job to turn his team members into the heroes who make connections between those people, places, and patterns." I could not have said it better. Engaging in active envisioning is relevant only if you build the structures around you to support and enhance the proactive approach to building a dream. Building dreams, by definition, must include the dreams of those you are soliciting, and the best way to do this is to create heroes out of those whom you hire and build them into your creation myth, build them into your story of belonging. Your CTO and their team are the heroes of the product; your VP of sales and their team are the champions and heroes of your customers; and your finance department is responsible for keeping the company afloat en route. If you have embraced the notion of the mature performer, you will be able to move others gently onto center stage as you continue to direct from the wings, assisting with the connections between the people who make up your team, the places they will need to journey to as part of your vision, and the patterns of trial and error that will occur along the way.

Here are just a few of the issues that will keep you up at night as an architect building a company of heroes: How much freedom does my team really need? How much do they want? Are my team members asking for structure, or are they really in need of clearer direction? When employees say they want opportunity, are they really communicating a greater need of certainty about their futures? How do I balance managing a team at a distance versus managing those back at home base? How do I know when the right time comes to promote someone into a VP position? Can one have too many VPs? How do I get my engineering, sales, and marketing teams to see eye to eye, or is it okay that they are always slightly at odds?

Dealing effectively with these kinds of issues requires a pretty hefty to-do list that is relentless in scope and length. Finding answers for these problems is less complex than you might think, however. There are really only five major approaches that I have learned in my journey toward effective architecting and in the making of heroes. By incorporating these notions into your management style, you will begin to find the answers to the myriad questions you are asking yourself as you build the connections between people, places, and patterns.

getting and keeping your hands dirty

If the challenge of Cycle One is about moving away from the notion of a dysfunctional family model, and the challenge of Cycle Two is about side-stepping adolescent self-doubt on the road to a refined vision, Cycle Three is about creating an engaged environment as you move from the original impulse that first started the company. In this third cycle of growth, when you have already reached a certain size and degree of success, you begin to realize that people are coming to work for your company for different reasons than they did in the beginning, when non-belongers came to you looking for a rebellious leader. So how do you maintain your entrepreneurial spirit and the original impulse that inspired you? Some entrepreneurs foster a sense of personal responsibility for their team members; others prefer

I view our company as 200 overachievers. In a sense, our organization is an incubator for learning how to combine work and life. It is a lifelong struggle and a romance between the two.

JONAS SVENSSON,
CO-FOUNDER AND
CHAIRMAN,
SPRAY NETWORKS

Innovation ultimately means interpreting a customer's experience as an opportunity to add new value.

MICHAEL MOON

to concentrate their energies on the creation of a customer-focused organization. I believe that maintaining the original impulse of the company is derived from the notion of getting and keeping your hands dirty.

A "customer-focused organization" is a well-recognized business mantra of the '90s. But in my experience, having this focus is not only necessary for direct sales but is also one of the best ways to maintain an entrepreneurial spirit as the company grows in the third cycle. If the new entrepreneur encourages everyone to participate directly with customers, team members, and industry associates as a means of maintaining an edge, a closeness to the trends and attitudes and needs of those who are most important to the health and wealth of the organization, then they derive two benefits:

- First, the original momentum and drive of the company is continuously renewed through everyone's active engagement in staying close to and interpreting a customer's experience as an opportunity to add new value that can be resold again (i.e., the features reflected in the next version of a software product, or a new product, for that matter).

- Second, just as a company's culture evolves, so does its brand. With a team that is collectively getting and keeping its hands dirty, you cannot help but stay close to changes in customer desires, wishes, and understanding. If and when it is necessary to begin to evolve your brand (what I call "eclipsing your brand")—from a service company to a product company, from a magazine publisher to a variety of digital online and print properties, etc.—you will be able to anticipate when it is time to shift your company's image, readjusting your language or icons quickly and effectively.

There are 15 behaviors that are desirable and learnable. Among them, we find "the team builder and hero maker. The successful entrepreneur is not a 'loner.' He or she makes 'heroes' out of the people they attract to the business, giving them responsibility and credit for their accomplishments.

ELIZABETH CHELL,
JEAN HAWORTH AND
SALLY BREARLEY,
*THE ENTREPRENEURIAL
PERSONALITY*

dip in, dip out

Jane Metcalfe, co-founder of *Wired* magazine, describes the role of her executive editor as "someone who lives in the future and reports back to us." In the magazine business, this is a pretty essential role to play in predicting trends in the world of digital media. To me, this also sounds like a good description of the role of the entrepreneur in the third cycle of their company. As you begin to build an effective management team and structures to support a well art-directed group of decision makers, you will be able to spend more time on the outside of your organization. In fact, that is where you should be spending a great deal of your time. You will talk to the press and to customers, meet with analysts, compare notes with associates in the same industry in different countries. You will process all these pieces of information, and, as a master of interpretation, you will "report back to the company." But as you move more and more within the external circles of influence, do not forget to continuously come back to home base and check in to ensure that your team is accurately understanding, buying into, and communicating the reports of the future that you are sending its way. Dip in and dip out regularly so that you make sure you have not left your team behind you in your own wake of interpretation.

fluid managing

Growing up, I spent my summers at a camp located on an island in Temagami in northern Ontario. This was a "free" camp, with little structure or scheduling requirements. In addition to water and land sports, you had to go on at least one canoe trip during the summer, regardless of your age or skill level. It wasn't until years later, when I returned to this same camp as a counselor, that I understood why it was important for kids to leave the camp behind for a few days and go out into the wilderness as a small group. Whether you were away for 3 days or 21 days, something happened the minute you left main camp. Kids who were not popular in main camp became heroes on the portages; those who were scared to try new sports at main camp were the bravest ones, eager and ready to conquer a particularly rough patch of white-water navigation. New friends were made, old alliances broken, surprising heroes emerged, and kingpins were brought down. When I asked the camp director why he was so intent on everyone going on a canoe trip, he said, "Because you realize that it is not the canoe trip that is so important, nor the particular skills they learn when they are away. It is the renewed understanding everyone has for each other when they return, an understanding that is crucial to growing up." And he was so right. As a counselor, I watched as everyone returned to main camp after a 10-day trip, dirtier, generally happier, but with a new view of their cabin mates and a visceral understanding that things are different when you take away the familiar structures and routines that you have come to depend on.

These canoe trips come back to me when I think about what happens to the teams that make up your entrepreneurial organization when you move into Cycle Three. Suddenly, people are traveling to faraway places. You may even need to relocate a few salespeople or engineers in a new city temporarily, away from home base. All the structure and processes that you have worked hard to set up in Cycle Two begin to lose their relevance. But as with a canoe trip, this is not such a bad thing. It provides a basis for discovering which of your staff, in fact, can work outside of the security of the structures of your organization, who you can depend on when the going gets tough. It also tells you who would rather stay at main camp.

The learning that happens amid team players when familiar structures and processes are taken away is particularly helpful in building respect and trust among various team members. For example, in a software company, the struggle to align engineering, sales, and marketing is a constant battle.

I think of a hero as someone who understands the degree of responsibility that comes with his freedom.

BOB DYLAN

A little knowledge that *acts* is infinitely more than much knowledge that is idle.

KAHLIL GIBRAN,
VOICE OF THE MASTER

One story that a software entrepreneur told me really hit home: "When we were launching our new software product, one of my most senior engineers and my most senior marketing person had to go on a three-day analyst road tour. The fact that these two people did not get along that well caused some alarm for me, but I decided that it was time to stop playing the mediator between two highly competent and highly valued executives within the company. To my surprise, when these two individuals returned, they seemed to treat each other differently in meetings. They were able to have more discussions and fewer arguments regarding the role of engineering and marketing within the context of the product launch. A week later, when I was able to ask the senior engineer how the tour went, he replied, 'It was one of the best experiences I ever had. There we were, sitting in a room with analysts, and suddenly we had to be on the same team. He was so good at breaking the ice, at providing an overview of the company and our philosophy without getting bogged down by engineering details. When it came to product information, I was able to map out our architecture and conduct a demo that was concise and thorough. For the first time, I think I really appreciated his expertise, and I am pretty sure the feeling was mutual. It was a team of equals and opposites.'" Providing contexts in which your team members will learn how to resolve their own differences is key to the maturation of your organization. As with the canoe trip, it is not the idea of the journey that is most important but what happens to each individual team member who goes on this journey and what they bring back with them on the other side of the experience.

"remember, ideas are not precious, people are"

Another important lesson for the new entrepreneur is the willingness to let go of any ideas that are no longer beneficial. In his approach to theater design, Michael Levine actively resists thinking that any of his ideas are carved in stone. Similarly, the new entrepreneur must also resist the temptation to hold too tightly to any one idea, because an idea should never be allowed to turn into dogma. As your company grows, some ideas will work out and others will not. Be ruthless about reassessing ideas, recognizing that they are supposed to be dynamic. If you can find a better way of making something work, do not hesitate to implement it.

In Geoffrey Moore's view, as the entrepreneur moves through the various stages of business (early market, niche markets, mass markets, and continuous innovations), they find that what is required for success in one stage is often the exact opposite of what is required for success in the next stage. For example, to succeed in the early market, you don't need to focus at all, but need to stay broad, accumulating customers that may have nothing in common. In the second stage, in niche markets, you do the exact opposite: you take on only customers that have a point of reference to each other, you narrow your focus and eliminate anything that does not support this activity.

The same is true for branding and for leading your company. Often what worked in the creation stage of the company will no longer work for the later stages of the company. The only way to ensure that you are on top of this is to recognize that as your organization evolves, you will need the flexibility to let go of what you may once have thought were "precious" ideas.

At the same time that you treat ideas with a certain flexibility, be careful how you treat your team members, how you dip in and dip out of your version of the future. Always assess what you are seeing and experiencing in the present. I always strive to remember that each member of my team is on the same "canoe trip" that I am on. I also keep in my mind that, when the journey is over, we will all have our own take on who we are. The best advice on managing people, places, and patterns of behavior during Cycle Three is "remember, ideas are not precious, people are."

lasting belonging

For the new entrepreneur, the challenge of creating, managing, and building a sustainable culture and a lasting place of belonging requires the ability to juggle myriad details, aligning them with the reality of the present and assessing the possibility of the future. Maintaining a state of mind of magical realism adds insight, as does understanding the mindset of the Knowledge Deal Makers who make up your company. The notion of seeing oneself as an architect rather than a leader is worth a try. And the constant promotion of active engagement keeps the necessary momentum of growth and development going. But as with all life challenges, there is no line you can cross where you suddenly are able to say, "Aha, we are all grown up now," or "Now we are the company we have always wanted to be."

In my experience, the first signs of graceful aging, of sought-after maturity, come when you can finally allow yourself to recognize the moments of peak performance amid your heroic efforts at creating mechanisms for change. Perhaps this will be the first time your management team reaches consensus about a contentious issue without you having to step in. Or perhaps it is an email you get from an employee about the way the company has changed their view of how business works, or a customer who congratulates you on your team of salespeople. There come times when you and your team are at peak performance, when all the hard work at adjusting, repositioning, and cajoling seems to make things fall effortlessly into place. It is at those moments that the relationship between focus and time intersect and a new cycle of growth—and chaos—begins. These are the moments that often take you by surprise, and they certainly keep you coming back for more. For that one hour, or those few days, you are reminded of why it is so important to be an architect who tries to build a

What is required at one stage is the equal and opposite of what may be required at the next stage in the company's growth.

GEOFFREY MOORE

These are the soul's changes. I don't believe in aging. I believe in forever altering one's aspect to the sun. Hence my optimism.

VIRGINIA WOOLF

destiny for people, places, and patterns and creates heroes who make the necessary connections between those three categories. At those times, seemingly without effort, you have slipped over the dividing line between an inexperienced entrepreneur and an entrepreneur who is aging gracefully.

When I asked Bill Buxton, chief scientist at SGI and at Alias Wavefront, to talk to me about his earlier days as a musician, he described what it was about playing music that was most exciting to him. "When you are really performing at peak level, you cross a threshold where things slow down rather than speed up. In fact, you appear to have all the time in the world. When our musical ensemble was really working, everything seemed to slow down and my perception grew and grew. But I really appreciated the notion of team and individual peak performance when I read an article on speed skiing. Here is an activity that is superficially as far away from music as you can get. Essentially, you put on a really tight suit and an aerodynamic helmet and go straight down the steepest hill you can as fast as you can. In makes downhill racers seem as if they are standing still. But this one athlete described what happened to him on good runs. He said that at a certain point, he crossed a threshold where, despite going faster and faster, things slowed down. He had time not only to think about what he was doing but was even able to resolve individual flakes of snow on the ground. This is similar to music, an expansion of time that comes with peak performance through focus, skill, and practice."

And that is exactly what happens in the entrepreneur's world every so often. Whether you are with your team and the pieces are all falling into place, or you are in a moment of reflection and all alone, time, which is so precious and in some ways your biggest enemy, slows down long enough to give you a moment of magic. When that happens, remember to look around and appreciate the collection of people, their skills, and all the practicing they have been doing in an attempt to be there with you for one absolutely peak performance. In a speed skier's terms, try to resolve the individual flakes of snow on the ground as you whiz by in slow motion.

The most exciting moments in entrepreneuring, as in music, are often those that go unheard.

AN ENTREPRENEUR

Heard melodies are sweet, but those unheard are sweeter.

JOHN KEATS,
ODE ON A GRECIAN URN

chapter 10

The Advantageous Burden of Money

En route to a long overdue family vacation, Jackson wondered for the umpteenth time if he should simply let his two daughters and his wife go on without him. How could he possibly take any time off now, knowing that the future of his company was hanging in the balance? Launching his product was contingent upon closing the second round of financing, which was precariously balanced between courier packages and legal documents. And then, with a look his wife had come to recognize as "This is the last time I will do this to you," he dropped off his family at the airport, deflecting the questions from his daughters and avoiding eye contact with his wife. He watched them walk into the terminal en route to the Caribbean and then quickly headed back to the office. What he didn't know was that this would *absolutely* be the last time he would do this to his wife, because when she returned from the holiday, Jackson would no longer have a company to keep him away.

Jackson, like many entrepreneurs, felt that he had always been an enterprising person—from his early days of newspaper routes to his first really ambitious stint at age 16, when he used his life savings of $700 to start a bike repair business. In the early 1990s, after working for a large technology company as a midlevel field engineer, he came up with an idea for a kind of graphics authoring software specifically built for graphic designers. Having cashed out on his stock options a few years earlier, he was able to pool $200,000 of his own money with $300,000 given to him by a long-time associate of the family—"an angel"—who truly believed in his abilities. With this money, Jackson got together a crew to build the prototype. Jackson was able to run a very tight ship and spend this money wisely. But, as many first-time entrepreneurs find out, things always take longer than you think they will. The predicted six-month lead-time turned into 18 months. He soon discovered that to launch his product properly, he would realistically need $4 million in outside funding. Since this was far beyond what he or his "angel" were able to invest, he began to shop around for the money required to launch his dream.

The market was ripe for this kind of product. The interest within the venture capital community was keen, and there was an atmosphere of great optimism regarding the kinds of returns that investors could make on the right software investments, optimism fed by stories such as the success of Netscape.

At this point, Jackson was approached by three major companies with whom he had worked in the past. Each of them was impressed with his prototype and offered him consulting contracts to create a customized version of his product for their exclusive use. These three contracts combined would have kept him afloat for a while and possibly offered a viable business model for future consulting. But when he thought about it, he knew that he had not come all this way just to get into the consulting business. He turned down the offers, knowing that it would only delay his ability to complete the product currently in development. Within weeks, Jackson questioned this thinking. Although, after making 25 presentations, he was able to generate serious interest within various venture capital firms, he could not get a buyer who was willing to commit to him within his time frame. He had only 60 days before his seed money ran out.

In the eleventh hour, Jackson was able to find a smaller venture capital firm (which was not on his original list of referrals he had collected from business associates) that was willing to put up the initial $2 million, contingent on Jackson's ability to find the additional $2 million within a 12-month time frame. Jackson was delighted to be thrown what appeared to be a lifesaver.

Over the next 12 months, Jackson "did" the investor circuit, flying across the U.S., meeting with and selling his business concept to would-be investors. What he soon learned was that many venture capital firms were hesitant to partner with his investor (whom we will call venture capital Firm XYZ). His instinct kicked in and red flags went up: Why the hesitancy? Was there some kind of secret pecking order within the venture capital community? By the end of a year, he had no takers. He was beginning to get a clear picture that he had signed up a group of people who were neither well liked nor respected within the investment community. At this point, meeting payroll was once again a problem. Jackson had little choice, and so he borrowed another $1.5 million from Firm XYZ, yielding control of his company in the process.

Finally, Jackson found a venture capital firm that was very interested in both him and his product. But then, things took a turn for the worse. During the negotiation process, Firm XYZ began to balk at various conditions of the term sheet being proposed by the new lead venture capital firm, ABC, stating that there were over a dozen deal killers. The next three

Merger: combination of two or more corporations. The dominant company absorbs the passive company, with the former continuing operations usually under the same name. Differs from a consolidation, where two companies combine and are succeeded by a new corporation, usually with a new name.

weeks, as Jackson now recalls, were a string of urgent telephone calls and meetings in which Jackson tried to accommodate the surprising and last-minute issues that Firm XYZ kept raising while simultaneously trying to minimize the growing frustration and disinterest of Firm ABC.

Although there were issues with getting the due diligence done on time for their closing date, and there were the usual stresses and strains of too many lawyers and too many accountants in the room at one time, things were beginning to gel. Given the circumstances, things were going well. *So* well, that the board encouraged Jackson not to cancel his vacation. But as we know, Jackson had second thoughts at the last minute and returned to his office rather than getting on a plane headed for the Caribbean.

Sitting down at his desk, still wondering about how he would make up this last-minute change of plans to his family, Jackson noticed an envelope from Firm XYZ marked "personal" sitting on his desk. He opened it up, and there, to his horror, was a letter addressed to Firm ABC. In essence, it was a "change in decision, need to turn down the deal" letter. And it had Jackson's name at the bottom, waiting for his signature. It was dated the day Jackson was expected back from his vacation.

Jackson sat down and began to go through his email—out of habit more than anything else—until he realized the absurdity of his actions. What was he doing? Ultimately he would be forced to sign the letter turning down the only money being offered to him. He had little voting power, because, with 65 percent ownership of his company, Firm XYZ had majority voting control on his board. It seemed that his ability to persuade them otherwise had run out. The deal was dead, and he was pretty sure that the product would never launch now, despite the fact that they were weeks away from completion. And Jackson knew it was just a matter of time before he was ousted from his own company, leaving a trail of meaningless documents and half-hearted handshakes behind him.

Why had the deal gone south? Why did other venture capital firms resist working with them? Why did Firm XYZ force him to turn down money that would have saved not only the company but also their investment of approximately $3 million to date? He had few answers. He had dreamed, prepared, sold, negotiated, and waited for money, believing that once he got it, he would be on his way. But once he got his initial investment, he had discovered that he had to worry about the kind of money he had gotten.

Two years and a couple of hundred hours of reflection later, Jackson sat with me in his new home. Having lost his company and his marriage, he is now living in a new city with a new job. But rather than display the despondency that one might expect, Jackson is a man who feels that he has learned some valuable lessons about entrepreneuring.

He told me that, as he had predicted, his start-up company folded soon after he was asked to leave. Jackson has a lot to teach about getting money

Valuation: appraising, setting a value.

IPO: initial public offering. A corporation's first public offering of stock, usually underwritten by a single investment banker or a pool of investment bankers and brokerage firms.

and investors. But as many of us entrepreneurs have learned, the real learning that money teaches us has as much to do with relationships, instinct, integrity, persistence, and contingency planning as it does with the green stuff deals are made of.

a monetary footnote

Jackson's story is unusual, tragic, and not by any means typical of the experience that most entrepreneurs have in working with investors. In fact, while we hear about the dramatic mega-mergers and acquisitions of the biggest company deals on Wall Street, the truth is that today, capital markets, in both private and public arenas, play a significant role in creating wealth and opportunity in the world of entrepreneurial business. "The private-placement market is just one example. During the first three-quarters of 1997, just over $250 billion was invested in these deals alone, according to Securities Data, which tracks the financial markets. That amount was nearly twice the $128 billion private-placement level of 1993."

Many entrepreneurs, including myself, have had very positive experiences with investors. The reason I am telling Jackson's story, however, is that every entrepreneur whom I have talked to has at one time or another had to deal with many of the elements that pepper his tale. Most important, Jackson's story painfully points out that there are many questions the entrepreneur needs to ask themselves if they wish to avoid some of the potentially devastating consequences of finding the *wrong* kind of money and investors.

As a speaker over the past few years, I have found that I get more questions about how to raise money effectively for a start-up software company than about anything else. This is not surprising, considering one hears reports that venture capital investment groups in the U.S. invested US$9.5 billion in 1996, a 25 percent jump over 1995. In Silicon Valley in 1997, 3,575 new businesses were launched, and venture capitalists poured a record $3.7 billion into start-ups, 60 percent more than the year before, according to PriceWaterhouseCoopers. Today, most start-up technology companies are successfully financed by venture capital, which is described as "a financial art form that Silicon Valley has perfected." The venture capitalists dotted along Sand Hill Road in Menlo Park, California, control around a third of America's independently raised venture capital and around a sixth of the world's total. One of those firms, Kleiner Perkins Caulfield & Buyers, has invested around $1 billion to help start 250 companies, which in 1995 had revenues of $44 billion and are worth $85 billion." That's a lot of money and represents a whole lot of opportunity for many start-up companies looking for outside investment. How to tap effectively into this kind of network of money and connections is high on the list of priorities of most new entrepreneurs—as it should be.

Investment, whether pre- or post-IPO (initial public offering), of course, is only part of the financial picture. The entrepreneur needs to learn a whole lot about banking and cash flow and balance sheets and P&L (profit and loss) long before they should even think about looking for outside investment. There are many other books and articles that address these issues in great detail, just as there are resources that list the kinds of investors you can look for, the kinds of formulas you can follow for creating a viable business plan, and the kinds of returns you can expect from your efforts. "Go On an Equity Hunt to Fund Expansion" by Jeff Wuorio in *Your Company* is one of many examples of informative articles. The *Journal of Business Strategy* and *Inc.* magazine's "How to Finance Anything" by Jill Andresky Fraser are also good resources.

What I would like to tell you about are the questions that no one told me to ask my potential investors, my team members, my board members, and most of all, myself, when I went out to look for money. Through my own experience of raising three rounds of investment totaling $17.5 million and through a collection of stories from investors and entrepreneurs alike, I hope to provide some answers to these much-neglected questions. In the process, I believe that, like Jackson, you will understand why seeking and getting money teaches you about a whole lot more than mere finances.

A recent survey conducted by Coopers & Lybrand indicates that small firms "bellied up to the VC [venture capital] bar for a record $10.1 billion in 1996."

YOUR COMPANY
MAGAZINE

stage one: on dreaming, thinking, and talking about money

THE NEW ENTREPRENEUR OPENS THE CHAPTER ON MONEY WITH ONE WORD: RESPECT. AS YOU LEARN TO RESPECT YOUR PARTICULAR STYLE OF ENTREPRENEURING, THE KIND OF COMPANY YOU WANT TO GROW, AND THE KIND OF TEAM YOU NEED TO BUILD YOUR DREAM, YOU WILL ALSO LEARN TO RESPECT THE KIND OF MONEY THAT CAN GET YOU THERE.

During a trip to Paris, I enjoyed the luxury of spending the day in the Musée D'Orsay with a friend of mine who is a well-respected art historian. As we were standing in front of one of the most beautiful Monet paintings, a tourist beside us went up to the index card beside the painting and said to her friend, "Oh yeah—Money, Monet—I've seen it spelled both ways." My art historian friend gasped, "Not only is that ignorant, but it is so disrespectful to Monet." And I agreed. But later that day, I thought about the irony that money and Monet—both highly valued, yet difficult to price—were compared in the same sentence. As ludicrous as the comment was with respect to the artist, it was also disrespectful to the notion of money. It reminded me that when entrepreneurs are looking for money, they like to hide behind various terms and words: investment, equity position, long-term financial partner, etc. But what they are really talking about is plain old *money* and what that means to the life and death of their company. Just as I believe the entrepreneur learns more by calling an "intelligent gamble" a "risk" and gains insight by redefining personal limitations as "fears," so, too, do they benefit from a more visceral approach to their monetary needs. The word is simple and straightforward and should be respected for what it is—money.

The entrepreneur begins with a dream for which they require a plan. Then they require the conviction that the dream and the plan will lend themselves to a notion of value. Only at that point does the entrepreneur begin to think about money. And in thinking about money, the new entrepreneur must respect it for what it is and respect its place within the dream and the plan that it will support. Bill Sahlman of Harvard University has seen many an entrepreneur who, he claims, "does not respect money very much. They have unrealistic expectations of how much of their company they are willing to give away, of how much their idea is worth, and of the relationships they will have to build to maintain an ongoing stream of money coming in to fulfill their dreams." Money, like technology, is in itself neither good nor bad. It is the people who find ways to use it constructively who count. While the new entrepreneur respects money by recognizing its value, it is wise for them to remember that there are those who abuse it and that there is always a price attached to its value.

If you fail to respect money, you may find yourself misunderstanding the role it will play in your life as an entrepreneur. This attitude will cause you much heartache and disillusionment.

Three notions about respect for money have helped me understand its role in my entrepreneurial journey:

- Should you choose to get outside money, recognize that it will probably be one of the most critical decisions you make in the history of your entrepreneuring career. Respect how this decision will inextricably be linked to your future.

- Understand that money is a hard currency. It is black and white. But at the same time, those who have the money to finance your entrepreneurial dream have the choice to buy and value the intangible—in the shape and form of your dreams and your ideas. Respect the power that these people have, and learn how to continually enhance their notion of long-term value.

- Remember that money is a tool (albeit a critical one) to be used to actualize your dreams. At the same time, however, money does not replace the impulse, careful planning, strategic thinking, and the necessary conviction and obsession

Bill Sahlman of Harvard University has seen many an entrepreneur who, he claims, "does not respect money very much. They have unrealistic expectations of how much of their company they are willing to give away, of how much their idea is worth, and of the relationships they will have to build to maintain an ongoing stream of money coming in to fulfill their dreams."

of the entrepreneur. Come to terms with your relationship to money, and respect yourself for it.

WHEN LOOKING FOR MONEY, EVERY POTENTIAL INVESTOR IS GOING TO WANT TO KNOW WHAT YOUR *EXIT* STRATEGY IS, IN OTHER WORDS, "WHEN WILL I GET THE HIGHEST POSSIBLE RETURN ON MY INVEST-MENT?" WHETHER YOU ARE FOCUSED ON A STRATEGIC BUYOUT OR AN INITIAL PUBLIC OFFERING, THE NEW ENTREPRENEUR REALLY NEEDS TO BE THINKING OF THEIR *ENTRANCE* STRATEGY, IN OTHER WORDS, "WHAT IS THIS MONEY GOING TO MEAN TO THE KIND OF ENTREPRENEURIAL VENTURE I WANT TO GROW? WHAT AM I ENTERING, EN ROUTE TO MY EXIT STRATEGY?"

When I was in university, my group of girlfriends and I used to refer to our contingency planning for a date gone bad as our "personal exit strategy." In looking for money during Bulldog's first round of investment, I could not help but smile when I first encountered the notion of an "exit strategy." Before you have barely met your investor, before you know how your "date" with him will work out (so to speak), they already want to know your exit strategy. As Jeff Wuorio writes, "The most daunting part of the investment process is developing an exit strategy to pay off investors. Most want their money back plus a hefty annual yield of at least 40 percent within three to seven years. However, depending on the amount of money that was raised and the success of the venture, very few owners can meet these demands purely from cash flow. That's why many venture capital recipients plan to sell their technology or their business to a competitor or corporate Goliath to compensate the investors and make money themselves; others take their company public."

This pressure for the entrepreneur to produce superhero returns continues to escalate in the investment cycle. "What the initial public offering market has done for venture capitalists these days is nothing short of astounding. In the 1980s a major venture capital success returned perhaps 20 times the investment in, say, five to six years. Now the homers harvest 30 to 100 times the outlay in as little as three years." Add to this the reality that given the risk involved in start-up investing, venture capitalists aim to multiply their money in any one company at least tenfold within four years, but ultimately, one in three investments produces a total write-off. The odds that the typical venture capital firm is playing were best described in terms of what one of the leaders in the high-tech investment community calculates it costs to train a member of a venture capital firm: Mr. Doerr likens training a venture capitalist to crashing a jet fighter. "It's probably going to cost you $20 million to $30 million. Hopefully, you can pull the ring and eject from the plane to fly again another day." As an entrepreneur, you want

Due diligence: the work performed by a broker or other representative in order to investigate and understand an investment thoroughly before recommending it to a customer.

to make sure that your investors do not pull the ring too early or too late on *your* investment.

All of this translates into a high benchmark of success in investment terms, and it can be an unrealistic benchmark for success in entrepreneurial terms.

what business are you in?

In traditional business thinking, one of the key factors to multiplying investment is how successful you are at planning and executing your exit strategy. But as an entrepreneur thinking about getting money, your focus should be first on the notion of an entrance strategy. Here is my reasoning. Exit strategies are *only* a financial construct built on the investor's notion of value: How much money will I get out, and how soon? And so it should be, because that is the business that investors are in. But that is *not* the business that the entrepreneur is in. As an entrepreneur, you are building something from scratch. Sometimes that company gets built incredibly fast, and you are able to leverage that into an incredible exit strategy all within two years. In a case like Xylan, a network-equipment company that went public in 1996, Brentwood Associates put $4 million into the company, and two years later, its shares were worth $400 million. Seagate Technologies brought a $56.5 million profit on the venture capital firm's original investment of $500,000.

In these cases, everyone did well financially—the entrepreneurs and venture capitalists alike. But these stories are not representative of the usual scenario. Even in a fast-paced industry such as high tech, it may take 5 to 10 years to build a truly viable and sustainable business to the level and velocity that everyone is looking for. This kind of fast maturation rate can and often will happen, but not necessarily with the speed with which your investors are banking on. And therein lies the paradox. In order to get a good valuation (the value of your company at the time you get an outside investment), you are often required to build a business case that is based on short-term expectations, or what I call "the standard $50-million sales projection within a two-year business plan." Wonderful, you get an exceptional valuation. And for a while in the mid-1990s, it seemed as if there was one generic miracle business plan template that every entrepreneur was using to build their company. While all this might look good on paper, you may unfortunately be putting yourself in a situation that I call "getting eaten up backwards." As you begin to slip and miss the completely unrealistic sales targets that you set in order to get a great valuation, you risk having more and more of your company ownership taken away from you as a means of making up for this. Or you simply live in a vortex of seeming to continually underperform, even though you are making headway by leaps and bounds, according to a more reasonable business plan. The ability of an entrepreneurial organization to cope with the pressure of having to perform at superhuman levels to make up for the potential collective losses

According to the Canadian Venture Capital Association, based on 106 venture capital investment groups across Canada, a total of 1,336 investments were made in 794 companies through 931 rounds of financing over the course of 1997. A total of $866 million went to first-time financing in 1997, up by 28% from the prior year, which underscores the continued attractiveness of the environment for entrepreneurs in search of capital.

of the investors' other deals may be part of the gamble that the investor is taking, but it is hardly a realistic expectation. Recognize that this is part of the game of odds that you are now part of.

When you are preparing for an IPO, this notion of an entrance strategy is, of course, heightened. Joy Covey, CFO of Amazon.com, an on-line bookseller, describes their valuation strategy as a kind of entrance strategy, in that they were willing to forfeit potentially higher valuation for the right kind of financial partner. As Joy advises, "Understand your own relative position well enough to know how hard to play for valuation." It is often important to recognize what a high-profile investor can bring to a company based on their relationships and experience, not just their financial contribution. "If you have a strong position, hold your line. If you don't, compromise intelligently, hold out for the most important things." She should know. Today, Amazon.com, a public company listed on Nasdaq, has served 4.5 million customers, employs 614 people, and is redefining the way books are bought, sold, and distributed. As the third largest U.S. book retailer, the company is worth about $5.5 billion. Like Amazon.com, by thinking entrance strategy, you can allow yourself to focus on the things that are really important for any new entrepreneurial venture: what you are building, what kind of money you can get to help you achieve your dream, and what kind of people are best to work with as a means of creating long-term, not necessarily short-term, wealth for all concerned.

ask yourself the right questions

What Kind of Dream Do You Want to Finance?

If your goal is to build and grow a small, but stable, business that will provide you with a good income, generate some fun and excitement, and perhaps create a working environment that people are proud to be part of, you may be able to finance your dream through a small loan and your line of credit. If you are not within a highly time-sensitive industry but feel you can build a good business over time, you may also be able to do this without looking for money from others. But if, on the other hand, your dreams are built on an attempt to be a major player in an industry or a leader in a new product category, your need for getting money from outside investors is unavoidable. In asking yourself what kind of dreams you want to finance, you also have to determine your comfort level with the associated risk. When Jackson was faced with the glum reality of having no interested investors and a 60-day window to meet payroll, he could have opted to take three large contracts from the customers who wanted him to do consulting for them. Perhaps he should have. But he stuck to his notion of entrepreneuring and took the risk of trying to create a product that he believed in. Today, he still does not regret his decision,

**Hortensio: I would not wed her for a mine of gold.
Petruchio: Hortensio, peace! Thou know'st not gold's effect.**

THE TAMING
OF THE SHREW
ACT I, SCENE II

Today's venture capitalists are pickier than ever, and they're interested only in businesses that can deliver annual pre-tax returns of 32 to 48%.

BUSINESS WEEK
MAGAZINE

though he does warn others that you have to be willing to lose it all before you take money from *anyone*.

Other entrepreneurs, such as Doug Humphreys of Skyrocket, use a less risky tactic. Doug believes in boot-strapping his new entrepreneurial ventures through his existing business until he is able to find the right investor or strategic partner who will take over. This process takes longer and risks the potential of missing a window of opportunity in an extremely fast-paced industry of new media. But for Doug, having control and total accountability for the financing of his ventures is much more important than being able to leverage his position to jumpstart a product faster through outside money.

The game is already risky enough. Venture capitalists generally expect that two out of ten investments will be big successes and hope that no more than two others will completely fail.

FINANCIAL WORLD
MAGAZINE

I have heard hundreds of other stories describing every kind of company and financing structure you can think of. But I have found that people who have really learned to respect money have one thing in common. They understand that they are building a dream first and foremost, with the persistence and conviction of seeing that dream through. With this firmly in mind, they are able to decide more clearly how and when outside money should play a role in their plans.

What Kind of Money Can You Live With?

Money always has a price. Playing in the big league, in a time-sensitive industry such as high tech, requires outside money, and often more than you imagined. In addition, software and high-tech start-ups are often based on products and services that are nascent, which means that many of these new ideas and products have few if any predecessors. Therefore, models of success to study and observe are hard to come by.

Understanding what kind of money you can live with is also about accepting what outside investors will take away—and not just in terms of dollars and cents. Seeking investment means potentially giving up control of how you manage your company, how it will be structured, and the operating decisions regarding the team that you have built. This is not always a bad thing. In fact, with the right kind of investors and advisors, you can potentially create a much more efficient and effective organization that benefits dramatically from the wisdom and experience of your board and investors. But the evolution of this company under these circumstances might, in the end, be much different than the entrepreneurial enterprise that you had originally imagined. As Tom Jenkins, CEO of Open Text Corp., says, "Make sure that you are prepared to give up the degree of ownership and control that goes along with third-party financing. Recognize that having a small piece of a big pie can be more satisfying that having a bigger piece [of a much smaller pie]. Otherwise, you're going to forever begrudge giving up what you had."

Who Comes With This Money?

The people attached to the money you get are much more important to the livelihood of your company than the dollars and cents written out on the check. Many experts tout the fact that there is too much money chasing too few ideas.

You want to know not only the trustworthiness of the investors, their reputations, but also their goals. Michael Pralle of G.E. Capital tells of a medical start-up that "formed a business for extracting bone marrow cells to reduce rejection rates during transplantation. While they were interested in making money, he notes, their primary goal was to save lives. A venture firm looking only to grow the business quickly will cause heartaches for the founders as time goes by."

Obviously, in Jackson's case, time constraints left him with little choice as to which venture capital firm to work with. Perhaps if he'd had the time to look closely enough at the track record of the people behind the money, he might have learned that their approach to managing start-ups did not gel with his. Or, more importantly, he might have set up different legal structures around the deal to protect himself when the going got rough.

I know one entrepreneur who has created a list of the qualities of the ideal investor. She keeps revamping this mental list as she meets and talks with other entrepreneurs, learning through both the right choices and the mistakes that they have made. She is not in the market for getting outside investment now, but when she is, I have no doubt that she will be a lot better prepared than most. She will be signing up investors for both the money *and the people* that they can bring to her business.

When Can I *Not* Afford to Get Money?

Too often, I hear young entrepreneurs tell me of the various experiences they had failing to raise money—particularly in the software industry. They are stupefied as to why, in the end, they were not able to close the deal, despite the interest investors had in their prototype, the respect for their credentials, and the work they had done scouting out the market and its potential. When I listen to these war stories, two things come to mind. The first harkens back to the notion that we discussed early in the book about the benefit of creating a product out of a service model. The key benefit to this approach in terms of attracting investors is the ability it gives you to build a customer base. Customers are the key to selling your potential product. If you have had the benefit of working with live customers in the creation of a prototype or even in the creation of the initial product spec document, investors are going to be a lot more interested in you and your potential.

The second issue is, When is it the right time to go out and get money? In my experience, and in that of many entrepreneurs in my industry, getting outside investment becomes necessary only if and when you are fighting

As one of many examples, in 1997, Geoffrey Yan of Institutional Venture Partners made $10 million, a 250% return on their original investment when Whitetree Inc. was sold to Ascend Communications for $66 million. That's what I call a happy exit.

BUSINESS WEEK MAGAZINE

against the clock. If you need to get your product or service to market and cannot support the need for capital within the time frame necessary, then you need outside money. I still advise you to do whatever you possibly can to self-finance your company and its growth until you are able to get a customer, or potential customer, who is going to provide the necessary reference for your product or service and testify to your abilities as a good entrepreneur and leader of your company. Tap out your VISA card, extend your line of credit at the bank, ask family members to give you a loan, do whatever you have to do. In the end, if and when you finally do have to get outside money to fully launch your software product, you will be valued at a much higher level for the organization you have built, for the experience you have gained, and for the customers you have garnered.

Do not get me wrong: If you have a great product and a business plan, and you can get the kind of valuation that you deserve right off the bat, all the better. Just be sure that you have asked and answered the following questions: Is this the right time for me to think about my entrance strategy? Do I have enough experience as an entrepreneur to know what kind of company I am capable of building? Am I ready to enter into a world and commit to relationships based on money that will change the course of my intended entrepreneurial dream?

As with most of the questions the new entrepreneur faces, there is no right answer. But by asking yourself these questions and truly understanding what your entrance strategy is, you will be much better equipped to map out an exit strategy that will satisfy both yourself and your potential investor.

"you are so money"

When I first started entrepreneuring, money was one of those nasty topics that I had to deal with but was not comfortable with it. When Bulldog was a graphics and multimedia design firm, I was able to limit my dealings with money to sales, balance sheets, and a good relationship with my bank manager. Had I known then that I would one day have to spend days and months of my life in rooms with financial experts, convincing them to part with their money to support my notion of a new product niche, I would have taken the topic of money a lot more seriously.

When dreaming, thinking, and talking about money, the new entrepreneur needs to take on the mantra "I am so money" in preparation for getting it. There are two key elements to being "so money."

Get Comfortable with Money as Soon as Possible

Many entrepreneurs that I have interviewed reveal a secret disdain for and/or fear of talking about money. Get over it. Whether you have a friend

Many large technology corporations have their own venture units which they use as a strategic investment tool as much as a financial one. For example, Motorola's venture unit, New Enterprises, looks for potential investment opportunities by identifying an industry of future strategic importance to the company. "First we consider the strategy, then the technology, then the management team, and finally the return on investment."

BOB BURTON,
GENERAL MANAGER,
NEW ENTERPRISES

in the investment community who is willing to lunch with you on a regular basis, or you subscribe to various magazines, scan the Internet, or revisit your university text books, make sure that you begin to get comfortable with talking about the various kinds of money available to you and how much each type will cost you.

This is not just my opinion. I spoke with one investment banker who said that, more often than not, he is shocked at the financial ignorance of the entrepreneurs who approach him. "As with everything that the entrepreneur must do, learning to talk the talk and walk the walk in financial terms is as important as anything else." Do whatever you can to familiarize yourself with money, investment, and investors.

Get a Money Mentor

When you talk to Robert Forbes of Glenmount International, an investment fund, the first thing he will tell you is that every entrepreneur needs a money mentor. "It is absolutely critical. Find yourself someone you know and trust. It is best if you can find someone who not only understands the world of investment but preferably has operations experience, hopefully somewhere close to your industry, so that when times gets tough (and they will), this person will be able to provide you with context. As you grow your company and as you potentially bring on outside investors, you are going to need someone who can provide you with a context for the financial decisions that you will face every day."

If you have been building your championship network, finding this kind of person is not as hard as it sounds. Entrepreneurs who have succeeded many times are often looking for the excitement of being back in the thick of things. David Schneider is a young restaurateur in New York who was able to find a mentor and an angel in one person—Norm Brodsky. The benefits for Norm were that he was attracted not only to the restaurant concept that David put forth but to the fact that David was interested in seeking his advice and assistance, not just his money.

When you find a money mentor, what can you offer them in return? Since money is probably the one thing that you do *not* have as a start-up, you can always offer them an advisory seat on the board and, with the proper legal advice, you can provide them with some form of equity in the company.

One word of warning about money mentors, however. Make sure that they are not hobbyists. As an entrepreneur, you are pouring your heart and soul into the creation and success of your company. In choosing a mentor, pick one who is committed to helping and advising you because it allows them to experience their own entrepreneurial challenge all over again.

Through money mentors, one can develop a respect and a comfort level with regard to talking and thinking about money. In this way, you can begin

The notion of the odds that the typical venture capital firm is playing was best described in terms of what one of the leaders in the high-tech investment community calculates it costs to train a member of a venture capital firm. Mr. Doerr likens training a venture capitalist to crashing a jet fighter. "It's probably going to cost you $20 million to $30 million. Hopefully, you can pull the ring and eject to fly again."

THE ECONOMIST

to map out when, where, and with whom your dreams and outside money may intersect.

stage two: on buying money

THE NEW ENTREPRENEUR DOES EVERYTHING POSSIBLE TO SELL THEIR CONCEPT TO POTENTIAL INVESTORS. BUT IN THE PROCESS, THEY RECOGNIZE THAT THEY ARE NOT ONLY SELLING THEIR IDEAS. THEY ARE ALSO IN THE MARKET OF *BUYING* MONEY.

It's damn tough to get a first-tier venture company to invest, even though each year there is $6 billion or $7 billion in new venture funding. There is a rigor and a discipline that venture capital companies look for.

COMPUTER WORLD MAGAZINE

When Jackson was traveling around the country looking for an investor to sell his business concept to, he was missing one important point: While selling his concept, he was also *buying* money. As with all purchases, you need to evaluate the person you are buying from, the quality of the merchandise, and the terms and conditions that are attached to the product that you are walking away with. If, during your initial stage of "thinking, dreaming, and talking about money," you have forced yourself to think about the kinds of people who are attached to money, then you are much better prepared for assessing investors, even when you are working against a clock that moves in double time. When you are entirely focused (and rightly so) on finding someone who wants to buy your concept, it is often difficult to remember to return to your initial ideas of the kind of money you want to buy.

profile of an investor

When looking for the first round of investment at Bulldog, the first thing I did was to ask people what kinds of investors I should consider in terms of my company's needs. This is certainly a reasonable question and one that most money buyers begin with. But if I were to go through the process all over again today, I would start with a list of the characteristics and attributes that *I* was looking for, the profile of the investor that would best suit the kind of money *I* was hoping to get. To understand the kinds of investors available to you, I suggest that you pick up a book or subscribe to a magazine such as *Red Herring, Upside, Inc.,* or *Fast Company,* which will describe the kinds of investors that are available. Some of these are venture capital firms, mutual fund institutions, angels, bands of angels, government grants, private individuals, etc.

These investors will each have a different set of requirements for their exit strategy. Some, like many of the venture capital firms, will want to get a substantial return—anything from a 20 percent to a 50 percent return—within a two to three-year time period. Others, such as mutual fund investors, will have a longer-term view of their investment, though they will want the same kinds of returns on their money.

A lot of attention has been given to angels and bands of angels, and rightly so. According to the university of New Hampshire's Center for Venture Research, "about 250,000 angels now invest as much as $20 billion a year in some 30,000 companies in America." Mr. Paul Allen, formerly of Microsoft, has a $17 billion fortune and looks for what he calls the "psychic reward" of investing in companies and ideas that interest him.

Today, of course, there are many alternative sources for funding to choose from—non-banking banks, barter credit companies, angels, niche investment firms. To paint a one-dimensional picture of these various investment sources is naïve and inaccurate. Many new players, who call themselves strategic investment developers, not venture capitalist firms, are as concerned with their ability to expand their network of alliances for future technology and product-development advantages as they are with a quick return on their investments. Other organizations, such as Idealab, which is backed by a diverse group of investors, including actor Michael Douglas and director Steven Spielberg, do more than just invest financially in companies. They also provide infrastructure support, such as health care, legal counsel, advertising, and public relations, as well as intellectual capital (in the form of regularly scheduled brainstorm sessions), for their numerous Internet companies, providing them with an incubator to develop ideas. Whether you turn to angels, venture capitalists, incubators like Idealab, or investment bankers, it is important to truly assess and determine where these potential investors fall on the spectrum between the business of financial returns and the business of entrepreneurial pursuits.

As with any important partnership, when choosing an investor, there are certain characteristics and attributes that I would put on my priority list. I recommend that any entrepreneur looking for money consider the following traits in assessing the kind of money they can buy: trust, a long-term player, mutual respect, enlightened self-interest.

I Trust You with My Life

Yes, getting outside money is a financial transaction, when you come down to it. But it is also one of the most important decisions you will make in your entrepreneurial journey. Once you have signed up with an outside investor, your life, to a large extent, is in their hands. Whether or not they have voting control, operational clout and influence, or terms and conditions surrounding additional funding, the truth is that they can make or break your business model. Your entrepreneurial life depends on them. As part of your entrance strategy, when you look into "the whites of their eyes," make sure that you see integrity and trustworthiness first and foremost. You do not have to like them (though you will probably develop some very strong relationships with some of your investors), and you do not have to see eye to eye on every major business decision (and believe me, you

To produce one megahit IPO such as Yahoo, venture capitalists sift through hundreds of ideas. At IVP, for instance, Geoff Yan and his seven partners look at 2,000 ideas a year. The good ones are relatively rare: IVP performs what venturers call "due diligence" on only about 100 prospects. All told, it invests in 12 to 14 of the 100 deals it closely examines.

FORTUNE MAGAZINE

won't). But in the end, you *do* have to have faith in their desire to help you keep your company alive and in the best possible position to achieve the benchmark of success that you have both agreed to.

The best means of determining the level of integrity and trust within a potential investor is through championship. As a new entrepreneur, finding champions in the investment community should be a top priority on your list. In the early stages of thinking and dreaming about money, make sure that you have talked to as many champions as possible within many different parts of the investment community. Ask around about possible investors even before you enter the negotiation stages with them. Some entrepreneurs, such as the founder of Silicon Spice, a start-up in the semiconductor chip business, found a trusting mentor *and* champion in Rob Ryan of Entrepreneur America. As Rob says, "I kept pushing Ian Eslick to build the prototype and find the people to round out his team. And he trusted me and followed my advice. We would get together regularly to review his work to date. Finally, we were able to put together a presentation at the ranch, and I was able to put him in touch with three or four top investors that I know. And, lo and behold, he secured financing."

When you are ready to develop a list of potential investors, always work through qualified referrals. Ask your money mentor to help you network with people who may be able to introduce you to investors whom they have done business with. In doing so, you will be working within a defined network of potential investors who are known entities to people who care about you and your business. This kind of self-referencing circle will reduce the chances of dealing with investors you may *not* be able to trust with your life. But in the end, remember *also* to trust your instincts. Some people may have an unscathed investment record, but you may not feel comfortable with them. You often do not have a lot of choice. But always assess the downside (potential mistrust) for the upside (life-giving injection of cash) before you sign on the line.

Long-Term Player

When you are signing on an investor, you are also creating your board of directors, who will guide you through the process. Despite the stories that we read in the newspaper of the unusual speed of success of high-tech companies such as Netscape and Yahoo, building a business from scratch takes time. Creating a business is not a sprint but a marathon. To achieve success, you will need the stamina and the mindset of the long-distance runner. You will also want to know that your investors (board members) are running the same race.

Make sure that you are prepared to give up the degree of ownership and control that goes along with third-party financing. Recognize that having a small piece of a big pie can be more satisfying that having a bigger piece [of a much smaller pie]. Otherwise, you're going to forever begrudge giving up what you had.

TOM JENKINS,
CEO, OPEN TEXT CORP.

Mutual Respect

When I asked my father what was the most important element of the relationship between an investor and an investee, he said, "Mutual respect. With respect comes trust and integrity and good intentions. If two people respect each other, they will both resist doing anything to jeopardize the relationship. But remember, respect is not something you can ask for." The entrepreneur respects the investors because of the value and experience they bring to the table. They should respect *you* for who you are, for the ideas that you have, and for the plan that you have put together. Sometimes, new entrepreneurs who know they have less experience than others forget to look for respect from their investors, thinking that they need to have more experience or money in order to gain it. The respect that others have for you may increase with time and experience, but an investment deal based on mutual respect right from the beginning is the best jumping-off point for selling an idea and a dream and buying the money to make the dream come true. Always look for respect from your investors. If you have to ask for it, watch out.

WHEN THE NEW ENTREPRENEUR IS IN THE MARKET TO BUY MONEY, THEY UNDERSTAND THAT EVERY INVESTMENT IS BUILT ON AN EQUATION OF MOTIVES THAT IS MADE UP OF EQUAL AND OPPOSITE SIDES OF ENLIGHTENED SELF-INTEREST. RECOGNIZING THIS FACT IS CRITICAL TO SUCCESSFUL RETURNS FOR BOTH SIDES.

In the early '90s, Michael A. Levine, partner at Goodman Phillips & Vineberg and chairman of Westwood Creative Artists Ltd., was acting on behalf of Associated Producers, pitching a historical documentary entitled *Hollywoodism*, based on Neal Gabler's *An Empire of Their Own: How the Jews Invented Hollywood*. Levine was in England visiting Michael Grade, then head of Channel Four. As Levine recounts, "With roots in Poland, Michael Grade came from a family that, in North American terms, would be characterized as moguls in the British entertainment industry. I knew I only had one chance to get funding from Michael, and I knew that the only way to do this was to sell directly to what he cared about most, what motivated him. I didn't walk in and say, 'Michael, I have this wonderful documentary to sell you that I think you will find interesting for your audiences.' Instead, I said, 'Michael, I'm making a movie that tells your father's life story and I know it will make great television.' I sold the deal in two sentences."

Well-known entrepreneurs are sometimes able to sell their business model to investors in two sentences because they have long-standing relationships. Sometimes, because they have a track record. Despite the fact that James Clark was the founder of Silicon Graphics, when he left the company, he forfeited millions of dollars worth of stock options. But a few years later, when he wanted to start another company, he was able to get support and

The computer-related sector continued to be the most active in terms of investment activity in 1997, with 191 computer-related companies attracting a total of $466 million.

CANADIAN VENTURE
CAPITAL ASSOCIATION

investment immediately because of his previous track record as a founder of Silicon Graphics. The firm he started next was Netscape, and when Clark made US$565 million when it went public only 16 months later, he became the stock market superhero, the icon of start-up, high-tech success for many an entrepreneur.

Enlightened Self-Interest

Just as Michael Levine sold his documentary film by focusing on his buyer's interests, beating out the competition within the private placement market requires an understanding of the modus operandi of the players you are courting, or what I call "enlightened self-interest." Of course, if you are a professional eclectic who has had previous experience in sales, then you are well aware of how to develop an understanding of a person's modus operandi through your experience with every buyer you have ever sold to. Getting money is no different.

There are many networks of angels today, often with a technology focus. Silicon Valley Capital Network, Saratoga Boys Club, and the Band of Angels are just a few examples. Others such as the Women's Growth Capital Fund in Washington, D.C., invests solely in women-owned businesses.

Even though, in a sense, you are always sitting on the opposite side of the table from your investors, there is a symbiotic relationship between the entrepreneurs looking for money and venture capital firms looking for ideas to fund. The size of the market alone, particularly in the high-tech industry, is indicative that something is working. According to John Doerr, between 1981 and 1990, "the value of the new personal computer industry grew from virtually nothing to $100 billion, the largest legal accumulation of wealth in history. More than 70 percent of these firms were venture-backed." Use your training as a professional eclectic to fine-tune your ability to detect the enlightened self-interest of those investors to whom you are selling. Find out about what kinds of investments they have succeeded with in the past, what kinds of jobs they have held, and what kinds of entrepreneurs they are most comfortable with. You may not be able to sell your concept in two sentences, but you could get close.

Based on my experience with a host of investors and entrepreneurs alike, I have come up with several ideas about how to capitalize on the enlightened self-interest of potential investors in balance with the interests of the entrepreneur.

profile of the entrepreneur as derelict genius

Let's not take this buying-money concept too far. The bottom line is that while you are in the market of buying money, you most definitely and undeniably are in the process of selling your idea and convincing well-heeled experts that there is a monetary value attached to your ideas. After collecting the advice of several investors and entrepreneurs alike, I have come up with a list of what investors are looking for in you, the entrepreneur, the seller of ideas and the buyer of money.

The Spartan Baby Theory

When I asked Robert Forbes of Glenmount what he looks for before investing in an entrepreneur, he sums it up as follows: "I focus on what I call the Spartan Baby Theory. The myth goes that in ancient Sparta, newborn babies were left on a hill for three days. If they were still alive when you came back, they were keepers. Whether this myth is true or not, I do not know, but it serves as a metaphor in the industry for survivability. Investors look for people who know how to survive, who have tried and tried, failed and come back around, again and again, because the business of success for the entrepreneur is based on the notion of 'survive to succeed.'" The concept of survive to succeed is made up of the following:

Flexibility. Anyone who has been in business is painfully aware of the unpredictability of the future. Investors know this. But when they are assessing a potential start-up venture and the entrepreneur behind it, they are really interested in the entrepreneur's ability to be flexible and to *adjust* to the unexpected turn of events. Stories and examples that reflect one's flexibility and the speed with which one is able to adjust to a new business reality are crucial to their evaluation of you as a good risk.

Patience and Stamina. Stamina and patience are both unsexy but crucial words for the new entrepreneur. The rule of the game of survival is that you only have to get up one more time than you are knocked down. And you will always get knocked down. So the investor is looking for your staying power, your ability to persist, and the innate stamina that will force you to revisit, revamp, and realign your plans as required to get up that one last time. As the story goes, you give up just as you have failed with a new drink called Six-Up. And then, some other entrepreneur with more stamina comes along and invents Seven-Up and makes a killing! Investors look not only for perseverance but also for a certain level of patience that will maintain the necessary stamina to stick it out.

Discipline. Gone are the days that entrepreneurs are able to "fly by the seat of their pants," hoping that they will land on their feet. When you are out looking for money, remember that those who are giving it to you want to be sure that you have a level of self-restraint, that you evoke discipline in the company you run, in the finances that you have managed to date, and in your approach to the customers you are servicing. When our investors first looked at our company, they were happily surprised by the fact that we were paying salaries to our top employees that were far beyond our own and that we had been doing this for a few years. They recognized that we were disciplined enough to know that we needed to provide our key employees with

Over the past five years, the ranks of angel investors have swelled to about 250,000, according to the founder of the Center for Venture Research at the University of New Hampshire. And there are at least 2 million individuals in the U.S. who have the potential, the wealth, and the know-how to become angel investors in the future.

YOUR COMPANY MAGAZINE

more incentive than our partners, who were banking on the future. As Jane Metcalfe says, "Your business is like a B movie in that all the money you have, gather, accumulate, or borrow is reflected in the movie itself. There is no extra money for anything that cannot be seen up on the screen."

Smarts. Just as the entrepreneur is happier to get smart money rather than dumb money, the investor is much happier to invest in people with the smarts. In my mind, this comes back to the notion of respect. Investors want to understand not only that you have a good product or service and are smart and competent but that you and the team you have assembled have a point of differentiation. For us at Bulldog, brand was a key differentiating factor in our pitch. We had competent people working for us and a track record in maintaining a lead position within the multimedia industry, but we also had an ability to build a following, a brand, and a presence in a new highly competitive industry in what, for us, was a new country (the U.S.). That takes smarts, and investors recognize this and are attracted to this differentiating factor.

The Pain Threshold. Investors like to invest in a product or a service that has a certain sense of urgency to it. This is particularly true in the high-tech world, where things move so quickly that developing the right product is a race against the clock as much as it is a race against any potential competitors. At Bulldog, I came up with a notion of the "pain threshold." As more and more companies began to invest in creating a variety of digital media to put on their Web sites and use for their print materials, training, and internal intranet needs, we determined that media asset management was a viable and growing concern. Through the learning we gained from existing beta customers, we were convinced that the highest level of pain, the strongest need for our product, did not lie within the corporate and pre-press industries, as we had originally thought, but was limited to two large and highly influential markets: entertainment and broadcasting. With this insight, we were able to target a more accepting initial customer base and not waste time and money on industries that were not at the right level of "pain" for our product to be valued by them within our time frame.

What reflects a high pain threshold? In our experience, it was the twentieth time a senior level executive from a major company told us that if he did not propose a viable alternative to all the money and time being wasted storing, retrieving, and repurposing video assets (or what have you), then he was going to lose his job. He needed to survive and we were his ticket. To survive and succeed requires that you first find the highest pain threshold and then sell to and own that market as much as possible. In doing your research, make sure that you are as focused as possible on products or services that will immediately relieve pain within an industry or a particu-

Datamerge is the creator of Venturetrack 2000, a CD-ROM packed with information on 500 venture capital firms. The CEO of the company, Spencer Klesner, is a former private eye and is able to get information the same way *Dateline* gets its stories: by sending in investigative reporters.

Investors look at the people, the opportunity, the context, and the deal. The primary notion is that there is a balanced perspective among each of these four elements.

BILL SAHLMAN

lar niche. Investors will relate to this, and you will have a much better chance of gaining their initial interest in your pitch.

the people, the opportunity, the context, and the deal

One of the best summations I heard of what investors are looking for came from Bill Sahlman of Harvard University. "Investors look at the people, the opportunity, the context, and the deal. The primary notion is that there is a balanced perspective among each of these four elements. They look for competent people trying to actualize an opportunity that they're uniquely qualified for in a context that is favorable—without adverse rules or regulations—a deal that relates to the specific use of capital and/or the suppliers that service it. Finally, they look for how the product or service will evolve over time in a sensible way."

stage three: laying the groundwork

Jackson shopped his deal to more than 75 investors in the span of eight months. Others, myself included, have found themselves in the position where they shopped their deal to only one very interested investor, therefore putting themselves in an extremely vulnerable position that they only barely squeaked out of. We at Bulldog learned from this experience. When we did go out for our second round of financing, we spent months preparing for, shopping for, and negotiating the final deal, trying to keep our options open. Understand that getting outside money will become your life. Here are a few words of advice that I give you to get mentally prepared for this adventure:

Know that Looking for, Finding, and Closing the Financing Will Take All of Your Time and Energy

If you have an existing business, ensure that you have structurally set your team up to support and replace you in the key functions in the company. When an investor calls with a question or a new crucial investor meeting is set up by your mentor out of the blue, you must be prepared to drop everything else.

You Are in a Game of Low Hit Rates

Some investors liken the process of looking for money to the success ratio of a direct-mail campaign where you expect a 3 percent reply rate. Silicon Spice, the start-up that Rob Ryan worked with at Entrepreneur America, had quite a few setbacks when one investor pulled out at the last minute. For the 23-year-old entrepreneur, this might have been earth-shattering.

Microlending, typically defined as business loans less than $100,000, is a positive trend for the entrepreneur. According to a recent survey by the U.S. Small Business Administration's Office of Advocacy, 478 banks across the U.S. are involved in a significant way in this market. The group increased microlending activity by 26% just from 1995 to 1996, raising its total level of involvement to $15.8 billion at last estimate.

INC. MAGAZINE

But instead, he simply went back out there to find a replacement as soon as possible. Setbacks in timing or last-minute maneuvering that occur with investors are often outside of your control.

But there are other times when you can actually benefit from a rejection. Bulldog had one investor who came to us based on an article they had read about the company. They were extremely thorough in their initial due diligence and spent a great deal of time with us. In the end, however, they rejected us with the mysterious statement, "We do not invest in people like you." Although they had taken away extremely valuable time from our day-to-day deadlines, as well as from other potential investors who wanted to meet with us, we did not walk away despondent. Instead, we called up our key contact at this venture capital firm and asked him to have lunch with us. At that lunch, we asked him to outline specifically why they did not invest in "people like us." As it turned out, a good part of their decision had to do with a lack of familiarity with the new product category that we were pioneering. But he also gave us great insight into how our method of presenting our case was too heavily weighted with unknowns. Because we had been studying, living with, and breathing these unknowns for two years, we were comfortable and confident with the risk involved. But for investors with less knowledge about our niche, it seemed as if we were positioning the business model in too risky a light.

We changed much of our presentation based on his input and rethought our sales model. We might never have realized we were missing this important repositioning had we not pursued and assessed why the other investor had turned us down.

Do not get discouraged by companies that are not interested in you. Instead, understand *why* they are not interested in the investment, and try to learn what you can from their perceptions, either directly or through your mentor or the champion who introduced you in the first place. That is the best way to reevaluate your business plans, your presentation, your assumptions, and your pitch for the next investor. Maintain your stamina and never give up.

Give Yourself as Much Time as Possible

When I went out looking for our first round of investment, I was told to give myself three to four months. In the end, it took us seven months to find the right funding. The amount of time you should allow yourself for getting money really depends on your present situation. If you are in an existing business with a product prototype, I would still suggest that you give yourself four months at a minimum. If you are just thinking about getting outside money and are looking for seed money to develop your prototype, add another month to thoroughly research and assess the players and get comfortable with how to think, talk, and dream about money. From that point on, you will need a good solid two months to develop a comprehensive business plan and presentation. This may sound like an outrageous amount of time, but it is better to plan for how you are going to survive while you are properly looking for money than to go out too early and potentially damage your chances of getting the right kind of interest.

the lowdown on the essentials for buying money

Rob Ryan of Entrepreneur America has a very specific notion of what it takes to get funding. When reviewing candidates to help them get their businesses together to attract potential investors, he suggests that they have four things already in place: a product or a service, customers, a well-defined team that reflects the energy and the requirements to build the business, and some kind of prototype. If entrepreneurs have not slowed down long enough to thoughtfully put these pieces or parts of these pieces in place, they will have a hard time looking and feeling viable to a potential investor. Rob Ryan has seen many a young entrepreneur come out of the gates racing directly toward the venture community. They spend all of their energy and whatever money they have begged or borrowed to fund the required travel, presentation, and marketing materials only to end up with a few meetings and a handful of no-thank-you's from potential investors. Unfortunately, you rarely get a second chance with those investors unless you already have a track record. Lets look at what the crucial elements of your "pitch portfolio" should be.

The Proverbial Business Plan

When Louis Rossetto of *Wired* magazine was asked to comment on all the Internet and new media companies that were not able to sustain their businesses, despite the hype of the Web, he succinctly said, "Well, it turns out that euphoria is not a business strategy." As an entrepreneur, almost by definition, you begin with an idea that is, hopefully, accompanied by the euphoria of your enthusiasm. But as soon as possible, that dream needs to be articulated and formulated. Enter the business plan. There are 1001 recommendations for the dos and don'ts of business plans. But in my experience, there are really a few essential guidelines for writing business plans. If followed, these will clearly dictate how to structure the plan, how much to say, what to focus on, and how to transform a euphoric dream into a tangible plan that people will want to buy into.

Disciplined focus

First and foremost, never forget that the business plan is a tool to force you to articulate your dreams in a very focused manner. Rather than think of it as the writing of a business plan, think of it as the architecture of your

Entrepreneurs may find it difficult to weigh the advantages of angel capital against those of traditional venture capital. In the end, it seems, the difference will be overshadowed by the terms of each deal and the working relationship a start-up develops with its investor, regardless of whether they are individuals or professional firms.

THE RED HERRING GUIDE TO TECHNOLOGY FINANCE

ideas. And as such, the discipline required to edit out what is unnecessary is as important a process as determining the core of the plan. It takes time and attention to make a business plan believable and viable. As one investor said, "Putting together your business plan is not a Friday-night exercise."

Remember that one of the most important areas in which to apply discipline and focus are niche analyses—the specific details of the market you are going after.

Investors want to see focus and discipline, not just in the document they are reading but in the context you bring to the plan itself. Ensure that you have scoped out your market, talked to customers, and brought a sense of reality to bear on your plan.

Contingency planning, or planning for the what-ifs

The purpose of the business plan is not to attempt to map out exactly what will happen over time with the business model you have scoped out for your product or service but, rather, to account for as many "what-if" scenarios as possible. If you ask any entrepreneur or investor about the original business plan that everyone signed off on and the one that actually took shape over time, nine times out of 10, they will tell you that there is little similarity between the two.

For example, owners of one company I spoke to recalled that their original business plan was based entirely on product sales of a customized sales database. As they began to sell their product, they found that many of their customers were only willing to buy the product if they could provide the necessary ongoing assessments required to integrate this new product into the various divisions of a given company. Although consulting was not in their original plan, they found that not only was this service essential to their product sales, but the revenue generated from this consulting was soon equal to, if not greater than, their product run rate. As this company discovered, what is constant is the intent and the intelligence behind the plans. What changes are the variables that become a reality as you move forward.

If you have put together a good business plan, you will have taken the time to scope out as many variables and assumptions as possible and build them into the thinking that makes up your plan. This is what investors are looking for. As one investor says, "Business plans never turn out the way you expect them to. That's not the point of a business plan. It is the contingency planning that alerts the investor to an entrepreneur who has sussed out his market, understanding that there is no *one* formula for success and that he has thought through how to survive to succeed."

Insightful numbers

There is an old saying: "Figures don't lie and liars don't figure." When it

Rather than trying to predict market success, the best option is to know what to avoid. It's like knowing not to stand outside during a rainstorm. This is best typified by the term discipline—the discipline to organize your resources based on your best estimate of market potential, plus the discipline to abandon your preconceptions if they appear to be off the mark and start the process again.

UPSIDE.COM

comes to developing your financial projections and the details of your spreadsheets, understand that an investor is not as interested in the extent to which you can create spreadsheets but in your ability to provide meaningful interpretations of these projections. Robert Forbes of Glenmount Investments sums this up best: "There is an inverse correlation between the level of detailed spreadsheets and the understanding behind them." When I ask entrepreneurs about their numbers, I hear, 'Well, I stuck the number here, and, to be honest, I've forgotten how I built this damn spreadsheet. When I changed this number, this goes up by this much and, oops, I just can't remember my rationale for this original number.' My recommendation? You can never afford to lose the connection between your spreadsheets and your original numbers.

Referrals, referrals, referrals

As Geoffrey Moore says, the first thing an entrepreneur needs to do is go out and get customers. For those searching for a software or hardware product, if you are in the service business, you are at an advantage in that you are able to provide your investors with referrals from customers who have a history with you. In addition, you are often able to have your customers help you fund your prototype through customized applications that they may ask you to construct for them. You might also be able to get these same customers to work with your prototype, helping you to increase its viability based on testing it in a real production environment. Getting customer referrals is absolutely critical to how a potential investor will valuate you. Prepare your customers for their role by making sure that they are comfortable with it. Find out if there are any concerns they have with you, your company, or the product you are pitching, and clearly brief them on the various investors who may call them during the due-diligence process. And, of course, any recommendations that they are willing to put in writing are always an advantage. For example, during one due diligence, one of our biggest customers sent a letter that said, "Your CTO and his team are among the most thorough and exceptional that I have seen in a long while." Quotes like this from real live customers are worth their weight in gold or stock options, as the case may be.

Business plans are about the discipline of focused market analysis, the insightful assessment of the dollars and cents required to leverage that focus. Most important, they are about contingency planning for the inevitable changes that will occur. Your success with investors will depend on your awareness of this fact.

To separate the gold-plated winners from the also-rans, venture capital firms such as New Enterprise Associates review 3,000 business plans each year and end up funding just 20 companies. Hummer Winblad Venture Partners culls through 1,600 plans to come up with 10 worth seeding.

BUSINESS WEEK MAGAZINE

There is an old saying: "Figures don't lie and liars don't figure."

money and storytelling

Nowhere is the power of storytelling so apparent as in the process of looking for and finding smart money. Assuming you have taken the necessary time to think and dream about money, found a mentor or champion to help you through your planning process, and put together a viable business plan based on your product or service, there is one more critical element that you need to focus on—storytelling.

Despite the level of knowledge and expertise within any group of investors, the level of familiarity and comfort with your particular product or service will vary dramatically from one investor to the other. So what in the end ties the pieces together? What creates a desire, a belief, and a conviction to part with precious money? *The story.* And what the investor is waiting to hear is your version of how you see your dream unfolding, with all the elements in place to ground that dream in the here and now. One entrepreneur described his storytelling strategy for getting seed money for his software product as follows: "I had nothing more than 20 PowerPoint slides and a very compelling story of how our product was going to intersect the growing need for authoring tools on the Web with television programming for children. I had no office, I only had two people in place, and I had no demo. But what I did have was a story of where the world was going, and I gave these individual investors a reason to want to belong to my version of leveraging the technological progress of the Web as a communication pipeline and my expertise in television programming as a means of capturing the imagination of kids and parents alike. I was able to tell my story with such conviction that I raised $500,000 from 10 private investors." Three years later, this company has sales of $20 million and is represented internationally.

Here are some important things that I learned about effective storytelling to investors:

Don't Try to Be a Flavor-of-the-Month Investment

When Bulldog went out for our first round of financing, the story that every investor was buying into was the Web. Web authoring, distribution, advertising, e-commerce—anything to do with the WWW was hot. When we looked at our story, our initial knee-jerk reaction was to position our whole story around the advent of the Web and how that was going to affect people's need for tracking, storing, rerouting, and repurposing digital media files for their Web sites. But when we reassessed our plan, we realized that this was shortsighted. And it was also short-selling our dream, which was channel independent. Instead, our story revolved around the notion that everyone has to store, repurpose, and retrieve their media files—whether they are in digital or analog form. Some companies within our target market would be highly dependent on the Web (such as certain entertainment companies who were repurposing their photos and graphics for sale on the

I always approach investors with the notion that I am selling to the uninitiated, the unconvinced, and the uninvolved.

According to John Doerr, one of the best known venture capitalists, between 1981 and 1990, "the value of the new personal computer industry grew from virtually nothing to $100 billion, the largest legal accumulation of wealth in history. More than 70% of these firms were venture backed." In 1995, 203 venture-backed firms went public, raising $8.2 billion.

THE ECONOMIST

Web), while other customers (such as broadcasters) were mostly concerned with effectively storing and retrieving video clips for their own internal and archival purposes, with little concern for anything to do with the Web.

By demonstrating how our media asset management system could be at the center of this growing concentric circle of media, in all forms, we were building a case that extended far beyond the Web and was not dependent on the success of one communication channel. This, in the end, turned out to be a key motivator for our potential investors. The long-term benefit of having a software product that had the potential to be the cornerstone of digital manipulation for Web distribution, without exclusively being used for that purpose, gave our potential customers and investors a comfort level. In a period when many start-up companies that were able to raise money based on the Web story line did not, in fact, deliver on their Web technology, we were able to bring investors into a much bigger story that outlasted the hot plot line at the time.

As Joy Covey of Amazon.com recommends, "Being straight and mature in your storytelling counts. It is most important to stay true to the core of your business and its strategic priorities rather than compromise yourself in the telling of your story to increase interest and value. If you get caught in this trap, you might find yourself impaired in your strategic flexibility later." Don't get carried away with notions of being a stock market superhero or the flavor of the month. Just tell a good and true story.

Train Like a Boxer

One of the best lessons we at Bulldog learned in the process of getting our first round of financing was the notion that no matter how much you rehearse your pitch, the investor is most interested in how you answer the unexpected questions. As one entrepreneur told me, "When you are in a presentation in front of two or three senior partners from a venture capital firm, you cannot show any weakness. To a large extent, investors are looking for holes or weaknesses. If you stumble or hesitate, they will detect it, and your chances for buy in are dramatically reduced. In an investor presentation, move like a boxer, deflecting the punches in real time, as required."

To move like a boxer requires that you train like a boxer. Besides rehearsing your 40-minute presentation, make sure that you also rehearse the unexpected questions as much as possible. You should be fully prepared to answer devastating questions such as, "So, let's assume that you meet your sales targets in the fourth quarter, as predicted in your pro forma, but then you dramatically drop sales in the next two quarters. What is the plan?"

Lastly, when you are in a presentation in front of investors, be sure that you have the right storytellers in place. Only bring team members into the presentation who are going to participate fully in the telling of the story and in deflecting punches—team members who are quick on their feet. The

Today, there are many more niche venture players. "We like to call it M&Ms, meaning misfits and mavericks, the kind of companies and executives that might otherwise fall through the cracks. We like the M&M niche because there's dramatically less competition here, and we believe that the potential returns are fantastic," says Ted Stolberg of Stolberg, Meehan & Scano, a niche venture group in New York and Denver.

INC. MAGAZINE

last thing an investor wants to see is any deadweight at the top of the company they are thinking of investing in. Choose your storytellers carefully, and try to find a balance between those who can deflect questions and those who can weave the plot line. Leave everyone else at home, no matter how important they are to your company.

the performance

If you follow the model of a service company that segues into a product company as a basis for looking for outside funding, then you will already have many of the pieces in place for a good story. Focusing on the high-tech industry, let's look at what is crucial to successful investor presentations.

Investors do not want to invest in a list of feature/functions. They want to invest in companies that are creating new ways of doing business, launching whole new industries.

KATRINA GARNETT,
PRESIDENT AND CEO,
CROSSROADS SOFTWARE

The Team

As Rob Ryan says, investors are not only buying into you as an individual but also into the caliber of team you are able to assemble. Aside from the smarts they want to see reflected in your point of differentiation, they are also looking at the dynamics of the group as a whole, watching to see whether they exhibit the necessary complementary skills that fill in the places where the lead entrepreneur may be lacking. If you have a team that has worked well together for a few years, its chemistry is palpable and registers with investors.

The Support System

During the highly charged, stressful process of getting investment, it is important that you have the support and insight of a top-notch group of supporters. In addition to the essential money mentor, having the right cheerleaders was invaluable to me throughout my various rounds of financing. For example, the right lawyer can offer invaluable input to your negotiations. Once when Bulldog was down to the final rounds of negotiation with what turned out to be the wrong investor, we instinctively sensed that there was something not right about the deal on the table, but we could not put our finger on it. It was our legal counsel who recommended that we call a face-to-face meeting with all the lawyers and accountants in one room and go through the term sheet line by line until we understood what the real issues of contention were. Placing his laptop on the boardroom table, our lawyer was able to record all the conversations in that room, allowing us to reexamine comments on paper that might otherwise have passed us by. That, in the end, saved us from buying the wrong kind of money for our needs.

In the actual pitching process, the most important person to have on your side is your money mentor. They will provide both the moral support and the wisdom of their experience by simply acting as the spectator throughout the meeting and presentation process. This is a critical role, as it will lend you the perspective that you will need when it comes to finally signing away a part of your company.

The Prototype

Often entrepreneurs seek out venture capital, looking for seed money to create a prototype. In my mind, this is the hardest route to take. Before you approach an outside investor, I strongly advise that you do whatever you can to seed a prototype, even if it is only a conceptual prototype with very little of the fully functional product that you are planning to build. When Bulldog first approached BCE, we had a working prototype. The value of being able to show something tangible to an investor will increase both your chances of gaining their confidence and gaining an advantageous valuation.

The demo

In the technology industry, there are two rules about when to show the demo: The first camp says, if you have a great prototype—if it is something that sizzles and easily demonstrates the power of your story—show it as early on as possible within the presentation. If you do not have a completed prototype, and/or your technology does not lend itself well to being demoed, save it until the end.

The second camp says that you should show the demo only after you have told the story, using the demo as a finale. I am in the second camp for one reason: While it may be true that you are selling a product or service, what you are selling, first and foremost, is yourself and your team as successful entrepreneurs. You are selling not only your interpretation of a market opportunity but your ability, guts, drive, differentiation, and determination to turn that interpretation into an actuality. By showing a demo at the beginning of a presentation, you risk the potential of your investors focusing on the details of the features/functions and faults of your product and getting distracted by them. Additionally, the conversation will be reduced to the product level at the onset of your presentation, making it all the harder for you to bring the investors back to the big picture. It is a lot easier to start with broad strokes, focusing on a story that people want to belong to, allowing them to imagine the possibilities before you provide them with a tangible representation. You can always dazzle them with your demo after you have created the desire to belong to what you are doing. At that point, if something goes wrong with the demo or if there are concerns and questions regarding the product, you can answer these questions from a position of strength. As Katrina Garnett of CrossRoads says, "Investors do not want to invest in a list of feature/functions. They want to invest in companies that are creating new ways of doing business, launching whole new industries."

Being straight and mature in your storytelling counts. It is most important to stay true to the core of your business and its strategic priorities rather than compromise yourself in the telling of your story to increase interest and value. If you get caught in this trap, you might find yourself impaired in your strategic flexibility later.

JOY COVEY

stage four: on negotiating and waiting for money

THE NEW ENTREPRENEUR RECOGNIZES THAT THE TRUE TESTING OF WHETHER OR NOT YOU ARE A VIABLE INVESTMENT COMES DURING THE NEGOTIATING AND WAITING STAGE. EVERYTHING YOU DO, FROM THE WAY YOU WAIT TO THE WAY YOU NEGOTIATE, INDICATES TO THE INVESTOR WHETHER OR NOT YOU ARE REALLY A GAMBLE WORTH TAKING. WAITING IS THE ULTIMATE SALES ARENA.

These are tumultuous times for bankers, who either must reinvent themselves or must figure out new ways to compete against those giants from their smaller regional bases. Either way, it boils down to a set of competitive pressures that are remarkably similar to those facing equity investors.

INC. MAGAZINE

Never forget that while your investors are looking for a passion and energy in your storytelling, they are also looking for a coolness in your negotiating tactics and a maturity in your ability to wait.

Let's assume that you have gotten through several presentations and have found what seem to be a few seriously interested investors. This is the point where your sales job comes into play, because it requires a lot of stamina and diligent attention to detail to move someone from interested investor to signed equity partner. Here is what negotiation and waiting is all about.

you are what you negotiate

The first time I went out looking for investment, I mistook negotiation for exactly what it was—a process of ascertaining the elements and issues that stood between my team (Bulldog constituents) and the other team (the investors) and carefully evolving a set of terms and conditions that would reflect the best possible outcome for all involved. But when we went out for our second round of financing, I saw the negotiation process not only as the ultimate sales challenge but as a chance to test my hand at playing out the paradoxical profile that we talked about in Part Two of this book, "dangerous diffidence," the kind of slightly detached involvement that is required as part of the paradoxical profile of the entrepreneur.

It is in the negotiating stage that your potential investors are truly scrutinizing how you conduct yourself—searching for the lethal combination of passion and commitment with a sense of objectivity—in the heat of the moment. If getting money is one of the most important milestones that you will make in your entrepreneurial life, then how you handle the various stages of due diligence, how you wait between meetings, and how you handle inevitable compromises to close the deal will reflect how well you will treat their money once it is in your company's bank account.

One investor admitted to me that if he encounters an entrepreneur who accepts the terms and conditions of his deal too easily or too quickly, without challenging and seriously scrutinizing the fine print, then he is wary about going through with the investment. His rationale is that when the going gets tough out in the marketplace, he wants his investment to be with an entrepreneur who is going to fight like hell to make sure they get their fair share in a dog-eat-dog world. If they can't reflect this when they are negotiating to give away a piece of their company, how can the investor be confident that they are going to be able to negotiate effectively out in the marketplace?

When Bulldog was looking for our first round of money, the fact that we were 10 days away from a potential disaster had to stay as far out of our minds as possible as we patiently went through the due-diligence process with BCE Capital. Were we desperate? Anxious? On the brink? You bet. But the only card we could afford to play was that of disciplined professionals juxtaposed with unswerving energy and a commitment to succeed.

trust your instincts

Of course, the notion of selling goes both ways. As you are in the final stages of hoping and praying that the potential investor in front of you will believe in your story, it is incumbent upon you to buy into their story as well. Take note of how they are handling the various negotiation stages, recognize signs of their bias in the terms and conditions that they are most apprehensive about or least likely to move on. Remember to take in others' perceptions (such as those of your own team and your money mentor) as well as your own.

And finally, trust your instincts. If you sense something is not right, make sure you examine it with coolness and thoroughness to help you ascertain what to do with your new insight. As they say, there is no better way to predict the future than to study the present.

Having heard the stories of many entrepreneurs and investors alike, I recognize now that no two deals happen in the same way. The last-minute maneuverings and the blind spots that can kill a deal come in all shapes and sizes. Though this is by no means an exhaustive list, here are a few things I would look out for in the final stages of negotiation.

entrechat

When I asked Jackson how he got into such a tight time frame in his first round of investment, he recounted a typical mistake that many first-time entrepreneurs are likely to make. After raising the seed money to build his prototype through a number of private investors, he stepped out into the venture community. Right away, he found one investor who was extremely interested in his deal. So interested, in fact, that after just one meeting, they asked him not to show his prototype to anyone else. Over the course of the next 45 days, he flew out to meet with these people several times, assuming that their request for exclusivity was indicative of a sure deal. When the 45 days were over, the deal was tabled at the partners' meeting (which is often the case in various investment firms) and it was turned down 3 to 5, based

When Louis Rossetto of Wired Ventures was asked to comment on all the Internet and new media companies that were not able to sustain their businesses, despite the hype of the Web, he succinctly said, "Well, it turns out that euphoria is not a business strategy."

If you sense something is not right, make sure you examine it with a coolness and a thoroughness to help you ascertain what to do with your new insight. As they say, there is no better way to predict the future than to study the present.

on a desire to watch the particular niche market that Jackson was playing in for another quarter or so. Unfortunately, the time and energy it took to court this one investor dramatically took away from his ability to find others and manage his company at the same time. In the end, the pressure to find money—any money—was heightened and, in some ways, may have led to his desperation to sign on the venture capital firm that he ended up with.

As entrepreneurs, it is easy to get dazzled by anyone who says, "Yes, I am interested." My recommendation? Be very careful. Interest in your business plan may be genuine, but it is not a guarantee of anything. As much as possible, try to get yourself in a position where you are negotiating more than one deal at a time, or if you are legally restricted for a period of time, at least have a back-door option ready. In the end, this kind of planning can save you.

In ballet, there is a beautiful step called the entrechat. As the ballerina jumps straight up in the air, she switches her right and left foot in front of each other several times, as quickly as possible, before she lands in a plié. That ballet step represents exactly the kind of juxtaposition you want to have with a couple of potential investors. If at all possible, while the deal is "up in the air," keep yourself balanced between the two of them as much as possible before you finally land safely on both feet.

the vanilla contract

In our second round of financing, we were heavily courted by a venture capital firm that seemed to have some knowledge about our specialized market segement. They flew in to meet us, saw our product, and indicated a very keen interest. So much so, they offered to conduct all the customer due diligence and technology partner referrals on behalf of all the other investors. We agreed that this seemed like a reasonable idea, since time was short and they were familiar with many of the players. Within 10 days, the venture capital firm sent us a transcript of all the telephone interviews they had conducted with our customers and technology partners. We were delighted with the favorable responses. At this point, we were already in the final stages of negotiation and documentation with several other institutional investors. Surprisingly, despite the intense interest from the first venture capital firm, we still had not received a term sheet from them. After several requests, they finally faxed over a term sheet at the eleventh hour. To our horror, despite the due diligence that they themselves had conducted and their presumed understanding of our market, they were offering us a number of unacceptable terms.

We got on the phone to them, determined to find out what was at the bottom of this. When we remarked that there were a number of deal breakers in their offer, they said, "We don't understand what the problem is. As far as we are concerned, this is a vanilla contract—you can't do any better. We would be very surprised if, in the end, you were offered anything better."

If you can't exactly predict where the market is headed, the next best thing is to know where it has been. Ray Noorda, former chairman of Novell, is quoted as saying, "I'm not a visionary, I'm a historian. At least if you know which direction the market is headed away from, that can give you some idea of which options to rule out."

UPSIDE.COM

With the help of one of our board members, we gracefully turned down the term sheet. Then we put the pieces into place to redo the due diligence and were on the phone, alerting the other investors that we had already turned down the offer of this particular venture capital firm.

What we learned from the experience was that in having this one venture capital firm conduct the due diligence, we allowed them, in some ways, to take on a leadership role that might influence the other investors both in terms of their proposed knowledge of the industry and in their direct contact with the customers. Had they tried in any way to communicate with the other investors, they might have seriously damaged our ability to maintain a more reasonable deal structure. The lesson? Never allow one investor to conduct your due diligence on behalf of a number of investors. And when you hear the words "vanilla contract," read "lowest possible valuation, highest degree of control."

face-to-face

Although it costs more and takes a whole lot more time to organize, try as much as possible to have face-to-face meetings in the negotiation process. Telephone calls are obviously necessary, especially if you are dealing with various geographic locations, but try to limit these calls to cover very narrow and specific topics. The worst possible scenario that you could be involved in is a five-way conference call that is an attempt to cover a whole range of issues, from legalities to logistics to questions regarding due diligence to timing. Invariably, these telephone calls create *some* level of confusion and can even set you back if someone misinterprets something that is said on the phone in an offhand manner. If phone calls are unavoidable, set your agendas very carefully, choose a chairperson to lead the conversation, and always follow up with documented notes of the meeting. If someone has an issue, they will be able to respond to the written word a lot more effectively than they will an "interpretation" of a conversation that no one remembers with any accuracy.

theories of creative anomalies

In the James Bond movie *Tomorrow Never Dies*, media tycoon Elliot Carver states his firm belief in the theory of creative anomalies—the theory that if something sounds too good to be true, you know that something is about to go seriously wrong.

In the final stages of negotiation with potential investors, you often come to a point when everything is going so well that it spooks you. If this happens, beware. In my experience, this is often a sign that the other side is saving some major potential deal breakers for the last minute. The vanilla-contract investors were a case in point. This doesn't happen because anyone is trying to be sneaky. This is just a savvy negotiation tactic. It is always easier

Oh, guess what? I'm looking at another $50 million company in five years. Astonishing! Oh, and what do you know? Here's a 20% margin. That's amazing; I've never seen that before!

BILL SAHLMAN

to negotiate with someone who believes a deal is done than with someone who is still in the earlier and less optimistic psychological mindset.

The best way to avoid testing out the theory of creative anomalies is to begin probing for the other side's hot buttons as early as possible. For example, if you suspect that control is the key issue, try to get a sense of what kind of voting structure the investor is going to ask for. If the investor has an issue regarding some former voting structure on an existing board or if a special condition on your line of credit is worrisome for them, try to suss this out as soon as possible. This is neither easy nor always possible. Try to gather as many crumbs of information as possible, and begin to *guesstimate* what you think the hot buttons are going to be. Begin to draw out the various contingency plans for how you are going to counter any potential deal breakers—because there will always be a few.

Real generosity toward the future lies in giving all to the present.

ALBERT CAMUS,
THE REBEL

The second tactic in sidestepping the theory of creative anomalies is to make sure that you already have both your own list and your prediction of the other side's list of deal breakers, the issues of contention, and the respective wish lists. Make sure that the deal breakers are distinctly separate from the issues of contention, and try to limit them to one or two points. As a good friend of mine who has been through many rounds of financing says, "Find the deal breakers and address them first. You can cover everything else by putting in the appropriate mutually assured destruction clauses. Always be willing and ready to concede to what you think is at the top of their wish list as long as it is at the bottom of your contention list. This formula usually keeps everyone relatively happy."

Sometimes the theory of creative anomalies is simply reflective of the idiosyncratic nature of people. There are times when the style of a particular investor or venture capital firm is not at all indicative of their interest level in the deal. In our first round of financing, we had one firm who sat through our presentation patiently and jotted down a number of notes. When the presentation was done, they did not have a single question for us. On the same day, we went back for the fifth meeting with another potential investor, who had yet another round of questions for us to answer. If you had asked me to guesstimate as to who was going to buy into our business, I would have said that the first investor was definitely out because they seemed to show relatively little interest and that the second investor was a 90 percent yes based on the details of their questions. In the end, the exact opposite was true. The first investor was so comfortable with our information and so confident in their investment interest that they had only a few questions for our broker, which they asked in a side telephone conversation. They ended up coming in with the largest financial commitment, while the second firm, in the end, turned down the deal.

a deal is not a deal until it is signed

One entrepreneur recounted a story that happened to him when he started his first company, a new media firm that specialized in creating multimedia programs for the retail industry. Through one of the projects they were doing, they came across a concept for a retail management system that could be marketed to smaller retailers who could not afford the premium-priced computers which were the industry norm in the 1980s. They began building this prototype, struggling to support their development efforts while they maintained their service business. And then suddenly, one of the large telecommunications companies heard of this concept and became very interested. Through four months of negotiation for a joint-venture partnership, this little company had all the right signals that this was a done deal. So much so that, in anticipation of a sure deal, they spent every last penny completing the prototype, despite the fact that they were behind in their rent. Just as they were worrying about how they were going to possibly make up for the debt they had gotten themselves into, they got a call from their potential strategic partner and investor, who said, "Congratulations! Not only have we decided to do the deal but we have also agreed to increase our investment in your product to enable us to conduct a more extensive marketing campaign. We will be sending the legal papers to you within the next two weeks. Congrats, it's a done deal!"

This entrepreneur describes how they were all so excited that, amid the leased computers that were in arrears and in the office space that they were risking being evicted out of, they danced around, popped the champagne, and called their mothers.

And then, five hours later, this same entrepreneur got another call. This time, the news was not so great. "Listen, I am so sorry to tell you this, but there seems to have been a bit of a mix-up at the committee level. Although we are still really interested in the product, we have had a loss on some unexpected deals and will not be able to go through with this one. I'm so sorry to have misled you."

Epilogue? The company scaled back, retrenched, and paid all their bills. They worked out of a home office for a year, until they were able to regroup and determine what their next product would be. The lesson? A deal is never a deal until all the documents are signed and the check is in the bank. Even then, wait until it has cleared and your investor calls you to be the first one to say congratulations.

There is a real difference between hot companies and hot products. We don't expect hot companies to be fully formed yet—they are too new, and they are still essentially one-trick ponies. The best of these have products that are leading their market and products that come in families. They scale.

HOWARD ANDERSON, FOUNDER, PRESIDENT, AND MANAGING DIRECTOR OF THE YANKEE GROUP AND CO-FOUNDER OF BATTERY VENTURES

stage five: on getting, managing, and worrying about money

There's an old saying, "Be careful what you wish for—you might get it." For weeks and months on end, your entire being has been focused on getting investors to decide that you and your company are worth the gamble. Even when you are attempting to diligently attend to every other detail of your company, your mind is constantly churning through the details of the term sheet. You are wondering whether you should call your legal counsel one more time to discuss the changes that you agreed to make in the last round of documentation, or you are revisiting a passing remark made by the accounting firm that conducted the due diligence. When you have signed every last document and look up into the face of your new partner, it is hard to imagine not having to be consumed with finding money.

Be careful what you wish for—you might get it.

We won! We won!—Now what do we do?

But don't fret. That euphoria lasts for only a few precious days. Almost immediately, your short stint of jubilation is followed by a whole new set of issues to worry about: how to integrate investment into the people, structures, and culture of your company. How to manage and worry about the money you just got.

the slow dissolve

In one of the most beautiful scenes of the French film *Betty Blue*, the two lovers are painting beach houses in the off-season of a vacation spot in France. At the end of the scene, against a brilliant orange sunset, they are leaning back against their car and looking at the fruits of their labor. Then all the other brightly painted cottages, the blues, oranges and reds and yellows, begin to blur. There is a slow dissolve of the scene, until you are not sure whether you are looking at the blur of the colored cottages or at the inside of the mind of the female protagonist and her interpretation of the colors.

This kind of cinematic technique is a great metaphor for what happens to your company, structure, and culture after you "get money." You slowly begin to feel as if your own company is slipping away from you. The people around you begin to reshape their expectations and understanding of their roles while your investors begin to become a very focused part of your life. This is not necessarily a bad thing, but just as the slow dissolve in *Betty Blue* left you wondering what you were looking at, so the entrepreneur begins to wonder what they are seeing—their company going through a genuine change or the perception of *real* change as seen through the minds of the players. Here are some of the elements at play in this slow dissolve.

stock options do not a culture make

In his article on building a company's vision, Jim Collins talks about the fact that "maximizing shareholder wealth does not inspire people at all levels of an organization." He goes on to say, "Motorola people like to talk about impressive quality improvements and the effect of the product they create on the world. When a Boeing engineer talks about launching an exciting and revolutionary new aircraft, they do not say, 'I put my heart and soul into this project because it would add 37 cents per share to our earnings.'"

Although Collins was talking about the vision of larger, more established companies, the same thing is true about start-up companies. When forming your core team prior to getting outside investment, the way you ration out pre-money stock options is a hotly debated topic. What I learned is that this debate does not end once the deal is done. Because you, as the leader, have been so focused on preparing for and ramping up the team to "get money," it is often hard to reorient your team and remind them what their reason was for joining the company and what their role within it is. It is not to determine, guesstimate, or speculate when and how their stock options will vest but to begin to perform like never before. Why? Because as soon as you actually have your investment in hand, the clock *really* begins to tick. Now you and your team are racing against time. You are working not only to beat the competition and maximize your market share and perception of leadership within your niche but to meet the investor milestones you set as a means of providing your investors with the return they are looking for. The only way to do this is to ensure that your team players focus on their jobs and recognize that their ability to perform against the set milestone is dependent not on speculation about their stock option plans but on their contribution to increasing the value of the company as a whole. Stock options can and should be used to attract talent. They can be used to reinforce the contributions that your team members have made and continue to make. They can be a good way to evaluate individuals within the company in terms of what they are contributing to the entrance strategy of getting money. But do not, under any circumstances, allow stock options to become a replacement for the active envisioning that you need to keep in place and the belonging that you want your team to feel for you and your company. If you do, you risk playing a never-ending game of who has more stock options. You may also lose the soul of the company along the way.

"Everybody Was Gauging the Distance between Here and There"

One well-heeled angel told me about a common error that first-time entrepreneurs make. They misinterpret the fact that they suddenly have a few million dollars in the bank as a sign that they are rich. Working capital is

Rapid-growth businesses use a variety of compensation practices. Entrepreneurs expressed the view that salary should be about 65% to 75% of total compensation. Profit sharing was the most often used method (in 72% of companies), but bonuses, commissions, and stock options were also frequently used.

NANCY ROBERTS AND BRIAN GOLDEN, "HOW ENTREPRENEURIAL COMPANIES ARE COMPENSATING KEY EMPLOYEES"

something that can make you feel rich, because it can sit on a balance sheet. Remember, there is no such thing as an overcapitalized start-up business.

Managing your perception of this sudden injection of capital is a big, big part of your job within your company. Suddenly, groups of people who were working together in a kind of fishing-camp mentality will be arguing over resources, all in the name of getting the job done, of meeting investor milestones. The best way to cut these requests off at the knees is during the next meeting of the management committee. Succinctly communicate to managers that they are the gatekeepers of this hard-to-come-by money that is sitting in the bank. Lead them through the process of determining, as a group, how much they think it will take to accomplish the goals set within each quarter, reinforcing the idea that you are all on the *same* team. As a team, decide what is more important to the bottom-line business model—to invest in a few more engineers to complete the product development or to spend the extra money buying a highly skilled salesperson who is demanding a higher salary than projected? Would it be better to hold off on creating the sales training manual or adding a sales administrator to build the customer database?

Once the management team comes to a decision, make sure that you allow one or two of them to present the plans directly to the board together with you. If there is any residual feeling within your management team that you and your company have newfound wealth, those feelings will be squashed pretty quickly at the board level.

This attitude must filter through the organization so that everyone understands that the longer you can survive on the money you have, the better chance you have of providing a healthy return on the investment over time—and yes, the more valuable everyone's individual stock options will be worth. Let your team gauge the distance between here and there, if only to ensure that they understand what it is going to take to travel the distance in between.

L'endurcissement

At one point in the book *Le Divorce*, the protagonist goes through a step-by-step description of the process of her sister's divorce, including the divvying up of the assets and other unpleasant arrangements that have to be made. One of the older, more experienced French matrons observes, "It is always like this, people start out in agreement. Then, the hardening. *L'endurcissement*. Perhaps that is only another word for experience or for growing up."

If you are an entrepreneur, getting outside money does create a certain element of *l'endurcissement* for both you and your team. People who have been loyal to you for years come under the scrutiny of a management team that is being asked by the board to cut costs. Your historical loose reporting structure is seen as a recipe for redundancy and inefficiency by your

Maximizing shareholder wealth does not inspire people at all levels of an organization.

JIM COLLINS,
HARVARD BUSINESS REVIEW

It is always like this, people start out in agreement. Then, the hardening. *L'endurcissement*. Perhaps that is only another word for experience or for growing up.

DIANE JOHNSON,
LE DIVORCE

investors, and any decisions that you made regarding how money was spent in the past are suddenly questionable to your new board. At this point, you can see why it is helpful to have moved away from the notion of a family-like culture to a company culture. Otherwise, the changes that you are forced to make when bringing in outside investment would be more painful than necessary, making the difference between here and there more dramatic.

the role of your board of directors

Learning how to work with and manage a board of directors will become a very big part of how you spend your time and energy. Maximizing the power and effectiveness of your board requires an understanding of the isolation factor.

The Isolation Factor

Bob Dylan once sang about serving the Lord or the devil; it always comes down to one or the other. This has become the theme song of many an entrepreneur who is suddenly faced with the challenge of working with a newly formed board. As Geoffrey Moore describes it, "The problem with the entrepreneurial paradigm is it doesn't make it clear that you *do* need to serve somebody. I think this paradigm often creates the illusion that you can serve only yourself. And there is no greater danger to both yourself as a person and to your investors than to try to do this."

This brings us back to the paradoxical profile of the "lone coach." Pre-money, many entrepreneurs find the task of coaching and encouraging their team while they themselves wrestle with their role of "bringing the water to their team members" challenging but doable. But when you have outside investors, you will find yourself in an even more isolated place, where you are trying to anticipate and answer to the financial goals of your investors, the operational needs of your team players, the product needs of your customers, as well as the visionary needs that cycle through your own mind. I have found that the following attitudes greatly minimize the pressure of trying to serve these often disparate groups:

Fault Tolerance

When you are negotiating for seats on the board, ensure that you are assembling, as much as possible, a group of people who represent a balanced portfolio of operational know-how and financial expertise. Get to know your potential investors, find out what their backgrounds are, and understand their biases. Not only are you looking for operational know-how within the board, but you are looking for what I call "fault-tolerant" individuals, who either have experience operating companies or entrepreneurial experience that is directly related to your particular niche. If you are lacking in the level

Be sure to take a board seat to guarantee yourself a voice in the future of the company. Make certain that you also appoint the same number of board members as your investors. Some equity agreements stipulate that an additional seat be given to a neutral party.

YOUR COMPANY MAGAZINE

of fault tolerance within the investor representation on your board, ensure that you have the ability to fill at least *one* seat on the board with the member of your choice—and then find that player yourself.

Today, fault tolerance comes in all shapes in sizes. In fact, a whole new host of "nouveau" venture capital firms, such as Softbank and Flatiron, are filling a gap in the marketplace by providing smaller initial investments to start-ups (from $500,000 to $5 million) that some of the more traditional venture capital firms can no longer afford to focus on. But perhaps more important, these fault-tolerant investors are fueling industry niches where they have particular expertise to complement the companies they invest in. For example, Colonna, which is the founder of Flatiron, has a lot of experience in publishing and media, which is particularly advantageous for Internet start-ups looking for knowledge and strategic input in a very new media-oriented business. These investors reflect fault tolerance based on their familiarity and direct entrepreneurial experience in media that is crucial for those entrepreneurs pushing the boundaries of where media and technology intersect. If you have a good level of fault tolerance on your board (whether that be through a strategic investor, an angel, or through traditional venture capital), they will be able to guide you and support you, often referring back to what they did (as operators, not investors) in a former life, when they were in similar situations, within similar industries. You will need this perspective that goes beyond quarterly report reviews.

One investment banker I know always says, "Information is the investors' food. So be sure to serve it to them in just the right proportions and with the right presentation. That way, they will never walk away from the table wanting more."

Investor Sustenance

One investment banker I know always says, "Information is the investors' food. So be sure to serve it to them in just the right proportions and with the right presentation. That way, they will never walk away from the table wanting more." I have found this to be true in my dealings with investors. When you first begin to hold board meetings, be sure that you have a chat with each of the board members to find out how they like to be communicated with, serving each individual's enlightened self-interest while creating an effective collective communication.

When it comes to your directors, provide them with a regular overview and assessment of your competition. Not only is this essential for your own information, but the discipline of doing this on a regular basis will help to counter any false alarms on the part of board members who may "hear" something without having all the facts, often introducing a sudden lack of confidence in you and your company until you have spent ample time refuting the false claim. Ask for their valuable input, seriously consider any information they pass on to you, and amalgamate it into your arsenal of competitive information, rather than react to the potential threat it may pose.

And never, never tell your board of directors that there are no competitors. First, this often indicates that the market you are in is not worthy of the attention of other players within your industry. Second, it can be an invitation to fuel fears that an unknown competitor is lying in wait to pounce.

on life after money

THE ADVANTAGEOUS BURDEN OF MONEY IS NOT TO BE FOUND IN THE FACT THAT YOU HAVE TO ANSWER TO SOMEBODY WHERE YOU DID NOT HAVE TO BEFORE. IT IS NOT TO BE SEEN IN THE STRUCTURE AND FORMALITIES THAT YOU DID NOT HAVE TO ADHERE TO IN THE PAST. INSTEAD, THE BURDEN RESTS ON THE FACT THAT WHILE YOU HAVE CHOSEN TO ACCEPT MONEY FROM OTHERS, YOU HAVE ALSO BROUGHT OTHERS INTO YOUR STORY.

keeping your heart and soul in the black

Whenever someone asks me what it is like to go from a completely privately self-funded company to one that has outside investors, I always say that I am living the life of someone who understands the "advantageous burden of money." In the entrepreneur's world, the bottom line is that you always have a choice as to how much money and what kind of money you infuse into your company. I, along with my partners, chose to forfeit a portion of control of our company in exchange for the money required to build toward a much bigger dream than we were able to finance ourselves. Yes, there is a sense of loss along the way, and yes, there is a hardening (*l'endurcissement*) that takes place, and yes, there is a whole list of compromises that you are forced to make that feel very far from choice. But this decision also provides you with one of the most expansive learning experiences about understanding people's motives that you will ever have. It challenges the strength of your communication, negotiation, and sales capabilities and tests your trust, faith, instincts, and guts.

Bringing investors into your company is part of the evolving plot line of the entrepreneur's tale. It becomes incumbent on you, then, to demonstrate to your investors again and again why it is worthwhile for them to *want* to become part of your epic. Amid quarterly reports and term sheets, retell your story, and you will ensure that you keep your heart and your soul in the black, even when your spreadsheets reflect the fact that, financially, you may temporarily be in the red.

I always say that I am living the life of someone who understands the "advantageous burden of money."

dream big dreams about smashing tiny particles

I call people rich when they are able to meet the requirements of their imagination.

HENRY JAMES,
PORTRAIT OF A LADY

Every entrepreneur has had a different experience in looking for and finding outside money.

Although it would appear that Jackson should have been devastated by what happened to him, he instead felt inspired to tell his story to others in the hope of passing on what money taught him. Jackson is determined to use what he has learned from his past experience to guide him in his future pursuit of his dreams.

To date, I have had very positive experiences in finding investment, though not without shake-ups, last-minute changes, and anxious moments. My experience has been limited to date to raising pre-IPO investment. I have no doubt that preparing for an IPO adds a whole new dimension to the notion of "money," as many entrepreneurs have recounted to me. As always, through the stories of others, we each begin to formulate our own insight and understanding in preparation for the unknown.

The key to getting money and utilizing it is to remember why you are going out to get it in the first place. Sometimes, that initial impulse is clear *only* to you, so it becomes your job to communicate its importance to all of your stakeholders. This idea became crystal clear to me one day when I read a headline in the front section of the *San Francisco Chronicle*: "Physicists dream big dreams about smashing tiny particles." The heading was ludicrous, but then I realized that in some ways, it was reflective of the experience of any entrepreneur who has ever tried to get someone to believe in their dreams. The physicists only *appear* to be obsessed with tiny particles. In reality, they are in the process of discovering important scientific revelations about the very nature of matter itself. In dreaming about this, they are able to find those who are willing to support them in their efforts. The same holds true for the entrepreneur.

If you are an entrepreneur who is considering getting outside money, you are missing the mark if you think that the sole purpose of all your efforts is to focus on how to exit with as much money as possible in your pocket. Instead, consider the world you are about to enter, remembering to ask the hard questions along the way. In the meantime, you will have had the chance to dream big dreams. And as for accumulating wealth? Whether you are able to smash tiny particles together, build a new form of educational software, or build a new volunteer medical program in a far-off country, you will have gained a wealth of experience. As Ralph Touchett says in *Portrait of a Lady*, "I call people rich when they are able to meet the requirements of their imagination."

storytelling

storytelling

storytelling

storytelling

chapter 11 # The Beauty of Imbalance

Sterling put down his handmade mug and relished the taste of the echinacea concoction that he had just made for himself as part of his New Year's resolution to avoid caffeine at all costs. He quickly printed out his presentation on the new laser printer that he had installed in his home office on the weekend. Then he changed out of his Dri-Fit jogging suit and got into the shower. Looking forward to his busy day, he mentally prepared himself for one of the biggest presentations of his career as a director of product development for High Tech Company Inc.

As the hot water pounded on his back, he visualized the route he would take home later that day to avoid the rush-hour traffic and arrive on time at his in-laws' anniversary dinner. This exercise helped to keep at bay the slight nervousness he felt creeping up his rib cage as he loofaed.

Meanwhile, Sterling's wife of five years, Becca, was already at the office and completing her second conference call of the day. She always arrived at 6:00 a.m. and worked until 9:30 a.m. without interruption. That allowed her to take a two-hour break in the late morning (which her personal trainer told her was her peak time for physical exertion) and attend the kick-boxing class at the gym down the street. Who said entrepreneurship stole your life away from you? She was still able to do everything she had always done—her three-times-a-week gym routine, lunch with a friend at least once a week, volunteer work—*and* she had maintained a good marriage. Frowning, she tossed aside a magazine that reported, "Not surprisingly, entrepreneurs in 1997 reported a divorce rate of 80 percent." Becca looked around her small, but growing, multimedia design firm and felt a moment of peace as she watched her three top designers conferring on the upcoming client presentation. They were neatly dressed and in the office every morning by 9:00 a.m. She felt confident about the team's ability to close the deal without her involvement. Or should I attend the presentation this time? she wondered. Too late, she thought. I don't want to miss my kick-boxing class. She whisked out of the office, speed-dialing her darling Sterling on his cell phone to wish him luck on his presentation. Thank God I made the decision to start my own company last year, she thought to herself. I don't know what all the fuss is about—imbalance, lack of control, and sacrifice? I feel in complete control. And with that, she sprayed her B-12 vitamist into her perfectly lipsticked mouth, simultaneously checking in with her assistant in case she had missed any urgent calls en route to the gym. [Pan to view of Golden Gate Bridge.]

I have yet to meet a Sterling and Becca, though I know that they probably do exist somewhere, whether in myth or in actuality: "See Dick (Sterling) work as a career man in Silicon Valley. See Jane (Becca) start up her own multimedia company after receiving her MBA from a top-notch college. See Sterling and Becca lead a balanced life as they both pursue their goals with a finesse and a sense of control that surprises even them." Just as the icons of the 1950s posed a dangerously perfect version of the North American family that people everywhere tried to emulate, so Sterling and Becca reflect an unrealistic image of the young up-and-coming entrepreneurial couple: people who are somehow miraculously able to juggle the demands of their start-up company, their family life, and their personal desires and interests with grace and confidence. Somebody, please stop the film, at least long enough for the truth to begin to seep in.

In the 1970s, life began to get serious again after the heady days of the '60s and the onset of the oil crisis. The 1980s will be remembered as the "Me Generation." In the past decade or so, we have been inundated with the notion of balance: balanced diet, balancing one's career and family life, balanced relationships, balanced ego—and the list goes on. I must admit I really *want* to like balance, I *want* to aspire to it, but as an entrepreneur, I know I cannot truly have it. Nor, I hesitate to admit, do I want to. Why? For two very good reasons.

the downsides of balance

balance holds a false promise

Balance is one of those words like "happiness" or "fulfillment" which present a concept that is unattainable. And after unsuccessfully striving to attain it for years on end, a person often finds themselves asking, "But *why* do I actually want it? When I get to 'balance,' what will I have to show for it except a rather symmetrical-looking scorecard that only *I* get to pull out of my night-table drawer every few months to remind myself that I have managed to stay as close to the little white line as possible.

I prefer an exciting life. Balance, as in nature, is death.

HARRIET RUBIN

We give permission to be saved from our worst nature, or to challenge our better selves, to put it that way.

DIANE JOHNSON,
LE DIVORCE

"balance, as in nature, is death"

So says Harriet Rubin, author of *The Princessa: Machiavelli for Women.* As someone who has spent my life entrepreneuring, I subscribe to this philosophy wholeheartedly. Those who choose to take on the challenge of entrepreneuring are misguided if they believe that balance is the goal of the exercise. It is not. That is not to say that you cannot strive to find a place where you can be true to yourself. But rather than focus on the notion of balance, I suggest you look for a little healthy imbalance, an acceptance that feeling slightly askew may be an indication that you are at the beginning of a trek which requires your full unabashed attention, and a belief that the unknown can become a place of familiarity and assurance.

That's why you are an entrepreneur—to not have balance!

DEIRDRE O'MALLEY

applied torque

Sociologists and academics have lots of words for the entrepreneur's personal style. They tell us that a high proportion of entrepreneurs are "high sensation seekers," workaholics, or individuals who suffer from "anxiety addiction" or "attention deficit disorder." All of these terms include the notion of being out of balance.

Extreme cases can be disastrous. But with practice and the right attitude, imbalance, like so many of the challenges of the entrepreneuring lifestyle, can be turned into a winning situation. I like to think of this process as applying a little torque. By maintaining a high level of torque in all that you do, you can use the imbalance in your life to help you to think clearer when the pressure is on, to maintain stamina when everyone else has lost theirs, and to reignite your passion and enthusiasm when the day-to-day stresses of entrepreneuring undermine your willpower. For the entrepreneur, the struggle to maintain just the right amount of torque is a never-ending battle of give and take, keeping you teetering on the edge of believing in future possibilities while ferociously trying to participate in the limitations of the present.

your own grand epic

As Manfred De Vries writes, "Entrepreneurs have an overriding concern to be heard and recognized—to be seen as heroes." This concern often leads to behaviors and lifestyle decisions that others see as obsessive or even destructive. As Keith Kocho of Digital Renaissance says, "I was constantly being told by my friends, 'Get a life.' And I'd look at them and say, 'You know, I kind of like what I do. I'm truly fulfilled by my desire to create my own story and to have an opportunity to create something, especially in the world of technology, which has never been done before.' I'd give up almost anything in my life to see this dream through. There's a spark in me that has the capacity to override just about everything. Well, almost everything."

Some do not believe that the desire to live heroically is a positive thing. Moses Znaimer claims that there is some kind of "damage" within the true entrepreneur, some kind of desire to destroy in order to create. Whether this means the destruction of the status quo within an industry in order to redefine a product or service, or the need to push through the bias of others, enabling you to create a new notion of success, there seems to be some kind of "obsessive messianic urge" that forces the entrepreneur to keep searching and pushing for the creation of what I call "your own grand personal epic." But De Vries reminds us that "the boundaries between highly creative and aberrant behavior can be blurred. The mix of creative and irrational is what makes entrepreneurs tick and accounts for many of their positive contributions." Perhaps the combination that De Vries is talking about is really another way of describing the entrepreneur's applied torque.

What a day-to-day affair life is.

JULES LAFORGUE

I get motivated by imbalance. Dream the perfect life, but if you achieve it—know there is something wrong.

JONAS SVENSSON

on exhilarating panic, enlightened anxiety, and the blurring of boundaries

Andrea Southcott, who works with her husband as the managing partner of Bryant, Fulton & Shee, describes her life as an "exhilarating panic." In *The 500 Year Delta* the authors describe "enlightened anxiety" as follows: "[It] cannot be erased, because anxiety is a natural reaction to a world in extreme flux. Rather, it must be embraced and used."

For anyone living with an entrepreneur or trying to grapple with the mindset of their newly found self (as a new entrepreneur), there is a heightened sense of urgency that comes from being needed in too many places at once, of a life that is marked more by the few rare moments of downtime between crises than by anything else. The entrepreneur's level of stress, feelings of panic, and yes, exhilaration (a by-product of creating a company from scratch) are perhaps similar to what doctors in an emergency ward or firefighters experience. That is not to say that responsibility and daily performance are reserved for the entrepreneur alone. But when the life and death of your company rests on your shoulders, it is hard to separate yourself from your entrepreneuring. As Lanny Goodman, a consultant to entrepreneurs says, "It's a mistake to think that owning your own business can be anything but personal." As such, your ability to draw the line between the time and energy you spend on you and your personal life and the energy you spend on your company becomes less and less clear-cut. More than that, there is an addictive quality to exhilarating panic that puts a new spin on Noel Coward's words, "Work is much more fun than fun." And therein lies the danger. Because exhilaration is so attractive, the entrepreneur cannot easily resist going back for more. In the process, friends and family can feel neglected and sacrificed.

Is there a way to reconcile this life of exhilarating panic with having a personal life of some sort? The notion of finding the right partners (friends, spouse, business associates) to share one's life with is at the heart of the new entrepreneur's ability to deal with the paradoxes and challenges of their life, both personal and business. Having studied and consulted with many working couples, Pepper Schwartz, a professor of sociology at the University of Washington, columnist and author, strongly believes that choosing a partner who can accommodate your need and desire to entrepreneur is crucial to attaining entrepreneurial success—someone who can hold to the flexibility, persistence, and vision required for long-term business gain while at the same time allowing you to take the scenic route along the way; that is, to also enjoy your life.

Joanna Lau, of Lau Technologies, suggests that those who are intent on running their own company must view their spouse as a partner in the business, whether or not they have an operational role and/or equity ownership. Joanna, by conferring with her husband on many of the decisions she has to make as an entrepreneur—from potential customer deals she is considering to ideas about how to handle human resource issues—is able to build both her company and her personal relationship around tangible elements of her day-to-day life.

Of course, each couple has to search for their own criteria for a relationship based on love, trust, respect, intimacy, and the idiosyncrasies of why people are drawn to one another. But aside from these universal needs, there are three guidelines to a meaningful personal partnership for the new entrepreneur. Each, in its own way, reflects an acceptance of the notion of imbalance.

Entrepreneurs are far more likely than corporate managers to intertwine their business and personal lives.

MARKETING NEWS

Spin control: the act of making something seem favorable.

spin control, or units of pleasure

Joy Mountford describes her job as her hobby. Pamela Wallin says that there is no particular end to her day and that her work is her life. Jonas Svensson of Spray cannot imagine life without a high level of critical decision making. Regardless of which industry these entrepreneurs have chosen to work and play in, all of them are talking about the same thing—the role played by imbalance in their lives. Many entrepreneurs often try to separate their work from their personal lives, when really what they might consider is bringing the two closer together.

The challenge for the new entrepreneur is to somehow find a way to gracefully combine the exhilaration and excitement of building a company with the responsibilities and joys of building a home life. Rather than creating false partitions between the two, one should try blurring the boundaries. For example, many entrepreneurs now bring their kids into the office with them on the weekends, allowing them to feel that the place where Mom and Dad work is comfortable and familiar—a place the kids can feel physically connected with.

Of course, for every couple, how one blurs the boundaries between work and home life will be different. Katrina Garnett and her husband successfully blurred the lines between their work and their personal lives by moving his consulting business into Katrina's software headquarters. In that way, they could see each other during the day and could both visit their newborn baby, who is cared for in a nursery down the hall. For this couple, the weekends are sacrosanct. "On weekends, no one would recognize us— we're just total bums," Katrina told me. "We're consumed by our kids. And all that matters to us is spending time with them." There is no set formula for how one successfully blurs the lines. What is comfortable for one couple may not work for another. But what is common is that each of them has found a way to stop seeing their world as divided into discreet units of pleasure and to begin to create their own unique version of a blurring of the boundaries that is immeasurable.

Work is much more fun than fun.

NOEL COWARD

You need to have a partner, a significant other, or someone who believes in what you're doing and has enough of their own life beyond you that they are comfortable with you giving all to the business for years on end, because that is what is— to a certain extent— going to happen.

ROB RYAN

"everyone knows one truth: life consists of how we choose to distort it"

WOODY ALLEN, *DECONSTRUCTING HARRY*

In the charming film *Deconstructing Harry*, Robin Williams plays a stand-in actor who suffers from the strange malady of being "out of focus." After many attempts at changing the situation, his entire family decides to wear special glasses that remedy the situation—at least for them. Although, on the outside, this appears to be a somewhat selfish (and quite humorous) solution, the element of commitment on the part of this character's family is what stands out as meaningful in my mind. To ensure that their father/husband remains in focus, this actor's family is willing, at times, to look at the world from his point of view. This is a great analogy for what sometimes needs to be done by the entrepreneur's spouse, partner, or family if there is to be a successful blurring of the lines between the work world and the personal world. At the same time, there is a limit to what you are willing to put off as a means of coping with the reality of the present, with a false promise of future happiness.

the big problem with the big happy

For many years, whenever I worked on a weekend and did not take time out to stop and relax for an hour to meet a friend for a drink or to drop in on my parents to say hi, I always justified this level of commitment by saying that I was building something for the "big happy." I was willing to forfeit the small moments that added up to a day or a week or a year for the ultimate moment when—what? When I would one day wake up and discover that I had a lot of unused smaller moments of happiness that I had never experienced? When I would be fully satisfied with my achievements, with the direction of my company, and with my entrepreneurial accomplishments? None of these answers made sense to me, because the truth is, for most entrepreneurs, there *is* no milestone that is good enough. As soon as you reach one big goal, you are immediately reaching for the next. It was not until I attended a lecture by author Anne Lamott that I realized that the notion of some "big happy" at the end of the entrepreneurial rainbow is a false one, and a bit of a cruel hoax at that. In talking about how to approach writing as a career, she advised, "Writing is a process that gets better the more you give in to it. Never hoard anything, but rather give your best to each page, to each day of the journey." As with writing, the key to successful entrepreneuring is found in realizing that the process of building the business is as important as the completed structure. As the old adage goes, you cannot achieve a good end with bad means. In fact, there *is* no real ending; the *means* are all we really have. When struggling to reconcile what you give to the here and now and what you hoard for the promise of the future, your personal relationships and your entrepreneurial venture *both* need to be accommodated in one equation.

The Chinese ideogram for *crisis* also means *opportunity*.

the chancing that happens

Workaholism is the term often used to describe those who do not know when to take a break and turn it off long enough to live in the here and now. In my experience, the notion of workaholism is not what is in question, because who is to say that what is "too much" for one person is not nearly enough for someone else? Workaholism is not what gets between an entrepreneur and their family. The real problem comes in people's blatant denial that they can't "have it all," that being an entrepreneur *does* require sacrifices, compromises, understanding, and adjustments from everyone.

After years of working as a senior executive in a large technology company, Philippe finally decided to take a chance and start up his own software company, based on a product that he had been working on in his free time. His family was excited by his enthusiasm and convinced that their lifestyle would not change dramatically, because of the careful financial planning that Philippe had attended to for 20 years. They believed that they had more than enough residual income and resources to carry them through any financial crunch his venture might cause.

A goal setter by nature, Philippe mapped out exactly what his plan was—to go public within a four-year time frame and get a 35 percent return on his initial investment. Despite the fact that he had no entrepreneurial experience, he found that within months of starting the company, he felt, in some ways, more comfortable working "within his own skin." Rather than shying away from the stresses and strains that every entrepreneur faces, he was energized by them and motivated to work even harder. This level of commitment to his business went on for years on end. Delighted with his progress and excited by the growth and success of his software company, Philippe kept working long hours. When his family complained about never seeing him, he kept saying, "I am building this for our future. In a few years, I will be able to be around full-time again like I was before."

This tenacious character actually *did* achieve his goal within four and a half years, and his wife and children hung in there with him, looking forward to the time when they could accept their father/husband back into the family. But of course, what none of them had predicted was that, while evolving his company over the years, Philippe, *too*, had evolved, for better or for worse. He was now a changed man. Though he loved his family dearly, he had also fallen in love with a different level of excitement and creative intensity that provided him with a kind of fulfillment he had never experienced before. As soon as he achieved his initial goal, he immediately went out to try to raise money for a new idea he wanted to bring to market. At home, it was not a happy scenario.

Eventually, Philippe was able to find ways to integrate his family life and his business world by agreeing to take an advisory role within his new start-up and to plan his family trips in conjunction with business trips he had to take. But in confiding his story to me, he wanted to stress one important point: It's not that he thinks entrepreneuring can and should be conducted at any cost. In fact, having almost lost his family, he feels quite the opposite. What he does stress is that it is essential that both the entrepreneur and his spouse and family recognize that entrepreneuring is not a career but, rather, a dynamic evolution, a living and breathing cycle of growth.

If one person in the family is entrepreneuring, it is essential that the rest of the family find ways to accept the fact that taking a chance on a company really means taking a chance on everything—business, family life, and the direction of one's personal growth. Along the way, the entrepreneur must realize that they will most definitely evolve through the mere act of entrepreneuring. Entrepreneuring is exciting and dramatic, but like any lifework, it demands that you manage the process—by finding ways to bring

"What'll we do with ourselves this afternoon?" cried Daisy. "And the day after that, and the next thirty years?"

F. SCOTT FITZGERALD,
THE GREAT GATSBY

I have to give a chance to the chancing that happens.

DAVID NASH

those you love along with you, by ensuring that all involved recognize and even celebrate the changes which will undoubtedly occur, and by working as hard as possible not to postpone the life you are living. As David Nash says of his art, "I have to give a chance to the chancing that happens." The new entrepreneur needs to ask of themselves, "Where can I find the courage to chance, and how can I manage the imbalance and the rewards that this chancing will bring on?"

situational love?

In an effort to understand the difference in attitude between entrepreneurs and corporate career persons, *Inc.* magazine hired Roper Stach Worldwide to survey the attitudes of 500 owners of small, fast-growing companies and 200 high-level executives at large corporations. When asked about their top reasons for entrepreneuring, 91 percent of the entrepreneurs cited "the right opportunity," 87 percent "the desire for more control over life," and 87 percent "the desire to create something new." To satisfy that drive, 74 percent of the entrepreneurs risked their own money, 66 percent their economic security, 40 percent their personal reputations, and 39 percent their professional reputations. The editor-in-chief of *Inc.*, George Gendron, gave his assessment: "The study underscores something we have said for years. When you start a business, everything you have is at risk. You don't think of it as a career; it's your life."

In the U.S., there are at least a quarter of a million co-preneurs who are working to find some kind of new model of marital and business partnership.

Despite the somewhat grim statistics regarding divorce rates among entrepreneurs, the percentage of entrepreneurial operations continues to grow. And despite the fact that the stakes are much higher for couples who choose to entrepreneur together, in terms of both personal *and* financial risk, the number of co-preneurs keeps growing. "Although no definitive figures exist on the number of husband/wife-owned businesses, some small-business experts believe they are increasing almost as fast as the number of woman-owned businesses. There are 7.7 million of these today, up from 4.1 million in 1987, according to the U.S. Census Bureaus and Dun and Bradstreet Corp."

As it turns out, "Couples decide to go into business together for myriad reasons. They want to spend more time together. They believe they have a chance of making more money. They think running a business will be more successful with a partner they already know intimately and trust."

Sometimes, couples choose to co-preneur as a natural offshoot of one or the other's vision of a product or service. John Evershed, founder of MondoMedia, recalls that when he first got into the multimedia design business, he knew he had a certain set of skills and that his wife Deirdre O'Malley had complementary skills. "So she came on to kind of fill in, neither of us thinking that we would become business partners. But over time, we have both become equally integral to the company. She brings a different kind of skill to bear on the company as it grows."

Many entrepreneurial couples recount similar stories, whereby they started off working together to tide things over, and the next thing they knew, they were long-term business partners. Having been through the experience myself, I have come to realize that this kind of setup pushes the envelope of imbalance one step further than most of us are comfortable with and really challenges the notion of a healthy blurring of lines. And yet, just as getting money teaches you much more than investment formulas, couples who entrepreneur together find a dynamic growth that is part and parcel of their journey.

You put your art into your work. I put it into my life.

FROM THE MOVIE
DECONSTRUCTING HARRY

total trust

In my many formal and informal interviews with entrepreneurial couples over the years, trust is the word that every one of them uses to describe the foundation of their entrepreneurial relationship. Deirdre O'Malley of MondoMedia describes it as follows: "I don't understand why people always say, 'I would never work with my spouse.' For me, I know that I have 100 percent trust in that other person, and in the rough-and-tumble world of entrepreneurship, that is really valuable." Sometimes, that trust is built on past experience working together, as in the case of Jane Metcalfe and Louis Rossetto. Jane says, " We had an incredibly strong foundation before we started *Wired*. We'd been working together since 1988 on another magazine, which, from one day to the next, our funding sources decided to stop funding. Everything that we had been building for three years was going to come to an end. The fact that we survived that setback is what gave me the strength and the sense to know that we could do it again."

However you blur the boundaries between work and pleasure, it is the trust between you that allows you to jointly agree to tilt the scales of balance just enough to get you through the hardest times. It is part of the chance of chancing.

complicated simplicity

In Chapter 9, we talked about the need, at some point, to evolve the start-up organization from a family model to a company model to permit the organization to grow and improve without the emotional overlay of a family atmosphere. Regardless of which model an entrepreneurial couple chooses, most experts point out that creating sensible boundaries is a real issue for co-preneurs. "Married owners can be as bad for the business as the business is for the marriage. Too often, couples make decisions for the good of their relationship rather than for their company's bottom line. In addition, their two perspectives have often melded into one, making it harder for a couple to come up with creative solutions to tough problems."

So what is the solution, if there is one? Most entrepreneurial couples, at some point in their journey, recognize that they will need to divide their responsibilities according to what they are *exceptional* at, not simply based on what they can do relatively well. For example, when Deirdre and John first started MondoMedia, they did not have enough time or people in the company to divide responsibilities. If a sale had to be made, whoever was available would make it; if payroll had to be paid, someone would tend to it. But as they matured as businesspeople and their company grew, it became evident that Deirdre was more of the process-oriented, managerial type and John was more of the creative type, the opportunity maker. And the truth was, once they began to separate their responsibilities completely, they were able to avoid a level of tension and confrontation that was unavoidable when they were interchanging each other in every aspect of their entrepreneurial organization. Deirdre says, "I would advise any entrepreneurial couple to assess what each of your strengths are and divide up the business. Have different responsibilities. Don't cross paths very often, and stay out of each other's territory. Define how you are going to work together, and know and trust that the other person is going to respect those boundaries as well. If you have complementary skill sets and you remember to divide and conquer, you will have a winning team."

The "divide and conquer" strategy not only provides benefits for the company and the other members of your team, it eases the tension in your relationship and provides benefits for you as an individual. By focusing on your individual role within the company, you open the doors to developing meaningful relationships within your working environment. If you divide and conquer equally, your team members will trust each of you more openly and you will both be able to develop separate alliances and working habits that reflect your individual contribution to the company rather than nurture compromised relationships based on a need to accommodate a couple's combined sensibilities.

When Chris and I decided to bring other business partners into Bulldog, they made it clear to us that it was important to them that Chris and I not be a single unit in terms of our decision making and day-to-day operating style. After six years of working with us, Tom Howlett should know that this is not our style. "Any hesitancy I had of partnering with Ellie and Chris as a couple disappeared when they came to me within the first few months of our business relationship and told me that they had made a deal to never discuss anything about the company that requires a decision without me in the room. I came to respect their discipline in this area, though I knew that during times of crisis, it must have been very difficult to honor."

Academics have noted that people tend to be attracted to romantic partners with similar traits—in other words, entrepreneurs are drawn to each other.

THE GLOBE AND MAIL

Married owners can be as bad for the business as the business is for the marriage.

STEVE KAUFMAN

"just don't step on my punch line!"

Regardless of the dynamics between any two people, every co-preneurial couple I know admitted that it is impossible to avoid falling into the personal role at work from time to time. "Let's all be honest," says one entrepreneur who co-founded a photography business with her boyfriend, "and admit there is no one who knows how to hit your hot button better than your spouse or partner." When things are going smoothly, this rarely happens, but when there is a decision that has to be made or a crisis that needs to be dealt with, everyone has their human foibles. The less opportunity you have for falling into this default position, the better for everyone involved.

Although Chris and I almost always agree on the end goal or objective at work, we often have different ideas about the best process for getting there. In some ways, this is comforting to both us and our partners, in that we often work harder to combine our various ideas, resulting in a much better solution. But inevitably, we, like many entrepreneurial couples, openly admit to some level of competitiveness within the relationship. To avoid unhealthy competition between us, Chris and I put together a list of our "rules of engagement," whereby we specifically divided our duties. By identifying each of our strengths, we agreed that it was okay to disagree on the process for achieving the goal within each of our areas of responsibility as long as we agreed on the final outcome. This not only saved us time and energy but enabled each of us to grow faster within our areas of expertise rather than feel hemmed in by the other person's attempt to assert control or influence as a spouse instead of a business partner.

But as with any human interaction, there is always the exception. When both of us are excited by an idea, we know each other so well that, once in a while, we find it hard not to finish the other person's sentence. In one particular situation, while Chris was recounting a customer presentation to the account group, I could barely contain myself and began adding details to lend drama to his story. At one point, Chris turned to me and said, "Add as many details as you like, just don't step on my punch line!" And as someone who was committed to the notion of bonding by dividing and conquering, I never did.

are we having fun yet?

I was once talking to a friend of mine—a freelance writer—who works out of her house. Her partner was an entrepreneur who ran a top talent agency. "It's just that by the time Joan comes home, she is so worn out that she never wants to do anything. Meanwhile, I've been sitting at home working on my computer, and all I want to do is go out. It's almost as if neither of us has the benefit of seeing each other at our best, which apparently occurs during the hours when we are working. It's hard to reconcile." I nodded,

You're up, you're down. In the end the house wins, but you can't say you didn't have fun.

FROM THE MOVIE
DECONSTRUCTING HARRY

If you have complementary skill sets and you remember to divide and conquer, you will have a winning team.

DEIRDRE O'MALLEY

but I must admit that I really did not understand what she was trying to tell me until I interviewed Andrea Southcott. "The best part about working with Jim as an entrepreneurial couple is that we get to see each other at our best. There is nothing like being in a meeting and watching your spouse deliver a particularly great client presentation or knowing that he is relishing the fact that you are motivating an employee whom no one else is able to help. We get to see and experience each other when we are 'on.' That is a big part of our relationship, and I cannot imagine not having that." So true. When a trusting entrepreneurial couple works together, you are able to enjoy and experience the nuances of moments with your partner when they are at their best, rather than meet up with them at the end of a long day, when they have given the majority of their energy, their creativity, and their passion to those they left behind at the office.

More than that, there is an instant level of empathy that is part and parcel of working together, an inherent understanding of how your day went, a visceral check-in point with the other person that is hard to match when both experience a huge success or a devastating blow. As one entrepreneur described it, "If something is going badly, it's going badly for both of you. You are on the same rhythm, and you are able to completely and utterly understand what the other person is going through. But when you have successes, there is nothing like sharing it with your spouse, and when you are going through a crisis, there is no one you would rather be with than your entrepreneurial spouse, who is as dedicated and as intertwined with the outcome as you are. You are more or less locking into the same pattern, and with it comes a bonding that is hard to replace."

Those who choose to work at a start-up company often find it difficult to balance their dedication and commitment to the company with their time away from the office. Jane Metcalfe recalls, "When *Wired* magazine launched, the single people and those who had a partner in another kind of business found it very difficult to keep their relationships going through the launch. If you are a couple embarking on the same adventure, it is very exciting. There is no doubt about it: You bond with people at work, and when one of those people is your life partner, you end up bonding very tightly. You've got a very different kind of relationship than if you go home to someone who doesn't really know the details of what you do all day every day."

> **When you have successes, there is nothing like sharing it with your spouse, and when you are going through a crisis, there is no one you would rather be with. You are more or less locking into the same pattern, and with it comes a bonding that is hard to replace.**

> **Entrepreneurship is like love. You're in or you're out. When you're in, you do whatever it takes and you do it gladly and with passion.**
>
> DOUG KEELEY

Top Ten Signs That You Have Forever Redefined *Fun*

1. When you look forward to snuggling up in bed with your partner to review the latest version of your business plan.

2. When you consider being in a client presentation with your spouse as "quality time" together.

3. When you consider reading the paper together on a Saturday morning at home as a holiday.

4. When you find yourself introducing your husband to someone at a cocktail party by saying, "Have you met my associate?"

5. When, unlike your employees, you think it is sweet that you both wear the same colors to the office on the same day.

6. When you congratulate yourselves on evenings when you have to spend only two hours reviewing the details of a particularly grueling day.

7. When your idea of the beginning of a romantic evening begins with reviewing your new corporate brochure.

8. When faced with a controversy at home, you both agree to retreat to the study and jot down the salient points on a flipchart you happen to keep there.

9. When your spouse suggests going out for dinner, and, without thinking, you both say, "What would the desired outcome of that expenditure of energy provide us?"

10. When you both start to refer to the company as "she."

It can be idyllic to share a vision, as well as love, by building a business together.

RHONDA ABRAMS, PRESIDENT, ABRAMS BUSINESS STRATEGIES

"I'm drowning, and you're describing the water"

One serious pitfall of co-preneuring as a couple is that imbalance can all too quickly turn into *extreme* imbalance if you are not careful. One entrepreneur working in the electronic publishing business described this situation as follows: "You spend so much energy as an individual and as a couple focusing on the growth and maturity of the business that you can forget to ask yourselves, 'Yeah, but are we growing as a couple?' To keep both the company and the relationship healthy, make sure you do not neglect your relationship. Do not always let the relationship take a second seat to the business. If you do, one day, five years down the line, you may look around and realize that you now have an exceptionally mature company but that both of you have grown apart, not together. You need to fight against that all the time."

Many co-preneurs eventually find that the only solution is to stop working together on a daily basis. After seven years of running the day-to-day operations of our company together, Chris and I decided to change the balance. In this past year, when I moved into an advisory role and Chris continued to run the company, we found that we were able to alleviate the potential extreme imbalance without losing the benefit of each other's contribution to the entrepreneurial venture.

upping the ante on imbalance: the business of elsewhere

Depending on the kind of business you choose as your foundation for entrepreneuring and the level of growth you are willing to accommodate, there is a by-product of entrepreneuring that can also tip the scale of imbalance—the element of doing business "elsewhere." Of course, the issue of traveling has long been discussed by executives around the world as an integral part of their lives. Despite the fact that we are able to communicate via video conferencing, email, faxes, and a steady stream of courier packages, the pool of road warriors has steadily increased, reminding us that relationships are, after all, at the cornerstone of business. In a recent article, *Inc.* magazine reported that there are nearly 280 million business travelers in the United States. That represents a lot of road warriors who must find a way to juggle these two worlds as demanded by our growing (international) businesses. Let's look at some of the effects that doing business "elsewhere" has on the entrepreneuring couple.

the two time-zone sense of home

When I first moved to California to explore the opportunities for Bulldog in software, I was in my early thirties. I don't recall ever having defined what I thought a sense of home meant prior to my arrival in California. Perhaps this was because I was always blessed with having a home to go to—whether my parents' or my own. But within the second year of my bi-coastal existence, I began to ask myself: Where is home? Is home the place where my husband is sometimes, though often not, because he too is traveling? Is home the place where I have friends and family whom I am having a hard time keeping in touch with because of the business? Or is home the place where my most immediate concerns are—in the shape and form of the meetings and phone calls that make up my day-to-day existence as I edge toward redefining the business of my company? Is it the place where my favorite clothes hang and my new horse is boarded? Or is it in the house that my husband and I renovated ourselves with four years' worth of collected oddities? When I began to talk to other entrepreneurs who are living a similar two-city life, I found that they, too, were struggling with these very questions. Most admitted to me that they preferred to simply define their lives as the times when they were "on the road" and the times when they were not. But I was not able to dismiss the notion of home that easily.

It's becoming more common for entrepreneurs to maintain a truly virtual office. I read that "There are more than 6 million Americans whose offices have license plates and seat belts, and that number is expected to increase 25% in the next five years."

COLORADO BUSINESS MAGAZINE

And then I watched the movie *Wings of Desire* by Wim Wenders, a beautiful black-and-white film about an angel who descends to earth and falls in love with a mortal. This character was, in a sense, homeless. As a displaced angel, he desperately wanted to exist on earth, though he was invisible to the people there. And yet one sensed that heaven was not really his home either, but more a holding place that he inhabited until he could descend back to where he truly wanted to be—earth. What struck me most about the film was how this character dealt with his dilemma. He did not focus on trying to figure out what attributes indicated "home" to him but, rather, gave his all to wherever he happened to be at the time. In that way, he reconciled the two very different places in himself.

And that is how I began to reconcile my own notion of home—as the place where I happened to be. I even found ways to create a home in my hotel room when I went on extended trips by committing to unpacking everything in my suitcase, no matter how short my stay. Somehow, the act of unpacking and setting out my clothes reflected a commitment to the place I found myself in. I committed to calling my husband and my family and friends at a convenient time in *their* time zones as much as possible, and I kept wardrobes in California and Toronto as a means of ensuring that I felt comfortable with the image I cut in both places. I kept books I was reading in both places. I put photos of people I cared about everywhere. Perhaps it sounds as if I am focusing on the small details instead of the big picture. But by building tangible elements into my revised notion of a home, I was able to travel between time zones, between cities, and within strange places with a level of comfort and a sense of self that was liberating. I created "postcards" in my mind that incorporated elements of one home along the way into another and allowed myself to be a true wanderer. I found that three things happened:

By instilling a high level of spin control, I was able to turn a feeling of homesickness for a mythological place in which I never seemed to be into the concept of a virtual home.

I was forced to stay flexible and open-minded no matter where I was and no matter how uncomfortable I truly felt. Maintaining a level of flexibility and open-mindedness is like working out—if you stop exercising any particular muscle group, it will atrophy, and when you finally do need to use these muscles, they may not work very well. I found that my stress level went down, because I was on a constant training program for accommodating the unusual. As an entrepreneur, I began to respect this element of training and appreciated the courage with which I faced new situations, no matter how foreign or unfamiliar they seemed.

I found a renewed sense of belonging. As I traveled around the world, I was able to tap into what I like to call a virtual community. I found that I was drawn to and able to relate to people who were in similar situations as myself, and with that came new friendships or a passing conversation that allowed me to feel grounded and, oddly enough, at home. Suddenly, the impersonal, distanced sense of communication that I had felt by using email became a link between my virtual community and me. As Jonas Svensson of Spray describes it, "It is almost as if I am part of a new tribe—a kind of virtual network that links me with a whole host of other people who, too, are living in limbo as we each move toward our own entrepreneurial goal." Needless to say, some of my best insights into entrepreneuring come from talking to or corresponding with someone whom I consider part of my virtual community—another wanderer in flux. In some cases, I met people who have become my close friends, and in other cases, I have been able to discover new customers and business alliances that I would never have established otherwise.

As a road warrior, you are experiencing a good portion of your present-day life in a virtual community—between flights, in hotel rooms, and between meeting rooms. There are times when all you want to do is put your feet up on a familiar couch and talk to someone you love and have known for longer than three days. However, there are ways to turn that longing into something that can translate into a renewed appreciation of your spouse or partner, allowing you to "bring them with you when you go." Whether one or both of the co-preneurs I have spoken to must travel much of the time, most told me that doing business elsewhere adds a sense of adventure and romance to their lives. This is especially true when the couple works together an average of 12 hours a day. As one entrepreneur said to me, "A structure that forces a separation for the sake of the business can be exciting. It reduces the day-to-day grind of having to let business come first and relationships come second (which often happens). When you reunite, you suddenly have a reason to put your relationship first and the business second. As someone who has worked with his spouse for over seven years, I see this as a real plus."

The new entrepreneur (individual or couple) has the potential to enrich their entrepreneurial experience by incorporating rather than separating the time you spend elsewhere, by exercising flexibility and finding courage in your day-to-day activities, and by allowing you to bring loved ones with you when you go. The new entrepreneur's sense of a virtual home makes room for imbalance to be *somewhat* beautiful.

is this intimacy or simply belonging revisited?

In the past decade, therapists and psychologists, group-therapy leaders, and perhaps even psychoanalysts were treating their patients for a kind of love malaise that reflected the aftermath of the Me Generation of the 1980s. The

It is almost as if I am part of a new tribe—a kind of virtual network that links me with a whole host of other people who, too, are living in limbo as we each move toward our own entrepreneurial goal.

JONAS SVENSSON

Instabond: a word to describe the instant bonding that happens between road warriors who do business elsewhere.

TED MCNICHOL

standard phrase bandied about these therapy rooms was: "I just can't find anyone to fall in love with. I'm lonely." Today, the therapists I know tell me that this statement has been replaced by "I just can't seem to be really intimate with my spouse/partner/friend."

Instead of jumping to the conclusion that we have all lost the fine art of intimacy, I suggest an alternative interpretation. Perhaps, if one is pursuing the entrepreneurial lifestyle, the notion of intimacy, like the notion of a home, simply requires a redefinition. It reminds me of a movie I once saw, in which the main character could only whisper "I love you" to his partner in foreign languages. Without the protection of language, he felt too vulnerable. As you can imagine, this is probably not a topic covered in the business journals that flood the newsstands, at least not yet. However, the need for redefining intimacy is very real for those who entrepreneur. I suspect this is another syndrome which has arisen due to the ever-increasing pressures and heightened demands in our working life.

the beckoning of intensity and the avoidance of intimacy

When you are an entrepreneur, particularly in the early days of your venture, you will feel invigorating stress, or what psychologists call "eustress." The truth is, to cope with eustress, entrepreneurs spend most of their workday avoiding intimacy, because creating this distance between themselves and others makes the difficult, but necessary, day-to-day tasks of entrepreneuring manageable. Firing a longtime employee, dealing with uncalled-for accusations from a disappointed customer, or answering to the financial shortcomings of your projected revenues on a spreadsheet with your board of directors all demand a certain level of avoidance of vulnerability.

Todd Logan expresses this concept well: "We're talking about a breakdown in the relationships we value most. Here's the pattern. We start our business. We're excited, nervous, and yet optimistic. It's hope, it's opportunity, it's personal and family fulfillment. Our spouses or significant others are right there with us, backing us all the way. We know and they know that, in the beginning, it's going to be tough and time-consuming, but that's okay, because once the business gets to a certain point, everything in the relationship and family will return to the way it was or the way we want it to be. Of course, the business, this complex entity, with seemingly a life and mind of its own, never gets to that certain point. We keep promising that with the next big deal, the next big year, we'll finally be there. And our spouses or significant others eventually stop listening to us. They've seen the movie and heard the song too many times already. We're angry that they don't understand or empathize with how hard it really is to own and operate a business successfully. They're angry that we're not there both physically and emotionally."

Some days the level of eustress can be exhilarating, and other days you

Take me with you when you go . . .

RACHEL KANE,
"GIFT OF THE MAGI"

Absence diminishes commonplace passions and enhances great ones.

DIANE JOHNSON,
LE DIVORCE

can let down your guard slightly because you have fewer negotiations and fewer issues to deal with. But the truth is, being an effective "lone coach," a great "freedom fighter," and a "long-term doer" requires a necessary level of self-preservation to get through the day.

Unfortunately, these characteristics pose a potential threat to one's personal relationships. As one entrepreneur expressed to me, "Regardless of how you approach the challenges of the day, you do have to don armor of some kind. Sometimes, it is easier just to leave your suit of armor on, rather than have to take it off at the end of the day when you go home and then put it back on the next morning." Jane Metcalfe was very open about the potential dangers that donning this armor produced in her relationship: "When you're an entrepreneur, you're busy being strong and being tough. You're keeping everybody else afloat, and you're fending off the challenges. But that armor is exactly what could be destroying your relationship with your partner."

Of course, this notion of armor is not reserved for the entrepreneur alone. Many executives in a variety of industries face the same challenges. But when you own your own company, it is harder to set limits, it is harder to determine the cutoff point between what you are willing to sacrifice for your company and what you *know* will take a toll on you as a person.

Many entrepreneurs I know would agree that it is not just limited to a romantic notion of intimacy. Keith Kocho of Digital Renaissance talks honestly about how entrepreneuring has its price in this arena. "I think in some ways, I've sacrificed any opportunity to have a meaningful sort of relationship with people. It seems that no matter what, people know me through my company, so immediate barriers go up. And it seems that I don't have time to engage in a social scene as much as I would like to. When I work 14 hours a day, seven days a week, even when I am socializing the odd time, I have a tendency to drift back to thinking about my company. In that way, *I* am putting up the barriers myself."

If one person within the couple is not entrepreneuring full-time, it is often easier to see the initial signs of distanced intimacy. In such cases, one's partner has an obligation to call the entrepreneur out on it before this distancing becomes a habit that is too hard to break. But with the co-preneurial couple, it is harder to detect and reverse the intensity/intimacy equation, because both people are often caught up in a redefined sense of intimacy and belonging that begins and ends with the rush of the business—the creativity, the passion, and the intimate details that require constant attention. At those moments, part of you is so excited to be sharing the intimate details of the business with the person you care about most, and part of you is wondering whether you have become business partners at the expense of life partners.

The only dependable aphrodisiacs, my worldly friends tell me, are not to be found in books. They are two in number, the first being the presence of a desirable woman (man), the second her (his) absence.

M.F.K. FISHER,
THE ART OF EATING

it's about renewal

The inability to be intimate with others is also connected with the inability to renew oneself. As we discussed earlier, the challenge of entrepreneuring is more like a marathon than a sprint. It is the continual getting up and renewing a commitment to finding a solution or revising a new strategy that is the sign of the true entrepreneur. Maintaining the required stamina for that kind of a life requires a constant fine-tuning. One must maintain just the right amount of torque to motivate, not destroy, the imbalance that exists. How one chooses to find renewal is an individual thing.

Geoffrey Moore has his own ideas on this matter: "There's a much broader set of choices in our society than we currently imagine. In other centuries, spiritual intimacy was very important. Today, there's a real interest and commitment to nature and the outdoors as well as to volunteerism as a means of establishing intimacy. And naturally, with that intimacy comes renewal. Without renewal, life can extract a very painful toll. I've seen the price paid time and time again by the entrepreneur who gets addicted not only to the work but to a false sense of intimacy that is created in the business environment."

A woman I spoke to who had entrepreneured with her husband for 20 years voiced her regret over her loss of intimacy with her children. Their company finally went public and achieved their benchmark of entrepreneurial success, but not without extracting a high price. "If you asked my two children today, I believe they would tell you that the business always came first and they came second. If you ask either my husband or myself, we would say our business relationship came first and our marriage second. It was not until we began to find a way to renew ourselves as a family through volunteering within the community that we realized just how far away we had gotten from each other. We have a long road of repair ahead of us, though I know we will arrive there."

Others I spoke with, such as Jane Metcalfe, discovered that it was only by tipping the imbalance scale completely that they were able to finally find a way to balance their lives. "I decided to have a baby, because I knew that nothing else was going to help me achieve the balance that I so desperately wanted. It was a very conscious decision, and it has forced us to redefine the blurring of the lines." The balance that Jane and her husband did find was in wisely choosing *when* to have children. "I'm not sure we could have started *Wired* if I'd had kids waiting for me at home. I don't think I would have made the choices that I made. I don't think I would have given the organization what it clearly needed to succeed."

Entrepreneuring will take more love and more energy and more attention than you probably know, but in the meantime, recognize that those moments along the way demand the same kind of dedication and determination as does the goal that looms somewhere in the distance.

AN ENTREPRENEUR

Top Ten Signs That You Work in the '90s

1. You lecture the neighborhood kids who are selling lemonade on ways to improve the process.

2. You get excited when it's Saturday, so you can wear sweatpants to work.

3. You refer to the tomatoes grown in your garden as deliverables.

4. You find you really need PowerPoint to explain what you do for a living.

5. You normally eat out of vending machines and at the most expensive restaurant in town within the same week.

6. You think that "progressing an action plan" and "calendarizing a project" are acceptable English phrases.

7. You know the people at the airport hotels better than your next-door neighbors.

8. You ask your friends to "think out of the box" when making Friday-night plans.

9. You think Einstein would have been more effective had he put his ideas into a matrix.

10. You think a "half day" means leaving at 5 o'clock.

"I felt a trifle unbuckled."

ELIZABETH MCCRACKEN,
THE GIANT'S HOUSE

the beauty and the beast: how to maintain healthy imbalance

Geoffrey Moore likens the mystique the entrepreneur holds for the general public to the mystique of the 1960s, when everybody wanted to be an artist: "But the point was, they didn't want to create art—they just wanted to be artists. And there's a version of that with entrepreneuring. In other words, I don't want to actually deal with the risk that entrepreneuring may bring to my life, to my work, to my family—I just want the mystique of being an entrepreneur." Unfortunately, entrepreneuring, like all life choices, is a package deal—it is at once beautiful *and* imbalanced, and with it comes personal risks that cannot be denied. Rather than provide an unrealistic benchmark to measure yourself against, let's look at the ways in which other entrepreneurs have been able to find a healthy level of imbalance, avoiding having to deal with an unmanageable beast.

haven time: threefold

While I was on a plane en route to Amsterdam, I read a review of a book called *The Marriage Spirit: Finding the Passion and Joy of Soul-Centered Love* by

Paul and Evelyn Moschetta. One of the ideas that struck me the most was the authors' concept of "haven time." In business, we talk about the need to have "face time" with a customer; in investment terms, we are always calculating the number of "person hours" it will take to complete a project. For the entrepreneur, personal time should be called "haven time." Haven time, as described by Paul and Evelyn Moschetta, is the space you carve out for yourselves that is absolutely precious. What you choose to do during haven time is wide open. What is important is that you commit to finding time to accommodate it into your life and recognize that it is sacrosanct to cancel or change it for any reason. An entrepreneur needs to take this notion of haven time and extend it into all three areas of their life: their relationships, their company, and themselves.

Haven Time and Your Relationships

A longtime friend of mine who has entrepreneured for more than 15 years suggests the following approach to haven time for a couple. Set aside a weekend every month or two during which you both commit to going away. You are not allowed to bring anything with you—no cell phones, no magazines or business-related reading material, no laptop, and no beeper. Before leaving, commit to *not* talking about business for the entire weekend. In the end, it does not matter where you go, only that it is a place where no one knows you, where you are not reminded of your life as business partners, and where you are focused on renewing both your own energy and that of your partnership outside of work. Once you commit to doing this, you both begin to rely on this haven time as a structured way of reintroducing intimacy into your relationship.

Once you get used to setting aside haven time for yourselves as a couple, suddenly the notion of doing the same thing with family and friends seems easier. I always found that an early-morning tennis game, before the unpredictability of the day could get in the way, was a great way to spend time with my mom on a regular basis. Jonas Svensson of Spray strongly believes that an annual vacation with his family allows him to plan something fun and unconnected to his business travel. The key to making haven time work is not judging yourself by how much of it you take but doing whatever you can to avoid canceling the haven-time events that you plan.

Haven Time and Your Company

It would appear that the best way to manage a healthy imbalance is to minimize the time you spend thinking about your company when you are away from it. I have found that allocating a certain amount of haven time for my company is as essential as allotting it for my personal life. All too often in your business, you are forced into a constant state of doing. It is at those times, when you are madly doing and not reflecting, that you are most likely to tip

The Betty Ford Clinic for dysfunctional executives has doubled in size in the past two years. Although there are few statistics on the burnout rate in Silicon Valley, 8,000 executives have been treated since it opened.

UPSIDE MAGAZINE

Remember, spring is what happens when you've completely given up hope. The same is true for weathering the endless hope required for entrepreneuring.

AN ENTREPRENEUR

the scales of imbalance *completely*. By setting aside haven time for reflecting on your company, you are ensuring that you renew your energy, excitement, and interest in your entrepreneuring without the pressure of having to act or react in the heat of the moment. Some people are disciplined enough to find a way to do this in the shower every day or on the commute home. However you find the time, building company haven time into your schedule is one way to renew your entrepreneuring in a structured manner.

Haven Time and Yourself

Every January, Lisa Jacobson sits down and plans her 12 personal days for the upcoming year. Some days involve going to a new restaurant in Manhattan by herself, followed by a two-hour massage. Other days she may take a train out to a new gallery she has read about. Some days involve visiting with long-lost friends for dinner. Whatever the activity, Lisa is absolutely set on committing to what she calls her "free days," regardless of what crisis evolves in the office.

Likewise, Keith Kocho finds that the only thing that helps maintain a healthy imbalance for him is hiking alone in the mountains for a week or 10 days at a time. "When you are standing on the edge of a mountain or in a valley between glaciers, you feel so small. Somehow it puts everything into perspective." Regardless of what you choose to do, every entrepreneur who embraces imbalance in a healthy way has found a way to ensure that they get some kind of haven time for themselves. They are as relentless about holding onto those precious hours as they are about their dedication to growing their businesses.

vocational hazards of entrepreneuring

In the early '90s, it became apparent to the many software executives in Silicon Valley that their companies did not actually have retirement plans for their employees. It was a simple case of supply and demand. These companies had no retirement plans, because they fully expected people to burn out and move on long before they needed to retire. I'd be willing to bet that if you asked any number of founders and managers of entrepreneurial start-ups what their priorities are today, the last thing on their to-do list would be to finalize a plan for retiring employees. This is not surprising when the average age in a given start-up in Silicon Valley is so low and when the possibility of burnout is extraordinarily high.

But what might be more germane to the health of an entrepreneurial team is an investment in a medical plan that pays for all kinds of specialized therapy to counteract the vocational hazards of entrepreneurial

His fingers kept slowly snatching at nothing, as if he had already made dozens of things disappear, rabbits and cards and rubber balls and bouquets of paper flowers, and had done this so brilliantly, even he could not bring them back.

ELIZABETH MCCRACKEN,
THE GIANT'S HOUSE

I have always found that things become utterly invisible just moments before they explode.

DOUGLAS COUPLAND,
*POLAROIDS FROM
THE DEAD*

environments, not the least of which includes burnout, depression, repetitive stress syndrome, and absenteeism. No wonder there is a market for a Web-based program such as PROACT from Wilson Banwell, which allows employees to get counseling on anything from dealing with burnout to couples' counseling in the privacy of their own homes—or in cyberspace, as the case may be.

For those who have chosen to entrepreneur their own company, there are a few new psychological terms that you may want to familiarize yourself with. Although they sound and look a lot like the more traditional vocational hazards of successful career building, they have a unique twist of their own. And, guaranteed, at some point in your dance on the tightrope of imbalance, you will experience any one of these. The bad news is that these syndromes are real and treacherous and can greatly affect you if you do not manage to find ways to bring them into perspective. The good news is that these really are manageable beasts of burden, and there are ways to head them off.

The pressure can crush you or turn you into the diamond version of yourself: hard and brilliant.

LYNDA OBST,
HELLO, HE LIED

The definition of *burnout* is "a state of mental or physical exhaustion often reached as a result of prolonged stress or frustration." But perhaps under "S" should be added a new term called "self-induced tailspin."

the self-induced tailspin (read: repetitive enterprising stress syndrome)

The definition of *burnout* in *The Encyclopedic Dictionary of Business Terms* is "a state of mental or physical exhaustion often reached as a result of prolonged stress or frustration." But perhaps under "S," a new term called "self-induced tailspin" should be added. Entrepreneurs, as we have discovered, are exceptionally good (either naturally or through proper training) with self-initiation. They can grab something out of the air and turn it into a concept that eventually becomes the basis for a product to sell. They can imagine a story line and begin to tell people about it, and before you know it, they are actualizing a dream that many people have already bought into.

The flipside of that talent is that the entrepreneur can be equally good at creating their own tragedy, in full Technicolor. Where rational explanation falters, vivid imagination can take over. Often this loss of perspective creates a relentless urgency to act upon a false new reality. In assessing the traits of the entrepreneur, Manfred Kets De Vries has found that there can be "a great discrepancy between the narrative truth and the historical truth: facts are arranged to suit the individual's needs. Splitting—a behavior pattern whereby everything is seen in extremes, black or white, friend or foe—is a defense mechanism used by some entrepreneurs."

One entrepreneur described a situation in which he was convinced that his two largest competitors had aligned themselves against him and were planning to overtake his largest three accounts. For two weeks, he experienced a sense of paranoia and imminent dread that affected everything he did, from his ability to conduct customer presentations to the way he handled his update phone calls with investors. Finally, unable to bear the burden of knowing that it was only a matter of time before he lost his largest account, he confided in a friend, an entrepreneur in a completely different industry. "When I finally said it out loud, I realized how ridiculous it all sounded. When my pal further questioned me, I admitted that I had overheard a passing comment from someone who worked for an investment firm that we chose *not* to go with in our last round of investment. Instead of assessing who made the comment, I immediately allowed it to penetrate and began to act instinctively. At that point, I realized my level of imbalance was way out of line, and I forced myself to take a few days off. Within a week, I was able to verify that it was simply an industry rumor that I was reacting to, and I moved on. Next time I will know that my talent for self-initiative does have its downside."

Whether or not the self-induced tailspin erupts from a real or imagined source, it is more important to understand what it is indicative of. Gideon Kunda, in his book *Engineering Culture,* sums up burnout in general: "On the face of it, burnout is a failure of self-management: a loss of control over role responses and the boundaries that separate and protect the self from the demand of the organization and an inability to sustain the façade of controlled ambiguity characteristic of the successful self."

As one entrepreneur confided in me, "Every entrepreneur finds themselves running straight into a blank wall. Recognizing your own personal need for rejuvenation and being able to factor it in *before* the need becomes critical is not so easy to do. Some people are naturally good at self-preservation. But most entrepreneurs I know find themselves much more likely just to keep giving and giving and giving, because it's that extra oomph that makes things happen. All I can say is, beware, because it can be a real trap and I don't know a single entrepreneur who has not fallen into it."

Look Out for Some of These Signs of the Self-induced Tailspin

- An inability to decipher the difference between narrative rumors, off-the-cuff remarks, and a valid comment that warrants further exploration. My advice? Stop eavesdropping, and always check with someone else on your team for perspective.

- Grandiose schemes for revenge against someone who once did you wrong. My advice? Revenge is a dish best served cold. Cool off first, then decide if it is worth the effort.

- An unreasonable pressure to play the game of comeuppance with inappropriate competitors. If you find that you are competing with your board members, your employees, and your family, recognize that this downward

For the first time in U.S. history, more millionaires are below age 50 than are above it. We are gaining wealth faster, sooner—and in greater-than-ever abundance. At the same time, more and more people are being diagnosed with depression: more than 17 million people in the United States suffer from some form of depression.

HARRIET RUBIN,
FAST COMPANY MAGAZINE

spiral requires an emergency brake. Go for a jog, get a massage or read a book about a heroic character who represents honor and courage.

is there a cure?

The most helpful advice I can give for avoiding the self-induced tailspin is based on simple common sense.

Articulate the source of the tailspin. Whether that means talking about it to a friend or your spouse or writing it down and reviewing it in the morning, make sure that you are as specific as possible about the problem. In reviewing your verbal or written articulation, you may find that there is really only one issue, rather than several. This strategy should also help you to reduce the one major issue to a manageable problem.

Compartmentalize the issue that is causing the tailspin. Once you have articulated the issue(s), then try to break down your concern into small pieces and deal with only one at a time. Having someone within your company who can assist you with this, such as a partner, is very helpful and makes the task seem less daunting.

Take a pause. Give yourself enough time to assess your options properly. Sometimes, a crisis truly is a crisis and you need to jump right into action, but most of the time, it is better to pause and determine your plan of action. Because you do need a plan of action; otherwise, your self-induced tailspin can reach "escape velocity," taking on a hallucinatory sense of perception found only in Henry James's novels. Once that happens, damage control is a lot harder to render effectively.

Recycle it. As Lynda Obst says, "The skill to managing a crisis is viewing it as a simple mess—a working debacle—that can be recycled and tilled into fertile new ground for more work."

deceptive de-skilling depression (read: temporarily vocationally incapacitated)

As Natalie Goldberg says in *Writing Down the Bones,* "We have an idea that success is a happy occasion. Success can also be lonely, isolating, disappointing." I call this condition "deceptive de-skilling depression," and it usually happens immediately following a great success or a grave disappointment. Many entrepreneurs admit to feeling this immediately after they finally sign on their investors. Others find that it occurs just after they launch their product. Whatever the trigger, DDSD can set in unexpectedly.

What are the signs of DDSD? Most entrepreneurs describe it as a feeling

You know you are in trouble when you define sheep as the sharks of the vegetable world.

DAVID NASH

of being "de-skilled." They wake up one morning and begin to question the one or two skills that have been exceptionally strong for most of their lives. When you begin to question your innate abilities, you know it is time to take out the dictionary and revisit the term "self-induced."

I know of one entrepreneur who worked harder than she ever had to get the money together to launch her new media authoring product at one of the largest shows in broadcast and entertainment, called NAB (National Association of Broadcasters). The day of the launch went very smoothly for her and her team, and they were bombarded with interest from the trade-show floor. On the third night of the five-day trade show, they had planned a celebration with their core clients and technology partners. Minutes before the party, this particular entrepreneur, who prided herself on her networking abilities, was sitting in her hotel room considering not showing up at her own event. The overwhelming success of something she had worked on for so long had triggered a sense of self-doubt, and she found herself questioning her networking skills—something she knew she intuitively possessed.

The good news is that DDSD goes away pretty quickly. Many entrepreneurs I have spoken with say that the best cure is to inject a little more imbalance into the equation as a means of triggering the opposite response. One entrepreneur cured his DDSD by beginning plans for a new project the day after he launched a project he had been working on for seven months. He knew that he would need to take a desperately needed break soon, but in the meantime, the act of beginning something new alleviated his feelings of uselessness and disappointment that the previous project had come to completion. Sure enough, his new ideas energized him. When he took a few days off the following week, he was happier, knowing that he had something in the creation stages to return to.

entrepreneurial malaise (read: burnout entrepreneurial style)

Steven Berglas of Harvard Medical School's Department of Psychiatry makes a clear distinction between stress and burnout: "Stress comes from facing demands that are beyond your sense of competence. Burnout, on the other hand, comes from facing goals that are too readily achieved or have already been met, which results in boredom or perceived worthlessness. The burnout mantra goes like this: Been there, done that, seen it, felt it, had the thrill."

Based on this definition, it is no surprise that burnout rarely hits the entrepreneur at the beginning of their entrepreneurial journey. In early-day entrepreneuring, there is no room for anything as undramatic as burnout. *Crisis?* You have that every day. *Fear?* You experience that many times a week. Fatigue and stress become routine after a while. But the entrepreneurial malaise of burnout is a condition reserved for entrepreneurs who

Being a champion is not about winning a fight. It's about getting knocked out and coming back to win again.

EVANDER HOLYFIELD

If you don't get quiet sometimes, how are you going to see things?

AN ENTREPRENEUR

have been at it for a while. Many entrepreneurs admit that although they feel frustrated that they have little time to do anything else, they cannot imagine *not* entrepreneuring. As Doug Humphreys of Skyrocket admits, "Some days, I suddenly look up and it is 5:00 p.m., and I say, 'Damn, I would love to go to the gym or go take a walk by the beach.' But I don't because I have two or three or five more hours of work to do. And sometimes that gets old. We focus on working and we like working, but I have so many other interests that basically have been put on the back burner for several years. At some point, they atrophy, and that is sad."

The burnout mantra goes like this: been there, done that, seen it, felt it, had the thrill.

STEVEN BERGLAS,
INC. MAGAZINE

How Entrepreneurs Stay Motivated (from a survey of the *Inc.* 500 CEOs)

- Find a new challenge inside the business, 63.9 percent

- Exercise, 8.5 percent

- Find a new challenge outside the business, 6 percent

- Take time off, 3.9 percent

- Pray, 3.2 percent

Entrepreneurial malaise sets in when you suddenly realize that things take longer and are harder to achieve than you expected. When I interviewed Deirdre O'Malley of MondoMedia, she admitted to me that entrepreneurial malaise comes and goes all the time. "You are catching me on a good day. But there are bad days. And there are days when that feeling floats over into my whole life. You try to put this kind of temporary mood into perspective, but sometimes you can't, because it is all-encompassing."

What are the signs of entrepreneurial malaise? You cannot think of anything else that interests you except your company, and the only conversation you can make at a cocktail party is about the brilliance of your strategy for how to maximize your airline points system. It is when you wake up one morning and feel one-dimensional—you have no hobbies, you have no friends who do not do what you do, you have no interests that stretch you or complement you. You are even starting to avoid risk in a way that feels foreign to you. Emotional boredom sets in, despite the fact that you have more on your plate than you can handle. Although you think that your company, your entrepreneurial quest, is the only thing that can keep you going, that, too, starts to look paler around the edges, and you may even begin to shirk responsibilities there. *That* is entrepreneurial malaise.

the "why" of entrepreneuring

One of the best ways of counteracting entrepreneurial malaise is by continually revisiting the "why" of what you are doing. In the very early days of entrepreneuring, "survive to succeed" *should* be your daily mantra. This concept overrides moments of doubt and overcomes disillusionment, though it certainly does not allow any room for a whole lot of balance. But as time goes by, the company will begin to stand on its own two feet, generating revenue and becoming a tangible representation of the original entrepreneurial quest. As the company evolves, it will reflect not only the ideas of the original entrepreneur(s) but also those of their partners and team members. At that point, it is important for the new entrepreneur to take a step back and revisit the original question they may have set out to answer: "Why am I doing this?" Some entrepreneurs are very clear about their reason for entrepreneuring—they want to make a lot of money. Others claim that they want to create a future where they will finally have free time. Still others want the excitement of creating something that is wholly their own. But whatever the reasons for entrepreneuring, the entrepreneur needs to revisit their understanding of *why* they are doing what they are doing and to ensure that not only are they devoting their time and energy to supporting the needs of the organization, but the organization they have built is *really* supporting their needs and desires as well.

Lanny Goodman, a consultant for entrepreneurs (and an entrepreneur himself), has concluded that "nothing nourishes a company so much as aligning its business aims with its owner's personal ones. And conversely, nothing starves a company like keeping those aims at odds." When he challenges entrepreneurs in his audience with the statement, "The sole reason for your company to exist is to meet your needs," he is met with shocked expressions and blank stares. Most entrepreneurs are so busy focusing on some form of the big happy that they are not aware of how far they have allowed their company to take them from their original desires and needs.

According to Goodman, the entrepreneurial organization *is* personal, reflecting, for better or for worse, the entrepreneur. Only by incorporating what he calls an element of "creative selfishness"—whereby you clearly outline what your desires and needs are—will your team members be able to clarify what *they* want to accomplish. Only in this way can you work together toward finding common ground. This is not easy to do, but perhaps it is well worth investigating, because according to Goodman, this "creative selfishness" makes for much healthier relationships and a much more vital and energetic company. Without this clear assessment, you risk fostering a muddled sense of direction and risk supporting a toxic environment. "If

It's a hideous, bone-chilling, stomach-knotting, now-or-never feeling.

NICKY SILVER,
ELLE MAGAZINE

Il a les défauts de ses qualités. (His faults spring from his very qualities.)

LE MOT JUSTE

your entrepreneurial organization does not support you in your life pursuits," says Goodman, "why bother? There are so many other ways to make a living in this world."

What Goodman refers to as "creative selfishness" is really a way to ensure that you are constantly reassessing the "why" in your entrepreneuring. In doing so, you will be able to minimize the impact of self-induced tailspins and manage the inevitable entrepreneurial malaise that can hang over you like a cloud.

But the real question, according to Goodman, is, "How can I create a life that I will look back on as an incredible shining adventure, and how can the business be a vehicle to help me accomplish that?" Having had the luxury of reflecting on my understanding of the beauty of imbalance, I have concluded that, ultimately, I want to be able to dream about the big happy while I fiercely live in the here and now. I want to be able to look back in time and be able to see how moments of exhilarating panic strung together with just enough torque to create a meaningful "why" in my version of an entrepreneuring life. Every new entrepreneur needs to create their own version of beautiful imbalance. Perhaps they will also find someone to share the scenic route along the way.

chapter 12 A Never-Ending Act of Doing

As the floatplane circled around Knight Inlet, on the northern coast of British Columbia, Chris could already picture himself recounting stories of his summer adventure to his university housemates. His mind alternated between visions of catching 60-pound salmon and imagining the roaring silence that is reserved for those who have fished along the northernmost reaches of that coastline. He hoped for a great experience and wondered what he would get out of this summer.

He could already taste the salt just around the edges of his lips as he stepped off the floatplane and threw his duffel bag down beside him. Working as a fishing guide for wealthy clients would be a dream job—he just knew it.

Bud, the camp manager, walked up to him and shook his hand. "Hey sport, I'm Bud. Change of plans, big guy. Damned if I know why, but the loggers' cook is getting married, and he's flying out tonight. Eating is *important* to the loggers up here. Not a whole lot else to look forward to, if you know what I mean. So you'll need to fill in for a few days. You'll find everything you need here. Got it?" And with that, Bud jumped into the floatplane, which soon disappeared downriver. And so did all of Chris's 17-year-old notions of fishing triumphs. A growing queasiness immediately set in, not so much a result of the rocky ride in the floatplane but because he had never cooked before in his whole life. He wondered what the loggers would have to say about *that.*

With the threat of hungry loggers and a need to ensure that he kept his summer job, Chris immediately plunged into the challenge of learning how to cook as quickly as possible. Bud's notion of "everything you need" turned out to be an oil stove (which took a minimum of three hours to heat up), a tattered copy of the *Joy of Cooking,* which had at least 30 pages missing, and a CB radio so that he could call for help should anything go wrong. Not really a beginner cook's survival kit, but it would do. With the determination to make those few days bearable, Chris read recipe after recipe and experimented with the contents of the deep freeze, not afraid to start over again when any of his concoctions did not quite work out.

**The whole point of being
an entrepreneur is that
you plunge.**

MOSES ZNAIMER

**While the most exquisitely
balanced dinner can
never be relived,
a book may evoke its
graceful ghost.**

M.F.K.FISHER,
THE ART OF EATING

What started out as three days of filling in as the camp cook turned into a full-time job, 12 hours a day for four months. By the end of the first three weeks, not only were the loggers happy with the good food served to them, but they also relished the variety of dishes that were not a part of the regular cook's repertoire. By the second month, word started to spread over CB radio, all up and down the inlet, that the best food in Knight Inlet was at Float Camp Two, and fishermen from nearby sites began to show up at dinner time. At one point, even some of the wealthy guests from the fishing camp overheard the fishing guides talking about the cook at Float Camp Two. Curious, they asked if they could dine there one evening. When these five guests arrived without any warning, Chris was at a loss as to how to turn his regular Thursday-night fried chicken into a special dish for the dignitaries. Before he could reach into the deep freeze, one of the fishing-camp guests came into the kitchen and, without a word, began working away with a speed and grace that was a pleasure to watch. As it turned out, the guest was a world-renowned chef from Seattle, and without any of the usual ingredients available in this remote kitchen, he taught Chris how to make *coq au vin*.

That evening, Chris served up his first truly gourmet meal. As the water lapped up against the logs supporting the float camp, and with the taste of the *coq au vin* lingering on his palate, Chris looked around the table. Here he was in the middle of nowhere, surrounded by people who had very little in common—from the northern B.C. loggers to the high-paying guests of the fishing camp to the young fishing guides. And yet, his preparing the meal had allowed them to share something special together.

It was then that he realized his wish had come true. The summer was truly turning into a great experience. But it was not great because of what he had gotten out of it but because of what he had given. By focusing on the desire to prepare food that people could truly enjoy, he had created a place where people wanted to belong, a table that people flocked to for the pleasure of experiencing good food. Along the way, he discovered a passion for cooking that he knew he would pursue with a zest and enthusiasm for the rest of his life.

In the years that followed, whenever Chris was asked how he got to be such a good cook, he would sit back and recount this story. He always ends the story by saying, "But what I remember most about that summer is that, in a strange way, it crystallized my understanding of not *what* I wanted to do with my life but how I wanted to *live* it. To this day, I equate the sheer delight and surprise of providing *coq au vin* at a float camp in the middle of nowhere with the optimism that unequivocally comes with the act of giving more than is necessary. In a strange way, that summer provided me with the initial stirring of what I thought entrepreneuring was all about. Perhaps opportunists are motivated by the question, 'What can I get out of this?' But enterprising spirits are motivated by the question, 'How can I work with the give and take that makes up our day-to-day lives?' And as for my wish for an incredible experience along the way? It is reflected in the entrepreneuring—and the cooking—I have been doing with and for people ever since that summer."

celebrating the give and take

Whether it is the preparation of *coq au vin* that keeps fishing-camp guests coming back for more culinary voyages or the articulation of "vision" in the shape and form of an unforgettable brand, entrepreneurs are constantly looking for ways to create powerful signs and symbols that represent their dreams. In the process of building their dreams, or "story," and encouraging others be a part of it, they are contributing more to their environment, to the culture, than they take from it. The new entrepreneur is a symbol, in some ways, of the spirit of giving.

I was fascinated to read that urban cultural anthropologist Jennifer James spends her time searching for all kinds of modern-day signs and symbols—from food preferences to job titles to the way people spend their Saturday nights—seeing these things as a signal for changing realities in our modern-day culture. Most important for the readers of this book, she points out how, by learning to read the signs of change, companies can stay ahead of shifts and anticipate trends that will affect their business. For example, casual dressing at work signals a flattening of hierarchy, and the fact that the male and female lawyers on the television show "Ally McBeal" share a unisex bathroom is a good enough reason not to invest in urinals!

Based on James's ideas, I began asking myself what critical cultural symbols signal not only the desire but also the need to integrate entrepreneuring into our lives. For me, there are two in particular that stand out. The first is the use of the term "free agents." In an economy where value and price are de facto, whether one is dealing with products or services, talent or perceived talent, I find it interesting that the word "free" is used to describe the people—the Knowledge Deal Makers—as they search for how best to increase the value attached to their talent, skill, and knowledge. Equally interesting is the use of the term "agent." What comes immediately to mind is the notion of representation; in this case, self-representation. When I put these two terms together, I am struck with a notion of an open-ended (free) sense of representation (agent). In 1998, temporary staffing in the U.S. was a $50 billion a year business. This growth of free agents (particularly in knowledge-based industries such as high tech) is really a reflection of the desire for individuals to tell their own never-ending story of how they are reinventing

Because that's what life is. Making yourself believe the best things you can.

ELIZABETH MCCRACKEN, *THE GIANT'S HOUSE*

But some of us must see the fish in order to see the water. The water may be too transparent to grasp without varieties of fish to show its texture.

SHUNRYU SUZUKI, "ZEN MIND, BEGINNER'S MIND"

themselves. Examples can be found in the graphic designer who becomes a computer programmer, the television producer who becomes a writer for interactive entertainment programs, and the banker who starts her own e-commerce consulting business.

The second cultural signal that I see is that of context. Regardless of whether one is a free agent, or just someone who is working *toward* a model of independence, the desire to own one's own destiny, to take care of oneself, is at the heart of the search. A systems engineer who works for one of the hottest new software companies in the Valley admitted to me that although he loves his work and is proud to be working for a hot new company, he is "starved for my own context." When I've spoken to many others in the technology industry, that sentiment is echoed time and time again. Enter the desire to become a new entrepreneur.

the power of providing a context of optimism

The power of entrepreneuring is that it provides a context for those who need to struggle with notions of freedom and reinvention. This is so, because the act of entrepreneuring itself is an exercise in the continuous refinement of "opportunity." In fact, some psychologists, such as Harvey Levinson, president of the Levinson Institute in Belmont, Massachusetts, suggest that in some ways, entrepreneurs work with a single-minded intensity because they are psychologically compelled to. Like artists, they invest their heart and soul into their work, motivated by the need for achievement and the opportunity for innovation. Of course, today, high tech provides the backdrop for this readiness to reinvent, the overriding need to achieve. The speed at which change occurs in this industry encourages those with an entrepreneurial spirit who wish to take advantage of the turnover cycles.

Even more important is the fact that entrepreneuring provides a context for optimism. Henry David Thoreau described the world as a mass of people leading lives of "quiet desperation," reflecting the belief that the only things possible are what we can see or touch. The philosophy of entrepreneuring, however, allows one to embrace a state of magical realism. In this way, those who entrepreneur can take their vision of never-ending possibilities and share it with others. Whether psychologically based or not, this optimistic attitude is magnetic and hard for others to resist.

Many cultural observers are claiming that in today's world, Generation Xers have fewer opportunities available to them than the baby boomers before them. By focusing on entrepreneuring, however, this philosophy can be turned on its head and viewed as a reflection of the need to reinvent success and the symbols of achievement. Entrepreneuring invites upcoming generations to base their lives and work not on the standards that others before them have set but on their own vision. This redefinition of success

Genius can be bounded in a nutshell and yet embrace the whole fullness of life.

THOMAS MANN

Cathy is a graphic artist who works for an advertising agency. Her boss gives her his view of the true superhero: "The ultimate superhero. Ready? He only has three super powers. Meet the mime: He can enclose himself in a glass booth; he can walk against heavy winds, or he can pull himself along on an invisible rope. But wait, there's four—he can lean on an invisible mantelpiece.

FROM THE MOVIE
BREATHING ROOM

is reflected in a shift in the business world from that of company employees to that of brokered talent—of individuals, services, and products. The optimism that entrepreneuring demands (but also provides) is an important stepping-stone for this collective and individual need for self-determination. If entrepreneurial stories reflect a more diverse notion of success, then in the process, these tales also encourage the notion of evolving symbols of change. In the true spirit of entrepreneuring, there is an inherent giving that takes place—in the meaningful stories that are told and in the learning that comes from an exchange between people that might otherwise not occur. There are three trigger points for maintaining and passing on this entrepreneurial spirit.

the act of doing is a never-ending way of seeing the world

Whenever I meet an entrepreneur who has multiple successes under their belt, the first question I always ask is, "If you could give someone one piece of advice, what would it be?" And I am always struck by the fact that, many times, the response is a variation of the phrase coined by Nike—"Just do it!" Further discussion often shows that what they mean by "Just do it!" refers to the notion that nothing really takes the place of action. At a certain point, only so much wisdom can be gained from reading, talking, listening, and observing. Regardless of what business you choose, the untrainable element of entrepreneuring comes only from the doing itself. Once you plunge into action, you realize that success does not come from following the way that Ted Turner, Sam Walton, or Carol Bartz did it. The real learning and the real self-definition comes from the need to overcome challenges in a creative way, through your own version of how to imagine yourself out of or into the situation.

I once read a quote that said, "There are three kinds of people in this world: those who make it happen, those who see it happen, and those who wonder what has happened. We all know where entrepreneurs fit in." When it comes to "doing," what is most important is not the accomplishments that one can actualize but the unbridled learning that comes with acting. As a new entrepreneur, you learn about people and possibilities, rather than merely how to implement the goals of others. Sometimes that learning can be a natural evolution of the direction you are already heading in, and sometimes it happens only when you take a random stroll into unknown territory or when you are forced into a sudden and dramatic pause in your doing. Being committed to "serial" doing provides not only the optimism that comes from uncovering new possibilities but a sense of renewal that is essential if one is to continue learning and growing as an individual.

Entrepreneur Heather Reisman has pursued a variety of businesses throughout her life. She began in social services, moved into change

Inspiration is the best word we have for appetite.

ADAM PHILLIPS,
THE BEAST IN THE NURSERY

Is that what they call a vocation, what you do with joy as if you had fire in your heart, the devil in your body?

JOSEPHINE BAKER

management consulting, moved into retail branding, and is currently building a series of cultural department stores for the book lover in the shape and form of Indigo Books & Café. Many have asked her about the connection between these seemingly different businesses. "Throughout my life I have always looked for the ultra-progressive and focused on understanding how people, business organizations, and consumers interact. By committing to 'doing' and actively seeking out the connection between people and their needs and desires, I have been able to accumulate knowledge and experience that has been a constant throughout my work life." For Heather, as with many entrepreneurs, by being one of those people who make it happen, she has been able to entrepreneur successfully time and time again. In the process she is celebrating the possible.

It is above all by the imagination that we achieve perception, and compassion, and hope.

URSULA K. LE GUIN

I don't develop; I am.

PABLO PICASSO

liquid leadership

Al West is the CEO of SEI Investments, a company that manages $121 billion in assets, mostly mutual funds. What is most surprising about this company is that, despite the cultural stereotype of the starched white shirt typically associated with financial services, SEI "exudes a sense of bottom-up informality." When asked to describe what is at the heart of his workplace, Al West replies, "We call it fluid leadership. People figure out what they're good at, and that shapes what their roles are. There's not just one leader. Different people lead during different parts of the process." For SEI, fluid leadership begins with doing away with walls, secretaries, and typical organizational charts and ends with everyone taking responsibility for their role in the company. But when I reflect on the term fluid leadership, it conjures up something that spills over beyond the boundaries of a company and into society at large. The notion of different people taking on different responsibilities along the way reminds me how important it is to avoid putting boundaries around the contributions that people make within any given process. In my mind's eye, the image of fluid leadership evolves into "liquid leadership," and, true to the properties of liquids, it has the ability to seep and spread into all kinds of places with a strange force of its own.

Peter Drucker, in his book *Innovation and Entrepreneurship,* identifies many examples of entrepreneurs who made their living in one industry and yet truly contributed to the society of their time in a completely different area. He refers to these people as social entrepreneurs. For example, Thomas Edison is best known for his invention of the light bulb and the phonograph, but perhaps his biggest contribution was the invention of the first industrial research lab in the U.S. in 1876, which revolutionized how new ideas are generated and tested. Michael Moon best sums up how the role of the entrepreneur extends far beyond that of company leader: "Entrepreneurs change how we live, work, and play. And the ones who have been the most successful overall are those who have brought something entirely fresh to how we perceive and understand new ideas and adapt to new concepts. What they give to society at large is where we all gain the most."

Liquid Leadership Is Not Always about Liquid Assets

In an article that Jim Collins wrote, called "The Foundation for Doing Good," he describes an unlikely commonality between the conservative Maryland-based Marriott Hotels and the casual, informal California-based sports-and-leisure clothing company, Patagonia: "You'd certainly have a hard time finding two executives with less in common than J. Willard Marriott Jr. and Yvon Chouinard. Yet . . . both see the corporation as a powerful tool for social change." Marriott launched a program called "Pathways to Independence," which provides intensive training to welfare recipients to prepare them for jobs within the company. Similarly, Patagonia tries conscientiously to give something back to society. "Patagonia's activities as an environmental activist date back to the early 1970s. Today, the company makes jackets out of recycled plastic bottles, produces clothing made exclusively from organic cotton, and donates 1 percent of its sales to environmental causes." These are just two of many examples of how established entrepreneurs are blurring the lines between their responsibility to their shareholders and employees and their responsibility to the society they work and play in.

What is even more exciting are the examples set by up-and-coming entrepreneurs who choose to give more than they take. Melissa Bradley is a prime example. Just one year out of college, Bradley created a consulting company that booked its first million-dollar year. But when she sold the business a few years later, in 1992, rather than put the proceeds into something for her own monetary gain, she used the money to launch the Entrepreneurial Development Institute, a nonprofit organization that teaches entrepreneurship to youth at risk. Coming herself from an underprivileged, single-parent household, Melissa decided that she wanted to help others like her to succeed as entrepreneurs.

There is a growing number of examples of entrepreneurial organizations that not only contribute to society through their checkbooks but "donate their acumen or invest in nonprofit groups' business ventures as a means of creating new wealth for community needs." Larkin Business Ventures is an organization that trains and supports youth at risk. They currently operate a Ben and Jerry's ice cream franchise in San Francisco. Founded in 1992, Business for Social Responsibility has 1,400 members—all small companies and start-ups that have won recognition for their innovative initiatives. Working Assets is another example. A privately held long-distance telephone and credit card company, it donates a percentage of revenue to support various ecological programs, as well as a host of other causes. In fact, when you pay your bill, they will prompt you to

One always learns one's mystery at the price of one's innocence.

ROBERTSON DAVIES

To bury the grape tendril in such a way that it shoots out new growth I recognize easily as a metaphor for the way life must change from time to time if we are to go forward in our thinking.

FRANCES MAYES,
UNDER THE TUSCAN SUN

contribute by saying, "Your bill comes to $25.34. Would you like to round that out to $27.00, and we will not only contribute the usual percentage but also the overage to our donations pool?"

The role of the organization, according to Jim Collins, is about collective contributions. "I think many people assume, wrongly, that a company exists simply to make money. While this is an important result of a company's existence, we have to go deeper and find the real reasons for our being. As we investigate this, we inevitably come to the conclusion that a group of people get together and exist as an institution that we call a company so that they are able to accomplish something collectively that they could not accomplish separately—they make a contribution to society, a phrase that sounds trite but is fundamental."

Nowhere is this truer than within the realm of the entrepreneur's world. In "Risk and Reward" (a recent study conducted by Roper Stach Worldwide), "92 percent of entrepreneurs and 82 percent of corporate executives believe entrepreneurial companies are role models for American business." Furthermore, 68 percent of executives in Fortune 500 companies agree that entrepreneurs are the heroes of American business (up from 49 percent in 1987). George Gendron, *Inc.*'s editor-in-chief, believes that part of this image of heroism is based on the fact that entrepreneurship is becoming more professionalized, bringing with it a certain level of sophistication.

Although entrepreneurs are often stretched for cash and resources, it is not the size of the altruistic project or activity they initiate that is important but the act of giving and the message this sends to others. At a time when, in some districts, 70 percent of high school students are interested in entrepreneurship, learning by example is critical in passing on the value of liquid leadership. Gun Denhart is the co-founder of Hanna Andersson, a mail-order clothing business that encourages customers to return their used clothes (which the company then donates to various children's centers around the globe) by allowing them to apply a 20 percent discount to their next order. When Gun's son Christian was asked, "What is a corporation?" he answered, "A corporation has many parts, just like the human body. It has a brain *and* a heart." The message that Christian's mother is passing on, through her own example, is what will help to create the next generation of liquid leaders. Teaching by example provides the necessary guidance and motivation for the generations who are watching and learning from our never-ending act of doing.

Some entrepreneurs choose to engage in an organized means of contributing to society, as some of the entrepreneurs noted above have done. Others take a personal interest by mentoring others in their vocational pursuits. Either way, at a very basic level, entrepreneurs have the opportunity to become local heroes and influencers through the stories they tell, the learning they choose to share, and what they give back to their

There are three ways to see the world. There is the three-dimensional approach, which is about the physicality of the world. There is the two-dimensional mode, which requires imagination in the adding of the third dimension. And then there is the third way, which demands that you put the three-dimensional viewpoint and the two-dimensional viewpoint together. Only by celebrating the possibilities are you truly able to create a new reality that is wholly your own.

DAVID NASH

environment. For example, Joy Mountford is proud of the University Workshop Project she started a number of years ago as a means of finding people with complementary interdisciplinary skills who would be able to work together on the technology research at Interval. But what started out as a means of finding the right people to hire, became a template for finding complementary skill sets between seemingly unmatched disciplines. Many of her program graduates have gone on to recreate this kind of interdisciplinary approach to research in their own fields. By doing so, they have not only found fulfilling jobs but are changing the way research is being conducted, adding more breadth and depth to an equation based on such diverse skill sets.

the entrepreneurial touch— living the life of your chosen hero

Roland Barthes once remarked that narrative "is international, transhistorical, transcultural: it is simply there, like life itself." The significance of this remark came back to me one night when I was sitting in an out-of-the-way jazz bar in Sydney, Australia. Narrative, as it turns out, can also be transvocational.

As the local jazz band played the last sweet bars of music, my friend Rawlston asked me, "So, what do you think? Can you see yourself sacrificing a few baroque concerts for one of these moments of musical bliss every once in a while?" Of course I *could*, but, hard-nosed admirer of classical music that I was, I was not going to give in that easily. "You know I like jazz, but it just doesn't have the same personal meaning to me as baroque music does."

Rawlston then said, "What if I told you a story that involved a trumpet player, a jazz bar, and an entrepreneur? Could that possibly provide you with the kind of connection you need?" I sat back and waited for the story to begin.

"I was always a pretty good piano player with a wide repertoire," Rawlston continued, "but what I really loved was playing jazz. As I got better and better and honed my skills, I would voraciously listen to the masters of the art, Oscar Peterson, Bill Evans, and Thelonius Monk, until the wee hours of the morning. Rather than being motivated, I began to realize that I would never be as inventive as Oscar Peterson or ever master the technique of Bill Evans, and surely I would never have the same powerful, dramatic life stories to pour into the piano keys—the way they did time and time again. And so, by allowing their stories, abilities, and musical inventiveness to overwhelm me, I allowed them to steal my own music from me. I stopped playing altogether. I let the dust settle on my Steinway, and I cringed whenever someone asked me if I was still playing piano.

Entrepreneurs change how we live, work, and play. And the ones who have been the most successful overall are those who have brought something entirely fresh to how we perceive and understand new ideas and adapt to new concepts. What they give to society at large is where we all gain the most.

MICHAEL MOON

What is a society without a heroic dimension?

JEAN BAUDRILLARD

"And then a strange thing happened. I was at a little bar late one evening, and I found myself talking to this guy—a Frenchman visiting Aussie land—who just happened to be sitting beside me. He was a horn player, and, as it turned out, we both loved jazz. 'Do you play an instrument?' he asked. 'Well,' I said, 'I used to play piano, but I don't anymore.' And then whether it was the atmosphere or his encouraging smile, I went on to tell him why I had stopped playing.

"'Let me tell you something,' he said after I had finished, 'and I hope you listen carefully. Three years ago, I was at the lowest point in my life. After years of hard work, I had finally graduated with a combined degree in law and accounting. I knew that my ultimate plan was to start my own consulting practice, and I was lucky enough to get a job, right out of school, at a hot new up-and-coming consulting firm, working with the best and the brightest *and* their high-profile clients. I was obsessed with learning everything I could from this firm. I strived to be the best in the firm, avoiding making a mistake at any cost, so that I, too, could one day be able to have what my employers had.

"'But after working there for two years, rather than being inspired to follow in the footsteps of my bosses, I was deflated with the thought that I would never be quite as good as they were, that I would never be able to build up the same kind of client roster that they had. In short, I began to falter at my job. The less inspired I was at work, the more time I spent at home playing my horn, which I had not touched in years. The more committed I became to my music, the more casual I became in pursuing my career. And then one day, it dawned on me. I was so busy trying to become someone else, looking for ways to fit myself into someone's model for success and fulfillment, that I had lost a sense of what was most important to me. Today, I do have my own consulting firm. But it does not have a particularly hot client list, and it does not attract the best and the brightest. Instead it is a small practice that I chose to build to allow me to have the time for playing my trumpet. I choose how much work I want, I determine how much money I *really* need to make, and I measure myself only against myself. And you know what else? I make mistakes, and I falter all the time, but rather than protect myself against them, I allow them to happen and hope that I will learn something along the way. Sure I have days when I wonder what it would be like to have gone a different route. But most of all, I have something that is wholly my own.'

"I nodded but I did not say a word. A few minutes later, he left and I never saw him again. But a month later, I was at a party where someone was goofing around on the guitar. I liked the way he played, and I recognized some of the pieces he was playing. Without a word, I sat down at the piano beside him and joined in. I did not care how bad I sounded, and my inner ear was no longer consumed by my musical heroes. Instead, I allowed myself to make mistakes, and I waited to hear *my* own music. I faltered and stumbled through the pieces, but I did not stop playing. When I left the party that night, I felt a deep gratitude toward that stranger I had met the previous month, because I realized that he had taken the time to tell me his story as a way of reminding me that we all need to find our own version of whatever it is that we are best at doing. I have been playing music with this guitar player ever since, which has been a lot of fun. But more than anything, I can now sit and listen to professional jazz, like we are doing tonight, and it has a personal connection for me. Ultimately, I have come to understand that we all choose to study and emulate the lives of various heroes. But it is only those of us who go on to create our own unique version of living who are the truly heroic. And that is liberating."

What struck me about hearing this story was not only what my friend Rawlston had learned but the giving the man in the bar had provided. His willingness to be vulnerable and to share the personal side of his life had made all the difference in the insight that my friend was left with. Suddenly, the literal translation of the French words *entre* and *prendre* that make up "entrepreneur" had a lot more relevance for me. To be the person who operates "between taking" is really another way of saying "giving." I suddenly realized that liquid leadership could reflect something even more visceral and immediate than social entrepreneurship in an organized fashion. Just as the anonymous man had shared his vulnerability and his personal struggles with my friend Rawlston as a means of inspiring him to play music in his own way, so, too, could entrepreneuring be about the learning that comes when you truly give of yourself in the personal telling of your stories to those you care about *and* to strangers alike.

When I read an interview with Steve Miller of Royal Dutch/Shell about his notion of grassroots leadership, what struck me most was his focus on teaching as a means of leading. "As a leader and as a teacher, you've got to open yourself up. You simply have to make it personal. A lot of executives I know can get up in front of an audience and give a presentation. They're very comfortable speaking in the third person: 'Here's what the company is doing.' It's a safe way of talking. They don't have to put an 'I' in very many sentences. But real teaching means giving of yourself. To reach people, I had to talk in the first person. . . . That creates a personal connection—and it changes how we talk with each other and how we work with each other."

To me, what is most powerful about entrepreneuring is the personal teaching, the one-on-one exchange of ideas that an entrepreneur, as a storyteller, has the power and the responsibility to give to others.

When Harriet Rubin asked Peter Drucker what he was most proud of achieving in his life, he quietly answered, "None of my books or ideas means anything to me in the long run. What are theories? Nothing. The only thing that matters is how you touch people. Have I given anyone insight? That's what I want to have done. Insight lasts; theories don't."

There is a strong, deeply held sense among those at the forefront of business that purpose, community, and sustainability are lasting values that inform the work we all do—and the future that we are all working toward.

FAST COMPANY MAGAZINE

Sixty-eight percent of executives in Fortune 500 companies agree that entrepreneurs are the heroes of American business (up from 49% in 1987).

THE ORANGE COUNTY REGISTER

much to do about giving

Choosing to be an entrepreneur requires not only the courage to push the envelope of perceived risk but also the attempt to create something that is a reflection of who you are. Along with this courage comes a responsibility—and, not surprisingly, a *personal* responsibility—to take Peter Drucker's advice, to "touch" someone else's life. By doing so, perhaps you will provide others with insights that will last. Just as there are many ways to play jazz piano without being an Oscar Peterson and many ways to entrepreneur successfully without being a Bill Gates, there are many ways to inspire others. But it always begins with personal storytelling.

There are two key elements that provide guidelines for effective personal storytelling. In *The Age of Unreason,* Charles Handy talks about the need to reinvent education as a means of preparing all of us for a world in which effective organizations need more intelligent people, where careers are shorter and more changeable, and where people need to be more self-sufficient. In his view, the reinvention of education will not be limited to the traditional notion of the classroom setting. Our success in preparing people to work effectively in looser, more dispersed organizations will be based, to some extent, on our ability to teach them to work well in an atmosphere of change and exploration, not in a climate of fear and risk aversion. We need to create a culture of excitement, focused on questions and experiment, of exploration and adventure. "That kind of culture cannot be imposed. It can only be encouraged by demonstrations of warmth for all that is good, by celebration, by investment in individuals beyond the bounds of prudence. That kind of encouragement is only possible if one genuinely cares for the people being encouraged."

If we build on this notion of trusting exploration and the celebration of caring, then what is new about the new entrepreneur is not the act of entrepreneuring itself. That concept has been around for centuries in one form or another. What is really new may be the commitment to communicating the values that are intrinsically part of this never-ending story of doing: namely optimism, open-mindedness, reinvention, personal exploration, and a redefinition of the word *opportunity.* This side of the new entrepreneur has very little to do with taking (*prendre*) and much to do with giving. The giving comes from caring about others—enough to tell them your personal stories, good and bad, successful and otherwise, and to encourage them to celebrate the act of exploration and find their version of adventure and ultimately the learning that comes with it.

I believe that more wealth will be created and people will have more fun by entrepreneuring than by anything else. We will serve ourselves if we increase the importance of entrepreneurship, but I also know that to entrepreneur without compassion, without some order, and without a real social safety net, can be a very selfish, egotistical game, one not worth playing.

MICHAEL A. LEVINE,
PARTNER, GOODMAN,
PHILLIPS & VINEBERG

the future of everyday life

I once read that physicists often do their best work before the age of about 26. Perhaps this theory is based on the idea that they begin to lose their idealism. They become afraid of what they think might never happen. It is almost as if their learning begins to get in the way of further exploring their own capabilities. I wonder what kind of stories physicists tell each other as a means of passing on learning and understanding that will live on and that will keep them inspired?

On days when entrepreneuring and all that it has to offer wears me out, I think about those physicists who must live with an imposed deadline on their potential contribution. I admire them for pushing past this day-to-day challenge of being limited by knowing too much. And it reminds me of what I love most of all about entrepreneuring. It is not only the tension created by the desire to push boundaries of "what if's," and it is not only the variety of the give and take that seems to arrive with each new situation one must navigate through and toward. It is also the unavoidable celebration of a future that elegantly sidesteps any deadline or end in sight. It reminds me that insight, inspiration, and meaning in entrepreneuring are constantly replenished by the mere reflection of the "future of everyday life."

One word that comes into my mind is *privilege*, as in lucky, as in blessed; because I can't think of a more ferocious way to live.

MOSES ZNAIMER

on never losing the poetry

I have often wondered whether the frequency with which one experiences déjà vu is something that is genetically passed on or a side effect of the strange workings of a mind deprived of sleep or a body subjected to too many airplane trips. I say this because I have had so many moments of déjà vu throughout my life that I have stopped referring to them as such. But in 1998, I experienced a different form of déjà vu, a moment of true learning for me as a new entrepreneur and a teller of personal stories.

A friend of mine in the banking industry called and asked for a favor. He wanted me to visit a friend of his, Finley, who had started a company and seemed to be at an important decision-making juncture. He thought I might be able to provide him with some much-needed advice. I was all too happy to help out my friend, who had always been willing to help me out throughout the years.

A few days later, I arrived at the address I was given. I was immediately struck by the design and ambience of this particular office—a warehouse space converted into a beehive of activity and urgency that permeated the

There are three kinds of people in this world: those who make it happen, those who see it happen, and those who wonder what has happened. We all know where entrepreneurs fit in.

office even at this late hour of the day. I heard music playing somewhere, and I recognized the specific heat that emanates from too many computers left on for too many hours. I felt a comfortable sense of déjà vu, as if I had been here before, though I knew I hadn't.

Unfortunately, my sense of comfort slowly eroded 20 minutes later, when I was still waiting in the reception area. There was no sign of Finley, nor had anyone else come forward to greet me. I read a headline or two from the local newspaper on the table, I scanned my voicemail messages, and then I got annoyed. Finally, 10 minutes later, I was approached by a young man dressed in jeans and a crisp, electric-blue shirt who combined an apology and an invitation to tour his office all in one breath. I told him I had half an hour.

Sitting in his small but comfortable boardroom, which displayed awards and samples of current work, I discovered that Finley was the proud owner of a multimedia design company. He had 25 employees, had been in business for three years, and was thoroughly enjoying the struggle of turning his initial dream of creating great digital design for corporate clients into something bigger. I was intrigued. As Finley showed me his portfolio of projects—from Web sites to interactive training programs—bookmarked on the boardroom computer, we conversed in shorthand. He recognized my familiarity and comfort with the work at hand. And then, with a glint in his eyes, he switched to another program on the computer and began to explain the work that he and his team had been doing on a software authoring tool they had created, based on the multitude of digital design projects that they had worked on over the past three years.

I did not need him to describe the difficulty of trying to support R&D for a product concept while simultaneously managing and growing a service business. I am sure that my incessant nodding indicated to Finley that I probably knew a lot more about the trials and tribulations he was going through than most of his boardroom guests. I was almost impatient as he described how he had worked through a business model that would allow him to segue over from the service business to a product business without the capital or enough human resources in sight.

Just when I was about to tell him how similar our entrepreneurial experiences were, he said, "I haven't really told anyone this, but for some reason, I feel compelled to confide in you. Maybe because you are a stranger, maybe because I sense that you will be able to help me. So here goes." He took a deep breath, and with it there was a noticeable shift in the mood of the room.

"Despite the client roster we've attracted and despite the ongoing work we are generating, we've been pretty well on the edge of financial disaster for the past two months. I know why. It's because I have been putting as much capital into the ongoing R&D for this product as I can because I believe in it. I know that I have something here, and I am determined not

If entrepreneuring is love, do you know how to make love last?

DOUG KEELEY

to lose my window of opportunity to get into the marketplace with it before someone else does. Two days ago, I was approached by a company—a very reputable one—that is interested in partnering with me in the service side of the business. If I bring these guys on, I could probably find a way to dedicate enough capital to produce a beta version of the product. I believe I could get the deal signed with them within the next month, save my existing business, giving us a chance at jumping into the software industry, which is what I always wanted to do."

"So why the hesitancy?" I asked. "It sounds pretty good."

"In exchange for their capital infusion, they would get voting control of my board, which I could live with. But to be honest, I don't sense that they truly see the possibilities of this product, and I'm afraid that I will never be able to see this idea through if I partner with them. I cannot *believe* that I've allowed myself to get to this point, where I am considering giving away my company and, with it, the potential to go one step further. I don't know what to do. You will probably start by telling me that I should never have gotten myself into this position in the first place. I know that you probably have never been in such a bind. But I don't really have any options, do I?"

It was then that I was hit by the most powerful sense of déjà vu I had ever experienced in my life. Not the gnawing "I feel like I've been here before" kind of background noise I had experienced hundreds of times over the last years, but an in-your-face, heart-pounding "nowness" that comes only when you *truly* have been exactly where someone else is standing. For a moment, I was tempted to give him sound advice about how to weigh the pros and the cons of his dilemma and compliment him on the product concept he had shared with me. But in a flash, I realized this was *not* what he was looking for, nor what he needed. From one entrepreneur to another, I had a responsibility. Now it was my turn to take a deep breath.

And I began to tell him my story. Not a third-person version of how our company grew or how we made equally tough decisions, but my personal story, including the pain, confusion, learning, and liberation that I went through and continue to go through in the entrepreneuring I have chosen to do. I began by reliving the moment when, just like him, I, too, could not understand how I had led myself and my company into a situation where we were teetering on disaster. I recounted the sense of confusion and self-doubt I experienced when I realized that I had allowed my company to become depleted of resources to the point where I was going to have to sign up for the wrong kind of partnership simply because I had no choice. But I also took the time to describe the moments of inspiration and revelation that had come to me along the way, and the guidance and strength I got from my angels of advantage. I not only divulged the "how" but the reason "why" I chose to say no to money I could not afford to lose

The only thing that matters is how you touch people. Have I given anyone insight? That's what I want to have done. Insight lasts; theories don't.

PETER DRUCKER

and the journey that this decision created for me in the never-ending tale of my entrepreneuring.

As the hours passed and I disclosed the specifics of my entrepreneuring decisions, Finley was not the only one who was furiously taking down notes. In choosing to be truthful about the exploration of my entrepreneurial journey and to take on the responsibility of personally telling my tale, I realized that I, too, was learning. I, too, was reinventing myself in the process, gaining insights and ideas that I did not want to lose when I left that room. In those few hours, I recognized that the act of caring enough to divulge the nuances of my experience had a benefit I had not understood before. No matter how far out of balance entrepreneuring might take me, no matter how hungry I might be to equalize the various paradoxical requirements demanded of me on a day-to-day basis, as long as I was committed to sharing my never-ending tale, I could, as Peter Drucker recommends, touch others in a way that mattered.

Many centuries ago, a Chinese poet wrote that being able to describe something in words was like living twice.

The hours whizzed by. When I felt that I had said as much as I could, I concluded, "So, that's my story—so far. You will have to determine your own version of entrepreneuring. The most important thing I can leave you with is the admonition to keep seeing beyond the possibilities that your current situation presents you with. If you do that, you will always be able to create your own story. And with it, you will never lose the poetry in the journey you have chosen."

When I left Finley's warehouse, I realized that my role as a new entrepreneur was not about describing what my angels of advantage are, but in becoming one for someone else.

In the never-ending search for new possibilities and self-determination, the new entrepreneur recognizes that there are many fairy tales waiting for the right entrepreneurial spirit to imbue them with purpose. As an entrepreneur, the potential to influence, teach, explore, and question is continuously renewed through the act of storytelling. In the process of retelling my story in these pages, as the ancient Chinese poet discovered, I, too, feel that I have lived my entrepreneurial journey (to date)—twice. The first time was the active doing, which is demanded of the entrepreneur. The second time is the giving that I hope my writing reflects and in my wishes to gently provoke and challenge. Maybe even inspire.

In Hebrew, there is a phrase that is often used: *Ein Breira*. Roughly translated, it means, "It's unavoidable." The new entrepreneur, in a commitment to retelling their stories, will ensure that learning will be passed on in the margins of their diary pages. And if one had to choose a symbol to scrawl in those margins that most closely reflects the entrepreneurial spirit and passes it on to others, it would be the left parenthesis (..... because of the endless possibilities that this symbol suggests. Some people will gain insight from their stories, sit back, and wonder. Others will take this learning and create their own stories, eternally pushing the boundaries of possibilities, extending the definition of the spirit of the entrepreneur. As it should be. *Ein Breira*. It's unavoidable.

*I have only made this longer
because I have not had the time
to make it shorter.*

BLAISE PASCAL

Endnotes

page xi *"boldness has genius, power, and magic in it."* Johann Wolfgang von Goethe, *Faustus: A Dramatic Mystery*, line 303, translated by John Anster, 1835. Cited by *The Home Book of Quotations Classical and Modern*, 10th edition. New York: Dodd Mead & Company, 1967.

chapter 1: the lightness of entrepreneuring

page 6 *"independent professional offering."* Daniel H. Pink, "The Talent Market," *Fast Company*. August 1998.

page 8 *as recorded in the early 1990s.* "My Brilliant Career," *Report on Business* magazine. June 1997.

page 8 *one in seven Canadians run their own business. The Vancouver Sun.* April 6, 1995.

page 8 *faster than the Canadian economy as a whole.* Industry Canada, *High Tech Growth through Investment.* May 30, 1997.

page 8 *$3.7 billion into these startups.* Andy Reinhardt, "No Slacking in Silicon Valley," *Business Week.* August 31, 1998.

page 8 *50 percent of businesses by the year 2000.* U.S. Small Business Administration news release no. 98-13. March 11, 1998.

page 8 *providing almost one million jobs.* Women Business Owners of Canada, web site.

page 8 *has become de rigueur in the 1990s.* Tom Richman, "Creators of the New Economy," *Inc.* magazine. The State of Small Business Issue, 1997.

page 9 *dependent on those below you for information.* Charles Handy, *The Age of Unreason.* Boston: Harvard Business School Press, 1990, 166.

page 9 *more than $200 billion a year.* "The Valley of Money's Delight," *The Economist.* March 29, 1997.

page 9 *the Canadian economy as a whole.* Industry Canada, *High Tech Growth through Investment.* May 30, 1997.

page 10 *over the previous year. Inc.* magazine (online). October 14, 1998.

page 11 *1,600 women start a new business.* "My Brilliant Career," *Report on Business* magazine. June 1997.

page 11 *business people who are "hungry to think."* Jim Collins, "What Comes Next?" *Inc.* magazine. October 1997.

page 12 List adapted from "Creators of the New Economy," *Inc.* magazine. The State of Small Business Issue, 1997.

page 13 *entrepreneurship is taught at about 400 universities.* Marc Ballon, "Campus Inc.," *Inc.* magazine. March 1998.

page 14 *One in seven Canadians run their own business. The Vancouver Sun.* April 6, 1995.

page 15 *call themselves independent contractors.* Joann S. Lublin, "Waiting for Payment Vexes Self-Employed," *The Wall Street Journal.* September 3, 1997.

page 19 *"You've got the rock of eye."* John le Carré, *The Tailor of Panama.* New York: Alfred A. Knopf, 1996.

page 19 *"best to leave the mystery there."* Diane Cole, "The Entrepreneurial Self," *Psychology Today.* June 1989.

page 22   *"Yearn: for infinity."* The rock group Tricky in *Post* magazine. 1995.

page 22   *"a seemingly miraculous power."* Hilary Stout, "Law Students Are Catching the Entrepreneurial Bug," *The Wall Street Journal Interactive Edition.* September 30, 1997.

chapter 2: relentless convergence

page 24   *Internet e-commerce alone will hit $327 billion, equal to 23% of the gross domestic product.* Robert D. Hof, "The Net is Open for Business: Big Time," *Business Week.* August 31,1998.

page 24   *converging with our everyday lives.* Charles Piller, "Macworld Dreamnet," *Macworld.* October 1994.

page 24   *By 2001, 268 million computers will be hooked up to the Net.* "The Wired World," *Toronto Star.* October 2, 1997.

page 24   *computers per capita.* Industry Canada, *Investing in Canada's IT & T Industry*, 1998.

page 25   *Zenith and Motorola are a good case in point.* Jim Collins, "What Comes Next?" *Inc.* magazine. October 1997.

page 25   *as flexible as possible as a means of preparing for the future.* Polly Labarre, "Report from the Future," *Fast Company.* October 1991.

page 25   *all forms of information, both for business and entertainment, can be merged together.* Alan Freedman, *Computer Desktop Encyclopedia.* New York: Amacom, American Management Association, 1996.

page 27   *producer-controlled consumer markets.* Jim Taylor and Watts Wacker, *The 500 Year Delta: What Happens After What Comes Next.* New York: HarperBusiness, 1997, p. xiv.

page 28   *stereophonic sound on a magnetic track.* Desi K. Bognar, *International Dictionary of Broadcasting and Film.* Oxford: Focal Press, 1995.

page 35   *just 4% claimed profitability.* Industry Canada, *Multimedia Industry Profile.* May 27, 1996.

page 36   *High-tech business has created 7,000 millionaires and a few dozen billionaires in the last 25 years.* "Youngest, Best Educated Population of Rich People in History," *Forbes.* July 7, 1997.

page 39   *"installment credit."* Shenandoah Valley Agricultural Research and Extension Center, Virginia. Online biography of McCormick.

page 39   *Ideas don't know what discipline they're in.* Daniel H. Pink, "Metaphor Marketing," *Fast Company.* April 1998.

page 41   *"upside-down thinking."* Charles Handy, *The Age of Unreason.*

page 41   *Peter Drucker's approach to entrepreneurship and innovation.* Peter E. Drucker, *Innovation and Entrepreneurship.* New York: HarperCollins, 1993.

chapter 3: my trip to mecca

page 43   *Some two-thirds of all websites are thought to have been created on Macintosh computers.* "Intellectual Property of Apple," *Time.* August 18, 1997.

page 44   *The day Apple Computers went public, approximately 40 employees became instant million-aires.* Robert Mamis, "The Apple Tree," *Inc.* magazine. August 1993.

page 46   *"if you understand the technical work of a business, you understand a business that does technical work."* Michael Gerber, *The E Myth Revisited.* New York: HarperCollins, 1995, 13.

page 53   *Object relational databases.* "Is Informix Toast?" *Fortune.* July 21, 1997.

page 55   *based on incremental revenue from licensing and increased business valuation.* Gistics Report, 1998.

page 57   *"depending on luck or chance in regard to either profit or loss. Unpredictable."* Mary A. Devries, *The Encyclopedic Dictionary of Business Terms.* New York: Berkley Books, 1997, 302.

page 57   *Informix bought Illustra for approximately US$400.* "Informix—In His Dreams," *Upside.* July 1, 1997.

page 57   *"Luck favors the prepared."* John Le Carré, *The Tailor of Panama.*

chapter 4: profile of the sensitive extrovert

page 65   *"To know, to go, to do, to be."* Charles Handy, *The Age of Unreason*, xviii.

page 70   *Many lunches are spent speculating about the nature of these moods, and these are profitable discussions.* Lynda Obst, *Hello, He Lied*. New York: Broadway Books, 1996, 44.

page 71   *"ride the horse in the direction it is going."* Ibid.

page 72   *"Entrepreneurs never fail, they just have learning experiences."* Gayle MacDonald, "Entrepreneurs Ban the F-Word: Failure," *The Globe and Mail*. September 25, 1997.

page 72   *"The world can be falling in around them, and they don't run for cover."* Ibid.

page 73   *the need to prove oneself against a rejecting father figure.* Ibid.

page 73   *"the big idea."* Jim Collins, "What Comes Next?" *Inc.* magazine. October 1997.

page 73   *it means more to the health of your company than anything else.* Ibid.

page 74   *"Trust everybody, but cut the cards."* Finley Peter Dunne, *Mr. Dooley's Philosophy*. Cited in *The Columbia Dictionary of Quotations*, Robert Andrews, ed. New York: Columbia University Press, 1993, 925.

page 75   *"It is an equal failing to trust everybody, and to trust nobody."* Cited in Andrews, 925.

page 75   *"dangerous diffidence."* John le Carré, *The Tailor of Panama*.

page 76   *"Don't look directly at [a situation]; look slightly to one side of it."* Harriet Rubin, *The Princessa: Machiavelli for Women*. New York: Doubleday Currency, 1997, 160.

page 77   *"Teach us to care and not to care."* T.S. Eliot, *Ash Wednesday*, Part I. *The Complete Poems and Plays of T.S. Eliot*. London: Faber, 1969.

page 78   *Michio Kaku describes the difference between a theoretical and an experimental physicist.* Michio Kaku, *Hyperspace*. New York: Oxford University Press, 1994, 315.

page 79   *"almost by definition, an enduring great company has to be built not to depend on an individual leader."* Jim Collins, "What Comes Next?" *Inc.* magazine. October 1997.

chapter 5: the developing entrepreneur

page 82   *circle of learning: question—theory—test—reflect.* Charles Handy, *The Age of Unreason*, 58.

page 84   *borrowing a term from E.M. Forster called "flat people."* Ibid., 183.

page 84   *Eclectic came to mean "selective, freely choosing, or borrowing."* William Morris, *Morris Dictionary of Word and Phrase Origins*. New York: HarperCollins, 1988.

page 84   *people who are of "whole cloth."* Lynda Obst, *Hello, He Lied*, 54.

page 88   *"can look forward to a dose of real-world experience."* Jim Collins, "What Comes Next?" *Inc.* magazine. October 1998.

page 89   *the seven categories of intelligence.* Charles Handy, *The Age of Unreason*, 219

page 89   *a social embarrassment to be unable to read music, sing, or play an instrument. An Anthology of English Medieval and Renaissance Vocal Music*. Noah Greenburg, W.H. Auden, and Chester Kallman, eds. New York: W.W. Norton, 1970, 20.

page 91   *Peripheral: "beside the point."* Roget's 21st Century Thesaurus. New York: Delacorte Press, 1990, 620.

page 94   *"A specialist is someone who does everything else worse."* Ruggiero Ricci, *The Daily Telegraph* (London), May 25, 1990, cited in Andrews, 303.

page 94   *"Selling requires a certain emotional makeup and a willingness to face the music, which is why it is easier to avoid."* Ron May, "What's Your Scam?" May 1997.

page 94   *Diane McGarry, CEO and president of Xerox Canada, began her career as a sales rep based in Fort Wayne.* Dianne Maley, "Canada's Top Women CEO's," *Maclean's* magazine. October 20, 1997.

page 95   *"portable skills can turn your life around."* The San Francisco Examiner. June 14, 1998.

page 96   *"I understand what you need."* Harry Beckwith, *Selling the Invisible: A Field Guide to Modern Marketing*. New York: Warner Books, 1997, 208.

page 96   *Arriviste: someone who will use any means to achieve success. The Encyclopedic Dictionary of Business Terms*, 269.

page 98   *"whose playing field is within the boundary of an established company."* Timothy D. Schellhardt. "Small Business: David in Goliath," *The Wall Street Journal*. May 23, 1996.

page 99   *3M introduced 500 new products in 1996.* "How to Make the CEO Buy Your Idea," *Fortune* magazine. February 5, 1996.

page 100   *Their universal stock option plan promises to pay employees twice their annual salaries after eight years.* "Power Players," *Fortune* magazine. August 5, 1996.

chapter 6: the f(email) factor

page 108   *"Wealth usually comes from doing what other people find insufferably boring."* George Gilder, *Recapturing the Spirit of Enterprise*. San Francisco, ICS Press, 1992, 8.

page 109   *Almost a third of businesses in Canada today are owned by women. The Globe and Mail.* March 16, 1998.

page 109   *"I've always said that we'll have true equality when we have as many incompetent women in positions as we have incompetent men."* Dianne Maley, "Canada's Top Women CEO's," *Maclean's*. October 20, 1997.

page 110   *"It doesn't matter what you look like or who you know. All that matters is that you sell."* Ibid.

page 110   *77% would consider pursuing a career involving computers. San Francisco Chronicle.* April 26, 1998.

page 111   *"Power in the entertainment business is about more than money."* "Who's Who in Hollywood," *Working Woman* magazine. November 1997.

page 112   *to go in the direction the horse is already going in.* Lynda Obst. *Hello, He Lied*, 74.

page 112   *focusing only on stories about balancing career and family.* The Witi Report: Business Impact by Women in Science and Technology, 12.

page 114   *"provocative disruption."* Women, Sex and Power," *Fortune* magazine. August 5, 1996.

page 115   *"never giving up her femininity."* Ibid.

page 115   *Nearly a third of all business launched in eastern Germany since 1990 were founded by women.* "Women Lead the Pack in East German Startups," *Business Week*. June 3, 1996.

page 116   *personal growth and self-determination.* Holly Buttner, cited in "Female Entrepreneurs' Different Priorities," *USA Today Magazine*. August 1997.

page 116   *"Princessas don't hold back."* Harriet Rubin, *The Princessa: Machiavelli for Women*. New York: Currency Doubleday, 1997, 16.

page 116   *"strange, courageous, irreverent, and not so comfortable friends."* "Cocktails at Charlotte's with Martha and Darla," *Fortune* magazine. August 5, 1996.

page 117   *"will is a product of desire."* Denis Diderot, *Elements of Physiology*, cited in Andrews, 232.

page 117   *"the distribution of matter in the galaxy."* "Microsoft Research," *Fortune* magazine. December 8, 1997.

page 117   *she knew deep down that someday she'd do something really extraordinary or different.* "Women, Sex and Power," *Fortune* magazine. August 5, 1996.

page 118   *"My 'fear' is my substance, and probably the best part of me."* Franz Kafka, letter to Milena Jesenska, cited in Andrews, 325.

page 118   *More Singaporean women than ever are starting businesses.* "Singapore's Women are Minding Their Own Business," *Business Week*. International edition, April 7, 1997.

page 118   *"all your experiences come together and make you multidimensional."* "Women, Sex and Power," *Fortune* magazine. August 5, 1996.

page 120   *"Do something every day that scares you."* Widely attributed to Kurt Vonnegut. Actually written by Mary Schmich, "Advice, Like Youth, Probably Just Wasted on the Young," *Chicago Tribune*. June 1, 1997.

page 122   *"I let my customers know I'm here to do business."* Business Development Bank of Canada, supplement to *Maclean's* magazine. November 3, 1997.

page 123   *"Power can be taken, but not given."* Gloria Steinem, "Far From the Opposite Shore," *Ms.* magazine, July 1978, cited in Andrews, 720.

page 125   *"I am in the world to change the world."* Muriel Rukeyser, *The Knowledge Cards: Women Writers.*

page 125   *by the year 2000, half of America's businesses will have a female owner.* Debora Vrana, *Los Angeles Times,* Home edition. March 1997.

chapter 7: secret recipes for a disordered world

page 129   *"maybe something that wasn't going to happen does."* Ian Stewart, *Does God Play Dice? The Mathematics of Chaos.* New York: Blackwell, 1989, 141.

page 129   *Chaos: a pattern or sate of order existing within an apparent disorder. Webster's New World College Dictionary.* Victoria Neufeltd, Editor in Chief. New York: Macmillan Press, 1996.

page 130   *"In all chaos there is a cosmos, in all disorder a secret order."* Carl Jung, "Archetypes of the Collective Unconscious," cited in Andrews, 131.

page 130   *"since they never repeated the same thing, they weren't periodic either."* Edward Lorenz, The Exploratorium. www.exploratorium.edu.

page 130   *"I dream, therefore I exist."* August Strindberg, *A Madman's Defense,* cited in Andrews, 253.

page 131   *"could throw boats off by 60 to 100 miles."* Sebastian Junger, *The Perfect Storm.* New York: HarperCollins, 1997, 134.

page 131   *"to find a form that accommodates the mess."* Samuel Beckett, conversation with John Driver, 1961, cited in Andrews, 130.

page 132   *compass heading, forward speed, and wind conditions.* Junger, 134.

page 132   *"right them from extreme angles of heel."* Ibid., 79.

page 133   *"the zero-moment point."* Ibid.

page 133   *"Everything can be undone, including success."* Lynda Obst, *Hello, He Lied,* 16.

page 134   *"from the dream outward."* Anais Nin, *The Knowledge Cards: Women Writers.*

page 134   *"You see things; and you say 'why?'"* George Bernard Shaw, *Back to Methuselah,* 1921, cited in Andrews, 962.

page 135   *"Envision: to imagine (something not yet in existence)."* *Webster's New World College Dictionary,* 455.

page 137   *"Hope was transubstantiated into belief incarnate."* Diane Johnson, *Le Divorce.* New York: Plume, 1996, 272.

page 139   *"Many of life's failures are people who did not realize."* Thomas Edison, cited in Victory Quotations, Cyber-Nation.com., 1998.

page 140   *"It takes a different skill to build a business."* Daniel Grebler, *Business Plus.*

chapter 8: exceptional emblems

page 144   *"It seemed so simple."* David Nash, lecture at CCAC, San Francisco. January 1998.

page 144   *"To eat is a necessity."* LaRochefoucauld, cited in M.F.K. Fisher, *The Art of Eating.* Indianapolis: Macmillan, 1990, 9.

page 146   *a 68.2 percent compound annual growth over a six year period.* Frost and Sullivan Report, 1998.

page 147   *"PR isn't public relations—it's personal reinvention."* Katharine Mieszkowski, "The Power of Public Relations," *Fast Company.* April/May 1998.

page 148   *Roots shoes were dubbed the "Gucci shoe of the crunchy granola set."* From *People* magazine, cited in Geoff Pevere, "The Roots of Roots," *Profit* magazine. October 1998.

page 150   *"By itself, reality isn't worth a damn."* Joseph Brodsky, *New York Review of Books*, 1981, cited in *Morrow's International Dictionary of Contemporary Quotations*. Jonathan Green, ed. New York: William Morrow & Company, 1982, 130.

page 152   *"Those are the information leaders."* Mike Warshaw, "They Hear It through the Grapevine," *Fast Company*. April/May 1998.

page 159   *"Fantasy ... is really only fact with a whimsical twist."* Daniel Gross, *Forbes' Greatest Stories of All Time*. New York: John Wiley & Sons, 1997, 124.

page 160   *"The image is more than an idea."* Ezra Pound, *Selected Prose*, cited in Andrews, 444.

page 161   *Bo Peabody is someone who certainly understands emotional branding.* "Cool Companies," *Fortune* magazine. July 7, 1997.

page 162   *"Could you make sure the wine doesn't get too cold?"* Peter Mayle, *Chasing Cézanne*. New York: Alfred A. Knopf, 1997, 156.

page 162   *how the idea of gossip columns came to be.* Eugene Sue, *Mysteries of Paris*. New York: Howard Fertig, 1987.

page 163   *"I saw the Web, and I thought, this is exactly what I am looking for."* Clive Thompson, "Welcome to Silicon Valley," *Report on Business* magazine. March 1997.

page 164   *"Myths which are believed in tend to become true."* George Orwell, "The English People," cited in Andrews, 615.

page 165   *"Metaphors are much more tenacious than facts."* Paul de Man, *Allegories of Reading*, cited in Andrews, 443.

page 165   *a book of photographs of statuary fragments.* David Robinson, with text by Dean Koontz, *Beautiful Death*. New York: Penguin, 1996.

page 167   *"You are nothing; your knowledge is everything."* Harriet Rubin, "Peter's Principles," *Inc.* magazine. March 1998.

chapter 9: the to-do list of architects and heroes

page 169   *"Generation X actively pursues the deflation of the ideal."* Margot Hornblower, "Great expectations," *Time* magazine. June 9, 1997.

page 170   *"Life is uncertain. Eat dessert first."* J. Walker Smith and Ann Clurman, *Rocking the Ages*. New York: HarperCollins, 1997, 84.

page 170   *"Permanence used to be the quality of greatest value."* Cathy Olofson, "Experience Collection," *Fast Company*. October 1998.

page 171   *"Number two would be so far down that it would be hard to find."* Michael Hopkins, interview with Michael Bloomberg, "What Should You Say When an Employee Quits?" *Inc.* magazine. March 1998.

page 171   *"Today, knowledge and talent are seen as a stock, not as a commodity."* Daniel H. Pink, "The Talent Market," *Fast Company* magazine. August 1998.

page 171   *In a survey done by Yankelovich Partners.* Stephanie N. Mehta, "Young entrepreneurs: starting business after business," *The Wall Street Journal*. March 19, 1997.

page 172   *A recent year-long study of 6,000 managers and executives.* Charles Fishman, "The War for Talent," *Fast Company* magazine. August 1998.

page 172   *"Building a visionary company requires 1 percent vision and 99 percent alignment."* Jim Collins and Jerry I. Porras, "Building Your Company's Vision," *Harvard Business Review*. September/October 1996.

page 173   *53% of U.S. workers expect to leave their jobs within five years.* Christopher Caggiano, "How're You Gonna Keep 'Em Down on the Firm?" *Inc.* magazine. January 1998.

page 173   *"Today's truly ambitious entrepreneurs see themselves not as entrepreneurs but as 'independent professionals.'"* Harriet Rubin, "Peter's Principles," *Inc.* magazine. March 1998.

page 173   *In a study conducted by the Boston-based Young Entrepreneurs Network.* Stephanie N. Mehta, "Young entrepreneurs: starting business after business," *The Wall Street Journal*. March 19, 1997.

page 174   *has captured the loyalty of millions of buyers in and outside of Canada.* Geoff Pevere, "The Roots of Roots," *Profit* magazine. October 1998.

page 175   *"Passion, emotion, and conviction are essential parts of the vivid description."* Jim Collins and Jerry I. Porras, "Building Your Company's Vision," *Harvard Business Review.* September/October 1996.

page 175   *"All human knowledge takes the form of interpretation."* Walter Benjamin, *Briefe,* cited in Andrews, 496.

page 177   *"Culture is what people fall back on when there are no instructions."* Michael Warshaw, "Have You Been Housetrained?" *Fast Company* magazine. October 1998.

page 178   *A new Statistics Canada study of 3,000 Canadian firms.* Mary Jane Grant, with the Richard Ivey School of Business, "Welcome to the Innovation Age," *The Globe and Mail.* October 3, 1997.

page 180   *Pat Kelly, the CEO of PSS/World Medical, is committed to "stoking the campfire."* Elizabeth Weil, "Every Leader Tells a Story," *Fast Company.* June 1998.

page 180   *He holds company picnics.* Matt Goldberg, "Cisco's Most Important Meal of the Day," *Fast Company.* February 1998.

page 180   *"in a chaos world, the company with the fewest rules wins."* Taylor and Wacker, *The 500 Year Delta,* 293.

page 181   *"what Seeing Eye dogs are taught."* Ibid., 288.

page 181   *"Fault tolerance."* Ibid., 287.

page 181   *"intelligent organizations have to be run by persuasion and by consent."* Charles Handy, *The Age of Unreason,* 166.

page 183   *"Strive for perfection; settle for excellence."* Peter Carbonara, "Sleep Is for Wusses," *Inc.* Technology no. 1, 1998.

page 183   *"Endotruths usually begin with the nature of the founder of the organization."* Taylor and Wacker, *The 500 Year Delta,* 286.

page 185   *"The teacher should encounter the child."* *Teaching Tolerance,* Spring 1998, 15.

page 186   *"Sometimes chasing someone out is as valuable as keeping them in."* Eryn Brown, "Rob Ryan's Big Sky Boot Camp," *Fortune* magazine. December 8, 1997.

page 187   *"The smallest moment of inattention turns out to be the most disastrous."* Diane Johnson, *Le Divorce,* 100.

page 188   *"The collective brainpower of your company."* Thomas A. Stewart, "Grab a Pencil—It's a Knowledge Quiz," *Fortune* magazine. December 8, 1997.

page 188   *"Imagine that you've been asked to re-create the very best attributes of your organization."* Jim Collins and Jerry I. Porras, "Building Your Company's Vision," *Harvard Business Review,* September/October 1996.

page 192   *"Perhaps the most common catalyst that creates whining is change."* Scott Smith, "Days of Whine and Neurosis," *San Francisco Examiner.* January 25, 1998.

page 193   *"Will they fit within our culture?"* Seek Conference 1998.

page 196   *"The successful entrepreneur is not a 'loner.'"* Elizabeth Chell, Jean Haworth and Sally Brearly, *The Entrepreneurial Personality: Concepts, Cases and Categories.* London: Routledge, 1991.

page 197   *"I think of a hero as someone who understands the degree of responsibility that comes with his freedom."* Bob Dylan, 1985 interview, cited in Andrews, 403.

page 198   *"A little knowledge that* acts *is infinitely more than much knowledge that is idle."* Kahlil Gibran, cited in Andrews, 497.

page 199   *"These are the soul's changes."* Virginia Woolf, *The Diary of Virginia Woolf,* vol. 4, cited in Andrews, 25.

page 200   *"Heard melodies are sweet, but those unheard are sweeter."* John Keats, *Ode on a Grecian Urn,* cited in Andrews, 612.

chapter 10: the advantageous burden of money

page 204   *"The private-placement market is just one example."* Jill Andresky Fraser, "How to Finance Anything," *Inc.* magazine. February 1998.

page 204   *"In 1997, $6 billion was invested in 1,100 companies."* "Is it Time to Bail Out From Big-Company Life?" *Fortune* magazine. March 2, 1998.

page 204   *"Angels, usually wealthy professionals and retired entrepreneurs."* "Would You Please Take My Money?" *Fortune* magazine. March 16, 1998.

page 204   *a 25 percent jump over 1995.* "Guess Who's Paying for Dinner?" Laton McCartney, *Upside.* March 26, 1997.

page 204   *in 1995 had revenues of $44 billion and are worth $85 billion.* "The Valley of Money's Delight," *The Economist.* March 29, 1997.

page 204   *60 percent more than the year before, according to PriceWaterhouseCoopers.* "The 21st Century Economy," *Business Week.* August 31, 1998.

page 205   *A recent survey conducted by Coopers & Lybrand.* Sheryl Nance-Nash. "How To Raise Venture Capital," *Your Company* magazine. February 10, 1997.

page 207   *"The most daunting part of the investment process."* Jeff Wuorio, "Go on an Equity Hunt to Fund Expansion," *Money.* February 3, 1998.

page 207   *"What the initial public offering market has done"* Shawn Tully, "How to make $400,000 in just one minute," *Fortune* magazine. May 27, 1996.

page 207   *one in three investments produces a total write-off.* "The Great Hunt For Hot Ideas," *Business Week.* August 18-25, 1997.

page 207   *"It's probably going to cost you $20 to $30 million."* "A Really Big Adventure," *The Economist.* January 25, 1997.

page 208   *two years later, its shares were worth $400 million.* Ibid.

page 208   *Seagate Technologies brought a $56.5 million profit.* "The Great Hunt For Hot Ideas," *Business Week.* August 18-25, 1997.

page 208   *According to the Canadian Venture Capital Association, based on 106 venture capital groups across Canada, a total of 1,336 investments were made in 794 companies.* "Key Observations on 1997 Venture Capital Activity," Canadian Venture Capital Association website.

page 209   *has served 4.5 million customers, employs 614 people.* Nathaniel Wice, "Bookish Amazon is Winning the CD Wars," *Digital Daily.* October 29, 1998.

page 209   *the company is worth about $5.5 billion.* "The Book Trade's Big Bet on the Net," *The Globe and Mail.* October 19, 1998.

page 209   *"Today's venture capitalists are pickier than ever."* "Fishing for Venture Capital," *Business Week.* Special report, October 13, 1997.

page 210   *"The game is already risky enough."* John F. Geer, "The Venture Capital Boom," *Financial World.* November 18, 1996.

page 211   *"A venture capital firm looking only to grow the business quickly."* "The Great Hunt For Hot Ideas." *Business Week,* August 18-25, 1997.

page 211   *Institutional Venture Partners made $10 million, a 250% return.* Ibid.

page 212   *"First we consider the strategy, then the management team."* Meryl Davids, "Money, Money Everywhere," *Journal of Business Strategy.* March-April 1997.

page 213   *David was interested in seeking his advice and assistance, not just his money.* "My Life as an Angel," *Inc.* magazine. July 1997.

page 214   *"It's damn tough to get a first-tier venture company to invest."* Howard Anderson, "What's Hot, What's Not," *Computerworld.* September 29, 1997.

page 215   *"about 250,000 angels now invest as much as $20 billion a year."* "Technology's Archangel," *The Economist.* November 15, 1997.

page 215   *"psychic reward."* "Technology's Archangel," *The Economist.* November 15, 1997.

page 215   *"To produce one megahit IPO such as Yahoo."* Shawn Tully, "How to make $400,000 in just one minute," *Fortune* magazine. May 27, 1996.

page 215   *Other organizations, such as Idealab, which is backed by a group of investors.* Laton McCartney, "Guess Who's Paying for Dinner?" *Upside.com.* March 26, 1997.

page 217   *The computer-related sector continued to be the most active.* "Key Observations on 1997 Venture Capital Activity," Canadian Venture Capital Association website.

page 218   *Clark made US$565 million when it went public.* James Staten, "Netscape raises more than $1 billion in IPO," *Macweek News.* August 9, 1995.

page 218   *"More than 70 percent of these firms were venture-backed."* "A really big adventure," *The Economist.* January 25, 1997.

page 218   *There are many networks of angels today, often with a technology focus.* Michael S. Malone, "Angels in the Valley," *Upside.com.* April 1, 1997; and Jeff Wuorio, "Go on an Equity Hunt to Fund Expansion," *Your Company.* February 3, 1998.

page 219   *Over the past five years, the ranks of angels have swelled to about 250,000.* Jeff Wuorio, "Go on an Equity Hunt to Fund Expansion," *Your Company.* February 3, 1998.

page 220   *Datamerge is the creator of Venturetrack 2000.* Emily Esterson, "Bulletin Board," *Inc. Tech* 1998.

page 221   *Microlending, typically defined as business loans less than $100,000, is a positive trend for the entrepreneur.* Jill Andresky Fraser, "How to Finance Anything," *Inc.* magazine. February 1998.

page 222   *Non-bank banking options abound.* Ibid.

page 222   *The process of deciding if a venture capital firm is right for you.* Meryl Davids, "Money , Money Everywhere," *Journal of Business Strategy.* March–April 1997.

page 223   *"Entrepreneurs may find it difficult to weigh the advantages of angel capital."* Michael Perkins, in "Angels on High," *The Red Herring Guide to Technology Finance.* 1997, 89.

page 224   *"Rather than trying to predict market success, the best option is to know what to avoid."* Jeffrey Geibel, "Predicting Market Success," *Upside.com.* November 1, 1994.

page 225   *"To separate the gold-plated winners from the also-rans."* "The Great Hunt for Hot Ideas," *Business Week.* August 18, 1997.

page 226   *"the value of the new personal computer industry grew from virtually nothing to $100 billion."* "A Really Big Adventure," *The Economist.* January 25, 1997.

page 227   *"We like to call it M&Ms, meaning misfits and mavericks."* Jill Andresky Fraser, "How to Finance Anything," *Inc.* magazine. February 1998.

page 230   *"These are tumultuous times for bankers, who either must reinvent themselves."* Jill Andresky Fraser, "How to Finance Anything," *Inc.* magazine. February 1998.

page 232   *"I'm not a visionary, I'm a historian."* Jeffrey Geibel, "Predicting Market Success," *Upside.com.* November 1, 1994.

page 234   *"Real generosity toward the future lies in giving all to the present."* Albert Camus, *The Rebel*, cited in Andrews, 359.

page 235   *"There is a real difference between hot companies and hot products."* Howard Anderson, in "What's Hot, What's Not," *Computerworld.* September 29, 1997.

page 237   *"Everybody was gauging the distance between here and there."* Marya Hornbacher, *Wasted.* New York: HarperCollins, 1998, 249.

page 237   *Rapid growth businesses use a variety of compensation practices.* Nancy Roberts and Brian Golden, "How Entrepreneurial Companies Are Compensating Employees." Richard Ivey School of Business at the University of Western Ontario, website.

page 238   *"Maximizing shareholder wealth does not inspire people at all levels of an organization."* Jim Collins and Jerry I. Porras, "Building Your Company's Vision," *Harvard Business Review.* September/October 1996.

page 238   *"It is always like this, people start out in agreement."* Diane Johnson, *Le Divorce*, 126.

page 239 *"Be sure to take a board seat to guarantee yourself a voice in the future of the company."* Jeff Wuorio, "Go on an Equity Hunt to Fund Expansion," *Your Company.* February 3, 1998.

page 239 *"fault tolerance."* Jim Taylor and Watts Wacker. *The 500 Year Delta,* 287.

page 240 *Colonna, which is the founder of Flatiron, has a lot of experience in publishing and media.* Laton McCartney, "Guess Who's Paying for Dinner?" *Upside.com.* March 26, 1997.

page 242 *"Physicists dream big dreams about smashing tiny particles."* *San Francisco Chronicle.* March 9, 1998.

page 242 *"I call people rich when they are able to meet the requirements of their imagination."* Henry James, *Portrait of a Lady* (1881). New York: Alfred A. Knopf, 1991.

chapter 11: the beauty of imbalance

page 246 *"We give permission to be saved from our worst nature."* Diane Johnson, *Le Divorce,* 160.

page 247 *"Entrepreneurs have an overriding concern to be heard and recognized—to be seen as heroes."* Manfred Kets deVries, "Creative Rebels with a Cause," *The Financial Post.* March 1998.

page 248 *"enlightened anxiety."* Taylor and Wacker, *The 500 Year Delta,* 286.

page 248 *"What a day-to-day affair life is."* Jules Laforgue, cited in Andrews, 280.

page 249 *"Entrepreneurs are far more likely to intertwine their business and personal lives."* Gail Gaboda, "Entrepreneurs Differ from Executives," *Marketing News.* November 10, 1997.

page 250 *"Work is much more fun than fun."* Noel Coward, The Observer Sayings of the Week, June 21, 1963, cited in *Macmillan Dictionary of Quotations.* New York: Macmillan, 1987, 625.

page 252 *"What'll we do with ourselves this afternoon?"* F. Scott Fitzgerald, *The Great Gatsby.* New York: Charles Scribner's Sons, 1925.

page 252 *"I have to give a chance to the chancing that happens."* David Nash, lecture at CCAC, San Francisco. January 1998.

page 253 *"situational love."* Jim Taylor and Watts Wacker, *The 500 Year Delta,* 292.

page 253 Inc. *magazine hired Roper Starch Worldwide to survey the attitudes of 500 owners of small, fast-growing companies.* Gail Gaboda, "Entrepreneurs Differ from Executives," *Marketing News.* November 10, 1997.

page 253 *"In the U.S., there are at least a quarter of a million co-preneurs who are working to find some kind of new model of marital and business partnership."* Jerry Unseem, "The Myth about the Mrs. in Husband-and-Wife Teams," *Inc.* magazine. January 1997.

page 253 *"Although no definitive figures exist on the number of husband/wife-owned businesses."* Steve Kaufman, "In the office and out, they're partners—for better or worse," Knight-Ridder/Tribune News Service. April 2, 1996.

page 253 *"Couples decide to go into business together for myriad reasons."* Ibid.

page 254 *"Married owners can be as bad for the business as the business is for the marriage."* Ibid.

page 255 *"Academics have noted that people tend to be attracted to romantic partners with similar traits."* Wendy Stueck and Dawn Walton, "Loving Couples," *The Globe and Mail.* September 28, 1998.

page 258 *"I'm drowning here, and you're describing the water."* From the movie *As Good As It Gets.*

page 259 *"In a recent article,* Inc. *magazine reported that there are nearly 280 million business travelers in the United States."* *Inc.* Technology no. 1, 1998.

page 259 *"There are more than 6 million Americans whose offices have license plates and seat belts."* Jack Sommars, "Colorado's Mobile Merchants," *Colorado Business Magazine.* August 1995.

page 262 *"Take me with you when you go ..."* Rachel Kane, "Gift of the Magi," from the album *Groundwire.* Adam's Rib Productions.

page 262 *"Absence diminishes commonplace passions and enhances great ones."* Diane Johnson, *Le Divorce,* 125.

page 262   *"We're talking about a breakdown in the relationships we value most."* Todd Logan, "Trapped," *Inc.* magazine. January 1995.

page 263   *"The only dependable aphrodisiacs."* M.F.K. Fisher, *The Art of Eating*, xvi.

page 265   *"I felt a trifle unbuckled."* Elizabeth McCracken, *The Giant's House*. New York: Avon, 1996, 40.

page 266   *"haven time."* Review of *The Marriage Spirit: Finding the Passion and Joy of Soul-Centered Love* by Paul and Evelyn Moschetta, in *Ladies Home Journal*, March 1998.

page 266   *"The Betty Ford Clinic for dysfunctional executives has doubled in size in the past two years."* "Stressed Out? Recycling Silicon Burnouts," *Upside.com*. May 29, 1998.

page 267   *"His fingers kept slowly snatching at nothing."* Elizabeth McCracken, *The Giant's House*, 7.

page 267   *"I have always found that things become utterly invisible."* Douglas Coupland, *Polaroids from the Dead*. New York: HarperCollins, 1996, 3.

page 268   *No wonder there is a market for a Web-based program such as PROACT from Wilson Banwell.* Inc. Staff, "Bulletin Board," *Inc.* Technology no. 1, 1998.

page 268   *"a state of mental or physical exhaustion often reached as a result of prolonged stress or frustration."* The Encyclopedic Dictionary of Business Terms, 269.

page 268   *"The pressure can crush you or turn you into the diamond version of yourself."* Lynda Obst, *Hello, He Lied*, 7.

page 268   *"a great discrepancy between the narrative truth and historical truth."* Manfred Kets de Vries, "Creative Rebels with a Cause," *The Financial Post*. March 1998.

page 269   *"On the face of it, burnout is a failure of self-management."* Gideon Kunda, *Engineering Culture*. Philadelphia: Temple University Press, 1992, 204.

page 269   *"For the first time in U.S. history, more millionaires are below age 50 than are above it."* Harriet Rubin, "Success Excess," *Fast Company*. October 1998.

page 270   *"The skill to managing a crisis is viewing it as a simple mess."* Lynda Obst, *Hello, He Lied*, 232.

page 270   *"You know you are in trouble when you define sheep."* David Nash, lecture at CCAC, San Francisco. January 1998.

page 270   *"We have an idea that success is a happy occasion."* Natalie Goldberg. *Writing Down the Bones*. Boston: Shambhala, 1986, 170.

page 271   *"Being a champion is not about winning a fight."* Cited by Jane Metcalfe in an interview.

page 272   *"The burnout mantra goes like this: Been there, done that, seen it, felt, had the thrill."* Steven Berglas, "The Big Lie," *Inc.* magazine. March 1996.

page 272   *"How Entrepreneurs Stay Motivated (from a survey of* Inc. *500 CEOs."* From *Inc. 500 Almanac*, 1997, cited in *San Francisco Chronicle*. April 26, 1998.

page 273   *"It's a hideous, bone-chilling, stomach-knotting, now-or-never feeling."* Andrew Essex and Jennifer Weisel, "Will Nicky Silver Sell Out? Let's Hope So," *Elle* magazine. February 1998.

page 273   *"Il a les défauts de ses qualités."* John Buchanan-Brown, *Le Mot Juste*. New York: Vintage Books, 1981, 79.

page 273   *"nothing nourishes a company so much as aligning its business aims with its owner's personal ones."* Michael Hopkins, "The World According to Me: Interview with Lanny Goodmand," *Inc.* magazine. January 1998.

chapter 12: a n e v e r - e n d i n g a c t o f d o i n g

page 276   *"While the most exquisitely balanced dinner can never be relived, a book may evoke its graceful host."* M.F.K. Fisher, *The Art of Eating*, xii.

page 277   *"Because that's what life is."* Elizabeth McCracken, *The Giant's House*, 55.

page 277   *"But some of us must see the fish in order to see the water."* Shunryu Suzuki, "Zen Mind, Beginner's Mind," *1997 Anchor Book of Essays*. Newport: Anchor Books, 1997. 305.

page 277   *cultural anthropologist Jennifer James spends her tie searching for all signs of modern-day signs and symbols.* Jennifer James, "Symbol Skills," *Fast Company.* April/May 1998.

page 277   *In 1998, temporary staffing in the U.S. was a $50 billion a year business.* Daniel H. Pink, "The Talent Market," *Fast Company.* August 1998.

page 278   *"Genius can be bounded in a nutshell."* Thomas Mann, cited in *The Soul's Code,* James Hellman, preface.

page 278   *entrepreneurs work with a single-minded intensity because they are psychologically compelled to.* "The entrepreneurial self," *Psychology Today.* June 1989.

page 279   *"Inspiration is the best word we have for appetite."* Review of Adam Phillips, *The Beast in the Nursery: On Curiosity and Other Appetites,* in *Elle* magazine. February 1998.

page 279   *"Is that what they call a vocation."* Josephine Baker, cited in *The Soul's Code,* James Hellman, xii.

page 280   *"It is above all by the imagination that we achieve perception, compassion, and hope."* Ursula K. Le Guin , accepting the 1972 National Book Award for Children's Literature. *Knowledge Cards: Women Writers.*

page 280   *"I don't develop; I am."* Pablo Picasso, cited in *The Soul's Code,* James Hellman, x.

page 280   *"exudes a sense of bottom-up informality."* Scott Kirsner, "Total Teamwork: SEI Investments," *Fast Company.* April/May 1998.

page 280   *the invention of the first industrial research lab in the U.S.* Henry Ford Museum and Greenfield Village, 1990.

page 281   *"One always learns one's mystery at the price of one's innocence."* Robertson Davies, cited in *The Soul's Code,* James Hellman, x.

page 281   *"To bury the grape tendril in such a way that it shoots out new growth."* Frances Mayes, *Under the Tuscan Sun.* New York: Broadway Books, 1996, 2.

page 281   *Working Assets.* Marilee Strong, "The Business of Change," *San Francisco Focus.* May 1996.

page 281   *"You'd certainly have a hard time finding two executives with less in common."* Jim Collins, "The Foundation for Doing Good," *Inc.* magazine. December 1997.

page 281   *"donate their acumen or invest in nonprofit groups' business ventures."* Larkin Street Youth Center, San Francisco. 1995 annual report.

page 282   *"I think that many people assume, wrongly, that a company exists simply to make money."* Jim Collins and Jerry I. Porras, "Building Your Company's Vision," *Harvard Business Review.* September/October 1996.

page 282   *"92 percent of entrepreneurs and 82 percent of corporate executives."* Gail Gaboda, "Entrepreneurs Differ from Executives," *Marketing News.* November 10, 1997.

page 282   *At a time when 70 percent of high school students are interested in entrepreneurship.* Lynn Beresford, "Young Guns," *Entrepreneur.* October 1996.

page 282   *"There are three ways to see the world."* David Nash, lecture at CCAC, San Francisco. January 1998.

page 282   *"A corporation has many parts, just like the human body."* Christian Denhart, in "Doing Good By Doing Well," *Ladies' Home Journal.* October 31, 1994.

page 283   *"What is a society without a heroic dimension?"* Jean Baudrillard, cited in Andrews, 402.

page 284   *"Caring nothing for the division between good and bad literature."* Roland Barthes, "An Introduction to the Structural Analysis of Narratives," in *A Barthes Reader.* New York: Hill and Wang, 1981, 251-252.

page 284   *What is a corporation?* Christian Denhart, in "Doing Good By Doing Well," *Ladies' Home Journal.* October 31, 1994.

page 285   *"None of my books or ideas means anything to me in the long run."* Peter Drucker, in Harriet Rubin, "Peter's Principles," *Inc.* magazine. March 1998.

page 285   *"Sixty-eight percent of executives in Fortune 500 companies agree that entrepreneurs are the heroes of American business."* Gail Gaboda, "Entrepreneurs Differ from Executives," *Marketing News.* November 10, 1997.

page 285 *"There is a strong, deeply held sense among those at the forefront of business."* "The Agenda:
          A Special Report," *Fast Company*. April/May 1998.

page 286 *"That kind of culture cannot be imposed."* Charles Handy, *The Age of Unreason,* 233.

page 287 *"the future of everyday life."* *The Age of Unreason,* 233.

page 291 *"I have only made this longer because I did not have time to make it shorter."* Blaise Pascal,
          Provincial Letters, cited in Andrews, 264.

thank you's

I HAVE COME TO UNDERSTAND THAT WRITING A BOOK, LIKE ENTREPRE-
NEURING IS ABOUT PUTTING YOUR HEAD, HEART AND SOUL INTO THE
PROCESS OF CREATING 'SOMETHING OUT OF NOTHING', WITH A NON-
NEGOTIABLE TENACITY TO BOOT. BUT, LIKE ENTREPRENEURING, IT BEGINS
WITH STORYTELLING AND LIVES ON BECAUSE OF THE INDIVIDUALS AND
TEAMS OF PEOPLE WHO BECOME THE HEROES ALONG THE WAY.

I AM SO GRATEFUL TO ALL THE PEOPLE WHO TOOK THE TIME TO TELL ME
THEIR STORIES, TO SHARE THEIR PERSPECTIVE AND LEARNING WITH
HONESTY AND IMAGINATION. THANK YOU . . .

Ted and Cindy Ackley   Steve and Sherry Alexander, Owners, Digital Focus   *Randy Anderson, Director, Consulting Services, The Bulldog Group Inc.*   MICHAEL BUDMAN, CO-FOUNDER, ROOTS CANADA LTD.   BILL BUXTON, CHIEF SCIENTIST, ALIAS/WAVEFRONT AND SGI   Perry Caicco, Merchandise and Consumer Products Analyst, First Marathon Securities Ltd.   *Cate C. Corcoran, Executive Editor of Hot Wired, Wired Digital*   Joy Covey, CFO, Amazon.com   DAN DADALT, PRESIDENT & CEO, REDRUM   *Madeline DaDalt, President, Studio 104*   CATHARINE DEVLIN, PRESIDENT, DEVLIN APPLIED DESIGN   NICK DEMARTINO, DIRECTOR STRATEGIC PLANNING, AMERICAN FILM INSTITUTE   Sara Diamond, Executive Producer, Television & Media, The Banff Center for the Arts   John Evershed, CEO, MondoMedia   *Robert Forbes, Managing Director, Glenmount International*   Patrick Ford, VP Production Studio, Fujitsu Interactive Inc.   KATRINA GARNETT, PRESIDENT & CEO, CROSSROADS SOFTWARE   *Linda Harnevo, President & CEO, TeamWorks Technology Ltd.*   Paul Hoffert, Executive Director, CulTech Research Center   Steven Horowitz, Chief Technology Officer and Creative Director, Palladium Interactive   *Tom Howlett, Creative Director, The Farm inc.*   DOUG HUMPHREYS, PRESIDENT & CEO, SKYROCKET AND RED SKY FILMS   LISA JACOBSON, PRESIDENT, STANFORD COACHING   *Natalie Jeremijenko, Associate Director, Engineering Design Studio, Faculty of Engineering, Yale University*   Dr. Sandra Kahn, Pacific Orthodontics   Marty Katz, President, Grosvenor Park Productions Limited   *Doug Keeley, President and CEO, The KE Group of Companies*   CHRISTOPHER KIDD, PRESIDENT, SEC.OPS   KEITH KOCHO, PRESIDENT, DIGITAL RENAISSANCE   Gideon Kunda, Department of Labor Studies,

Stanford University   *Maire Kushner, Director US Operations, & Technology/ Deployment, SHL System House*   Joanna Lau, President and Founder, Lau Technologies   *Tara Lemmey, Founder, Narrowline*   DAVID LEVENTHAL, GENERAL MANAGER, FIGHTBACK.COM, INCORPORATED   MICHAEL A. LEVINE, PARTNER, GOODMAN PHILLIPS & VINEBERG AND CHAIRMAN, WESTWOOD CREATIVE ARTISTS LTD. *Michael Levine, Production Designer*   David Livingston, Senior Vice President, GTA Division, Toronto Dominion Bank   Jane Metcalfe, Co-founder, Wired Ventures   MICHAEL MOON, DIRECTOR, EXECUTIVE PROGRAMS & PRESIDENT, GISTICS INC. *Geoffrey Moore, Chairman and Founder, The Chasm Group, and Venture Partner, Mohr Davidow Ventures*   *Joy Mountford, Interval Research Corporation*   BARBARA MOWAT, PRESIDENT, IMPACT COMMUNICATIONS LIMITED   Caroline S. Ohlsen, MouseHouse   Deirdre O'Malley, Director of Marketing, MondoMedia   *Anne Perlman, President and CEO, Moai Technologies, Inc.*   HEATHER M. REISMAN, PRESIDENT AND CEO, INDIGO BOOKS MUSIC & CAFÉ   HARRIET RUBIN, AUTHOR, *THE PRINCESSA — MACHIAVELLI FOR WOMEN*   Alex Rubin   Lotte Rubin   Rob Ryan, Founder and Principal, Entrepreneur America   *William Sahlman, Associate Dean of Business Administration, Harvard Business School*   PEPPER SCHWARTZ, PROFESSOR OF SOCIOLOGY, UNIVERSITY OF WASHINGTON   EVAN SOLOMON, CO-FOUNDER AND EXECUTIVE EDITOR, *SHIFT* MAGAZINE   *Andrea Southcott, Managing Director, Bryant, Fulton & Shee*   Paul Stewart, Associate Vice President, Imperial Bank Entertainment Group   Jonas Svensson, Chairman and Founder, Spray   *Deborah Szekely, Founder, Golden Door and Rancho La Puerta*   WILLIAM UNGAR, PRESIDENT, NATIONAL ENVELOPE CORPORATION   PAMELA WALLIN, PRESIDENT, THE CURRENT AFFAIRS GROUP   *Nigel Warren, Investment Development Director, Australian Trade Commission*   Rene White, VP Marketing, Harmony Software   Beata Wickbom, Spray   PAUL WOLLASTON, EXECUTIVE PRODUCER, NIMM NEW MEDIA   SUSAN WORTHMAN, SENIOR DIRECTOR, ZD STUDIOS   *Moses Znaimer, President, Citytv*

IT HAS BEEN A PLEASURE TO WORK WITH SUCH A WONDERFUL GROUP OF PROFESSIONALS THAT MAKE UP THE HARPERCOLLINS CANADA TEAM. THANK YOU...

First and foremost to my editor, Don Loney, for his true love of books, his discerning eye and his ability to constantly cull the best somethings out of every line of copy. To Iris Tupholme for taking chances and knowing when it matters. *To Judy Brunsek for her ability to inject reality into the process with wit and expertise.* TO NEIL ERICKSON, DORE POTTER, AND SUSAN THOMAS AND THE SALES TEAM FOR THEIR PROFESSIONALISM AND HARD WORK. A SPECIAL THANKS TO NICOLE LANGLOIS FOR HER PERSONAL DEDICATION TO THIS PROJECT AND HER ABILITY

TO MANAGE ALL OF US THROUGH THE FINAL EDITING AND PRODUCTION STAGES WITH CARING AND FINESSE.

THANK YOU...

To Thomas Burdan, Geri Savits-Fine, Jordana Greenstein, Laura Heutschi, and especially Robin Kalbfleisch for their research assistance. To Anita Junnarkar, Caroline Martinez and Virginia Resner for their administrative support through chaotic times.

A SPECIAL THANKS TO THOSE WHO HELPED ME OUT IN SO MANY WAYS...

To Chris Loudon and to Kate Fllion for always being available to listen and to advise. TO RON DAVIS FOR HIS GENEROUS, ELOQUENT REFERENCES. TO VALERIE APPLEBEE FOR HER DESIGN INPUT. *To Doug Rier and Bill Duncan for keeping me technologically and digitally operational throughout.* To Stephen Brown for keeping me fit and to Michael Suza for keeping me on the tennis court. To my speaking agents, Martin and Farah Perelmuter, for their entrepreneurial spirit. *To the boys at the Farm for putting up with me.* AND TO ALL THOSE WHO HAVE BEEN A PART OF BULLDOG AND HAVE NOT ONLY TAUGHT ME A LOT BUT MADE STORY-TELLING SO WORTHWHILE.

TO MY CHAMPIONS WHOM I COULD NOT HAVE DONE WITHOUT. THANK YOU...

TO JOHN MACDONALD FOR HIS ONGOING SUPPORT AND HIS DESIRE TO SEE GOOD BUSINESS IDEAS SUCCEED. *To Michael A. Levine for being the first one to hear my story and for being a true champion in every sense of the word.* To my agent and my own chaos pilot, Bruce Westwood for his wisdom, his guidance and his ability to constantly give me the "why" so I could find the "how" throughout the process and to his whole team at Westwood Creative Artists especially Hilary Stanley for her professionalism and her diligence. To my designer, Shauna Rae, for her incredible ability to turn words into eye candy as she has done for me time and time again throughout the years. TO JOY PARKER FOR HER EXCEPTIONAL COACHING, ENCOURAGEMENT AND CONSTANT HONING THROUGHOUT THE LONG STORMY MONTHS OF EL NIÑO.

TO MY FRIENDS AND FAMILY WHOSE CARING IS CONSTANT AND VITAL. THANK YOU...

To Wanda and David, Richard, Courtenay, Sharon, Wendy, Ilan, Ted and Michael on the West Coast. TO MY PARENTS AND BENJAMIN, FOR ALWAYS BEING THERE, AND TO MARTY & LAURA, TOM & JIM, MICHAEL & JEFFREY, AND JUDY ON THE EAST COAST. THE BIGGEST THANK YOU TO AMY AND MADDY

FOR KEEPING ME BUOYANT. *A special thanks to my sister Leslie for sharing her lessons in art with me and much much more.* And to Lola for her constant bi-coastal company.

THE BIGGEST THANK YOU OF ALL...

Is reserved for my husband, my best friend, and my kindred spirit, Chris Strachan—whose love and optimism gave me the courage to begin this adventure in the first place. He is also the reason that I will keep searching for many more adventures in the near and distant future.

Index

1001-day plan, 137–138
500 Year Delta, The, by Jim Taylor and Watts Wacker, 180, 181, 183, 248

A

A&P, 34, 35
Abandonment of business preconceptions, 39
Action, importance of, as exemplified by the entrepreneur, 279–280
AFI, 163
Age in entrepreneuring, 71–72
Age of Unreason, The, by Charles Handy, 89, 286
Agility, strategic, 26–37
Alias Wavefront, 41, 200
Allegories of Reading, by Paul de Man, 165
Allen, Paul, 215
Aloneness of the coach-entrepreneur, 69–70
Amazon.com, 209
American Film Institute, 163
Anderson Body Ltd., 122
Anderson, Lisa, 122
Angels (investors), 215
Angels of Advantage, 46–50
    for woman entrepreneurs, 121–124
Anxiety, enlightened, 248–249
Apple Computers, 20, 32, 33, 43–44, 121, 150
Asper Centre for Entrepreneurship, University of British Columbia, 88
Autodesk, 124
AutoNet, 36

B

B.C. Home Business Report, 115, 149
Backdoor relationships with other companies, 32–33
Balanced life, impossibility of, for the entrepreneur, 246–247. *See also* Imbalance
Banwell, Wilson, 268
Barad, Jill Elikann, 115–116, 118
Barthes, Roland, 283
Bartz, Carol, 124
BCE Capital Inc., 6
Beautiful Death, by David Robinson, 165
Beckwith, Harry, *Selling the Invisible*, 96
Beers, Charlotte, 114, 116, 122
Belief systems, need for, 134
Bell Canada, 4
Bencher, harried, 75
Beside-the-point companies, value of experience in, 90–93
BioWare Corp., 36
Board of directors, content and role, 239–241
Boundaries, breaking of, 17–18
Bradley, Melissa, 281
Brand building, 29–30, 143–168
    eclipsed branding, 162–166
    emotional branding, 161–162
    errors in, 166–167
    essence of, 157–159
    existential branding, 145–147
    experimental branding, 159–161
    extensive relationships, 148–157
    personal nature of, 105–106

Brentwood Associates, 208

Brodsky, Norm, 213

Bryan, Fulton and Shee, 178

Budman, Michael, 174

Built to Last: Successful Habits of Visionary Companies, by Jim Collins, 11

Burgoyne Centre for Entrepreneurship, Brock University, 88

Burnout
    in employees, preventing, 193
    in entrepreneur, 268, 269, 271–272

Burns, Red, 85

Business for Social Responsibility, 281

Business plan, importance and content, 223–225

Butterfly Effect, 129

Buxton, Bill, 41, 90, 200

C

Cachet, 19–21

Calkin, Joy, 114

Canadian Association of Women Executives and Entrepreneurs, 124

Centre for Entrepreneurship, Ryerson, 88

Centre for Management of Technology and Entrepreneurship, University of Toronto, 88

Chameleon personality profile, 70–71

Champions
    types, 148–150
    use of, in finding investors, 216

Championship, 18–19, 148–157
    and partnership, 151
    building, 151–157

Chanel, Coco, 161

Change in a developing business
    managing, 169–200
    resulting from influx of investors' money, 236–239

Chaos, subjecting oneself to, 39

Chaos piloting, 129–142
    navigational tools, 133–141

Chaos Theory, 129–130

Chasing Cézanne, by Peter Mayle, 162

Cheerleader champions, 149

Choice, importance of recognizing, for woman entrepreneurs, 115–117

Chouinard Yvon, 281

CIBC, 35

Circle of learning, 82–83

Citytv, 47, 147, 158

Clark, James, 217

Coaching role of the entrepreneur, 69–70

Collective thinking, 181–182

Collins, Jim, 73, 79, 105, 172, 188, 237, 282
    Built to Last: Successful Habits of Visionary Companies, 11
    "The Foundation for Doing Good," 281

Collision, purposeful, 152–154

Colonna, 240

Communication with and among employees in Cycle One, 179–180

Company model, the need to evolve from family model, 177–178

Content and context in handling convergence, 37–40

Contingency planning in business plan, 224

Convergence, technological, 23–41
    definition, 25
    how to use advantageously, 35–37
    preparing for, 37–40

Cooper, Douglas, *Delirium*, 163

Co-preneuring, 249, 253–259

Covey, Joy, 209, 227

Creative selfishness, 273–274

Creativity of entrepreneurship, 58

Crombie, Peter, 6

CrossRoads Software, 98, 123

Cunningham, Andy, 147

Customers, direct participation in handling, 195–196

Cycles of growth, 173–200
    Cycle One, 173–183
    Cycle Two, 183–193
    Cycle Three, 194–200

D

Dadalt, Dan, 152, 159

Dangerous-diffidence personality profile, 75–76

Darling magazine, 176

De Mann, Paul, *Allegories of Reading*, 165 [de Man?]

Dead reckoning, 131–132

Deal making, 40
    environment for, 191

Delirium, by Douglas Cooper, 163

Demand for entrepreneur's service or product, importance to investors, 220–221

Demos in presentation to investors, 229

Denhart, Gun, 282

Depression after success or disappointment, 270–271

Desire, importance of, for woman entrepreneurs, 116–117

De-skilling, deceptive, 270–271

Detachment, value of, 75–76

Development of company, cycles of growth, 173–200

DeVries, Manfred Kets, 247, 248, 268

DeVries, Peter, 52–53, 72

Diamond, Sarah, 168

Digital Renaissance, 174, 175, 180, 185, 193

Disaster, averting (the righting moment), 132–133

Discipline in investors' ideal entrepreneur, 219–220

Distributed Objects and Connectivity Group, 98

Dobson Centre for Entrepreneurial Studies, McGill University, 88

Doer champions, 150

Doerr, John, 207, 218

Doubleday Currency, 116

Douglas, Michael, 215

Drucker, Peter, 41, 170, 285
  Innovation and Entrepreneurship, 280

Dubinsky, Donna, 123

Dyson, Esther, 124

E

E Myth Revisited, The, by Michael Gerber, 46

Eclecticism in entrepreneuring, 83–85
  in portfolio-building, 97–98

Edison, Thomas, 280

EDS Canada Ltd., 109

Ego control as strategy for woman entrepreneurs, 112–114

Emblems. *See* Brand building

Emotional effect of brands, 161–162

Employees
  advantages to them of traveling, moving, 197–198
  communication with and among, in Cycle One, 179–180
  expectations in Cycle One, 174–175
  in-house training in Cycle Two, 191–192
  letting go of, 186
  preventing burnout, 193

support for in Cycle One, 175–176, 182–183

support for in Cycle Two, 184–187, 191–192, 193

treating as individuals in Cycle Two, 191

value of experience as, 90–93

young, profile, 169–171

Empower Computerware, 15, 42–43

Endotruths, 183–184

Engineering Culture, by Gideon Kunda, 269

Enigmatic nature of brands, 158

Entrepreneur America, 71

Entrepreneurial Development Institute, 281

Entrepreneuring
  programs at Canadian universities, 88
  tools needed in, 105
  training and experience for, 81–106
  within large organizations.
    See Intrapreneuring

Entrepreneurs
  general profiles, 65–78
  profile of investors' ideal, 218–221

Envisioning, active, 134–139. *See also* Vision

Esergy rate, 179

Essence of brands, 157–159

Eustress, 262

Evershed, John, 178, 192, 253–254, 255

Evolution of brands, 162–166

Expectations, 103

Experience for entrepreneuring, 81–106

Experienced-hipster personality profile, 71–72

Experimenter partner, value of, 78–79

Extendicare Inc., 114

Extroversion, sensitive, 67–69

F

Failure as key to success, 51–52, 72–73

Failure in sales as valuable experience, 95–96

Family atmosphere and evolution to company model, 177–178

Fear, importance of understanding, for woman entrepreneurs, 119–121

Fighter personality profile, 77–78

Financing. *See* Money, raising

Firing employees, 186

500 Year Delta, The, by Jim Taylor and Watts Wacker, 180, 181, 183

Flatiron, 240

Flexibility
  in Cycle Three of company development,
    198–199
  in investors' ideal entrepreneur, 219

Fluid leadership in entrepreneuring, 197–198,
  280

Focus
  in business plan, 223
  on single goal as strategy for woman
    entrepreneurs, 111, 113–114

Fool's gold personality profile, 73–74

Forbes, Robert, 213, 219, 225

Ford Motor Corporation of Canada, 114

Forster, E.M., 84

Four see's, the, 138–139

Fraser, Jill Andresky, "How to Finance
  Anything," 205

Free agent, meaning of, for entrepreneur,
  277–278

Freedom-fighter personality profile, 77–78

G

G.E. Capital, 211

Garnett, Katrina, 98, 114, 118, 120, 121, 123
  136, 174–175, 229, 250 Gaunt, Bobbie, 114

Gendron, George, 253, 282

General Motors, 40

Generalist approach
  in entrepreneuring, 85–88
  in sales, 94–97

Gerber, Michael, *The E Myth Revisited*, 46

Gistics, 36

Giving nature of the entrepreneur, 281–291
  in experience and advice, 283–291
  in social responsibility, 281–283

Glass ceilings as means to evolution, 35

Glenmount International, 213

Goal setting, 103

Goldberg, Natalie, *Writing Down the Bones*, 270

Goodman, Lanny, 248–249, 273–274

Goodman Phillips & Vineberg, 217

Grade, Michael, 217

Green, Don, 174

Groves, Andy, 88

Growth, cycles of, 173–200
  Cycle One, 173–183
  Cycle Two, 183–193
  Cycle Three, 194–200

Growth of business, management of,
  169–200, 236–241

Gut response, 16

H

Handy, Charles, 41, 79, 82, 84, 181
  The Age of Unreason, 89, 286

Hanna Andersson (company), 282

Harried-bencher personality profile, 75

Haven time, 265–267

Heisenberg, Werner, 35–36

Hello, He Lied, by Lynda Obst, 70, 96, 112

Heroic nature of the entrepreneur, 247–248

History of the business, development of,
  175–176

Hoffert, Paul, 90

Hoffman and Associates, 123

Hoffman, Isabel, 123

Holden Corporation, 93

Horowitz, Steve, 194

Howlett, Tom, 3, 31–32, 194, 255

Humphreys, Doug, 130, 170, 171, 175, 177,
  178, 184, 186, 210, 272

Hyperspace, by Michio Kaku , 78

I

Idealab, 215

Ideas, willingness to let go of, in Cycle Three,
  198–199

Illustra Technologies, 54–56, 159

Imbalance in life of entrepreneur, 245–274
  healthy, maintaining, 265–267

Impact Communications, 115, 149

Independent percolation, 117–118

Indigo Books & Café, 114, 280 [& or and?]

Indispensability, rule of, 92–93

Influencer champions, 149–150

Informix, 57, 144

Innovation and Entrepreneurship, by Peter
  Drucker, 280

Intel, 88

Intelligence in investors' ideal entrepreneur,
  219–220

Intercom Ontario, 90

Interpretation vs. invention, 15–16

Interval Research, 115, 121, 283

Intimacy in personal relationships
  difficulty of achieving, 262–263
  ways of achieving, 264–267

Intrapreneuring, 98–102
    appearance of observing formal rules, 101
    careful choice of employer, 103
    conditions needed for, 99
    duplication of effort, 100–101
    need for vision compatible with
      employer's, 100
Intuition
    and skill in chaos piloting, 131–132
    calculated, 16–17
    in woman entrepreneurs, 121–122
    need for and use of, 47–48
Invention vs. interpretation, 15–16
Investment in nonsellable assets, 33–34
Investors. *See also* Money, raising
    courting enlightened self-interest of, 218
    expected returns, 207–208
    importance of the kind of people they are,
      211
    profile of ideal, 214–218
    profile of investors' ideal entrepreneur,
      218–221

J

Jacobson, Lisa, 267
James, Jennifer, 277
Jenkins, Tom, 210
Job searching and selection for good
    experience, 102–103

K

Kaku, Michio, *Hyperspace*, 78
Kindred spirits, 79–80
Kirkpatrick, Todd, 150
Knowledge Deal Makers, 169–171
Kocho, Keith, 174, 180, 193, 247, 263, 267
Kodak, 32–33
Kunda, Gideon, *Engineering Culture*, 269

L

La Rochefoucauld, François, 144
Lamott, Anne, 251
Larkin Business Ventures, 281
Lau, Joanna, 90, 249
Lau Technologies, 90
Le Carré, John, *The Tailor of Panama*, 19,
    57–58, 75
Leadership
    fluid, 197–198, 280
    liquid, 280–283

Learning, circle of, 82–83
Learning, openness to, 73–74
Learning Technologies Centre, Miramichi,
    New Brunswick, 37
Leonardo da Vinci, 85
Leventhal, David, 177
Leverage, 54–55, 56–57
Levine, Michael, 76–77, 142, 198
Levine, Michael A., 217
Levinson, Harvey, 278
Liquid leadership in entrepreneuring,
    280–283
Listening, value of, learned in sales, 96–97
Logan, Todd, 262
Lone-coach personality profile, 69–70
Long-term doer personality profile, 65–67
LookSmart, 36
Lorenz, Edward, 129–130
Luck, role of, 57–58

M

Mac Cosmetics, 165
Mac Temp, 15–16
MacDonald, John, 4, 5–6
Malaise, entrepreneurial, 271–272
Management
    fluid, 197–198, 280
    liquid, 280–283
Management team in Cycle Two, 188–191
Managing business through cycles of growth
    and change, 169–200
Marimba, 124
*Marriage Spirit, The: Finding the Passion and Joy
    of Soul-Centered Love,* by Paul and Evelyn
    Moschetta, 265–266
Marriott Hotels, 281
Marriott, J. Willard Jr., 281
Mars Group, 188
Mattel, 115
Maturity of entrepreneur, 71–72
Mayle, Peter, *Chasing Cézanne*, 162
McGarry, Diane, 94, 110
McKnight, Bill, 99
Media Asset Factory, 36
MEDITrust, 3, 4
Mental health problems of the entrepreneur,
    267–272
Mentor for money matters, importance of,
    213–214

Metcalfe, Jane, 141, 144, 145, 146, 159–160, 196, 220, 254, 257, 263, 264
Microsoft, 117
Microsoft Studios®, 40
Miller, Steve, 285
Miramichi, New Brunswick, economic revival through use of technology, 37
Mistakes, admitting to, 182
Mitchell, Jerry, 93
Molson, 164
MondoMedia, 176, 178, 185, 191, 192
Money
    clear decision on role it will play in your business, 209–210
    importance of people who have it, 211
    importance of understanding, 205–207, 212–213
    respect for, 205–207
Money, raising, 201–242
    business plan, 223–225
    customer referrals, importance of, 225
    elements of "pitch portfolio," 223–229
    entrance strategy, importance of focusing on, 208–209
    exit strategy, 207
    knowing interests of investors, 218
    presentations to investors, 228–229
    profile of ideal investor, 214–218
    profile of investors' ideal entrepreneur, 218–221
    Stage One, dreaming and thinking, 205–214
    Stage Two, buying money, 214–221
    Stage Three, preparing for presentation to investors, 221–229
    Stage Four, negotiating, 230–235
    Stage Five, managing money, 236–241
    storytelling in, 226–228
    timing and readiness for, 211–212
Moon, Michael, 30, 36, 37–38, 163, 280
Moore, Darla, 116, 122
Moore, Geoffrey, 13, 28, 86, 87, 99, 139, 144, 147, 148, 166, 173, 183, 198 225, 239, 264
Moore, Gordon, 88
Morse, Kenneth P., 88
Moschetta, Paul and Evelyn, *The Marriage Spirit: Finding the Passion and Joy of Soul-Centered Love*, 265–266
Motorola, 25
Mountford, Joy, 115, 121, 249, 283

MouseHouse, 36
Movie Network, 35
Mowat, Barbara, 115, 122, 149
Multitasking, 65–67
Musical intelligence, value of, 89–90
Mutual fund investors, 214
Mysteries of Paris, by Eugene Sue, 162

N

Names of businesses, 29–30
Narrowline, 175
Nash, David, 144, 253
National Envelope Company, 133
NB Tel, 3, 4
NBCC Miramichi, 37
NCompass, 36, 123
Negotiating, 230–234
    things to beware of, 231–235
Negroponte, Nicholas, 150
Netscape, 218
Networking, 148–157. *See also* Champions; Championship
New Brunswick Telecom, 3, 4
New Media School, 85
Northern Telecom, 3, 4, 32, 33
Numbers, meaningful, in business plan, 224–225
Numetrix Ltd., 36

O

Objectivity about the business
    maintaining while staying in touch, 196–197
    value of, 75–76
Obsession
    in woman entrepreneurs, 123
    vs. passion, 46–47
Obst, Lynda, 84, 133, 270
    Hello, He Lied, 70, 96, 112
Ogilvy and Mather, 114
1001-day plan, 137–138
Open Text Corp., 210
Openness to learning, 73–74
Optimism, context for, as provided by the entrepreneur, 278–279
Oracle, 57, 98, 144
Organization types
    flat, 180, 187–188
    hierarchical, 188
Orwell, George, 164

Outsider role as learned in sales, 95
O'Malley, Deirdre, 178, 182, 253–254, 255, 272

P

Palladium, 194
Palm Computing, 123
Panic, exhilarating, 248–249
Paranoid, trusting, 74
Partners
    and championship, 151
    choosing, 79–80
    value of, 31–32, 78–80
Passion vs. obsession, 46–47
Patagonia, 281
Patience in investors' ideal entrepreneur, 219
Peabody, Bo, 161–162
Peak performance, recognizing, in Cycle Three, 199–200
Percolation, independent, 117–118
Performance
    in entrepreneuring, 139–141
    in making presentations to investors, 228–229
Peripheral companies, value of experience in, 90–93
Personal life of the entrepreneur, 245–274
    blurring the boundaries with work life, 249–250
    difficulty of achieving intimacy in, 262–263
    effect of travel on, 259–261
    maintaining a healthy imbalance, 265–267
    mental health problems, 267–272
    need for renewal, 264–267
    postponement to a time that will not arise, 251–252
    ways of achieving intimacy in, 264–267
Personal nature of brands, 105–106, 145–147
Personal nature of entrepreneuring, 248–249, 273
Personality of the entrepreneur, 63–80
    profiles, 65–78
Perspective
    in visualizing changes, 138–139
    value of, 76
Polese, Kimberley, 124
Portfolio of developing entrepreneur
    balance in, 103–104
    eclecticism in, 97–98
Postcard theory, 136–137

Power for woman entrepreneurs, 123
Practical partner, value of, 78–79
Pralle, Michael, 211
Princessa, The: Machiavelli for Women, by Harriet Rubin, 116, 247
PROACT, 268
Professional eclecticism, 83–85
Profiles
    of ideal investor, 214–218
    of investors' ideal entrepreneur, 218–221
    of new entrepreneur, 65–78
Prototype in presentation to investors, 229
Purposeful collision, 152–154

Q

Quality of life for the entrepreneur. See Personal life of the entrepreneur
Questions, finding the right ones to handle convergence, 41

R

Rambus, 87
Realism, magical, 21–22
Rebellious leader, 173–174
Red Dog beer, 164
Red Sky Films, 130
Redrum, 152, 159
Referrals, customer, in money raising, 225
Reisman, Heather, 114, 122, 279–280
Renewal
    of brand, 162–166
    personal, to encourage healthy imbalance, 264–267
Resilience, value of, 92–93
Resourcefulness learned in sales, 95
Righting moment, the, 132–133
Risk, 14–17, 45
    in branding, 159
"Risk and Reward," 282
Robinson, David, Beautiful Death, 165
Rock, Arthur, 88
Role-shifting ability, 70–71
Roots Canada, 148, 174
Roper Stach Worldwide, 253, 282
Rossetto, Louis, 141, 159–160, 223, 254
Royal Dutch/Shell, 285
Rubin, Harriet, 116, 117, 120, 121
    The Princessa: Machiavelli for Women, 116, 247
Ryan, Rob, 71, 79, 86, 88, 186, 216, 221, 228

S

Sacrifice, 48–50
  in woman entrepreneurs, 122–123
Sahlman, Bill, 14, 64, 79, 88, 206, 221
Schneider, David, 213
Schwartz, Pepper, 249
Schwartz, Peter, 41
Seagate Technologies, 208
Second Cup, 35
SEI Investments, 280
Selfishness, creative, 273–274
Selling the Invisible, by Harry Beckwith, 96
Selling, value of experience in, 93–97
Sensitive-extrovert personality profile, 67–69
Service business, importance in product
  development, 28–29
SGI, 32, 33, 144, 150, 200
Shattuck, Roger, 76
Shift magazine, 130, 172
Sierra On-line, 117
Silence in allowing brand to evolve, 164–165
Silicon Graphics, 217
Silicon Reef, 33, 192
Silicon Spice, 216, 221
Silicon Valley, author's trip to, 42–59
Sinclair, Gerri, 123
Single-goal focus as strategy for woman
  entrepreneurs, 111, 113–114
Sisters of Success, 115–123
Size of business, appearance of, 30–31
Skyrocket, 130
Small companies, value of experience in,
  90–93
Social responsibility in the entrepreneur,
  281–283
Softbank, 240
Solomon, Evan, 130, 136, 185, 187, 189
Sony Pictures Entertainment, 6, 40, 57
Soul centers, 192–193
Southcott, Andrea, 178, 248, 257
Southcott, Jim, 178
Spartan Baby Theory, 219
Specialist approach
  in entrepreneuring, 85–88
  in sales, 95
Spielberg, Steven, 215
Spirit of the new entrepreneur, 275–291
Spouses as business partners.
  See Co-preneuring

Spray (company), 33, 69, 82–83, 145, 147,
  176, 179, 182
Stamina in investors' ideal entrepreneur, 219
Step Ahead, 124
Stewart, Martha, 116, 122
Stock options, 237
Stonebreaker, Michael, 54
Storytelling
  in entrepreneuring, 13–14
  in passing along experience and advice,
    283–291
  in raising money, 226–228
  need for, for woman entrepreneurs,
    124–125
Strachan, Chris, 3, 31, 94, 275–276
Strategies for woman entrepreneurs, 111–114
Stress. *See* Eustress
Style for woman entrepreneurs, 117
Submarine environment in Cycle One,
  177–178
Successful failure personality profile, 72–73
Sue, Eugene, *Mysteries of Paris*, 162
Sun Microsystems, 57, 144
Svensson, Jonas, 69, 82–83, 145, 176, 179, 249,
  261, 266
Sybase, 98

T

Tailor of Panama, The, by John le Carré, 19,
  57–58, 75
Tailspin, self-induced, 268–270
Tandem Computers, 54
Taylor, Jim, and Watts Wacker, *The 500 Year
  Delta*, 180, 181, 183, 248
TD Bank, 35
Teaching Tolerance, 185
Team selection for making presentations to
  investors, 228–229
Technology and business opportunities, 23–41
Technology Ventures Co-op Program,
  Stanford University, 88
Theoretician partner, value of, 78–79
1001-day plan, 137–138
Time scale for planning major changes,
  137–138
Timing for woman entrepreneurs, 117–118
Torque, applied, 247
Traditions, development of, in Cycle One,
  175–176

Training for entrepreneurs, 81–106
   programs at Canadian universities, 88
   programs for women, 124
Travel
   advantages to employees, 197–198
   author's trip to Silicon Valley, 42–59
   effect on entrepreneur's personal life,
     259–261
Trend-hopping, 26–37
Tripod, 161–162
Trusting-paranoid personality profile, 74

U

Ungar, William, 133
University Workshop Project, 283
Unknown territory, entrepreneuring as lead-
   ership into, 280–283
Unrules, 180–181

V

Vanilla contract, 232–233
Venture capital firms, 214
Vision. *See also* Envisioning, active;
   Visualization
   communicating to employees, 171–172, 184
   revising, 184
Vision statement, 172
Visualization, 136–137. *See also* Envisioning,
   active
   perspective in, 138–139
Vivid (company), 192

W

Wallin, Pamela, 90–91, 132, 148, 249
Weisskopf, Victor, 78
West, Al, 280
Westwood Creative Artists Ltd., 217
Whittaker, Sheelagh, 109
Williams, Roberta, 117–118
Wired magazine, 141, 144, 146, 147, 150,
   159–160, 165, 196
Wired Ventures, 141
Wollaston, Paul, 44–45
Women as entrepreneurs, 107–126
   Angels of Advantage, 121–124
   developing a comfortable style, 114–115
   elements of success, 115–123
   storytelling needed, 124–125
   strategies, 111–114

Women's World Banking, 124
Working Assets, 281
Writing Down the Bones, by Natalie Goldberg,
   270
Wuorio, Jeff, 207
   "Go on an Equity Hunt to Fund
     Expansion," 205
Wurman, Richard Saul, 150

X

Xerox Canada, 94
Xylan, 208

Y

Yankelovich Partners, 170
Youth in entrepreneuring, 71–72

Z

Zenith, 25
Zero-moment point, 133
Zimmerman, Adam, 148
Znaimer, Moses, 47, 48, 136, 142, 147, 158,
   165, 248

HOW TO

US

FOR MORE INFORMATION ON THE THEMES EXPLORED IN THIS BOOK

AS WELL AS A LISTING OF UPCOMING EVENTS, PLEASE FEEL FREE TO VISIT OUR WEBSITE AT

www.bulldog.com

AS PART OF THE ONGOING PURSUIT OF INTEGRATING ACTS OF ENTREPRENEURING INTO OUR

WORK AND LIVES, I AM MOST INTERESTED IN YOUR COMMENTS AND QUESTIONS.

PLEASE FORWARD YOUR QUERIES TO **spirit@bulldog.com**

AND I WOULD BE HAPPY TO RESPOND.

ELLIE RUBIN SPEAKS AT VARIOUS ORGANIZATIONS IN A WIDE RANGE OF INDUSTRIES ABOUT THE

DEFINITION OF THE ENTREPRENEURIAL SPIRIT AND WHERE AND HOW IT WILL EVOLVE.

FOR MORE INFORMATION ON BOOKING ELLIE RUBIN FOR A SPEAKING

ENGAGEMENT, PLEASE CONTACT SPEAKERS' SPOTLIGHT @ **1•800•333•4453**

OR VISIT THEIR WEBSITE: **www.speakers.ca**